Republic
of Taste

EARLY AMERICAN STUDIES

SERIES EDITORS

Daniel K. Richter, Kathleen M. Brown, Max Cavitch, and David Waldstreicher

Exploring neglected aspects of our colonial, revolutionary, and early national
history and culture, Early American Studies reinterprets familiar themes
and events in fresh ways. Interdisciplinary in character, and with a special
emphasis on the period from about 1600 to 1850, the series is published
in partnership with the McNeil Center for Early American Studies.

.

Republic of Taste

Art, Politics, and Everyday Life
in Early America

Catherine E. Kelly

PENN

University of Pennsylvania Press

Philadelphia

Copyright © 2016 University of Pennsylvania Press

Published by
University of Pennsylvania Press
Philadelphia, Pennsylvania 19104-4112
www.upenn.edu/pennpress

Printed in the United States of America on acid-free paper

1 3 5 7 9 10 8 6 4 2

A Cataloging-in-Publication record is available from the Library of Congress
ISBN 978-0-8122-4823-4

For Richie:
$M \times FF \times D$

Contents

Color plates follow page 184

The American Republic of Taste

Henry Cheever, an academy student in Massachusetts, was determined to hone his prose, molding it to meet the standards laid out by Hugh Blair's *Lectures on Rhetoric and Belles Lettres* and by Henry Home, Lord Kames's *Elements of Criticism*. He filled his commonplace book with epigrams culled from the works of Milton, Goldsmith, Dryden, and Pope. Keen to demonstrate his mastery of the fine style prescribed by the rhetoricians and exemplified by the poets, he set out to describe the summer sunset he had just witnessed. In July 1829, after beseeching the "Omniscient Potentiate" for guidance, he wrote that the "borders of the western horizon" glowed "like a golden flame," their light punctuated by "blue pyramidial mounts like [a] sudden flash of spirit in raging roaring flames."[1] In crafting his tortured summer sunset, Cheever marked himself not just as a reader and writer but also as a looker, as an active and engaged spectator whose "golden flames" and "blue pyramidial mounts" derived not just from a particular way of reading and writing but also from a particular way of seeing.

Lucy Sumner, newly married and intent on embodying the virtues that spelled republican womanhood, had fallen into the habit of visiting Daniel Bowen's Columbian Museum. The paintings, taxidermied birds, wax figures, and curiosities provided her circle with "rational and refined amusement," especially when compared to the risqué and "disgusting" circus that had been attracting far more patronage than she thought proper. But Sumner valued the Columbian for more than its admirable collection. The museum encouraged a distinct—and distinctly rewarding—sort of spectatorship. When one spent time at the Columbian, she explained to her friend Eliza Wharton, "the eye is gratified, the imagination charmed, and the understanding improved." Far from "palling on the taste," the interplay of familiar exhibits and novel additions had an animating effect on intellect and imagination. At the Columbian, she declared, "I am never a weary spectator."[2]

Sometime in the late 1780s, Samuel Powel, one of the wealthiest and most influential men in Philadelphia, paid tribute to his friend and fellow revolutionary, George Washington, by tracing his silhouette and inscribing "General Washington" on its back. We have no information about the circumstances under which Powel made the profile, although family lore held that he used a recently invented Argand lamp to project Washington's profile on the wall. We know only that the Powel family took pains to save it, passing the memento from one generation to the next until it finally found a home upstairs in their elegant townhouse, now a museum. The impromptu likeness testifies to the so-called Patriot Mayor's close personal and political relationship with the pater patriae. Its preservation testifies to his family's lasting pride in that association. But behind this all-too-predictable story about prestige and personal connection is another set of stories, even if we cannot recover them. What impulses led one powerful and cosmopolitan man to amuse himself by drawing the rough silhouette of another? What impulses led a revolutionary hero known for his reserve to amuse himself and his friends in this way?[3]

A teenaged academy student. A minor character in the United States' first best-selling novel. One man of affairs nearing the end of his life and another already securing his place in history. At first glance, the individuals at the center of these three vignettes seem to have little in common with one another. But in describing a sunset, touting the moral benefits of museum attendance, or creating a profile, each claimed citizenship in the republic of taste. To situate Henry Cheever, Lucy Sumner, Samuel Powel, and George Washington in the republic of taste is to place them at the intersection of the early republic's material, visual, literary, and political cultures. They knew that the exercise of their taste was caught up in the material world. It depended on taxidermied animals and Argand lamps. It demanded both beautiful vistas and books that contained a vocabulary capable of describing those vistas. Whether they believed that their distinguishing taste was inborn (and therefore a marker of breeding and station) or acquired (and thus the product of application and study), they understood that it was predicated upon, demonstrated through, and confirmed by reading, writing, and looking—processes that they believed to be inextricably bound together. Cheever, Sumner, Powel, and Washington also believed that their shared aesthetic sensibilities connected them to other like-minded individuals.

Figure 1. Samuel Powel, *Silhouette of George Washington*, Philadelphia, before 1790. The likeness is now part of the permanent exhibit at Powel House. The note attached to the profile tells the story of its creation and preservation. Courtesy of the Philadelphia Society for the Preservation of Landmarks.

They trusted that these shared affinities, which provided so much personal pleasure, also advanced the public good and thus held out great promise in the American republic. Never mind that the newly formed United States lacked the Old World's aesthetic infrastructure. In their eyes, the nation itself constituted a kind of gallery, a series of real and imagined spaces in which republican citizens could display and affirm their sensibility, their taste, and their virtue.

The intellectual underpinnings of the American republic of taste stretched back a century and spanned the Atlantic. European, and especially British, thinkers had been preoccupied with questions about taste, visuality, and aesthetics since the early decades of the eighteenth century. Whatever their differences, David Hume, Edmund Burke, and Hugh Blair all linked aesthetic dilemmas to political ones by the middle of the eighteenth century. Moreover, they did so in terms that invited the engagement of a growing middle class. Around the same time, prominent and well-connected painters-turned-theorists like Sir Joshua Reynolds insisted upon art's broadly didactic purpose, imbuing it with civic value. This wide-ranging body of thought, which encompassed philosophy, belles lettres, and the fine arts, contributed to a new understanding of the world. It simultaneously helped shift authority from the state to society and defined a terrain on which society could define and organize itself. Its high-minded aesthetic ideas were distilled and popularized through Britain's flourishing periodical press, starting with the *Spectator* (1711–1712), whose essays, published daily, titled simply by number, and reproduced widely, would influence aesthetic theory and literary culture on both sides of the Atlantic well into the nineteenth century.[4]

Before the American Revolution, educated and affluent Anglo-Americans sought access to the tasteful world that emerged from the pages of these texts in order to strengthen their ties to the metropole, in order to become more Anglo and less American. During and after the American Revolution, however, they invested this transatlantic discourse with enormous and explicitly republican significance.[5] Exploiting the similarities between aesthetic and political dilemmas, American thinkers explored questions about taste and beauty in order to wrestle with questions about power and authority. Thus, in 1776, John Adams imagined representative assembly as "in miniature, an exact portrait of the people at large"; more than ten years later, Anti-Federalists repurposed Adams's metaphor to attack the proposed Constitution, which failed to provide a legislative body that could serve as a "likeness" of the people. Indeed, Federalists and Anti-Federalists explicitly invoked debates over the relative importance of uniformity and variety as components of beauty in arguments over issues including representation and the separation of powers.[6] In much the same way, debates over the nature of taste (Was it innate or learned? Was there a single standard or were there as many standards as there were individuals?) directly informed debates over political and social authority. Precisely because the imagination posited by eighteenth-century aesthetic theory demanded both creative freedom and critical restraint, it provided Americans with an intellectual framework for considering the limits of liberty. Thinking about art, architecture, literature, poetry, or the theater thus became vehicles for thinking about and thinking through political issues ranging from government structures, to legislative representation, to qualifications for citizenship, to the meaning of liberty itself.

If taste accommodated social aspiration and encouraged political debate, it also suggested the possibility of affinity grounded in a shared national identity. Putatively free from the Old World's decadence, taste promised to be a vehicle for discovering and exercising a distinctly American genius. And putatively free from sectional prejudice and partisan strife, taste provided a platform that would encourage men and women to rise above their differences. Like "manners" and "sensibility," the period's other shibboleths, taste promised to bind the disparate citizens of a republic together while setting them apart from Europeans. Thinkers as different as Thomas Jefferson and Joseph Dennie, whose views extended across the early national political spectrum, clung to the hope that a republic could be forged at least partly out of taste. With so much at stake, it is small wonder that aesthetic preoccupations peppered the pages of the U.S. periodical press and turned up in speeches given to mark everything from college graduations to July 4th celebrations. Thus did a transatlantic republic of taste distill into an American republic of taste.

This is by now a familiar story; its narrative outlines have emerged over the past thirty years from the work of literary and cultural historians, including Jay Fliegelman, David S. Shields, Eric Slauter, and Edward Cahill.[7] But despite all that we have recovered about the resonance of taste for American political discourse, for all that we now know about the centrality of aesthetics more generally to American intellectual life, we have scarcely paused to ask whether, much less how, the eighteenth century's aesthetic turn figured in the lives of women and men who were not intellectuals in any canonical sense of the word. Did the early national vocabulary of taste, with its privileged visuality, register beyond the debates over the ratification of the Constitution or outside the pages of the *Port Folio*? Did it extend past political and politicized discourse to inform the imaginative structures and material forms of everyday life? *Republic of Taste* affirms that it did, although not in ways that anyone could have predicted at the conclusion of the American Revolution.

In the years following independence, ordinary women and men sought membership in the republic of taste because it afforded them cultural capital and personal pleasure in equal measure. They assured themselves that taste revealed larger truths about an individual's character, about his or her potential for republican citizenship. The man (or woman) of taste was disinterested, capable of seeing past particulars to grasp universal truths. At the same time, he was sensitive to the feelings and experiences of others. He was sensitive, indeed, to the world that surrounded him. Although his taste was to some degree innate, it was also the product of careful and sustained cultivation. He was thus knowledgeable, for in fostering his own taste he had become familiar with things that were appreciated by other people of taste. This familiarity with the texts, objects, and images that signaled taste was not only intellectual. It was also material. The tasteful life was graced by exquisitely bound books and mass-produced engraved prints, by decorated ceramics and schoolgirls' needlework. It was expressed in the graceful curves and swoops of penmanship and in the serenely composed faces that looked out from oil portraits and ivory miniatures. Taste conjured soft fabrics and polished surfaces just as it conjured intellectual and imaginative aspiration.

The valorization of taste was thus well suited to the early republic's Janus-faced culture of class, which simultaneously promised opportunity and reinforced distinction.[8] In theory, taste operated freely, unconstrained by either hereditary status or financial net worth. By and large, Americans preferred thinkers who treated taste as a capacity that responded to careful cultivation over those who believed it to be an absolute. But however taste was theorized, it operated within a constellation of texts, images, objects, and persons that placed it well beyond the grasp of people whose occupations, wealth, or race excluded them from the ranks of an emerging middle class.[9] Lack of money and standing did not necessarily signal a lack of taste. Indeed, the laboring men and women who created refinement's props often insisted that the quality of the goods they produced reflected their taste as well as their skill. That said, one was far more likely to discover a capacity for taste in a young woman whose once-respectable family had been rendered destitute by hard times than in a young man bent on clawing his way out of hardscrabble poverty.

Broad as taste's compass might have been, when Anglo-Americans attempted to define or to account for it, they turned time and again to metaphors and examples that hinged on sight and seeing. For Americans as for their British counterparts, taste and its cognate words—imagination, fancy, discretion, and, to a lesser extent, connoisseurship—were grounded in the eye.[10] The countless Americans schooled in taste by the rhetorician Hugh Blair, for example, learned that taste was "ultimately founded on a certain natural and instinctive sensibility to beauty" and that beauty was first encountered visually. Those who read the *Spectator* knew that Joseph Addison had singled out sight, "the most perfect and most delightful of the senses," as *the* critical component of his "Pleasures of the Imagination"; they understood that discretion was like a "well-formed Eye" capable of commanding "large and extended Views."[11] The logic connecting taste to vision was reiterated in the pages of the American periodical press. Writers and editors regularly reminded readers that the "finer organs" of a tasteful person could see beauty that was "hidden from a vulgar eye"; that taste turned a "nicer eye" on the works of nature; and that tasteful objects were those that "please[d] the eye."[12] The same set of associations appeared in the formal speeches made by college students like John Wales, who promised listeners that they could improve their taste while taking their daily strolls simply by noting which things appeared "pleasing and beautiful" and which did not. In no time, he assured them, they would establish a standard by which "everything was easily and readily ajudged."[13] Whether imagined as a badge of genteel discernment, an avenue to personal pleasure, or both, taste was imbricated in visuality. It depended equally on the perception of the subject and on the appearance of the objects and images within the field of vision.[14]

Opportunities to exercise one's taste—to scan the surroundings with a knowing and receptive eye—increased in variety and quantity during the early republic. As the eighteenth century gave way to the nineteenth, bourgeois Americans acquired access to more books and magazines, more paintings and prints, more museums and galleries. They encountered a visual field that was increasingly crowded, courtesy of an expanding consumer market. The language that women and men used to describe their aesthetic experiences offers one register of the growing influence of commerce, commodities, and consumer capitalism. Consider the word "taste" itself. A key word in the eighteenth-century British aesthetic lexicon, "taste" appeared in political treatises, oratory, and children's books. It also made regular appearances in letters written by and to the nation's founders: Jefferson urged the design of a capitol that would "form the taste of our young men," and he fretted over how John Adams's "want of taste" would be received in Europe. For his part, Adams took pains to distinguish between the artificial "Amuzements" and the "higher Taste" displayed in England's romantic country gardens. Even George Washington hailed Julius Caesar as a "man of highly cultivated understanding and taste."[15] These men, like their counterparts on both sides of the Atlantic, invoked "taste" in reference to physical sensations as well as to individual preferences and predilections; they used it to describe the appreciation of beauty in nature, art, and literature. "Taste" was an elastic word, conjuring an individual's reactions to endless external stimuli. But for all its value as an index of the external world, taste was also deeply and intrinsically internalized. This, in fact, was precisely what made taste so potent for men like Jefferson, Madison, and Washington: it simultaneously summoned gentility and moral character.

Not so the word "connoisseurship." If taste depended upon fundamentally internalized qualities and abilities, connoisseurship derived solely from a familiarity with objects outside the self. Connoisseurs were distinguished by their knowledge of category and quality, by their expertise in a world of goods. Defined by his or her relationship to particular things, the connoisseur was a creature of the market. It is telling that the same founders who never hesitated to appeal to taste rarely invoked connoisseurship; when they did, it was usually to declare that they lacked it. Thus Washington confessed that he was "not much of a connoisseur" of dinner plates and "profess[ed] not to be a connoisseur" of poetry. Jefferson was "so little of a connoisseur" that he found the paintings of Adriaen van der Werff and Carlo Dolci superior to those of Peter Paul Rubens.[16] To be sure, there was always the whiff of gamesmanship in disavowals like these. A preference for Dolci over Rubens might have ruffled the feathers of connoisseurs, but it also trumpeted a far deeper knowledge of art history than most Americans or Britons could claim. But by pointedly distancing themselves from connoisseurs, Jefferson and Washington implicitly juxtaposed connoisseurship's studied pretense against taste's authentic simplicity in order to announce themselves as republicans and to lay claim to an aesthetic and moral high ground.

Suspect in the eighteenth century, "connoisseur" and its variations triumphed in the nineteenth. Americans seized on the word to describe their connection to the material world. The early national periodical press provides a rough index of the ascent of the connoisseur. Initially, the word was associated solely with high culture and the fine arts. Connoisseurs judged painting, sculpture, and (much less frequently) literature; their approbation was invoked in announcements for gallery exhibitions and essays on Benjamin West's oeuvre and Henry Fuseli's lectures on painting.[17] But the range of objects that commanded the connoisseur's attention quickly expanded beyond the exquisite and the rare to include the everyday and the accessible. Newspaper and magazine advertisements invited connoisseurs to peruse engraved prints, perfumes, and wines or to enjoy mechanical panoramas, philosophical experiments, and turtle soup.[18] Arkansas land, merino sheep, cream cheese, and a special shade of red that could be produced only with a dye made from sheep's dung—all provided fodder for connoisseurs.[19] "Connoisseurship" never eclipsed "taste." Indeed, the two words were often linked. Eventually, they became all but synonymous. Nor was the exercise of taste ever entirely divorced from the material world. Nevertheless, the nineteenth-century ascendance of "connoisseur," a word that appeared only rarely in eighteenth-century Anglo-America, should alert us to the increasingly active and volatile presence of the market in the republic of taste.

The market ensured that the very visual and material cultures that helped materialize the United States' republic of taste also served to undermine it. The republic of taste had always been an abstraction, an idea. Like all theories, it proved vulnerable to praxis. Yet as it was imagined and constituted in the United States, this particular abstraction proved to be especially vulnerable to the material forms that were meant to embody and to shape it. For one thing, most of the texts and objects that structured the world of taste, even in its most allegedly American iterations, were European or, more likely, British in origin. An exclusively "American taste" was an oxymoron. Sovereignty produced neither cultural nor economic autonomy. Most Anglo-Americans did a very good job of overlooking the extent to which their tasteful texts and things derived from English originals. That said, Englishness (and the recent history of political rupture and economic dependency it implied) popped up more than anyone might have liked. Put simply, U.S. citizens' continued reliance on British texts, objects, images, and styles complicated their narratives about national distinctiveness and disrupted their claims about a singularly American republic of taste.[20]

More to the point, regardless of provenance, most of the objects and images constituting the American republic of taste were commodities. Circulating across the Atlantic and within the United States, taste's props were part of a protean consumer market that was both a source and a symbol of political, economic, and social change. Commodification undermined the lofty promises held out by the abstraction of taste not because it produced tawdry, tacky goods (although it assuredly did) or because it extended taste's compass across all sectors of society, thereby democratizing national culture (which it did not). Instead, commodification created the space for an imaginary that transgressed the unifying, disciplinary logic that undergirded the republic of taste.

Painters, museum keepers, printers, and producers of aestheticized objects more generally might have aspired to serve the republic by elevating citizens' taste. But they were also entrepreneurs who needed to make a living and tried to make a good one. Competing in increasingly crowded markets, they clamored to attract new clients by catering to a growing range of preferences and budgets. They angled to attract repeat business by catering to the public's desire for novelty. The resulting variety of goods ran the gamut from the ephemeral to the substantial. Promising only to suit the particular taste of individual patrons, producers made no claim to advancing a single standard of taste, much less yoking consumers to a particular form of collective identity or action.[21] The commodification of taste was by no means unique to the United States. But precisely because Anglo-Americans had endeavored to situate taste near the heart of the republican project, its commodification bore different and more urgent implications in the United States than it did in Britain. This was especially true when the commodities in question were intended to instill national spirit, cultivate republican sensibilities, or commemorate the Revolution. It was one thing for women's gowns to fall victim to the caprices of fashion, another for the same fate to befall likenesses of George Washington.

This book weaves together two related lines of inquiry in order to explore Americans' contradictory attempts to create and inhabit a republic of taste. The first explores the process of translating aesthetic ideals into everyday practice. How could a transatlantic culture of taste be rendered *American*? How could it be refined to meet the pressing needs of the republic? Just as important, how could women and men secure their claims to inclusion in this American republic of taste? And how could they use that status to consolidate their authority in the American republic writ large? As urgent as they were unresolved, these questions dogged attempts to create a culture capable of securing the republic. To forge an American republic of taste, individuals reinvested older ideas, imaginative structures, and material forms with new meanings. Capitalizing on taste's promises to identify and elevate the worthy few, women and men projected their aspirations for themselves onto their aspirations for the republic, thereby collapsing the personal and the national. Capitalizing on taste's penchant for distinction, they guarded the boundaries that elevated them above those who lacked their fine eyes and genteel sensibilities. To be sure, Anglo-Americans had been using taste (along with gentility and sensibility) as an instrument of social calibration since at least the early eighteenth century.[22] But following the Revolution, they also used it as a barometer of civic and political capacity. During the same decades, the expansion of the market guaranteed that there were more producers and more consumers, more images, objects, and texts jockeying for recognition and precedence. Americans thus sought to materialize their republic of taste in a social, economic, and cultural context that was inherently unstable, a context that all but guaranteed that attempts to create a republic of taste would ultimately undermine it.

The book's second line of inquiry focuses on the connections that early national Americans drew between visual and material cultures, on the one hand, and literary cultures, on the other. *Republic of Taste* is as concerned with texts, and texts that refer to things, as it is with things in and of themselves. This is intentional. Recent years have witnessed exciting work both on visual and material cultures and on literary culture.[23] That said, we have a remarkably underdeveloped sense of how the textual, the visual, and the material operated *together*. This is unfortunate, for in the late eighteenth and early nineteenth centuries, the visual and the textual were interwoven in distinct and specific ways.

An expansive, transatlantic literary culture provided educated women and men with structures for organizing visual perception, structures that operated much like the carefully mapped sight lines in a theater, which simultaneously ensure that audiences see the action on the stage and discourage them from peering into the spaces around them. These structures were as disciplinary as they were enabling. Belles lettres endowed readers with far more than the vocabulary necessary to translate a sweeping field of vision into words. The rich textual world elaborated in manuscript and print, in private exchange and public academies, showed women and men where and how to look and then helped them anchor what they saw in the things they read and wrote. The densely knit web of associations that emerged from all this reading, writing, and looking— the particular form of subjectivity it created—was hardly a natural effect of human nature. Instead, it was historically specific, grounded both in ideas about perception and selfhood and in an expansive world of images, objects, and texts.[24] This dynamic, triangular process was central to the ways in which individuals experienced, understood, and valued texts, images, and objects. It proved crucial to attempts to imagine the United States as a republic of taste.

The chapters that follow sketch the history of the American republic of taste. The story they tell does not aim to be comprehensive, as if such a story could be told comprehensively. Instead, its trajectory unfolds through a series of roughly chronological, topical chapters. Chapter 1 examines pedagogy and curriculum at postrevolutionary academies and seminaries to consider how ideas about taste, aesthetics, and seeing were introduced into the discursive and social practices of young women and men. Very little of this aesthetic education was new, and perhaps even less of it was unique to the United States. What *was* new in the years following the Revolution was the scale of the enterprise on the one hand and its political resonance on the other. Young men and young women, especially, increasingly pursued educations that injected ideas about aesthetics, habits of observation, and particular kinds of objects and images with an explicitly republican, explicitly national significance. Academy students, with their carefully schooled taste and their heightened sense of visuality, became newly visible to their fellow citizens as aestheticized embodiments of republican taste and virtue. The academy movement, as it is often called, produced several generations of students whose educations had imparted appetites as well as taste. Their desire to indulge their taste and exercise their eyes, a desire that continued long after they left school, was satisfied by growing numbers of painters, museum operators, and art teachers. These aesthetic entrepreneurs, the subject of Chapter 2, were eager to profit from the growing market for taste. But they were just as eager to claim some of their patrons' respectability—some of their polish—for themselves. Eager to qualify for membership in the republic of taste, they celebrated their visual discernment rather than their technical skill. Setting themselves up as arbiters of their patrons' taste, they were nonetheless vulnerable to patrons' whims and pocketbooks.

Aesthetics, both as theory and praxis, thus served as a vehicle for people of different genders and ranks to consolidate their social, cultural, and even economic power in the early republic. But what kinds of authority, precisely, could taste enhance? What kinds of visibility could it engender? Chapter 3 focuses on miniature portraits of two women, one black and one white, to explore these questions. Portraits were, by a large margin, the most popular form of painting in early America. By the turn of the nineteenth century, ivory miniatures were arguably the most common form of likeness among members of a growing middle class. This extraordinarily successful medium was celebrated not least for its capacity to depict complexion. It was governed by aesthetic principles that put the ideals celebrated in the republic of taste in the service of visualizing and maintaining categories of race, gender, and class. The portraits of Elizabeth Freeman, a former slave, and Betsey Way Champlain, a working artist, illuminate how ubiquitous ivory miniatures helped shore up the hierarchies that structured the early republic. And yet the images in question were only partly successful in this regard. Read alongside an unusually rich documentary record, these portraits gesture both toward the fundamentally aspirational nature of an exclusionary American republic of taste and toward the challenges that could be leveled against it.

Ironically, the kinds of images, objects, and practices sketched in the book's first half worked to undermine republican authority as often as they worked to shore it up. British originals gave the lie to fantasies about American exceptionalism, while the logic of the capitalist market made the meanings of goods as well as the uses to which they were put especially malleable. The timeless truths commemorated in the republic of taste were ultimately no match for the solvent of commodification. The chapters in the second half of the book trace the open-ended, unstable result of efforts to create an American republic of taste. In Chapter 4, a country villa opens up questions about the persistence of Anglophilia, the continued appeal of British commodities, and the problems posed by the reintegration of loyalists in the years following the war. The Woodlands, located just outside Philadelphia on a bluff overlooking the Schuylkill River, was the lifework of William Hamilton, a loyalist and confirmed Anglophile. By the 1790s, Hamilton had eased himself back into elite society, using his exquisite house and gardens to clear the path. Less than twenty years later, Hamilton's estate was widely celebrated in paintings, prints, and published texts and manuscripts as proof that taste could and would flourish in a republic. The same visual, material, and literary cultures that secured The Woodlands a prominent place in a national, nationalist imaginary demonstrate how deeply contradictory that imaginary could be.

Yet even institutions that were, from the outset, conceived and executed as vehicles for republican knowledge and taste were vulnerable to the logic of the market and the illogic of consumer desire. Early national museums, for example, were explicitly didactic. They claimed to serve the republic by connecting the right kind of observation and the right kind of reading to the right kinds of objects. In fact, museums—the subject of Chapter 5—generated forms of looking and reading that defied republican protocols and gestured toward a political imaginary that was every bit as likely to undermine republican pieties as to reinforce them. Not even George Washington, the ur-founder, was insulated from the contradictory effects that aesthetic practices had on political culture, a political imaginary, and on politics proper. Chapter 6 traces the multiple contexts in which Anglo-Americans and others produced and viewed representations of Washington from the Revolutionary War into the nineteenth century. Washington himself leveraged both his likenesses and his person, creating a visual politics calculated to secure his political position and his place in history. His efforts were almost immediately dwarfed by the endless work of painters and engravers, sculptors and metalworkers, who saturated the market with depictions of his face. The relentless reproduction of Washingtoniana underscores the promise held out both by the republic of taste and the intersection of aesthetics, on the one hand, and by the market, on the other. Washington—as man, as myth, and as commodity—was both the product and the culmination of the American republic of taste. This book concludes with a brief epilogue that uses the Marquis de Lafayette's triumphal return to the United States in 1824 as an opportunity to take stock of the American republic of taste.

CHAPTER ONE

Learning Taste

"Saturday morning we defined the word Sensibility." So wrote Caroline Chester in the copybook that she kept while attending Sarah Pierce's Litchfield Academy in 1816.[1] Chester was proud enough of her own definition to record it in her journal: "True sensibility is that acuteness of feeling which is natural to those persons who possess the finer perceptions of seeing, hearing and feeling. It may very easily be distinguished from the false as the former has the effect upon the heart while the latter affects only the nerves." This sort of exercise was a typical part of an academy instructor's repertoire: Students parsed words like "useful knowledge," "discretion," "taste," and "sensibility" in order to nurture those qualities in themselves and reward them in others.

"Sensibility" was an obvious choice for the pantheon of virtues that Pierce aimed to inculcate in her students. In the narrowest terms, the word described an organic, physiological sensitivity—Chester's "finer perceptions." But for Pierce and her students, it meant much more than that. Since the middle of the eighteenth century, sensibility had been a catchphrase and a catchall. By the time that Caroline Chester put pen to paper, legions of philosophers, popularizers, ministers, and novelists had touted sensibility as the ideal marriage of reason and feeling. They had also enshrined it as both a prerequisite for and a crucial component of the development of taste, a quality that promised to reinforce moral as well as aesthetic judgments. In fact, "taste" and "sensibility" were so closely linked in everyday usage that one conjured to mind the other. Judgments afforded by taste were suffused with feelings that flowed from sensibility.[2]

If it is not surprising to find that sensibility was included among the key words of an early national academy student, neither is it surprising to learn that Chester associated it first with the "finer perceptions of *seeing.*"[3] The same transatlantic discourse that defined and celebrated "sensibility" underlined the connections between physical perception, intellectual apprehension, and affective realization: Information about the world entered the individual through the eye, or the mind's eye, causing a nervous reaction and igniting emotion. That emotion manifested itself first in the individual's bodily appearance—in flushed cheeks, sparkling eyes, and pooling tears—and then in his or her behavior. One person's capacity for sensibility was thus immediately visible to others who were similarly endowed. Comparable processes were at work in the exercise of taste. Although taste operated on all kinds of phenomena, ranging from landscapes to texts to music, it generally depended on visual perception. Taste shaped what people saw and how they chose to be seen. Just as the man of taste picked his discerning way through the world guided by his eyes, so, too, did he mark his identity in ways that would render him visible within the republic of taste. The logic of sensibility and taste locked men and women of feeling into a sensory feedback loop that was predicated upon and driven by assumptions about the significance of vision and visibility for subjectivity, taste, and cognition. To be sure, these closely linked constructs posited individual virtue in ways that aligned morality with class. Yet Pierce and her contemporaries recognized that these qualities could be maximized in almost everyone. Toward that end, early national academies placed considerable emphasis on the cultivation of sensibility and taste.

These preoccupations were invested with new political and social urgency in the years following the American Revolution. Educated and influential citizens insisted that sensibility and taste could contribute to the harmony of both domestic relations and civil society. Imagining that manners and affect, taste and feeling could bind an increasingly diverse, increasingly contentious society together, Americans likewise imagined a republic in which the putatively personal became explicitly political. At the same time, the values and practices associated with sensibility and taste reinforced Americans' fundamentally contradictory ideas about status and opportunity. Based on capacities that could be cultivated if not precisely taught, sensibility and taste held out the promise of improvement to an infinite number of citizens. And to the extent that these qualities were, at root, predicated on one's ability to distinguish between good, better, and best, they reinforced any number of social distinctions. Simultaneously elevating individual and society, sensibility and taste, linked self-cultivation to public service.

This broad consensus on the public importance of taste and sensibility accounted for their prominence among the characteristics that early national academies aimed to inculcate in youth. An equally broad consensus on how these qualities were constituted and how they operated led educators to situate visuality near the center of the academy experience. But academies were more than crucial sites for the enculturation of taste and sensibility in young women and men. They were also crucial sites for projecting the notion that taste and sensibility were central components of the republican project. The curricula and culture that defined these institutions, like the endless discussions of education that swirled in newspapers and magazines, served as a charged fantasy, an idealized picture of what the nation should look like. Grand pronouncements about education in general and academy education in particular allowed a very select group of young men and women to stand in for the nation as a whole. These discerning students, in turn, served a particular vision of the republic, one that was exclusive rather than inclusive, hierarchical rather than egalitarian.

The Academy in the Republic

The academic world that produced Caroline Chester's copybook, with its studied definition of sensibility, was as much the product of an institutional matrix as an intellectual one. Colonial education had been a patchwork affair. Notwithstanding a handful of state-sponsored Latin grammar schools in New England, education was largely a private concern. Throughout the colonies, enterprising men and women opened up ad hoc venture schools, providing a paying clientele with training in any number of skills, practical and otherwise: Advertisements for various eighteenth-century venture schools enticed students with geography, French, fencing, drawing, and dancing along with reading, writing, and arithmetic.[4]

By the middle of the eighteenth century, academies of various sorts had begun to appear. Ranging widely in curricula, organization, constituency, and financial support, early Anglo-American academies defy the tidy categories that historians usually aim to impose: Any provisional definition collapses before the sheer variety of schools that were deemed academies by their contemporaries. Indeed, that very flexibility was central to their success. Depending upon circumstance and market, academies might offer the rudimentary English of a common school, the classical curriculum of a grammar school, the eclectic mix of a venture school, or the ambitious program of a college. Generally speaking, they were more catholic than grammar schools and more systematic and more permanent than venture schools.[5]

Predictably, access to any of these schools was mediated by the inequalities that structured Anglo-American society. The Virginia scion who devoted himself to the works of the Roman historian Sallust under the careful direction of a Princeton-trained tutor was far removed from the anonymous young men who labored at "Arithmetic and Book-keeping" at a Philadelphia night school. And women were, by definition, excluded from Latin grammar schools and colleges. Still, by the 1750s, children of the elite and the merely prosperous found it far easier to secure some form of advanced education than their parents would have. Although precise figures are elusive, the number of schools and students was increasing by the mid-eighteenth century. Why? A dynamic, complex economy rewarded men who possessed at least a modicum of learning. Protestant denominations, eager to secure their share of the faithful, looked to schools to inculcate piety. Political conflict, especially following the Stamp Act Crisis, increased interest in the public prints and sharpened colonists' textual engagement with civic life. Finally, the pursuit of gentility encouraged some individuals to seek out more extensive schooling than the minimum demanded by market, church, or civil society.

If the war for American independence disrupted this energetic, diverse collection of institutions and strategies, the creation of the American republic famously reinvigorated it. The ideological commitment to a culture of learning, broadly defined, ran wide and deep. Benjamin Rush may have been remarkable in asserting that a national school system could "convert men into republican machines," but he was downright pedestrian in believing that "the business of education has acquired a new complexion by the independence of our country."[6] Throughout the early national period, Americans manifested enormous faith in the capacity of learning to transform individuals and society. Countless essays, tracts, speeches, sermons, and letters affirmed that education, republican style, did more than create an informed citizenry. It also fostered a virtuous one. In Rush's words, formal education could make a man "immutable in his character, inflexible in his honesty," and prepare him to "feel the dignity of his nature and cheerfully obey the claims of duty." Only education could free men and women from the shackles of self-interest, from the parochial and the particular.

The expansion of education in the decades following the Revolution took many forms, encompassing the creation of common schools and colleges, the organization of learned societies, and the proliferation of print culture. Yet no one form was as visible, either for contemporaries or subsequent scholars, as the academy. Numbers alone account for much of the academy's prominence. By 1800, the United States boasted only twenty-five colleges, but it had launched literally hundreds of academies.[7] Academies flourished because they were well suited to a nation that was simultaneously convinced of the urgent importance of schooling, uncertain about how to fund it, and divided over the extent to which it should create new opportunities or reinforce old hierarchies. Most depended on multiple revenue sources, confounding modern distinctions between private and public. Funding was secured through gifts, subscriptions, and, especially, tuition, which varied widely among schools. But many academies also looked to state legislatures for support, ranging from monies raised by the sale of confiscated and public lands to outright land grants to tax exemptions. Whatever form it took and however limited it might have been, state support forged powerful ideological connections between "public" and "education."[8]

Conflicts over curricula, which quickly ballooned into ideologically charged debates over the kind of education most suited to a republic, also contributed to the notion that academies were central to the well-being of the republic as a whole. Consider the debate over classical languages. On one side were those who urged educators and students to eliminate or at least minimize the emphasis on Greek and Latin. As early as 1749, Benjamin Franklin had begun to champion a more utilitarian approach to education.[9] Following the Revolution, other voices joined Franklin's critique of the classics, inflecting it with the imperatives of postrevolutionary politics: Rush and Noah Webster, for example, advocated the careful study of English and condemned the classics as difficult, impractical, and altogether unsuited for a republic that demanded the diffusion of "universal knowledge." And any number of wags published jokes about farm boys whose academy stints had bestowed a smattering of comically bad Latin while doing nothing to remove the rust from their English.[10] On the other side of the debate, traditionalists like Joseph Dennie worried that, by "removing the foundations of intellect" from education, Americans were poised to "sacrifice intellect itself." John Adams wrote that he "should as soon think of closing all my window shutters, to enable me to see," as he would "banishing the Classicks, to improve Republican ideals." Defenders of the classics insisted explicitly that ancient languages and texts were the building blocks of advanced education. Implicitly, they correlated learning with social class. All citizens may have needed an education, but they did not need the same education.[11]

Neither side prevailed. The virtuous learning advanced by early national academies never fit into a single mold. Most men's academies managed to incorporate classical languages into their curricula. The pedagogy remained stultifying, and few students ever actually used the languages outside the academy or college. Instead, the persistent appeal of Latin, especially, testified to the political resonance and cultural cachet of all things connected to the ancient republics.[12] But with the exception of a handful of schools like Phillips Academy (where well into the nineteenth century, students studied Latin, Latin, and more Latin), the ancient languages typically formed one optional component of a far more general curriculum. School catalogs and advertisements promised students a sort of intellectual smorgasbord: The classical program of study was balanced by an English one, which included instruction in reading, spelling, grammar, composition, and polite letters. Arithmetic, including the useful but tedious "rule of three," was ubiquitous. History, which offered clues to the developmental trajectory of the American republic, and geography, which situated the nation in a global context while describing its vast and varied terrain, became common by the 1790s. By the turn of the nineteenth century, these standard offerings were often supplemented with modern languages; natural philosophy or natural history; music; a smattering of purely vocational skills including bookkeeping, surveying, and navigating; and an entire battery of "ornamentals." Some schools required students to follow a set course of study. But far more offered them a series of choices: English or classical, with extras like French, geography, or music added on, usually for an additional fee.[13] Withal, the precise course of study depended on both the competencies of available instructors and the expectations and desires of potential students. The options served up by early national academies derived less from a fervent commitment to the importance of, say, Latin, than to a complicated calculus of supply and demand.

If the much-ballyhooed debates over the classical curriculum in particular and truly republican cultures of learning in general did not determine what most academies actually offered, they did serve to amplify the political resonance of the curriculum as a whole. Academies could and did claim that their courses of study, regardless of their specific content, furthered the "diffusion of knowledge" and thus contributed to the "improvement of society." Such claims were freighted with republican significance. As the Reverend Simeon Doggett intoned at the dedication of the Bristol Academy in Massachusetts, education did more than determine the shape of the state. It endowed citizens with a "knowledge of the rights of man, and the enjoyment of civil liberty." Only education could forge a nation that was "happy at home and respectable abroad."[14] That said, institutions like the Bristol Academy granted students considerable latitude in deciding on the particular components of knowledge that were most desirable and, by extension, most republican.

This aura of civic importance extended from the curriculum to the students. It was not simply that an academy education could help initiate young men and women students into the ranks of a republican citizenry. Academies promised to extend that education—and all it represented—to an unprecedented number of students.[15] White women were the most visible beneficiaries of the postrevolutionary expansion of higher education. Their access to education is evidenced through not only the founding of female and coeducational schools but also those schools' rising enrollments. A few examples from especially well-documented schools can suffice: In 1798, Sarah Pierce's Litchfield, Connecticut, academy claimed thirty students; four years later, it claimed at least seventy. The Moravian female seminary in Bethlehem, Pennsylvania, tripled its enrollment between 1787 and 1790. One year after it opened its doors, the Young Ladies' Academy of Philadelphia enrolled one hundred pupils. Susanna Rowson's Boston school opened with five students in 1799; by the end of that year, it had more than a hundred.[16]

Analogous figures for male academies are both more elusive and less dramatic. The inaugural class of the Moravian Nazareth Hall in Pennsylvania, for example, included eleven students. Fifteen years later, in 1785, the school enrolled forty-five, and by its fiftieth reunion, the school boasted of educating more than eight hundred men and boys—an average of about sixteen new students per year. By 1803, Massachusetts's preeminent Phillips Academy enrolled a mere fifty-seven students.[17] These numbers, which pale next to those for female academies, probably testify more to supply than to demand. Young men could choose from a greater number of academies; in an increasingly crowded and competitive market, no one institution was likely to secure enormous enrollment increases. Anecdotal evidence suggests that these schools did broaden education's reach by serving a population that extended well beyond the college-bound sons of the elite. For example, when Josiah Quincy, the product of a prominent New England family and the future president of Harvard University, entered Phillips Academy at the precocious age of six, he sat next to a thirty-six-year-old Revolutionary War veteran.[18]

Indeed, one of the most regular registers of academies' popular appeal can be found in the chorus of complaints that they had become all too popular. As one critic explained in 1791, the "easiness of access, and the smallness of the expense," tempted farmers and mechanics to imagine brilliant and altogether unrealistic futures for their sons.[19] He need not have worried. Notwithstanding the striking increase in early national academy enrollments, only a minority of American women and men gained admission. Indeed, that minority may have been as small as 6 percent of the population. The cost of tuition and board, questions about the market value of an advanced education, and lingering suspicions that individual ambition owed less to virtue than to vice all ensured that the vast majority of Americans never pursued advanced education. And academies, for their part, were careful to pitch themselves to potential students who were, at the very least, "respectable"—a term that by definition excluded entire categories of people, most obviously African Americans and members of the laboring class.[20]

Although most Americans would never attend an academy, the public prints relentlessly cast those who did as exemplars of republican virtue, as citizens who served a unified public interest. Lofty claims about the value of education, delivered to students and then published for the benefit of the reading public, collapsed a very select group of women and men into a depiction of the nation as a whole. Female scholars, for example, may well have been drawn to academies by a love of learning or by the need to acquire practical, even marketable, skills. But they were celebrated for their salutary influence over the nation's manners. As the Philadelphia merchant, politician, and man-of-letters John Swanwick explained to students at the Young Ladies' Academy in 1787, "the luster of your examples, and the intelligence of your minds" would "dispose others to similar qualifications." Addressing the senior class of the Philadelphia Academy, James Abercrombie assumed that the purpose of the young men's education was the fulfillment of civic duty. Individual ambition played no part in Abercrombie's depiction of the liberal education afforded by the academy. Instead, schooling taught these soon-to-be-citizens how a "strong and energetic *Government*" and "undefiled *Religion*" together produced "real liberty." More than that, it taught them how "securely to curb the phrensy of faction, and effectually restrain the 'madness of the people.'"[21] By acquiring an academy education (at least as described in the prints), students pursued a distinctly republican, deeply politicized form of virtue—for themselves and for the nation.

This discourse was never the mechanical reflection of a social fact. It was also a charged fantasy of nation formation. Oafish farm boys with their comically bad Latin; evenhanded young men of affairs who could be trusted to rise above faction, pulling the rest of the electorate up with them; serene young ladies who elevated the nation's conversation before marriage and reared its citizens afterward: These were stock characters in a national discourse that used the academy movement to articulate an idealized, albeit contested, picture of the republic. Representations of male students marked the conservative boundaries of acceptable political culture. They reduced the threat of "leveling" to a joke and encouraged readers' faith in the handful of good men who could and would secure the republic and lead the nation to greatness.

Or consider the remarkably energetic discussion of women's education and female intellect that filled up the pages of early national newspapers and magazines, to say nothing of the catalogs, prospectuses, exercises, and broadsides published by academies themselves. Unlike discussions about men's educations, which danced around questions about class, discussions about women's education generally focused on the role of female intellect in a republic. Here, the issue was not so much educating the wrong girl as giving the right girl the wrong training. Should she learn rhetoric or French? Read history or novels? Learn to dance or to paint?[22] Certainly, the endless and endlessly repetitive discussions of the "fair sex" served as a response to the growing numbers of young women who attended academies and as a vehicle for debating women's social and political roles. But those same discussions also used the expansion of women's education to demonstrate the distinctive virtue of the American republic.

Commentators routinely appealed to philosophical and literary conventions that conflated women's status and national character. They gestured toward a political theory that located republics, including the American one, as landmarks on the journey from barbarism to civilization. John P. Brace, Sarah Pierce's nephew and right-hand man, regularly reminded Litchfield students that they had been spared the cruel indignities piled upon the women of Greenland, China, and Burma. They knew only second-hand what their "sex once suffered when the night of ignorance covered the world." Like the tales of "Oriental" seraglios that proved so popular in the 1790s, texts that focused on women's education implicitly and explicitly situated the United States on a spectrum of civilization bounded by heathen primitivism on one end and aristocratic decadence on the other. As Mary Magdalen M'Intosh put it in an 1825 commencement essay when comparing American and Turkish women, "They were educated as slaves; we as the legitimate heirs and children of Freedom."[23] Indeed, the remarkable prominence of educated women in early national discourse may have owed less to demographics of academy enrollments or even to battles over gender equality than to the powerful resonance of the appropriately educated woman as a symbol of American virtue.

The elements of a republican education were never imagined as a series of intellectual abstractions. When academies sought to turn students into the pillars of the republic, they prepared them to assume roles as spectators and players within a national spectacle. In effect, an academy education furnished young men and women with the skills to execute an infinite number of performances in the larger world. There, students would be judged not only on their ability to declaim in Latin and read a map, but also on whether they had internalized the moral example set by Cato and how well they knew the nation's geography. There, students would become objects of emulation, standard-bearers whose virtues would be reproduced across space and over time. And there, students would use the heightened perception and keen discretion they had acquired at school to monitor the nation's progress, keeping a sharp eye out for the rogues and coquettes, the factions and demagogues that threatened the republic. Like virtue itself, the subjectivities and social relations fostered by academies depended on the cultivation of sensibility and the exercise of taste. They were, in other words, aestheticized. For that reason, a concern with aesthetics—broadly defined and embedded in a rich visual culture—pervaded curricula at academies throughout the early national period.

Taste was central to the rhetorical study that anchored the curricula of the overwhelming majority of early national academies. Classes in English language and literatures (variously called "composition," "composition and rhetoric," or "composition and criticism") aimed to teach students more than the mechanics of grammar and the rudiments of style. Instead, they were intended to immerse young men and women in an aesthetic world that encompassed criticism as well as composition. As Sarah Pierce put it at the close of one school term, the goal of studying rhetoric and composition had been "to create or direct taste."[24] Toward that end, students at academies and seminaries throughout the country read in, if not all the way through, the eighteenth-century British aesthetic canon. This project was facilitated by an expansive print culture that made works by Joseph Addison; Edmund Burke; Henry Home, Lord Kames; Archibald Alison; and, most especially, Hugh Blair available in multiple forms that were more or less comprehensive and more or less costly. By the turn of the nineteenth century, Blair's *Lectures on Rhetoric and Belles Lettres* or Kames's *Elements of Criticism*, for example, were available as full-length books, in either imported or domestic imprints; as abridged editions; or excerpted into volumes like the one compiled in 1784 by James Rivington, which included extracts from Blair, Sterne, "Kaimes," Burke, Chesterfield, Addison, Steele, and the "Authors of the Connoisseur."[25]

This extensive, transatlantic discourse on taste, elaborated over the course of the long eighteenth century, was hardly monolithic. It encompassed significant disputes over whether the capacity for taste was the result of nature or nurture and generated arguments over whether there was a single standard of taste or many. But by and large, Americans were far less interested in the disagreements within this discourse than in its overriding consensus on the importance of taste as a measure of character and civilization. After all, as Blair observed in his enormously popular *Lectures*, educators "in every age" had been duty-bound to "tincture" youth "early with relish for the entertainments of Taste" because it was "more or less connected with every good and virtuous disposition." Taste increased "sensibility to all the tender and humane passions" and diminished the "more violent and fierce emotions." If these capacities made taste central to civilized society, they made it critical to a republican one.[26]

Given the stakes, debating taste was less important than affirming it. One mode of affirmation was explicitly textual. To recognize the connections between beauty, sensibility, and taste or to understand the standards of taste that governed the production of polite letters and fine arts, scholars were directed year after year to works by Addison, Kames, Alison, or the ubiquitous Blair. From these longer texts, they excerpted key passages, which they then read silently and aloud, memorized, recited, and transcribed. When Caroline Chester spent an afternoon in 1815 writing that a good letter called for "ease and familiarity, simplicity, sprightliness and wit" and that poetry was the "language of passion, or of enlivened imagination, formed most commonly into regular numbers," she demonstrated her knowledge of polite letters and her ability to reproduce their generic conventions in her own writing. But she also demonstrated that she had internalized the precepts from Blair's lectures on "Epistolary" and "The Nature of Poetry." More than fifteen years later, a Philadelphia student, Sara Gratz Moses, transcribed extracts from Addison, John Dryden, and William Cowper along with Blair's assessment of their rhetorical strengths and weaknesses. Sandwiched between these critiques were her own attempts to craft prose that would meet the standards that had been set out by Blair more than fifty years previous.[27]

Other modes of affirmation operated at the intersection of the textual and the visual, for one sign of a good stylist was the ability to communicate in tasteful words what the tasteful eye perceived. Indeed, according to Blair, the "high power" of prose and poetry obtained precisely in their capacity for "Imitation and Description," which allowed a writer to "represent" an original "in colours very strong and lively." Accordingly, student diaries, letters, and essays reveal a sustained and self-conscious attempt to train their eyes, articulate sensation, and thereby register taste. Henry Cheever, whose reading of John Milton, Alexander Pope, and Oliver Goldsmith inspired his description of a summer sunset, was hardly alone in using the books he read to help him recognize and describe the beauty of the natural world. While studying at Litchfield, Mary Ann Bacon regularly began her morning with a walk in the garden of the house where she boarded; after each walk, she recorded in her diary that she "went upstairs contemplating the beauties of nature."[28]

These habits of seeing and writing, conditioned by reading, stayed with young women and men outside the confines of school. Hetty Anne Barton, for one, took them with her on a family junket from Pennsylvania to Virginia in 1803. Standing on the banks of the Susquehanna River, she adopted the perspective of the picturesque tourist: "The scenery from the middle of the river is very beautiful, the eye can scarcely reach the misty distance, so extensive is the view while nearer objects seem more immediately to command attention. . . . The hills along the bank are richly fringed with woods," while "those more distant, assum[ed] the different shades of blue and purple, the warm colouring of the setting sun." The next morning, the shifting light of sunrise combined with the movement of the carriage to create a landscape that was "continually changing before us." This play of light and motion, a by-product of travel, was itself worthy of comment: "Every moment . . . unfolded new beauties, each scene, varying in richness, and highly cultivated, formed a continual picture for the eye to rest on." Barton parsed her field of vision according to the precepts laid out by eighteenth-century picturesque writers like Thomas Whately or William Gilpin; she described it in rhetoric informed by Blair.[29]

It was no accident that Cheever, Bacon, Barton, and countless other academy students were attuned to the "beauties of nature" or to beauty in general. For eighteenth- and early nineteenth-century thinkers on both sides of the Atlantic, the beauty that one encountered on the page was connected to the beauty one saw in the world. Beauty was connected, in other words, to visual perception. Consider Hugh Blair. His *Lectures* focused on elevating rhetoric and imbuing it with taste. But because he defined taste as the "power of receiving pleasure from the beauties of art or nature," he had no choice but to consider beauty. And beauty was, in the first instance, visual. Thus, hundreds of pages of lectures detailing sentence structure, cautioning against hyperbole, and explicating genres ranging from lyric poetry to legal summation were preceded by a discussion of "sublimity in objects" and a disquisition on beauty as it was grounded in color, shape, and motion and as it was manifested in the human countenance and in "artful design."[30]

Texts that expounded on beauty had to look the part. Academies thus placed great emphasis on penmanship, which one authority declared was "generally considered a strong evidence of a polite education."[31] Projecting the abstract realm of sentiment and thought onto the smooth surface of the page, penmanship demonstrated more than a writer's physical mastery of pen, ink, and letterforms. It also revealed his or her social rank, education, taste, and character. Penmanship signified so powerfully partly because writing had been an exceptional skill in the colonial era and partly because it acquired new meanings after the Revolution. Throughout the seventeenth and eighteenth centuries, Anglo-Americans viewed reading and writing as separate and only tangentially related skills. Although significant percentages of colonial men and women learned to read, if only to read the Bible, writing remained the province of a far more select group. Ministers, doctors, lawyers, wealthy women and men, and, especially, merchants could wield a pen. As the expansion of commerce increased the demand for writing in the second half of the eighteenth century, the expansion of education increased opportunities to acquire it. But if writing became less rarified, it did not become less resonant. The proliferation of print in the second half of the eighteenth century tightened the association between handwriting and selfhood. Unlike the mechanized, impersonal regularity of a typeface, the small idiosyncrasies that marked one man's round or Italian hand also signaled his temperament. In the years following the Revolution, this association became far more urgent. Educational theorists who posited republican society as the guarantor of a republican state attempted to identify the particular script best suited for a republic. At the same time, pervasive anxieties about authenticity compelled some readers to seize on a "good hand" as one more proof of an individual writer's character. Thus, a "good hand" rendered both text and writer legible.[32]

With so much riding on the stroke of a pen, handwriting could not be left to chance. Although the ability to write was a prerequisite for admission to an academy, an ongoing emphasis on penmanship was a routine component of the curriculum. Some academies hired writing masters outright; others made do with teachers already on staff who claimed some competence as "writing instructors." Whatever form the training took, students could expect to be judged on their proficiency with the pen. The younger students at the Bethlehem Female Seminary, for example, kept both individual writing books and a collaborative daily school journal. All these books were evaluated on the grounds of "writing and language." Congratulating the girls on their improvement in "writing a fair hand," school principal Jacob Van Vleck admonished them not to rest on their laurels but rather to continue "giving all possible pains in obtaining this noble art." The Bethlehem students were not alone. Well into the nineteenth century, academy students spent hours and hours copying words, phrases, and epigrams into their penmanship books: "By commendable deportment we gain reputation." "Virtue preserves friendship." "Xenocrates recommended virtuous employments." "Commend good men." "Merit creates envy." "Wisdom and virtue are ornaments of the soul."[33] The more advanced the student, the longer the passages. During their second year, the young men at Nazareth Hall graduated from short epigrams to business correspondence: "Rec'd from Francis TrueMan the Sum of Forty Seven Pounds Pennsylvania Currency being in of a Debt due by Mssr.s Trueman and Wilson." Even when students moved beyond the rote copying of the penmanship book, they were expected to continue honing their hands at the same time that they composed letters and filled up commonplace books and diaries.[34]

This was not a matter of elevating style over substance. As one educator put it, a good hand bestowed a "grace to composition." Thus Cheever understood that he was expected to fill his journal with his "feelings just as they are, and if possible in good style and fair writing." The quality of handwriting mattered well beyond the walls of the academy. To hear Stephen Salisbury's parents tell it, his wretched handwriting spoiled the letters he sent them from a Massachusetts academy. "Your father rec'd your careless Scrawl, & desires me to ask you if any of the other Scholars send such scraps of paper folded up as letters," his

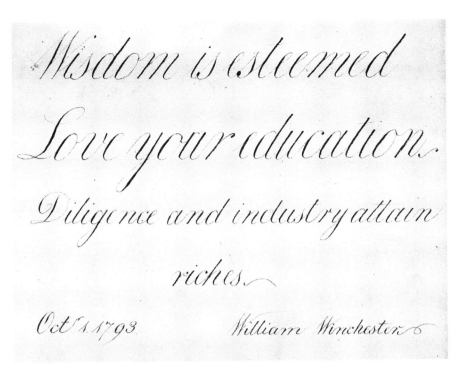

Figure 2. William Winchester prepared this example of the running hand for the Oct. 1793 examination at Nazareth Hall. Samples of the students' writing were preserved in a volume marked "Specimens of Writing Made by the Scholars in Nazareth School for the Autumnal Examination." Courtesy, The Winterthur Library: Joseph Downs Collection of Manuscripts and Printed Ephemera. Winterthur Museum and Library.

mother wrote. Ignoring the letter's contents—which recounted her son's life at school—she issued a warning: "It is time you did better Stephen." The quality of the medium and the message were of a piece.[35]

The conventions governing students' penmanship paralleled and amplified the conventions of their compositions. Both were governed by the aesthetics of emulation and the mechanics of reproduction. The work submitted by students at Nazareth Hall for their 1793 examination, for example, certified them as masters of the running hand, which was the script of choice for commerce and the professions. But the samples also certified the boys as masters of the copy. Almost to a one, they replicated the example provided by the teacher so closely that it is all but impossible to distinguish one writer from another. Only the small notation of names on some of the entries makes it possible to distinguish one boy's work from the next. For these boys and countless others, the goal was not legibility so much as submission to the conventions of a codified style. This discipline ensured consistency across the pages of script penned by a single

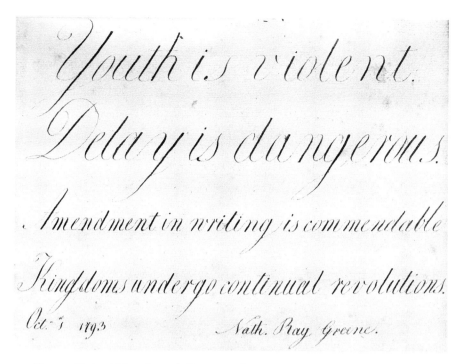

Figure 3. Nathaniel Ray Greene's "specimen," prepared for the same examination as William Winchester's, is nearly identical to it. Courtesy, The Winterthur Library: Joseph Downs Collection of Manuscripts and Printed Ephemera. Winterthur Museum and Library.

writer as well as consistency among all the student writers. An observer might recognize a particular penmanship sample as an example of the running hand but he would not immediately identify it as the product of any particular individual's hand. The uniformity of the script appears effortless. Along with the identities of the writers, the labor necessary to comply with the model has been effaced.

Like the return of the repressed, traces of labor that have been erased in one place reappear in others. Occasionally, students' everyday writing—marked by careening slants and misshapen letters—hint at the effort required to produce writing that met the standards held up by instructors and parents. Penmanship books, like the one kept by Samuel Salisbury in the summer of 1780 provide a clearer picture of a good hand in the making. For two months, Salisbury alternated daily between copying pages of single letters and pages of epigrams. Gradually, his lettering became more consistent, his script more fluid. Salisbury's book evidences his labor, but does not remark on it.[36]

Memoirs are more explicit on this point, recording both the effort and its value. Mary Jane Peabody recalled that the girls at her "boarding school" were required to write abstracts of Sunday's sermons. By the time she left, she had filled several books with summaries set down in "round, clear hand writing." But although the précis were easy to read, she was not satisfied with her writing. "Determined to write better, more like a lady," Peabody found a "good copy to imitate" and took "infinite pains." Her progress was measured on paper, in a book that began in her "usual hand" and ended in "very delicate neat writing." While Peabody described her pursuit of a good hand in a memoir, Samuel May inscribed his in the front covers of the same penmanship books he had filled as a boy. Near the end of his life, he wrote that because he had but a "cramped and awkward hand" at the age of twelve, his father arranged for him to leave the public Latin school for an hour and a half each day to take "at least 110" private writing lessons with the Reverend John Pierpont, "a penman of the very rarest excellence & good taste." At the minister's house, he traced sloping, parallel lines to memorize the ideal slant of the running hand and repeated single letters for pages at a time. Only then did he graduate to words and, shortly after that, to an "intermediate" writing school. In May's telling, his work with Pierpont was as significant a step on the road to Harvard's entrance examinations as the time he spent at the public Latin school.[37]

Chirography—the art of writing—involved more than the hand-eye coordination necessary to form letters. A penman "of the rarest excellence" produced legible text and did so in a way that commentators routinely described as "useful and polite" or "easy and correct." These stock phrases make clear that a "good hand" was defined as much by the person manipulating the pen as by the letters inscribed on paper. While we might trace Salisbury's progress as a penman by the changing appearance of his handwriting, his contemporaries would also have considered the changing appearance of his body as he wrote. Polite penmanship was a total body effort: That was the message drilled home by the "practical" writing guides published in the late eighteenth and early nineteenth centuries. Claiming to duplicate in book form the training offered by writing masters, authorities like George Fisher and Nathan Towne dictated the correct placement of every finger in the hand that held the pen and cautioned students never to allow the "ball and fleshy part of the hand" to touch the paper. But they also prodded would-be writers to pull their elbows in close to their sides, to keep their pens inclined toward their right shoulders. They insisted variously that writers sit "pretty upright" or that they lean forward over the table, making sure to keep their heads within the same plane as their spines.[38]

These dicta obviously helped novice writers learn to control the flow of ink and to protect their sleeves and cuffs from stains. But they also prescribed a bodily aesthetic. Like the pen-wielding sitters painted by John Singleton Copley

Figure 4. John Singleton Copley (American, 1738–1815), *John Hancock*, 1765. Oil on canvas, 49 1/8 × 39 3/8 in. Museum of Fine Arts, Boston. Deposited by the City of Boston, L-R 30.76d statement. Photograph © 2016 Museum of Fine Arts, Boston.

or Charles Willson Peale, the writers conjured by Fisher and Towne could turn gracefully from their work to acknowledge observers. They arranged themselves, their pens, and paper to communicate that they were engaged with but never consumed by the texts they produced. Real writers and painted ones drew attention to the performative and social contexts of penmanship, underscoring an aesthetic that encompassed process as well as product.

Learning to cultivate and demonstrate one's taste, like learning more generally, was an intensely embodied process. For one thing, the richly aestheticized education promoted by early national academies depended on the senses, especially sight. It was manifested materially, physically. Thus it is not surprising that teachers paid careful attention to the students' bodies. For another, educators, parents, and students were heirs to a long-standing western tradition that elevated a mastery of the body into a hallmark of gentility, imagining it as a central element of what one scholar has called "the civilizing process." An individual's mind and affections correlated with his or her physical form.

This inclination to view the body as the initial register of character was invested with new political and cultural significance after the Revolution, when Americans were keen to find evidence of themselves as a people who were truly republican and intensely worried that they would come up short.[39] The same assumptions and anxieties that connected the life of the mind to the body politic also connected the life of the mind to the bodies of students themselves. Accordingly, many academies incorporated into their curricula what we might call a course in physical education, one that started at the washbasin and ended in the ballroom.

First, students learned to pay close attention to their bodies. Philadelphia's Episcopal Academy included instructions about hygiene in the school's long list of rules, requiring "Cleanliness in Dress and Person" and directing students to take care that "the head be combed and the hands and Face washed before coming to School." Young women were also encouraged to heed their appearance. Every week, students at the Litchfield Academy were directed to inventory their bodies as well as their souls. Just as they "prayed to God in whose hands your breath is" they were to review whether they had "been neat" in their "persons" or careless with their clothes, whether they had combed their hair with a "fine tooth comb" and cleaned their teeth every morning. This preoccupation with the well-groomed body as a manifestation of inner character worked its way into book learning. "Neatness is the natural garb of a well ordered mind and has a near alliance with purity of heart," wrote one Litchfield student, pointing out that "Richardson whose taste was exquisite as his imagination glowing has painted his Clarissa as always dressed before she came down for breakfast."[40]

Regular and diligent grooming was a precursor to physical grace. In repose and in motion, students were taught to conform to the kinetic conventions of refinement. The goal was a kind of erect ease through the torso and neck, leaving one's arms, legs, and head free to trace Hogarth's line of beauty. Failure to master those conventions was a matter of real concern. Elizabeth Way, who operated a school for girls in eighteenth-century Delaware, was especially vigilant in policing the bearing of her charges. Way reportedly hung necklaces of "Jamestown-weed burrs" round the necks of students who let their heads hang forward and strapped both steel rods and "morocco spiders" to the backs of young girls inclined to slouch. In 1802, fourteen-year-old Lucy Sheldon shamefully reported that when she and her peers at Litchfield assembled to hear "Miss Pierce tell our faults," she had been singled out for "holding my arms stiff which made me appear awkward, and which I shall certainly endeavor to correct."[41]

If steel rods and public scoldings discouraged bad posture, dancing fostered physical grace and infused it with politeness. Both a physical discipline and a mode of interaction, dancing represented the union of genteel body and genteel sociability. Accordingly, many schools made dancing lessons available to male and female students for an extra charge. As Mary Bacon put it in an 1820 composition, dancing was "professedly an essential part of a good education as correcting any awkwardness of gestures giving an easy and graceful motion to the body." She was not alone. Speaking before Philadelphia's Young Ladies' Academy, Swanwick suggested that dancing promoted health and rendered "the figure and motions of the body easy and agreeable." The principals of the Clermont Seminary went further. They promised parents that dancing lessons combined with a close supervision of their sons' manners would impart "a taste and relish for decorum, and politeness," which was "no small part of education." Indeed, the Reverend James Cosens Ogden told the notables assembled for the dedication of the Portsmouth Academy in 1791 that dancing contributed decisively to a broader social good by dispelling "the rust of prejudice." When diverse and even divided men and women see one another in their "best dress and most pleasant face," he enthused, "spleen flies—harmony reigns." Amid the rancorous political climate of the 1790s, some observers hoped that society could serve as a balm to the wounds of partisan politics.[42]

Certainly, dancing attracted its share of critics. The novelist and educator Hannah Webster Foster surely spoke for many when she listed dancing among "the most fascinating, and of course the most dangerous," of accomplishments. The dangers were especially acute for women. A woman might well appear "polite and elegant" while executing the steps of a cotillion. But the thrill of self-display and the gratification of public recognition all too often lead to "unbounded wants," to psychic ambitions and physical desires that could not be satisfied within the realm of propriety. Because the ballroom was the setting for collaborative, ensemble performances, a woman who aspired to command center stage was surely headed for trouble. The boundary between the polite and the erotic was disconcertingly porous. Even Bacon, who credited dancing with erasing "awkward gestures," worried that "modern manners may however have carried the fondness for this accomplishment to an immoderate extreme." She wondered whether "exceling in this particular does not inspire too great a fondness for dissipated pleasures and proportionably abate the ardur for more retired virtues." After all, she reasoned, "a woman who can sparkle and engage the admiration of every beholder at a birth night or a ball is not always content with the grave office of managing a family."[43]

Removing dancing from a school's curriculum did not remove it from its culture. Many of the same schools that excluded dancing from their course lists included balls on their social calendars, suggesting that educators and parents expected students to have at least a passing familiarity with the basics. At single-sex and coeducational academies, balls were typically staged to mark holidays like July 4th and to celebrate the close of the school year. And at some schools, balls and dances were organized far more often than that. Certainly that was the case with Litchfield Female Academy. Although the school did not offer dancing lessons, student diaries and journals are punctuated with references to "pretty agreeable" balls, "very agreeable" balls, "school balls" composed of students only, and "public balls," where scholars mingled with select townsmen and -women.[44]

The point of dancing was not simply to school the body in grace but also to put the graceful body in the service of polite society. If student balls were rehearsals, public balls were auditions. Students were judged on their dancing and on the number of partners they attracted. But observers also took note of their dress, mien, conversation, and charm. Scattered accounts from diaries, letters, and memoirs suggest that young women were ranked more on appearance; young men, on their social skills. In both cases, the stakes were high. Most obviously, balls served as very public vehicles for initiating courtship. They also served as a proving ground for polite society. As a middle-aged woman quipped after watching the "heels fly this way and that" at a Litchfield ball, "This is solemn business." Or, in the words of her companion, a law student seeking the admiration of Litchfield's loveliest belles and the respect of its best families, balls "could make toil of pleasure as the old man said when he buried his wife."[45]

Like mastery of the body, mastery of the politesse that made balls such serious business was a formal part of academy educations. Especially around the turn of the nineteenth century, academies and seminaries took pains to assure parents and patrons that they could train citizens who were as well mannered as they were virtuous. Schools promised to police sloppy table manners, hush loud laughter, and calm boisterous behavior. But they also pledged to inculcate the sort of manners appropriate to a harmoniously hierarchical social order. Prominent among the "rules" that students at Litchfield Academy copied every year, for example, was a definition of politeness that directed "Every real Lady" to "treat her superior with due reverence" and her "companions with politeness." According to the trustees of New Hampshire's Atkinson Academy, precisely because politeness formed the "basis of honour & happiness to individuals, the foundation of harmony to society & felicity to nations," students must extend respect to superiors, friendship to equals, and courtesy to inferiors. At Leicester Academy, students were required to leave their heads uncovered when a tutor was present in the yard, even though they might be older than the tutor. Looking back on the practice some fifty years after the fact, John Pierce, who had served as an assistant preceptor in the 1790s, conceded that the practice probably seemed "extreme" to those who had grown up a generation or two later. But surely, he insisted, this rather stuffy past was preferable to the present, in which all forms of deference had fallen by the wayside.[46] Pierce understood that the outmoded rules of his youth had ensured order within the academy and beyond it. They prescribed clear channels of deference for students whose age or family background might otherwise allow them to claim precedence over instructors and schoolmasters just as they primed students to assume their proper social place after graduation.

The codification of etiquette also underscored the explicitly *social* ends of an academy education. Far from cultivating intellect for its own sake, academies groomed young men and women to take their places on a larger stage, one that began immediately outside the academy yard. Consider, for example, the cautions, prohibitions, and exhortations for student behavior on the streets. On their way to and from school, students were to refrain from "uncouth noises and gestures." They were to keep to the public roads and not trample across private property. They must not be "rude to any Person" and should extend themselves by "paying a handsome compliment to the passing stranger or citizen, by pulling off the hat or otherwise, as propriety & genteel conduct may require." They were in short, to "manifest, by [their] whole deportment, respect for the quiet of the place," and thereby "win the respect of the residents" for themselves and their teachers.[47] The imperative to maintain good-neighbor status accounted for much of this concern. No academy could afford to have its students associated with rowdiness or impropriety by the surrounding community. But more than town-gown diplomacy was in play.

Admonitions about students' public behavior, read alongside contemporary descriptions of students and reminiscences about academy life, reveal a self-conscious sense of young women and men on display. Especially in provincial towns and villages, where local academies were associated with brilliant careers and sparkling sociability, students constituted a special—and especially

　　　　　　　　　　　CHAPTER ONE

observed—group. This was as true in church as it was in the street or in the ballroom. Students at many academies attended church as members of a group, with the academy "family" sitting alongside the congregation's other, natal families. Numbers alone would have rendered them conspicuous. But some students sought seats that afforded them maximum visibility. In Litchfield, for example, Sarah Pierce's decorous young ladies preferred a "select" group of benches up front, where they were both free from immediate adult supervision and visible to the rest of the congregation. One student recalled that when "out girls" (farmers' daughters who lived "out" as "help" in village families) arrived at church early to commandeer the choice pews, a surreptitious battle of "pinching, pin pricking, and punching" ensued until the "school girls" could reclaim their turf the following week. Some seventy miles north in Massachusetts, male students from the Monson Academy were consigned to rear pews. But they nevertheless imagined themselves to be visible, at least to those who mattered most. Decades after leaving the academy, Charles Hammond could still summon to his mind's eye the "dioramic procession of the fathers and magnates of the town" as they promenaded with their families past the scholars to seats at the very front of the church. The front seats of the old-fashioned, three-sided pews were occupied by the heads of households, who sat with their backs to the minister, facing their wives and children. But in Hammond's telling, the notables kept their eyes "always directed toward us"—the academy students. As he "watched them in turn," Hammond judged them to be exemplars of "personal gravity."[48] In this fantasy of mutual recognition, the "fathers and magnates" served as a mirror into the future, allowing Hammond to anticipate his own "personal gravity."

Not all the fantasies spun by this sort of visibility were so uplifting, especially where young women were concerned. Poised on the brink of courtship, female students often figured as objects of sexual desire. This was certainly the case in Litchfield. There is no doubt that Sarah Pierce, a devout Christian and a shrewd politician, held her charges to the strictest standards of decorum. Yet the proximity of Tapping Reeve's law school meant that the young women faced a steady stream of potential suitors, to say nothing of men who were less interested in securing wives than in testing their own appeal. The charged atmosphere that resulted reverberates through student diaries and letters and into late nineteenth-century memoirs of life in "olden times." Recalling his arrival in Litchfield as a new law student, Edward Mansfield wrote that one of the "first objects that struck [his] eyes" was a procession of "school girls." Some fifty years later, he could still recall the scene: He stood atop a hill, looking down onto a parade of "gaily dressed" ladies who passed beneath "lofty elms," moving in time to the music of a "flute and a flageolet." He was entranced. In subsequent months, he confessed, "one of [his] temptations" was to time his walk in order to "meet the girls, who . . . were often seen taking their daily walk." This fascination with the town's concentration of eligible "girls" was more than the nostalgia of an old man who found a wife among Pierce's students. The "private journals" of John P. Brace, who taught at the school in the 1810s, are shot through with erotic tension. Frankly assessing his students' charms, Brace vacillated between swaggering proclamations that were he not a teacher he could triumph as a beau and nagging fears that he would never measure up to the ladies' exacting expectations. And a law student, George Younglove Cutler, filled up a journal with comments about the appearance and dress of Litchfield's belles that he illustrated and then circulated among male and female friends. It was no secret among his intimates, then, that Miss Hart appeared "most horribly fashionable in her accouterments," that Miss Talmadge was "certainly elegant," and that when Miss Munson dressed with fewer ruffles, her shoulders appeared "infinitely more to advantage than common."[49]

For women like the Misses Hart, Talmadge, and Munson, the politics of this highly eroticized visibility cut in multiple directions. Pleasure and power (if young men like Brace are to be believed) were countered by concerns about feminine reputation. Overexposure or improper exposure, especially before the wrong sort of spectator, could do permanent damage to a young woman's social and moral standing, undermining her prospects for a good marriage and a secure place within the community. That was the lesson driven home to Caroline Chester in 1816, when she and several schoolmates trekked to Little Island on the Bantam River. Splashing from stone to stone to reach the island, the girls got wet and one fell into the river. "Some one" proposed that because the island was "so retired a place," the girls could safely take off their shoes to wash their feet. The wettest also took off their "frocks" to dry across a bush. Alas, Little Island was not "so retired" as they hoped. After "spying two gentlemen" on a hill about "a quarter of a mile distant," the young women threw on their clothes and beat a fast path home. Within twenty-four hours, exaggerated accounts of their indiscretion had reached Pierce. Chester and her friends managed to prove that they were "careless only & not improper" and that they had been "unjustly accused." Still, for days afterward they were lectured about the uneasiness and unhappiness they had brought to the school. They were assured that *some* citizens continued to suspect them of the "most flagrant breach of propriety & delicacy." They were exhorted "like Caesar's wife [to] beware of being even suspected." After hearing for the umpteenth time that she should never even "approach the boundary line of propriety," Chester concluded that were she to "stay in Litchfield 100 years I would <u>never, never</u> walk to Little Island."[50]

98   August. 13.

This figure looks
very much like
A Miss – not
the face merely
the form –

Miss M
her ear
hat – ov
her fac
done fr
memory
the for
is rathe

ing – which could not however be w
avoided, taking into consideratio
state of the delineators imaginatio
– the figure is rather too straight –
bonnet does poke up near enough
                                    it

Figure 5. Page from the diary of George Younglove Cutler depicting Miss Munson, August 13, 1820. Litchfield Female Academy Collection, Litchfield Historical Society, Helga J. Ingraham Memorial Library, 7 South Street, P.O. Box 385, Litchfield, CT 06759.

More striking than the story's predictable moral—that a "woman's fame is easily tarnished"—or the way that it maps feminine propriety onto the town's geography, is the way that Chester's narrative illuminates the importance of seeing and being seen. Spectatorship pervaded the academy experience. The anonymous men on the hill who may have glimpsed the girls, or the spectators who may have hidden on the island itself, were no different from Mansfield, the would-be suitor who timed his walk to coincide with the students'. The citizens of Litchfield who decried the girls' scandalous undressing on the island were the same people who applauded their fashionable attire at balls. Those citizens, in turn, were little different from teachers like Pierce, who trained an eagle's eye on her charges' posture.

There was more to this than the imperative to submit rigid discipline of society; politeness was not an end in itself. By training young women and young men to mind their grooming, their posture, and their manners, academies instilled a doubled sense of self. As the objects of observation and as increasingly adept observers, students learned simultaneously to inhabit their world and to imagine how they must appear to others as they inhabited it. The ultimate aim was what the literary critic Peter de Bolla, following Adam Smith, has termed a "spectatorial subjectivity," which was "precisely not positioned in the eye of the beholder but, rather, in the exchanges that occur in the phantasmic projection of what it might feel like to be constituted as a subject by looking on the onlookers of ourselves." Or, as Chester came to understand after the disastrous trip to Little Island, the key to looking, like the key to looking good, was to understand immediately and intuitively how one looked to others.[51]

Academic Art

The close connections between taste, beauty, and selfhood coupled with the porous boundary between the textual and the visual prompted many academies to provide students with access to books and images aimed at sharpening their visual literacy. The same institutions were likely to offer some form of hands-on instruction in the fine arts. Although textile arts ranging from ornamental embroidery to worsted work remained the exclusive preserve of young women, other pursuits, especially drawing, attracted both genders. Whatever the media, students' artistic productions were meant to reinforce their book learning. The same themes dominated the images they created and the books they wrote. Like composition and chirography, drawing and embroidery were predicated on emulation. Both sets of practices, like the academy experience more generally, were calculated to ground students in a gendered republic of taste.

The haphazard nature of early national academy records makes it difficult to know for certain exactly which art books and images any particular school supplied or how many schools supplied them, but scattered references are suggestive.[52] Some libraries contained books that focused on art history, theory, or practice. The library of the Bethlehem Female Seminary, for example, acquired *Paston's Sketch book*, *Smith on Drawing*, and an edition of Leonardo da Vinci's *Treatise on Painting*.[53] Many more schools would have made do with books like Richard Turner's *Abridgement of the arts and sciences* or William Duane's *Epitome of the arts and sciences*, which were specially "adapted to the use of schools and academies." These books provided rudimentary definitions of an art form like architecture ("the art of building or raising all kinds of edifices"); broke it down into subcategories (civil, military, and naval); and identified its key styles (Tuscan, Doric, Ionic, Corinthian, and Composite). Written with recitation in mind, these texts unfold as a series of formulaic questions ("How many sorts of paintings are there?") and answers ("Five: oil, fresco, water-color, glass, and enamel").[54]

At best, such books were sparsely illustrated. In the first edition of his *Epitome*, for example, Duane included woodcuts illustrating mythological figures and natural phenomena like waterspouts, but he saw no point in picturing the difference between Doric and Corinthian columns. Authors like Duane and Turner were less interested in feeding students' eyes than in training them. They seem to have assumed that their readers already had access to paintings, sculpture, and architecture or to the representation of those arts in prints. That is, they provided the tools to translate what readers observed elsewhere into a shared language and to turn that language back onto images and objects in the form of criticism.

In order to provide objects for their pupils' criticism, educators called on a variety of sources. Printed images were an obvious choice. Judith Foster Saunders and Clementina Beach, who operated a female academy in Dorchester, Massachusetts, amassed a print collection that included prints based on Angelica Kauffman's paintings, scenes from Shakespeare's plays, and the Bible. Nazareth Hall early on acquired Johann Daniel Preissler's eighteenth-century German drawing manual, *Die durch Theorie erfundene Practic*, which worked its way from studies of single body parts like eyes, noses, and feet through the whole human form and then culminated in classical figures, both nude and clothed. The Bethlehem Female Seminary began acquiring prints in the eighteenth century and continued at least through the 1820s. Catalogs for the Germantown Academy in Pennsylvania boasted that the school had built a print collection to "interest the students in the productions and nature of art."[55] Illustrated books offered educators another obvious source for visual materials.

The plates in Charles Rollin's *Ancient History* and Pope's translations of the *Iliad* and the *Odyssey*, for example, introduced students to the visual conventions of classicism, regardless of their ability to read Latin. The Litchfield Academy purchased an edition of the Count de Buffon's *Natural History* that included a "great number of cuts." At a Massachusetts boarding school catering to younger girls, the scholars were allowed to look at two images in a large, lavishly illustrated Bible every Sunday as a reward for good behavior. Teachers and schoolmasters and mistresses also took advantage of resources outside the academy walls when they could. Madame Rivardi, who operated Philadelphia's Seminary for Young Ladies, regularly dispatched groups of chaperoned girls to the city's galleries and museums. Pierce made certain that an itinerant artist who performed demonstrations with a perspective glass and a set of English landscapes put in an appearance at her school.[56]

The cultivation of students' taste extended beyond criticism to hands-on training in the fine arts. Male and female students regularly studied drawing; women were also likely to have their choice of painting, fancy needlework, and a whole range of other "ornamentals." Unlike the study in composition or history, which might progress over several years, classes in the arts were generally designed to last but a single term. And unlike courses in composition or history, which were required and included in the standard tuition, courses in the arts were optional and almost always required an additional fee. Contemporary scholars have paid scant attention to this training. Historians generally regard it as a frivolous distraction from bookish learning—from the *real* work of republican education. Women's historians, especially, have condemned it for tainting serious learning with domesticity. Art historians have compared it to the formal studio training available to aspiring academic painters in Britain and on the continent in the eighteenth and nineteenth centuries and found it lacking. Yet the sheer numbers of young women and men who sought art instruction, and who paid extra for it, suggest that this training occupied a far more important place in the early republic than scholars have recognized.[57]

Female and coeducational academies were especially likely to offer some instruction in the fine arts. Indeed, it is far easier to list women's schools that excluded the ornamentals, like the Young Ladies' Academy of Philadelphia, than to count the ones that included them. In his seminal study of American women's education, Thomas Woody found that between 1742 and 1871, 162 female seminaries offered more than 130 courses in the visual arts. And this number probably underestimates the percentage of schools that offered such training during the early national period, for Woody's calculations do not distinguish between the curricular offerings before and after the 1820s, when the "ornamentals" suffered increasing, and increasingly sharp, attacks.[58] Figures on the number of men's schools that offered art instruction are far harder to come by, in large part because a far smaller percentage of them offered these courses. Nevertheless, drawing lessons were hardly an unusual component of a young man's education. In Philadelphia, the Clermont Seminary (later Carre and Sanderson's Seminary) included drawing lessons in their program to inculcate "a taste and relish for decorum, and politeness." So did the Round Hill School in Massachusetts, the New Haven Gymnasium in Connecticut, and Nazareth Hall in Pennsylvania. Drawing was common enough that in the "Desolate Academy," a poem satirizing the vagaries of learning at men's academies, Philip Freneau poked fun at drawing lessons along with math, history, Greek, and Latin.[59]

Even when academies excluded drawing from the formal curriculum, it was often available off-site from independent teachers. This was especially true in urban centers, where, in the words of Charles Willson Peale, foreign and native-born artists had by the 1790s "become so numerous that I cannot undertake to make any account of them." Looking to supplement their incomes, these men (and a few women) established drawing academies whose hours were carefully coordinated with the schedules of surrounding seminaries. For example, James Cox, who operated a "Drawing and Painting Academy" in New York and Philadelphia, taught "ladies" from 2 until 4 and "gentlemen" from 4 until 6, beginning his classes at precisely the time that students would have been released from their other studies. In a gesture of respect for the social distinctions prized by his patrons, he offered a separate "Evening School" to attract "gentlemen" who worked during the day. Although it is impossible to know how many students, male or female, attended schools like Cox's, the number of drawing masters who sought their patronage suggests that there must have been a steady demand for their services.[60]

If both sexes studied aesthetics and some form of fine arts, they did not study in quite the same way or toward quite the same ends. The most obvious differences derive from conventions governing the gender division of labor: A young woman would have been very likely to produce a piece of ornamental needlework, something ranging from an alphabetic sampler to a large, embroidered picture; a young man would never have plied a needle. While a young woman might have chosen classes in fancy needlework or drawing, she might also have chosen to learn calligraphy, painting, japanning, waxwork, or worsted work; a young man learned to draw. A young woman with the inclination and the financial resources might have opted to pursue some form of "the ornamentals" throughout her school years; a young man typically relinquished his drawing class in favor of more focused attention on the classics or branches of English and mathematics that might serve useful in commerce. But gender

Drawn by W^m. Hamilton R.A.

Engraved by Lawson.

He saw her charming, but he saw not half

The charms her downcast modesty conceal'd.

Autumn.

Figure 6. "Autumn," illustration from James Thomson, *The Seasons: With the Castle of Indolence* (1804). Library Company of Philadelphia.

Figure 7. Needlework picture depicting Palemon and Lavinia, created by Sarah Ann Hanson while she attended the Moravian Seminary for Young Ladies in Litiz, PA. Pictorial embroidery of silk, chenille, spangles, paint, and ink. Private collection; photograph courtesy of Old Salem Museum and Gardens.

Figure 8. Embroidered picture of Mount Vernon, ca. 1807, made by Caroline Stebbins when she was a student at Deerfield Academy. Her father paid $5 (the equivalent of a half year's tuition) to have the embroidery framed. Silk on silk, 13¼ × 16⅞ in. Courtesy of Memorial Hall Museum, Deerfield, MA.

also shaped the kinds of art that young women and men produced as well as its meaning.

The pedagogical and thematic parallels between young women's book learning and their "ornamental" studies are arresting. Both were structured by emulation, by the belief that in copying appropriate models, students might transcend mere mimicry and internalize the style and substance of their betters. Students' commonplace books and journals might have included their own observations, poetry, and even drawings. But they were largely devoted to "improving" extracts transcribed from published sermons, essays, poetry, and conduct and letter-writing manuals.[61] Their painted and embroidered pictures were based on popular prints, usually selected by their teachers and produced in a style specified by—and identified with—those same teachers.[62] The arts, in fact, were believed to be especially useful for inculcating the habit of emulation in young women. Thus, when one young woman turned up her nose at the ornamentals offered by the Bethlehem Female Seminary, her guardian was dismayed. "Her unwillingness to undertake any of the ornamental branches, shews her totally devoid of that emulation, without which nothing can be acquired almost induces me to believe that she is not <u>compos mentis</u>," he fumed. Never mind that the girl displayed "no taste for the arts": the arts fostered the habits demanded by other branches of study. "I want her <u>mind exercised by every possible means</u>," he continued, demanding that the girl be kept at "worsted work as long as you can control her" and that she begin drawing lessons immediately. This, he hoped, "may prove the inception to other undertakings, which may diminish if not destroy" the girl's "indolence of mind."[63]

It was not just the process of emulation that linked literary and ornamental work. It was also the sort of original that female students copied. The same themes and turns of phrase that young women recorded in commonplace books and schoolgirl essays to demonstrate their mastery of polite letters were embroidered on samplers. Inscriptions testifying to women's religious faith and practice dominated both media. But samplers, like commonplace books, also testified to young women's participation in the transatlantic community of letters that shored up the republic of taste. If quotations from Isaac Watts were especially popular, girls also selected verse from Pope, Goldsmith, and Cowper. With needle and pen, girls praised nature, whose "beauteous works" when "fitly drawn" "please the eye and the aspireing mind/To nobler scenes of pleasure more refined." They yearned for immortal friendships that might "outlive . . . the stars survive . . . the tomb." Anticipating death, young women anticipated the passing of time, youth, and beauty. In prose and embroidered inscription, they reminded themselves that only virtue and intellect withstood the test of time. As one young woman put it, "Rear'd by blest Education's nurturing hand/

Behold the maid arise her mind expand/Deep in her heart the seeds of virtue lay/Maturing age shall give them to the day." Or, in the words of another, "Beauty will soon fade away,/But learning never will decay." All of these lines, culled from late eighteenth- and early nineteenth-century samplers, could as easily have been drawn from copybooks from the same period.[64]

Literary themes and print culture more generally also dominated young women's pictorial embroidery and their paintings. The characters and plots of much-loved books, mediated by imported, engraved prints, provided scores of young women with fodder for needles and paintbrushes. Many students, for example, worked from illustrations from James Thomson's perennially popular book of verse, *The Seasons*. Following the lead of British painters and engravers, teachers and "schoolgirl" artists were especially keen to reproduce the plate for "Autumn," which showed the gentleman Palemon confessing his love to rustic Lavinia. Others favored themes that infused polite culture with civic duty and nationalism. In 1804, a student named Mary Beach created a large needlework copy of a Francesco Bartolozzi engraving taken from Angelica Kauffman's painting of Cornelia, Mother of the Gracchi. Cornelia was a figure revered in the early republic for her eloquence as well as her maternal strength. By choosing Cornelia, Beach (or, more likely, her teacher) simultaneously signaled her republican commitments and her familiarity with the cosmopolitan world of engraved prints. Similar sentiments were at work in the many pieces of art honoring George Washington. Elaborate renditions of prints depicting the Washington family were common subjects. Washington's death in 1799 predictably prompted an outpouring of mourning art. Even Mount Vernon attracted its share of attention from academy instructors and their students.[65]

Whatever they depicted, these images were created explicitly for display. The paintings and embroideries created by female students were generally framed, often at great expense. One Connecticut man recalled that any young woman who had attended an academy was "expected to bring home . . . some evidence of proficiency in her studies. Those who could, exhibited elaborate water color drawings which have hung ever since on the walls of . . . [local] Parlors." In fact, the imperative to display girls' accomplishments was so strong that frame-making began to employ significant numbers of artisans when and where schoolgirls began to make art.[66]

It is far harder to generalize about the artistic work of boys and young men, if only because so little of it has survived. That, in and of itself, is suggestive. Whatever happened to those drawings and paintings, they were not encased in expensive frames, hung up in family parlors, or passed lovingly from one generation to the next. They were never, in other words, intended for display outside the walls of the academy. But the short life of the final product (pictures) does not mean that the process (learning to draw) was unimportant. On the contrary. Thomas Jefferson took pains to ensure that the University of Virginia included drawing and painting in its curriculum. At the prestigious Nazareth Hall, drawing was a mandatory and integral part of the curriculum. In an 1815 poem celebrating the school's effect on its students, the principal W. H. Van Vleck ranked the transformative power of drawing alongside that of the classics:

> There first with rapt'rous eye, the page sublime
> Of classic Rome and Greece I wandered o'er;
> Now dared with, with venturous pencil, to portray
> Fair Nature's smiling face in mimic hues. . . .

Clearly, the ability to draw signified. But how exactly?[67]

The extraordinarily rich collection of surviving student drawings from Nazareth Hall can suggest some answers to that question. The young men who attended Nazareth Hall between 1785 and 1830, much like their female counterparts at academies throughout the country, learned to draw by copying examples selected by their teachers. And by the 1810s, a small number of students produced images analogous to the ones painted and embroidered by female students—botanical drawings complemented by Latin names and root systems, landscapes, and genre scenes. One young man, whose ambition outstripped his talent, painted a copy of Benjamin West's *Death of General Wolfe*, an image that had circulated widely through the colonies as an engraved print. Yet the majority of images produced at Nazareth Hall bear little resemblance to these polished, detailed images and even less resemblance to the painted and embroidered pictures that young women created.[68] The lion's share of the young men who learned to draw at Nazareth Hall did not reproduce complete images, much less images that thematized an expansive, transatlantic print culture. Instead, their training conformed more or less to the trajectory advocated in the drawing manuals that circulated on the continent and in Britain from the sixteenth century on. (In this case, the manual was the multivolume treatise written by Preissler, who served as the director of the Nuremburg Academy of Art in the early eighteenth century.) Academic artists and drawing masters began with the assumption that pictorial representation unfolded systematically; perceptual deconstruction preceded pictorial reconstruction. A draftsman first learned to break complex forms down into composite parts, which were in turn reduced to the most basic geometric shapes, lines, and proportions. Only after mastering the pieces, after learning to recognize and reproduce the basic elements of each constituent element, could the artist

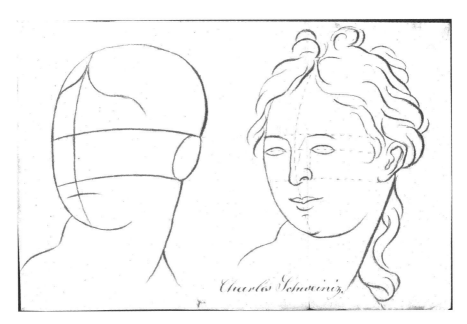

Figure 9. Charles Schweiniz was one of many students at Nazareth Hall to copy this head from Johann Daniel Preissler's drawing manual. Nazareth, PA, 1789. Nazareth Hall Collection. Courtesy, The Winterthur Library: Joseph Downs Collection of Manuscripts and Printed Ephemera. Winterthur Museum and Library.

aspire to the whole. The studies of eyes, heads, and feet completed by the Nazareth Hall students stand at a midpoint in this trajectory. The young draftsmen have moved beyond curved lines, geometric shapes, and basic outlines; they stop short of full compositions. The drawings do not signal an interrupted process; the students have progressed as far as their teacher intended. The schematic, formulaic figure studies that the students completed were of a piece with their architectural drawings, which aimed at familiarizing them with classical styles and proportions and the basic principles of mensuration.[69]

This was not preprofessional training; it did not impart a salable skill. Instead, the lessons were as much about learning to observe and to recognize as learning to draw.[70] These exercises, which had become a routine component of an English gentleman's education by the first half of the eighteenth century, taught republican gentlemen to see with a draftsman's eye. This carefully schooled perception was simultaneously a physical and intellectual process. It was likewise a metaphor for a way of being in the world. It enabled individuals to look beyond incidental variations and petty distinctions and seek out the transcendent and the universal in nature and society. It resonated with scientific convictions that pictorial representation could mirror a legible natural world.

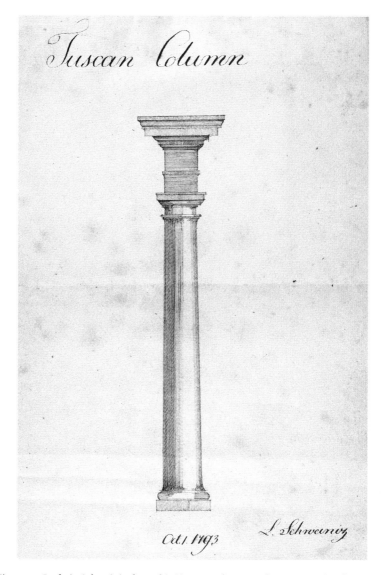

Tuscan Column

Oct 1. 1793   *L. Schweiniz*

Figure 10. Ludwig Schweiniz drew this Tuscan column to demonstrate his familiarity with the classical orders of architecture for an examination. Nazareth Hall Collection. Courtesy, The Winterthur Library: Joseph Downs Collection of Manuscripts and Printed Ephemera. Winterthur Museum and Library.

Of course, this visual proficiency was as prescriptive as it was mimetic. It instilled a set of standards that could be used for judging artistic representations and for assessing the merits of real objects and individuals. Just as important, the visual skills taught through drawing lessons held out the distinctly republican promise of access. The elegantly reasoned world represented in sketches of faces and columns is within the reach of diligent schoolboys.

Setting the extant drawings from Nazareth Hall alongside abundant examples of schoolgirl art, we can begin to see how the gendered production of art shaped the cultural meanings of emulation. The male students' drawings, like the engravings in Preissler's manual, do not depict any particular face, foot, or column. Instead, they describe a series of ideal types. Recapitulating assumptions that stood at the center of the Enlightenment project, the drawings' techniques and subjects champion the universal over the particular. The draftsmen are not intended to develop individual styles; their studies bear only the most attenuated relation to specific objects. Drawing lessons are analogous to moral philosophy; sketches of eyes and columns form a pictorial corollary to the universalizing maxims that students transcribed into their commonplace books.

Young women's pictures gesture toward a closely related intellectual milieu, the transatlantic world of polite letters. And, like the young men's drawings, their painted and stitched pictures are predicated on emulation. But where young men's art proclaims universal truths, young women's art illustrates narrative. It figures contexts and characters, choices and dilemmas. Just as important, young women's art concretizes and elaborates its origins in the material world in ways that young men's art does not. Women's pictures reproduce particular heroines drawn from particular engraved prints and particular illustrated volumes, insisting on the material underpinnings of the republic of letters. More than that, it trumpets their access to exclusive visual resources and expensive materials. If male students' art testifies to the circulation of ideas, female students' art testifies to the circulation of ideas-as-commodities. Depictions of Palemon and Lavinia or of Cornelia, Mother of the Gracchi, with their tiny stitches and delicate washes of color, inscribed the American republic not as a republic of letters but as a republic of taste, where virtue resided in the propertied discernment of the connoisseur rather than the earnest, workaday morality of the artisan.

This was hardly a neutral substitution. Literary critic Michael Warner has famously argued that, in the years following the Revolution, growing numbers of Americans laid claim to print culture as a means of articulating their citizenship and defining their place in an emergent public sphere. But if these men and women aggressively pursued books and periodicals, they did not gain access to costly illustrated books; they enjoyed far less exposure to fine, imported engravings. Female students' grandest productions underscored the fact that print cultures, like the citizens who participated in them, were not equal. Culled from exclusive books and prints, fashioned in silk and watercolor, and executed by graceful young ladies, "schoolgirl" art ensured that the highly restrictive republic of taste would work to counter the more protean republic of letters.[71]

An academy education, encompassing art and composition, penmanship and politeness, was ultimately calculated to culminate in the production of a virtuous citizenry. More immediately, though, it culminated in the production of academy examinations and exhibitions, where students displayed the fruits of their learning before a public audience. Colonial colleges had long sponsored public commencement ceremonies. But in the years following the Revolution, with the growing insistence on the connections between the quality of education and the health of the republic, examinations and exhibitions became more common, more public, and more elaborate. As rituals, examinations were intended both to demonstrate that students were fit to join a republican culture and to provide an idealized picture of that republican culture. The academy exhibition was the public sphere writ small.

The ceremonies typically took place in school halls, drawing townsmen and -women into the school proper and underscoring the public ends of private education. And they were routinely covered in the local press. Reportage ranged from cursory announcements to full-blown stories that ran for inches and included the names of especially impressive students, male and female alike. Either way, the press made the proceedings available even to those who were unable or unwilling to attend. It is difficult to know for certain exactly who turned out for exhibitions. William Bentley, Salem's indefatigable minister, made a point of attending local academy examinations just as he did Harvard's commencement. Joseph Dennie was a regular at the annual exhibitions at the Philadelphia Young Ladies' Academy. Harriet Beecher Stowe recalled that the "literati of Litchfield" always turned out for exhibitions at Pierce's academy. It is likely that audiences grew to include more than local literati, given that newspaper accounts regularly reported audiences numbering in the hundreds. By the 1800s, many schools were publishing broadsides that advertised the dates, times, and order of exercises for their exhibitions in order to encourage attendance.[72]

The precise format and content of these exhibitions varied from school to school. The trustees of the Atkinson Academy promised audiences that their exhibitions "shall not exceed four hours," while students at the Bethlehem Female Seminary thanked the audience for their "kind indulgence" after five days of public examination and exhibition. Exhibitions might include musical interludes or full-blown plays, complete with stage, scenery, and wardrobes "in true theater style." Some schools concluded their exhibitions with a public ball, where students could put their dancing lessons to good use. Regardless of the program's duration, audiences could count on hearing oratory, recitation, salutations, and staged "conversations" encompassing a variety of topics. Patriotic odes and essays on the significance of education in a republican society were popular among male and female students. But audiences might also hear students perform a dialogue such as "On Civilization, between a Fop and a Farmer," "On Taste," a "Latin dissertation on Electricity," or a "Lecture on Wigs."[73]

Academy examinations and exhibitions were public performances that literally displayed students' learning, sensibility, and suitability for civic life. Indeed, the emphasis on performance was so pronounced that some educators hastened to reassure parents and audience members that the public examinations would offer an accurate representation of student ability. Principals of the Clermont Seminary promised that *their* students appeared "in their true and natural state both of mind and body." Genuine accomplishment rather than hollow performance was the order of the day. "No one of our pupils is made to learn particular pieces of prose or poetry to recite," they insisted, "that he may shine a moment like a meteor in the darkness."[74]

If these "true and natural" displays depended on the spoken word, they also depended on a careful attention to visual detail. Even elementary student oratory was yoked to stylized gestures that underscored the speakers' meaning. A successful speech depended almost as much on choreography as recitation. As a consequence, efforts to reinforce the import of students' words with the movements of their bodies could become quite elaborate. Consider the dialogue "Astronomy and the use of the globe," performed at Nazareth Hall as part of the 1793 examination. The performance culminated when one of the boys explained how the stars, which were "calm, regular, & harmonious, invariably keeping the paths prescribed them," were "ranged all around" the earth. As he spoke, his classmates turned themselves into a human orrery. Quietly forming a semicircle around the globe, the students stood in for the stars that "ranged round the earth." The boys embodied the very qualities that the speaker explained governed the stars—regularity, harmony, and the determination to follow "the path prescribed them." By their positions onstage, as much as by the work they had submitted for examination, the boys suggested that the laws regulating the movements of the heavens could also regulate republican society.[75]

The visual dimensions of academy exhibitions extended well beyond choreographed oratory. Samples of penmanship, arithmetic, composition, drawing, painting, and embroidery were set out for audiences to inspect. Even commonplace books, diaries, and personal letters were mandatory submissions.[76] Students' bodies, especially those of young women, also came in for a fair amount of scrutiny. Visitors took pains to note how young women's virtue and accomplishment registered in their appearance as well as in their work. At Susanna

Rowson's academy, for example, an observer reported that the "ladies [were] attired with the greatest simplicity; no ornament whatever appearing among them." At Bethlehem's 1789 examination, the girls arranged themselves before the audience "in the form of a half-moon, and were mostly dressed in white." And in 1814 John P. Brace noted that on examination day the Litchfield "girls were all arranged in their best apparel" around the schoolroom. Only after the visiting "ladies and gentlemen had looked as long as they pleased" at both the girls and the specimens of their work could he announce the students' credit marks.[77]

Jacob Marling's *May Queen* (*Crowning of Flora*) (1816), which captures a May Day celebration at North Carolina's Raleigh Academy, plays on the fascination with female display and performance that informed this exhibitionary culture. The young women who dominate the canvas have honored Mary Du Bose of Georgia, their "favourite girl," by electing her May Queen. Surrounded by her loving peers, Du Bose sits in the center of the canvas, facing an audience that includes faculty, townspeople, children, and slaves. As the queen is wreathed with flowers, her fellow student, Ann W. Clark, recites an address that simultaneously celebrates the pleasures of spring, when "all nature is now attired in its loveliest robe," and warns that those pleasures are bound to fade. The fate of the season and of the students is the same. The "blooming crown" of spring blossoms will soon decay, reminding Du Bose of "beauty's transient glow, while its fragrant sweetness forcibly inculcates the superior charms of virtue." Quoting lines from Cowper that were as suitable for a commonplace book or a sampler as they were for an address, Clark pronounces "the only amaranthine flower on earth, is Virtue—the only lasting treasure, Truth."[78]

Perhaps. But Marling's painting is more concerned with display and publicity than with "amaranthine flowers" or "lasting treasures." The celebration of aestheticized, feminized publicity plays out on multiple levels. Marling himself was among the audience, perhaps invited because his wife was the academy's art teacher. He sketched the scene as it unfolded in order to share the moment with a larger audience who frequented his "exhibition gallery." A lengthy description of the event, including Du Bose's and Clark's names, a transcription of Clark's speech, and a discussion of Marling's planned painting, was reported in regional papers and approvingly reprinted in both the *New-York Weekly Museum* and the *Port Folio*. The fusion of taste and learning enabled a virtuous, distinctly feminine publicity.[79]

Marling painted a romantic May Day celebration rather than a sober annual examination; Du Bose was singled out for her popularity rather than her intellect. Nevertheless, the *May Queen* reproduces many of the conventions of the academy exhibition: the white-gowned young ladies; the staged accomplishment; the attentive, genteel spectators; and the multiple varieties of publicity. More than that, the painting helps us to recognize the pronounced resemblances between the female students who assembled to exhibit their learning and skill and the painted and embroidered female figures who populated their artwork. The same aesthetic—which might be summed up as the willful physical projection of a deeply internalized taste and sensibility—is at work in the painting, in abundant samples of schoolgirl art, and in young women's studied self-presentation. And why not? For if one of the main aims of an academy education was, in Pierce's terms, "to create or direct taste," then these young women had surpassed the goal. More than acquiring taste, they had become it. And they had done so in a context where, as we have seen, taste had considerable moral and political purchase.

But that process of becoming cut in multiple directions. On the one hand, it allowed women to stake a claim to the republic of taste and to play a crucial role in maintaining its boundaries. On the other hand, it raised questions about the legitimacy of women's claims to full participation within the republic of the United States. The same commonplace books, pictures, and performances that registered virtuous taste also summoned to mind the threatening specter of luxury, commodities, and consumption that haunted the public discourse on reading and accomplishment. This specter was made manifest at academy exhibitions, not only in the skills and supplies that schoolgirl artists purchased, but also in the ways that their paintings and embroideries emulated and referenced luxury goods. Worse, young women's accomplishments revealed the degree to which republican self-fashioning and republican taste were tangled up with consumption. After all, women's public presence was articulated through images, objects, texts, and performances that simultaneously connected them to republican refinement and to luxurious consumption—connections made all the more potent by the resemblances between students and the art they created.

Academies gave life to the American republic of taste. These institutions valorized taste as a crucial component of republican manners and genteel subjectivity. Just as important, they concretized it. Academy students learned to recognize beauty in texts, images, and objects. They learned that taste was realized in their posture and their penmanship; it was expressed in their belletristic essays and elegant embroidered pictures. The curricula and culture of early national academies helped ensure that students experienced taste as a way of being in the world and not merely as a philosophical abstraction. And by cultivating an appreciation for taste, academies also helped create a market for it.

Young men and women left academies with identities and subjectivities that had been deeply influenced by their aesthetic, aestheticized educations. Certain that their taste signified national and personal merit, these students-turned-citizens retained the habits and appetites that their instructors had worked so hard to impart. They continued to want and need objects and images on which they could exercise their taste. They sought out cultural spaces where they could perform their taste alongside others. Stepping outside the academy and into the larger world, students encountered growing numbers of aesthetic entrepreneurs, eager to make a living off of the appetite for taste.

CHAPTER TWO

Aesthetic Entrepreneurs

In the spring of 1806, Ethan Allen Greenwood traveled from New York City to Hanover, New Hampshire, for his final term at Dartmouth College. Like so many of his peers, Greenwood's years at college had been interrupted by stints teaching at regional academies in order to earn money for his own education. And like so many of his ambitious peers, he anticipated a career in law. But Greenwood was also an aspiring painter and a voracious consumer of culture, and culture was the purpose of the winter he had just spent in New York. While he was in the city, he read a "great deal." He frequented the theater, where he saw *Othello*, *Richard III*, *Romeo and Juliet*, *School for Scandal*, and a production of *Hamlet* starring Thomas Apthorpe Cooper, one of the most acclaimed actors on the American stage. He went to see the nation's largest pipe organ before it was shipped to a church in Philadelphia. He attended a variety of churches and visited the New York Academy of the Fine Arts. But mostly Ethan Allen Greenwood painted. He had arranged to study with the celebrated artist Edward Savage, best known now for the painting *The Washington Family*. Strapped for cash, Greenwood offset the cost of his training by offering drawing and painting lessons to Savage's daughters. By the end of his tenure with Savage, he had painted copies of ten portraits "among which was Jefferson, Franklin, John Adams, head of Washington, & [Gilbert] Stuarts full length of Washington, Cleopatra & others" in addition to "painting my own likeness."

Back in New Hampshire, Greenwood determined to make a name for himself by turning the fruits of his New York stay into an exhibition. He displayed the portraits he had painted alongside the prints he had purchased in his college rooms and invited all of Dartmouth to admire his accomplishments. To Greenwood's delight, "the government of [the] college, their families, & some other ladies called . . . to see my pictures" and several of the "ladies" stayed on to have their profiles taken. That April day, the college student became newly visible to Hanover's better sort. But he also became visible in new ways—as a painter who could render a likeness, as a connoisseur whose taste could compel and instruct, and as a painted face, as the object of others' discerning looks.[1] The memory of that heady afternoon may well have stuck in Greenwood's mind, for by 1813 he was ready to turn his back on the law and declare that his "attention now will be given strictly to painting." He spent the following five years painting hundreds of portraits; purchasing prints, books, and statuary at auctions; and *looking*—at art, at curiosities, at entertainments. In 1818, he bought the contents of Edward Savage's museum in order to form the core of his New England Museum and Gallery of the Fine Arts, which opened its doors in Boston on July 4.[2] Launching a career as a museum proprietor at the age of thirty-nine, Ethan Allen Greenwood had finally realized the promise of his college exhibition.

To a large extent, the American republic of taste depended on the efforts of individuals like Greenwood. As producers and impresarios, proprietors and teachers, their unlikely careers contributed much to the efflorescence of aesthetic objects and experiences following the Revolution. They catered to the needs and desires of men and women whose appetites for taste had been whetted by an academy stint. Perhaps more important, they helped extend that appetite to people whose fortunes or life courses ruled out the kind of formal aesthetic education promoted within academies. Their success depended on their ability to surmount a series of challenges and hone a battery of seemingly unrelated skills.[3]

Ethan Allen Greenwood offers a case in point. Before he could begin to imagine a vocation in the arts, he had to acquire a painter's technical, manual skills. In addition to training his hands, he needed to train his eye, to cultivate an intuitive appreciation for the beautiful, the curious, the instructive. He needed to know, immediately, what kinds of images and objects would appeal to his patrons' tastes. He also needed to convince them that he was as good with his eyes as he was with his brush: As a portrait painter, he needed to be able to seize on the traits that would render sitters' character visible on canvas; as a museum owner, he was responsible for curating the exhibits that would entertain visitors' eyes. Skill and taste, however, were not sufficient. Turning portraits and exhibits into cash required both the careful management of existing markets and cultivation of new ones. Success as a portrait painter and museum keeper demanded that Ethan Allen Greenwood become an aesthetic entrepreneur.

To describe Greenwood and his peers as aesthetic entrepreneurs is to capture the dual elements of their careers, to situate their lives in the history of looking as well as in the history of laboring and commerce.[4] On the one hand, Greenwood was simultaneously a product of the period's deep preoccupation with taste and a promoter of its rich visual culture. His career as a portrait painter and museum proprietor was made possible by a society that had embraced the sort of aesthetic precepts promoted by academies and seminaries. He found his clientele among a generation of women and men who were adamant about the cultural and political importance of taste, even if they were sometimes vague on its qualifying characteristics. Greenwood's patrons literally looked for new objects and spectacles upon which to exercise their taste just as they looked to print culture and educational institutions to legitimate it. Indeed, it was precisely this growing market for taste, manifested in multiple forms, that enabled many men (and more than a few women) to seek out careers as painters, art teachers, museum proprietors, or critics. This preoccupation with taste and visuality did more than expand consumer markets and open up employment opportunities. It also stood at the center of artists' self-fashioning. Artists of varying ability and success understood that they transformed the abstractions of taste into tangible objects and images. They defined themselves in terms that qualified them for inclusion in the republic of taste.

On the other hand, emissaries of taste were also makers and sellers of commodities. If artists had one foot in the republic of taste, the other was lodged squarely in the marketplace. They worked with their hands as well as their eyes in order to master the technical skills that could make taste visible. They made and sold paintings, portraits mainly. Artists, in other words, made and sold luxury goods. And the demand for luxury goods proved vulnerable to the slightest economic fluctuations. Operating in a sector of the economy that was unstable even by the standards of the day, aesthetic entrepreneurs had no choice but to sharpen their business skills and expand their markets. In the process, they and their patrons acquired new kinds of visibility within the early republic.

Finding a Vocation

Near the end of his long and remarkable career, Charles Willson Peale disputed the "generally adopted opinion" that "Ginius for the fine arts, is a particular gift, and not an acquirement. That Poets, Painters, &c are born such." A decade later, in 1834, the painter-turned-art-historian William Dunlap poked fun at apocryphal stories about the painter whose genius drove him to "scrawl, scratch, pencil, or paint as soon as he could hold anything wherewith he could make a mark."[5] From the artists' perspective, the problem with these hoary celebrations of genius was the way they ignored both the contingency that led to a career in the arts and the laborious training necessary to produce proficiency. Greatness, as Peale and Dunlap well knew, was not foreordained. From the historian's perspective, the problem with these narratives is that they work backward. Beginning with the polished work of a master painter, they seek evidence for its origins in the artist's biography. The clichéd stories derided by Peale and Dunlap are premised on the distance that separates canonical painters at the apex of their careers from the ranks of mere practitioners. That seemingly insurmountable gulf is then projected back in time, to the moment when training began, when "giniuses" and practitioners alike were novices. Reversing this perspective (and setting aside questions about a painter's eventual greatness) affords a far clearer understanding of the cultural and economic environments that enabled men like Peale, Dunlap, or Greenwood to forge careers as aesthetic entrepreneurs.

Painting was not an obvious vocation in the early republic. Academies and seminaries may have valorized taste and pushed male and female students to develop an eye for art, but they stopped well short of encouraging them to make a living by it. Men from the middling and upper classes found that the decision to make a living by painting, much like the decision to make a living by writing, was potentially suspect. The choice was well outside the conventions of masculine respectability. Landed wealth, commerce, the learned professions: *These* were the respectable ways for men to acquire and maintain property; the property thus accumulated was meant to culminate in disinterested civic service (in the eighteenth-century imagination) and partisan political engagement (in the nineteenth-century imagination). The arts, in contrast, were suitable for leisured contemplation and criticism or, at most, for dabbling. This ideal was hardly an easy fit for men whose talents and inclinations drew them toward careers in the arts.[6]

If painting was not a secure source of masculine identity, neither was it a secure form of financial support, as the fathers of many aspiring painters pointed out. Indeed, accounts of early national painters' lives echo with anecdotes about young men from propertied families who turned to art despite the objections raised by their fathers. In his 1841 autobiography, John Trumbull recalled his father's persistent attempts to push him into the law, widely heralded as "the profession which in a republic leads to all emolument and distinction." Dismissing his son's fantasies about the "honors paid to artists in the glorious days of Greece and Athens," the former governor drily observed that "*Connecticut is not Athens.*"[7] Indeed, the decision to paint is regularly depicted as a rebellion against patriarchal authority in *History of the Rise and Progress of the Arts of Design in the United States* (1834), William Dunlap's monumental survey of the careers of American artists. Henry Sargent's "irresistible" desire to paint "deranged or interrupted the sober avocations of mercantile life" that his father, an eminent merchant, had planned for him. Thomas Sully's father, a theater manager, initially placed him with an insurance broker who returned the boy in short order, complaining that although he "was very industrious in multiplying figures, they were figures of men and women." Only then could Sully persuade his father to apprentice him to a French portrait painter. Lawyer-turned-miniaturist Charles Fraser, orphaned at the age of nine, desperately wanted to pursue a career as an artist. But his guardians "did not yield to his desire for instruction in that art," Dunlap wrote, speculating that they feared committing the boy to a future some "might deem less certain" than the learned professions.

Such concerns were not limited to families that might reasonably expect to situate their sons as merchants or lawyers. Even Joseph Wood's father, who was merely a "respectable farmer" from Orange County, New York, expected the boy to follow in his footsteps.[8] Aspiring painters whose fathers were artisans or farmers not yet touched by the Village Enlightenment could also encounter the disapproval of older generations. Chester Harding, for one, recalled that his grandfather dismissed his career in terms that cast aspersions on both his honor and his manhood: The old man regarded it as "very little better than swindling to charge forty dollars for one of those effigies" and insisted that he "settle down on a farm, and become a respectable man."[9]

The decision to paint professionally was, of course, least likely for women. Those who attended academies might have discovered aptitudes for drawing and painting, but they were not supposed to find careers. On the contrary. Paid work was supposed to find them, and then only in emergencies, occasioned by, say, the death of a father or the financial reverses of a husband. Not surprisingly, the extant letters and diaries written by female artists and the biographies written about them during the nineteenth century have nothing to say about how, or even whether, they consciously chose to commence their careers. Particular women may have experienced an awakening of ambition and a hunger for distinction. Yet in their personal writing and in the few accounts written about them, their initial aspirations are either subsumed within household strategies or presented as fait accompli.[10]

There was thus no single path to this unconventional vocation. Family connections surely steered some women and men toward careers as painters. Charles Willson Peale famously named a number of his children after eminent artists and did everything in his power to push them into the family business. So, too, did Cephas Thompson, a self-taught portrait painter from Massachusetts, whose children Cephas Giovanni Thompson and Marietta Angelica

Thompson supported themselves as artists. Kin could serve as examples, teachers, and partners. Family connections may have been especially helpful for female artists, whose access to training, travel, and patronage was markedly constrained.[11] Academies, which provided students with a stylistic vocabulary along with at least rudimentary training in drawing, could also serve as a bridge to a career in art. Even a college education seems to have provided a small handful of very privileged young men with the opportunity to enhance their training. Although John Trumbull's father sent him to Harvard in hopes of squelching his artistic ambitions, the teenager seized the opportunity to scour the college library for engraved prints and treatises on painting and perspective; Samuel F. B. Morse began painting in earnest while he was studying at Yale.[12]

The trades provided a far larger number of men with the skills necessary to take up painting. Ezra Ames, for example, painted coaches in Albany before he painted likenesses of the state's legislators. Chair making and sign painting provided an initial entrée to painting for Chester Harding, who eventually attained both fame and wealth, and his brother Horace, who did not.[13] Many of the men who became portrait painters moved back and forth between art and artisanship as business dictated. Every city boasted tradesmen-turned-painters "who would occasionally work at any thing," sniffed John Wesley Jarvis, who had the good fortune to launch his career with an apprenticeship in Edward Savage's studio.[14]

Serendipity played no small role in the choices of many. Men who suffered from chronic ill health, like Joseph Steward and Eliab Metcalf, turned to art only after deciding that it was a profession suited to those with "impaired health and debilitated frame[s]."[15] John Vanderlyn began to discover his vocation as a consequence of clerking for Thomas Barrow, New York City's "only dealer in good prints." Henry Inman's "early delights were concerned with pictures," but his aspirations took flight when he read Madame de Genlis's *Tales of the Castle*, a children's anthology that included biographical sketches of famous painters and sculptors.[16] A chance encounter with a children's book, a lucky clerkship, a bout of poor health: These random circumstances were as likely to steer a person toward a career in art as an analogous apprenticeship or formal education.

Learning to Paint

However one acquired the desire to paint, obtaining the requisite training was notoriously difficult.[17] Anglo-American artists worked at a remove from the protocols that dominated European and especially English painting, and had—at best—limited access to formal studio training. Would-be American artists had to do more than learn to paint. They also had to invent that training that would teach them to do so. When Maryland saddler Charles Willson Peale decided to try his hand at painting in the mid-eighteenth century, for example, he quickly realized that "he had seen very few paintings of any kind, and as to the preparations and methods of using colours, he was totally ignorant of them." Although he could jerry-rig a palette and easel at home, he had to travel to Philadelphia for paint. When he arrived at the "colour shop," he realized that he was "at a loss to know what to purchase, for he only knew the names of such colours, as are most commonly known." Ever resourceful, Peale went straight to James Rivington's bookstore, where he picked up a copy of Robert Dossie's *Handmaid to the Arts*. After four days of study, he returned to the shop prepared to purchase the paints with which to launch his new career. For the next several years, he simultaneously painted portraits up and down the Atlantic seaboard and immersed himself in the work produced and collected by men like John Hesselius, John Singleton Copley, and John Smibert. By 1767, he had progressed enough that some of his Maryland patrons raised the money to send him to London for "close study" with Benjamin West, by then the director of the Society of Artists. When he returned to Maryland two years later, Peale had acquired skills in oil and watercolor painting, sculpture, and mezzotint engraving; he had mastered full-length portraits and ivory miniatures.[18]

An aspiring artist in the early republic would have faced challenges not much different than the ones Peale overcame a half-century earlier. Indeed, one rationale for establishing early national art academies like the Columbianum (1794), the Pennsylvania Academy of the Fine Arts (1805), and the New York Academy of the Fine Arts, later renamed the American Academy of the Fine Arts (1802), was to provide young artists with the sort of streamlined, systematic training that Peale, Dunlap, Trumbull, and others had enjoyed in London, courtesy of Benjamin West and the Royal Academy. Yet American artists never succeeded in establishing such an institution, not least because they disagreed bitterly about whether and how an academy modeled after a hierarchical organization tied to a royal court could meet the needs of a republic. As a consequence, through the first decades of the nineteenth century, men and women who wanted to learn to paint well enough to live by their brushes pursued strategies that recalled Peale's haphazard early training.

Learning to draw was only the beginning. Color posed daunting challenges. Before ready-ground pigments first became available in the 1830s, artists had to mix their own paints. Coming up with "receipts" that delivered consistent, long-lasting color in a form that was easy to work with was an ongoing concern, even for painters like Copley, Peale, and Washington Allston, who had considerable technical skills.[19] Then there was the question of application: How could painters learn to combine multiple colors—to say nothing of underpainting, toning, varnishing, and glazing—in order to reproduce what they saw in the world around them, much less the stylistic conventions of other paintings? Painters snatched up studio training when and where they could. But the kind of sustained study that Greenwood enjoyed with Savage during the winter of 1806 was elusive. Established painters were not always interested in taking students. Gilbert Stuart, for one, was willing to dispense snippets of advice to a long list of early national painters, but he extended formal studio training to a very select few. Painters like Savage and his pupil John Wesley Jarvis, who were willing to offer systematic training, were only accessible in eastern cities.[20] In the absence of formal training, loose-knit networks of like-minded individuals provided one avenue for sharing technical information. Most of these exchanges unfolded in informal, catch-as-catch-can conversations, but some took the form of correspondence. The canonical John Singleton Copley and the obscure Mary Way, for example, both wrote letters to their painter siblings in which they detailed long bouts of trial and error at the easel and suggested solutions to technical problems ranging from manufacturing paint to lighting a sitter.[21]

Even artists with considerable formal training found that the acquisition of basic technique could be a lifelong process. Dunlap, who trained with West, supported himself more or less successfully as a miniaturist for months in western New York and Boston despite being ignorant "even in the knowledge necessary to prepare ivory for the reception of color." The deficiency was only corrected when Edward Malbone learned about Dunlap's methods while the two were chatting at a dinner party. Malbone took pity and, reeling from a champagne hangover the next morning, walked Dunlap through the process.[22]

However a painter acquired discrete skills, he or she needed to incorporate them into a finished picture that conformed to established standards and conventions. Thus, painters sought out opportunities to copy paintings by Old Masters and American masters. These paintings, which were usually copies of copies, grounded practice in emulation. When actual paintings were out of reach, artists looked to engraved prints as guides for composition and templates for future work. Thus Dunlap and Sargent spent hours as teenagers copying mezzotints of Copley's renowned "shark painting."[23]

If ambition, finances, and luck aligned, an American artist's training culminated on the other side of the Atlantic. London was the most common destination, not least because of Benjamin West, who helped train three generations of American painters. But occasionally Americans like John Vanderlyn made their way as far as Italy or France. Access to European training obviously varied greatly. For Dunlap, blessed with an indulgent father who was a successful merchant, or Trumbull, possessed of impeccable social and political connections, European training was relatively easy to acquire. But it was not beyond the reach of the self-taught Harding, whose impoverished father had been more interested in devising a perpetual motion machine than in procuring "bread and butter" for "his hungry children." To be sure, Harding had to postpone the trip until he had saved enough to support his family and himself while he was abroad; he sailed for England as a means of enhancing an already successful career, not launching one. Nevertheless, shortly after he turned thirty, Harding, a former chair maker and sign painter, walked into Britain's Royal Academy to view one of Raphael's original cartoons.[24]

Predictably, women had a far more difficult time making their way through every step of this fragmented trajectory. The most privileged and talented were stymied in their attempts to advance beyond the skills taught at academies and seminaries. When the Pennsylvania Academy of the Fine Arts announced its first annual exhibition in 1810, President Francis Hopkinson grandly invited women to participate. "I hope and trust the walls of our academy will soon be decorated with products of female genius; and that no means will be omitted to invite and encourage them," he told the academy's board of directors. Despite the Pennsylvania Academy's endorsement of "female genius," only three of the hundreds of pieces included in the exhibition were produced by women. Two of those women were members of the extended Peale family.[25]

Training, rather than genius, was to blame. The proficiency required of an academy-approved artist was simply beyond the reach of most female painters. Formal studio training with an established artist was all but impossible for a woman to obtain, unless—like Anna Claypoole Peale, Maria Peale, Rosalie Sully, or Marietta Angelica Thompson—she could receive it from a male relative. Instead, aspiring female painters fell back on lessons from itinerant teachers. Miniaturist Sarah Goodridge, for example, who became successful in the 1830s, benefited from Gilbert Stuart's criticism and encouragement, but she received her extremely limited formal training from an unknown painter from Hartford, Connecticut, who briefly offered lessons in Boston. European study was out of the question for women. Consider Anne Hall, the daughter of a "physician of eminence" who enthusiastically encouraged her talent, albeit within the parameters dictated by gender conventions. Hall's father made sure that she had top-notch supplies and her brother, a wealthy New York real estate developer, sent her paintings that he purchased during his European travel. Knowing that she would need more training than she could hope to glean in Pomfret, Connecticut, her father arranged for her to travel. But where an affluent father sympathetic to his son's ambitions simply dispatched him to London, Dr. Hall sent Anne first to Rhode Island, to visit friends and to take lessons from Samuel King, Gilbert Stuart's first teacher, and then to New York City, to live with her brother and study with the noted Alexander Robertson.[26] Despite her many advantages, Hall painted in a world constrained by gender.

Print culture helped painters compensate for spotty formal, institutionalized training. Technical manuals, aesthetic treatises, and illustrated books and magazines increased in both number and variety in the years following the Revolution. These texts, both imported and domestic, promised to train painters who were affluent and laboring, urban and provincial, male and female. Drawing and painting manuals, especially, aimed to provide introductory, sequential training, showing reader-artists how to see by providing them with a schemata, a series of formulas for representing figures and landscapes in accord with conventions stretching back to the Renaissance.[27]

As the nineteenth century progressed, manuals became more systematic. Carington Bowles's *The Artist's Assistant*, an English text reprinted in Philadelphia in 1794, advised students to begin by copying "the several features of the human face"—eyes, nose, and mouth, borrowed from Charles Le Brun's drawings—which were included in the book before progressing to outlining profiles, full faces, and figures. By the 1830s, Rembrandt Peale's *Graphics* insisted that anyone could learn to draw. "Try" was spelled out across the bottom of the book's title page; subsequent editions added the promise that "Nothing is denied to well-directed Industry." Assuming that his readers might never have seen an actual painter at work, Peale began by explaining how to hold a pencil and position oneself in front of an easel. He proceeded through penmanship, lines, and geometric shapes before showing readers how to identify the angles that gave shape to, say, a human nose.[28]

The market for such books was partly, perhaps mostly, fueled by growing numbers of amateurs, keen to acquire the kind of polite and useful art offered in academies. But the boundary separating amateur and vocational training was porous at best. Would-be professionals benefited from many of the same texts that were sold to amateurs. Archibald Robertson pitched his drawing and painting manuals, like his school, at amateurs and professionals alike. And when teenaged William Dunlap took painting lessons from William Williams as a means of mastering his craft, he was surprised when his teacher presented him with a drawing book "such as I had possessed for years."[29] One man's preprofessional textbook was another's leisure reading.

Manuals were useful for more than teaching a reader how to depict forms on paper or canvas. They borrowed heavily from the Anglo-American aesthetic canon to weigh in on what kinds of forms displayed the finest taste and why. Thus Robertson's *Elements of the Graphic Arts* included essays on the "Theory of Painting" and the "Picturesque and the Beautiful" as well as instructions for schematizing the human profile as a series of triangles.[30] Painting and drawing books surely compensated for the absence of flesh-and-blood instructors and paucity of academic training. But they also composed yet another strand in a wide-ranging discourse on taste. They grounded painters in a shared set of aesthetic principles. Manuals thus helped distill taste into technique. In so doing, they worked to align the sensibilities and expectations of artists and patrons.

The Artist's Eye

Mastering the manual skills and the technical knowledge that painting demanded was no small matter; the obstacles were considerable. Yet, when we read early national artists' diaries, memoirs, and letters, it is striking how little they have to say about the acquisition of technique (exercised by the hand) and how much they have to say about the acquisition of taste (manifested in a good eye). In the narratives they spun about themselves, the difficulties of learning to treat canvas or ivory, to mix colors, to paint are eclipsed by the challenges and rewards of learning to see. Never mind that all their painstakingly acquired training took aim at both their eyes and their hands. In their telling, the process of becoming a painter was dominated by vision, yoked to intellect and imagination.

This emphasis, which amounted to a rhetorical dematerialization of the practice of painting, served to locate artists' work in the realm of the "liberal" rather than the "mechanical" arts. It recapitulated the venerable, transatlantic hierarchies that were rooted in writings by the Earl of Shaftesbury, popularized in any number of encyclopedias and treatises on art, reinforced in belles lettres, and painstakingly copied into the commonplace books of academy students. As one authority, writing for an American encyclopedia, put it, the "noble" and "ingenious" liberal arts (which included painting, poetry, and music) depend more on the "labour of the mind that on that of the hand." The "mechanical arts" (which included the "trades and manufactures" like weaving, clock making, carpentry, and printing) depended on "the hand and body" more than the mind. Or, in the words of Connecticut miniaturist Betsey Way Champlain, "Bright Fancy guides the pencil while I draw,/Who spurns at mechanisms servile law."[31]

Such easy dismissals of the merely mechanical offered a distorted representation of the lived experience of the majority of American painters, who struggled to acquire even basic technique. So, too, the hard and fast distinctions between the work of the eye and the work of the hand, for there was no denying that, on a fundamental level, painting was a manual art that owed much to the delicacy and dexterity of an artist's hand as it moved a brush over a piece of canvas or ivory. Yet the dematerialization of the practice of painting was a useful gambit precisely because it reinforced artists' claims to membership in the republic of taste. Small wonder, then, that it appeared so regularly in artists' textual self-representations. The selves fashioned by painters like Greenwood, Dunlap, and Harding gained (or squandered) cultural and financial capital with their eyes rather than their hands.

Greenwood's extant journals, for example, simultaneously mark his progress as a painter and museum keeper and figure that progress as the development of visual acuity. He succeeded at painting and museum keeping because he had learned to succeed at looking.[32] Greenwood's interest in art is apparent almost from the journal's earliest entries, which note his acquisition of canvases stretched on "frames suitable for painting" and his early efforts at portraiture. During the years when he vacillated between a career in law and a career in art, Greenwood made cursory notes about his painting output. The entries changed in frequency and tone after 1813 when Greenwood decided to devote himself "strictly to painting."[33] He began to take greater care in recording details about his artistic output. He was more likely to list his subjects individually and to single out exotic and unusual sitters like "Wha-Shing, a Chinese gentleman," "John Smith a dwarf 18 years old," and "Mr. Harry Gates of Hubbardston," whose "face was distorted by a wound on Bunker Hill." He noted subjects who were especially difficult to paint, like an eighty-three-year-old woman who was "so feeble" she could only "sit in position" a few minutes at a time.[34]

Greenwood also began to record purchases that signaled attempts to cultivate his eye and to demonstrate his taste. He subscribed to Joseph Dennie's *Port Folio*, which set itself up as a national arbiter of culture and the arts, and spent $25 to procure back issues. He purchased the published works of Sir Joshua Reynolds, including the *Discourses*, which provided a civic justification for art and codified the eighteenth-century Anglo-American aesthetic. He stepped up his acquisition of engraved prints and copies of European paintings and began to purchase plaster busts. By the end of 1817, he was able to boast that, notwithstanding several months' illness, he had managed to "increase my Library, my collection of painting, prints, statuary &c. very considerably."[35]

The entries in Greenwood's journal are so terse that it is tempting to treat the whole as an account book for tracking pictures painted and objects purchased. But if the journal functioned on that level—and it certainly did, especially after he opened the New England Museum—it also bore witness to Greenwood's visual engagement with the world and his sustained attempts to develop his taste. The acquisition of things and experiences, like the notations that fixed them in his journal, served as a kind of commonplacing. Both sets of practices internalized a conventional set of aesthetic values and marked his growing connoisseurship. And both enabled him to position himself as someone who looked out at the world from the perspective of the tasteful few.

Occasionally his looking was dilatory and aimless, as it was on the December afternoon when he recorded that he "went to auction a little, & elsewhere a little, & thus littled away the day." But generally it was purposeful and directed. He sought out private collections in and around Boston, the better to learn from others' taste. Thus he traveled the ten miles to Milton to see the elegant paintings belonging to Miss Lucy Smith, a woman distinguished by her "good sense and elegant manner" and "Waited on Miss Hannah Adams" in order to see "Bonaparte's pictures, St. Domingo, &c." While painting a portrait in Pomfret, Connecticut, he sought out Anne Hall's father and his "fine & valuable collection of pictures which he has shown me very politely."[36] And when he spent an evening at Boston's Mansion House in order to view "the very valuable collection of paintings & pictures" owned by John Hancock's widow, he wrote that he hoped to be "improved by this examination."[37]

Traveling exhibitions offered Greenwood another opportunity for improvement. He took in panoramas of Paris, Constantinople, and the Battle of Waterloo, the last of which he attended with a fellow artist, Sarah Goodrich.[38] When American painters with academic ambitions displayed their masterpieces in Boston, Greenwood was invariably on hand. In 1815, he paid to see Henry Sargent's *Landing of the Fathers*, which depicted the Pilgrims' arrival at Plymouth Rock, and he may well have supplemented his viewing by reading the *New England Palladium and Commercial Advertiser*, which offered its readers step-by-step instructions for studying the painting, carefully dissecting the appropriate movement of the eye over the canvas.[39] A few months later, he made arrangements to exhibit Samuel Morse's *Dying Hercules* when it arrived in Boston from the Royal Academy, where it had received "the highest approbation and applause." He obtained both the enormous painting and the plaster model that Morse had made to help resolve the technical difficulties of representing the reclining figure. The exhibition, which took place in Greenwood's painting rooms, generated revenue directly, through the 25-cent admission he charged, and indirectly, by increasing his visibility among potential clients. But housing the two pieces together also afforded Greenwood a rare opportunity for sustained, close study of a grand manner painting along with the even rarer opportunity to copy the painting by using the original painter's method of looking back and forth between the three-dimensional model and two-dimensional canvas. The majestic painting had been in his rooms less than a week when he began to copy it. Whatever his profit from exhibiting the *Dying Hercules*, Greenwood made sure he capitalized on the chance to duplicate Morse's method.[40]

On the rare occasions when Greenwood ventured outside New England, he recorded his attempts to consume the world with his eyes. The year before he opened the museum, he traveled south and, like other American travelers, recorded his experiences as a series of views: He was disappointed by the appearance of Lancaster, Pennsylvania, a "Principally Dutch" town marked by "a want of elegance in everything, no taste in buildings, dress, or manner." The moment he crossed into the slave South, the "misery and stupidity," the "ignorance & total want of taste" were to be seen everywhere. When he entered Washington, D.C., he "saw its desolation & barrenness." In livelier cities, his looking became far more urgent. He devoted himself "diligently to seeing every curious thing" in Baltimore; in New York, he vowed "to see & examine everything relating to the fine arts." Over the course of a single month, he spent time at the Peale family's museums in both Baltimore and Philadelphia; visited the studios of painters ranging from Charles Bird King to Mary Way; browsed bookstores, print shops, and gilders' workshops; attended concerts and the theater; and toured the U.S. Mint and the Philadelphia Athenaeum.[41]

Subsequent trips to New York and Philadelphia found Greenwood equally determined to "view . . . every interesting curiosity I could meet with." During a twelve-hour stay in New York City in 1821, he saw the gallery of wax figures at the Shakespeare Gallery, the Rotunda where John Vanderlyn displayed his panoramas, the American Academy of the Fine Arts, the Mechanical Theater, Scudder's Museum (which he visited twice, once during the day and again at night), and the theater.[42] A few years later, during a week divided between New York City and Philadelphia, Greenwood's agenda included the Peale, Scudder, and Sharpless museums; a medical college museum; both the American Academy of the Fine Arts and the Pennsylvania Academy of the Fine Arts, where he saw "West's great picture of Christ Healing the Sick"; and a morning in New York spent "in still further examination of everything curious with Col. Trumbull." "In fact," he wrote of this flying visit, "I looked at everything with all my might."[43]

Like the curiosity cabinets assembled by wealthy collectors, these cities provided Greenwood with fodder for observation, consideration, and criticism. His compressed visits served, in heightened form, the same purpose as his more mundane habits of looking at home in Boston. The notations in his journal helped him to internalize the value of what he perceived and provided a forum for exercising his taste. Greenwood's habits of looking and recording paid off: By 1821, the young man who had once hoped to "be improved" by Boston's State House pictures could pick out the "good heads" in the Shakespeare Gallery and dismiss the rest as "gaudy trash." He could commend the "elegance of arrangements & nature of the articles" in Scudder's museum and regret that there was so very little at the American Academy of the Fine Arts to afford "entertainment or improvement." By the time the journals end, in 1825, Ethan Allen Greenwood had become a connoisseur.[44]

If Greenwood's journal gestures toward the central role that looking played in artistic self-fashioning, William Dunlap's autobiography, published as part of his monumental *History*, expounds on it. The multivolume *History* unfolds mostly as a chronologically organized biographical compendium. Over the course of thirty chapters, he plumbs the lives of American artists, native born and otherwise, for insights about national character analogous to those that could be found in biographical compendia celebrating the nation's founders. As he explains to readers in the book's introduction, just as readers "earnestly desire to know every particular relative to the first settlers who raised the standard of civilization in the wilderness," so, too, did they want to learn about the artists "who raised and who supported the standard of taste, and decorated the social column with its Corinthian capital."[45] Accordingly, the first volume of the *History* begins with colonial migrants like John Smibert and Robert Feke, picks up speed with Benjamin West and John Singleton Copley, and assumes a distinctly national character with the ascendance of Charles Willson Peale, Gilbert Stuart, John Trumbull, and Dunlap himself.

Dunlap made no apologies for including himself in this pantheon and no apologies for taking up so many pages in it. His account of his own life is longer than his treatment of either Benjamin West or Gilbert Stuart and about the same as his coverage of Thomas Sully and Washington Allston combined. Dunlap began the *History* when he found himself in poor health and worse financial straits; his diary entries for the year leading up to the publication of his history of American art are a dismal catalog of diarrhea, laxatives, laudanum, and dwindling bank balances. Old and infirm, Dunlap may well have felt compelled to validate a career that had secured him neither economic stability nor public adulation.[46]

Why Dunlap chose to place his life story at the center of American art history matters less than how he told that story. In the *History*, he cast his life as an instructive flop. Where the lives of West, Copley, Trumbull, and Allston could help train up a young painter in the way he should go, Dunlap's own conduct "stood as a beacon to be avoided by all."[47] He readily admitted that his was a failure of discipline, maturity, and nerve. But in the autobiography, Dunlap depicts these shortcomings as a failure of vision. The capacity for a certain kind of sight, he insisted, was the precondition for the creation and appreciation of art. It was also the quality that he himself most lacked.

Before Dunlap wrote about his problem, he painted it. He depicted his compromised vision in two miniature self-portraits, painted in 1805 and in 1812, years that saw him returning to art after failed stints in the theater. Both likenesses are dominated by the artist's depiction of his eyes. The left eye is large, dark, and alert, whether it looks off into the distance or over his shoulder at the

Figure 11. William Dunlap, self-portrait, ca. 1812. Watercolor on ivory, 3 × 2½ in. Yale University Art Gallery. Gift of the Estate of Geraldine Woolsey Carmalt 1968.12.1.

viewer. The right eye, blind as the result of a childhood accident, is clouded over. There is no iris, no pupil, and no mistaking this eye's blindness. The absence of color signals the absence of sight. These portraits become more suggestive when paired against the portrait of Dunlap painted by Charles Cromwell Ingham for the National Academy of Design in 1838. Ingham's likeness repeats the poses Dunlap had used on the miniatures. But in Ingham's portrait, both eyes are large, dark, and apparently focused, as though reading. Ingham's portrayal suggests that although Dunlap may have been blind in one eye, his appearance did not immediately announce the fact to observers who did not know him. Yet the inability to see mattered enough to Dunlap that he rendered it visible.

Dunlap's autobiography spells out what his early self-portraits imply. He returns repeatedly to sight in his account of his early years and his decision to

Figure 12. Charles Cromwell Ingham, *William Dunlap*, 1838–1839. Oil on canvas, 30 × 25 in. Courtesy of the National Academy Museum.

become a painter, which occupies the first third of the narrative. The only child of "indulgent" parents, he received "no education in the usual acceptation of the word." His boyhood schooling was interrupted first by war and then by injury. The latter interruption was the one that mattered: While playing outside with a group of boys who were pitching wood chips at one another, Dunlap was hit in the face and his right eye was "cut longitudinally." "Weeks of confinement to my bed and more to my house" sufficed to restore his health, he recalled, but he never regained "the sight of the organ" (244, 250). During his convalescence and after, Dunlap developed a taste for drawing. By the time he recovered, his copies of engraved prints borrowed from the neighbors "might almost pass" for the originals.

Encouraged by the admiration these drawings solicited, Dunlap settled on painting as his profession. The war made it difficult to secure a regular teacher, so he resolved to learn by doing. He painted his father first, moved on to other relatives, and when he had exhausted his supply of family, he turned to his friends. The moment he began to get applications from strangers, he "fixed [his] price as three guineas a-head" and "thus commenced portrait-painter in the year 1782" (250–251). To be sure, this was something less than a serious bid at a livelihood. "Living as the only and indulged child of my parents" removed the pressure of subsistence, he explained. But Dunlap's efforts were promising enough that by 1784, his father was willing to send him to London to study with Benjamin West.

West did his best by Dunlap. He confirmed the young man's talent on the basis of his "specimens"; helped him secure cheap lodgings with Robert Davy, a portraitist and art teacher; loaned him plaster casts to draw; and secured his admission to the Royal Academy. Nevertheless, as Dunlap explained, a trip that should have gone a long way toward securing his future career as an artist proved a fiasco. Hours that should have been spent in the studio were wiled away in drinking, dining, and then drinking some more. Entire weeks were dissolved into visits to the theater and pleasure trips into the countryside. Dunlap abandoned Davy's rooms (and Davy's tutelage) for more fashionable quarters and took up with a group of "half-pay officers" fresh from America who congregated at a local porterhouse (257–262). He never studied at the academy and although he was a regular guest at West's dinner table, he managed to avoid his purported teacher's studio almost entirely. He completed a few paintings— portraits and historical pieces—but saw little progress. This "life of unprofitable idleness" came to an abrupt end in 1787 when his father heard about his antics and summoned him home (265–266).

Looking back on what he judged a misspent youth, Dunlap found much to regret. And as he considered his failure, he returned time and again to his inability to see the world with a painter's eye. Color posed the most fundamental obstacle. Because he taught himself to draw by copying engraved prints in ink, Dunlap worried that his "eye became satisfied with light and shadow" and learned to care little for "the excitement of colour." He imagined that early intervention in the form of a knowledgeable teacher might have helped him to overcome this hurdle. But that was all in the realm of the hypothetical. Whether "from nature," or injury, or training, he "did not possess a painter's eye for colour" (250).

Unfortunately, his experiences in England only confirmed a shortsightedness that should have been apparent before he left New York. The nadir came during one of the few lessons West managed to give Dunlap. While painting a landscape, the great artist "elucidated the doctrine of light and shadow," a doctrine "long . . . familiar to every artist." First, West drew a circle on a blank canvas, then touched in light and shadow with white and black chalk, leaving the canvas itself to show the "half-tint and reflexes." Next he directed Dunlap to examine the patterns of light and shadow on a piece of statuary to observe how the theory worked in practice. To extend the lesson from black and white to a full range of color, West returned the young man to his own unfinished landscape, pointing out that the "masses of foliage . . . were painted on the same principle." The lesson was humiliating. That West felt compelled to return his prodigal student to first principles was "perhaps proof of the little progress I had made in the art I professed to study." Once again, Dunlap demonstrated that he had a "better eye for form than for color" and was "discouraged by finding that I did not perceive the beauty or effect of colors as others appeared to do" (258–259).

Whatever the cause of Dunlap's poor eye for color, it quickly became a metaphor for his poor taste and poor judgment more generally. The aspiring artist was all but blind to the art that surrounded him in London. On his first visit to West's London studio, Dunlap remembered passing through a long gallery "hung with sketches and designs" that opened into a high-ceilinged room filled with "gigantic paintings" before entering the studio proper. "I gazed, with all the wonder of ignorance and the enthusiasm of youth upon the paintings," he recalled. There was no overcoming this well-intentioned gawking. Despite living amidst "wonders of art," he remained "blind as a savage." In and around London, he "looked upon pictures without the necessary knowledge that would have made them instructive" (256). On an expedition to Burghley House, whose grounds had been designed by the picturesque landscape architect Capability Brown and whose rooms housed more than five hundred paintings, Dunlap took in pictures of "Madonnas and Bambinos, and Magdalens and Cruxifictions," which "did not advance me one step" (263). The dazzling collection of the Duke of Marlborough offered "some pleasure" but "little profit." After three years of this futile looking, his father summoned him home to New York. There, he was greeted by his father's slaves, whose "black faces, white teeth, and staring eyes" held up a mirror to Dunlap's own failure of vision (266). Despite the finest opportunities money could buy, William Dunlap returned little changed from the youth who had once "admired [Charles Willson] Peale's gallery of pictures" simply because his ignorance led him "to admire every thing" (251).

Chester Harding succeeded where William Dunlap failed, and against far longer odds. Born into a rural New England household that lacked money, education, and pedigree, Harding had looked to the military, tavern keeping, and chair making for his livelihood before he learned to paint. He began with signs and moved on to portraits. Eventually, as his skill and reputation increased, he became one of the most successful academic-style portraitists working in the antebellum North.[48] Harding told the story of his remarkable rise twice. He wrote the best-known version, *My Egotistigraphy*, in 1865, near the end of his life, at the behest of his children and friends. Harding tells his life story in the first half of the memoir; in the book's second half, letters and diary entries piece together his travels through Europe.

The Harding who comes to life in the first half of the *Egotistigraphy* is the one everyone remembers, and with good reason. *This* Harding is as unpretentious as he is funny. He gets rich but never forgets his humble beginnings. He pokes good-natured fun at his clients' airs even as he values their trade. His is a workaday account of how he learned to paint and how he turned his genuine love of the practice into a lucrative career. There are no high-falutin' claims to genius, no paeans to taste. Indeed, those two words are all but absent from the first half of the memoir, although they turn up often enough in the diaries that Harding kept while he was abroad.[49]

To be sure, Harding was alive to the magic of a good likeness. He began to paint portraits after becoming "enamored" with the second-rate efforts of an itinerant he hired to paint him and his wife. The prospect of painting consumed him; he "thought of it by day and dreamed of it by night." And when Harding made his own stab at a portrait, a picture of his wife, he "became frantic with delight; it was like the discovery of a new sense I could think of nothing else."[50] But his growing ambition, an ambition first articulated as the desire to become a painter and then as the desire to become a fine one, was realized by *doing*. Success was the culmination of hard work, endless practice, and close attention to the technical demands of his craft. Success was also the product of business acumen, including the real estate investments that helped support his family while he worked as an itinerant. Harding measured his progress by the rising profits he could demand from an increasingly genteel clientele. In the first half of *My Egotistigraphy*, Harding sketches the artist as a self-made everyman.[51]

Some thirty years before his family coaxed the *Egotistigraphy* out of him, Harding told his story differently. In a long letter written for inclusion in Dunlap's *History*, Harding recounted his transformation from sign painter to portrait painter in terms that drew sharp distinctions between painting signs ("a useful art," "a vocation") and painting faces (a "profession," an "honourable" profession, a "newly discovered goddess"). In the narrative he produced for Dunlap, Harding traveled constantly not to earn money but to educate his eyes. He went from Kentucky to Philadelphia in order to spend "five or six weeks in looking at the portraits of Mr. Sully and others"; a few years later, a trip to Boston was "chiefly . . . a pilgrimage to Stuart." Trips to the East Coast were intended to hone his eye rather than his technique. Visual acuity naturally resulted in technical acuity.[52]

Harding took pains to define himself as a "self-taught" artist in ways that removed his work and, by extension, himself from the ranks of mere craftsmen.

Speculating on the success he enjoyed in Boston in the 1820s, when he claimed to have attracted more sitters than Gilbert Stuart, he considered the possibility that affluent patrons were attracted by the novelty of sitting for a painter who was a "backwoodsman, newly caught." Patrons and "superficial observers," he concluded, invested the phrase "self-taught artist" with misplaced cachet. More knowledgeable judges, he sniffed, understood the label as a symbol of labor, signaling "no other virtue . . . than that of perseverance." But for his part, Harding used the term only to indicate that he did not have "any *particular* instructor"; he did not owe his success to the tutelage of a Benjamin West or an Edward Savage.[53] Sidestepping the manual labor suggested by "perseverance," he explained, "It matters little how an artist arrives at a sort of midway elevation, at which all with common industry may arrive." What counted was genius, which enabled someone like himself to soar "above the common level," leaving "his less favoured brethren to follow in his track with mingled feelings of envy and admiration."[54]

Harding realized his genius not as an itinerant canvassing the American frontier, but as an explorer surveying a "wilderness of art" in London. At first, he confessed, the overwhelming number and variety of paintings dulled his senses, making him "indifferent to all the sublime works that were within my reach." Still, he persisted in looking and "by degrees" began to "see new beauties every day" in the Old Masters. Just as his eyes began to open, his money began to run out. He fell back on portraiture to support himself and immediately attracted a devoted and aristocratic clientele. His sitters provided much more than cash; they ushered him into a world of exquisite taste and sumptuous art collections. Noble patrons invited him to spend weeks at the "splendid" Hamilton Palace, seat of the Duke of Hamilton and home to one of the finest picture galleries in Great Britain. They enabled him to visit Holkham Hall, a seat of "luxury and elegance" belonging to the Coke family. There, he told Dunlap, his mornings "were chiefly spent looking at the 'old masters,'" his afternoons in hunting wild game, and his evenings benefiting from the dinner conversation of the aristocrats, politicians, and artists who were congregated around the seventy-year-old Lord Coke and Coke's twenty-one-year-old wife. For readers of the *History*, Harding cast the time spent at England's magnificent country houses as leisurely opportunities to soak up art, taste, and what he called the "high life."[55]

In fact, Harding's forays to these storied estates were, at best, busman's holidays. The account he penned for Dunlap bears slight resemblance to the one he recorded in his diary, which reveals him as a laborer, albeit an elevated one. He noted that his first attempt to gain admission to Hamilton Palace was rebuffed, despite the fact that he carried a letter of introduction from the Duke of Sussex, because the family was "constantly annoyed" by inquiries from ven-dors and tradesmen of all sorts. During the two weeks he spent at Holkham Hall, he painted four portraits, including a "kit-cat"-sized likeness of "Mr. Bla-kie, Mr. Coke's Steward." A working artist, he was constantly at his easel. His status was confirmed in the Holkham Hall account books, which list him as a "limner."[56]

Harding's inflated account of the time he spent in England was a savvy business strategy. His immersion in the world of Old Masters and tasteful aris-tocrats was calculated to enhance his American reputation. It seems to have worked. In the coda Dunlap added to Harding's "frank and manly" letter, he took pains to celebrate the former "backwoodsman" as a gentleman, possessed of pleasing manners and appearance, who had purchased his "own beautiful country seat." And he confirmed Harding's account of himself with a personal recollection: Years earlier, Harding had called on Dunlap in his painting room, introduced himself, and provided "proof of a true eye and taste" by "immedi-ately" picking out "the best head" Dunlap had set out for display. Together, Dunlap and Harding gave readers a portrait of the artist as a man defined by his eye and by his taste.[57]

Why did thirty years make such a difference in the way Harding told his story? In 1834, seven years after returning from Britain, he was solvent but hardly renowned. He was still rebuilding his network of Boston-based patrons and making a name for himself as a painter of statesmen in Washington, D.C. Naturally, he was keen to distance himself from his earlier, backwoods per-sona. With one eye trained on potential patrons and the other on fellow art-ists, the Harding of 1834 was bent on establishing his credentials as a man who warranted inclusion in the *History* not because of where he came from but because of what he had become. By 1865, Harding wrote for an audience of family and friends that included men of influence from New England to Washington, D.C. He counted John Quincy Adams, James Monroe, Daniel Webster, John Marshall, and Bushrod Washington among his clients. Secure in his social, financial, and professional success, Harding could frame his life story as a distinctly American picaresque. Then, too, around midcentury many Americans had begun to turn away from romantic conceptions of the artist, endorsing instead the ideal of the artist as a hardheaded businessman. By 1865, the life story of an artist whose self-making depended on the work of his hands as much as his eyes and whose self-fashioning resulted as much from time spent in Paris, Kentucky, as time spent in Paris, France, had an appeal that it lacked in the 1830s. Both the 1834 narrative and the 1865 narra-tive depict an artist in the American grain. Placed side by side, they show us how much that grain had changed.[58]

CHAPTER TWO

Painters' emphasis on what Dunlap called their "true eyes and taste," their dematerialization of the physical process of painting, generated a distinct form of cultural capital. Locating their identities in their eyes, rather than their hands, artists cast themselves as emissaries of taste. And by the 1810s, the most authoritative claims to taste assumed the form of claims to connoisseurship. By the end of the eighteenth century, the word "connoisseur" acquired both new connotations and new appeal. It no longer applied solely to wealthy male collectors, who were distinguished by their encyclopedic knowledge of stylistic and technical minutiae and their broad understanding of art's philosophical character. Disinterested and acute observers of literature, language, manners, and experience could also count themselves as connoisseurs. Most obviously, women and men capable of calibrating quality in the welter of market goods could count themselves as connoisseurs.

In a world that was rapidly filling up with more images, more texts, more exhibitions, and more aestheticized commodities, painters-cum-connoisseurs had an edge. They elevated themselves above workaday craftsmen and above painters whose likenesses were merely mechanical. Donning the mantle of connoisseurship also helped painters finesse the distinctions of social class, providing them with a means of setting themselves above the genteel ladies and gentlemen who became their clients. Locating their "genius," their "fancy," their "connoisseurship" in their eyes, painters endowed themselves with ways of seeing and ways of knowing that many of their patrons lacked. Unlike later generations of romantic artists, whose genius set them outside bourgeois society, early national painters cultivated and publicized a capacity for seeing that could distinguish them within that society.[59]

Thus, when Mary Way, her sister Elizabeth (Betsey) Way Champlain, and Eliza Way Champlain (Betsey's daughter) attempted to forge careers as painters in the 1810s and 1820s, they laid claim to connoisseurship.[60] Vision and visual discernment were recurring motifs in the hundreds of letters these women exchanged with each other and their friends as they moved back and forth between New London, Connecticut (where all three were born), and New York City (where Mary Way moved in 1811). At the most basic level, a painter's eye anchored each woman in the world of art, signifying her capacity to see and reproduce natural forms as pictures. But it also enabled her to observe and judge the world around her, signifying her status as a connoisseur. "Connoisseur" was, in fact, among the women's favorite words. They used it to invoke their painstakingly acquired visual literacy, their professional and personal aspirations, and the imaginative and material worlds of their patrons and social superiors. Certainly, the three women boasted a funny sort of connoisseurship. None could boast formal or even systematic training in the arts. Their status as connoisseurs owed little to the sociable performance of judgment and still less either to collecting or to the close and sustained scrutiny of particular art objects. Hardly disinterested observers, the women were working painters whose discerning eyes were verified by their skilled hands. Nevertheless, all three cast the qualities they cultivated as painters—their educated eyes, their superior taste—as badges of connoisseurship that allowed them to transcend the minor indignities and perpetual anxieties generated by the market; all three insisted that their connoisseurship exempted them from mundane social hierarchies.

Mary Way, by far the most successful of the lot, portrayed herself as a woman who had mastered her art by learning, through sheer force of will, to see. In a long letter to her sister, written a couple of years after she had left New London for New York City, Way recounted her progress in terms that recapitulated the tropes used by Greenwood, Dunlap, and Harding. Shortly after she began to advertise her business, the city's "painters, engravers, critics" (to say nothing of "connoisseurs in every shape and form") "flocked" to her rented room in order to size her up. They wanted, she wrote, to "examin my works [and], question me respecting the corse of my studies and mode of practice." They came speaking a language she did not understand, a language of demi-tints, half tints, local tints, opposing tints, and harmonizing tints. It was more than talk. They could see color in a way that she could not. As Way explained, the brightest colors were obvious to anyone. But the best, most satisfying ones—the "thousand nice gradations, soft tones and delicate tints"—escaped the observation of those who were "ignorant they exist." "This," she ruefully admitted, "I know from experience."[61]

Mary Way resolved to learn to see. She turned to a coterie of established painters including William Joseph Williams, John Wesley Jarvis, Joseph Wood, Anson Dickinson, and Samuel Waldo to criticize her style, correct her technique, and loan her paintings. She relentlessly copied three reproductions of Rubens's scriptural paintings, which a distant relative had stored in her rooms pending their sale at auction. Day after day, she studied paintings so beautiful they awed even "the connoisseurs." Her work paid off. Although her finances remained precarious, her eye and her painting improved. More than that, her way of being in the world was forever transformed. For just as Joseph Addison had promised nearly a hundred years before, as a woman of taste, a "connoisseur," Way had acquired a "kind of Property in everything" she saw.[62]

Like other early national artists, Mary Way, her sister, and her niece believed that the path to improvement lay in the education of the eye and in endless attempts to copy the work of one's betters. And like other early national artists, they framed this two-fold process in terms that gestured to the eighteenth-century British aesthetic canon. As Way put it, portraiture, in particular, demanded that the artist "exercis[e] judgment by seeing, and comparing the works of other painters, and varying your stile by copying those paintings approved by amateurs." Copying sharpened more than mechanical skills. It also conditioned a painter's eye. After exhorting Eliza to borrow and copy a friend's valuable paintings of the king and queen of France, Mary Way explained that these copies "should always be before you when you paint a likeness." Copied paintings did more than set a standard: They helped the painter see the sitter, to recognize in the sitter's face the very qualities that should be represented in miniature on ivory. They reminded the women what an accomplished painter was supposed to see when she looked at her subjects.[63]

Painters' sight was privileged sight, a point driven home by Mary Way's loss of vision in the late 1810s. On the brink of blindness, when she could "scarcely distinguish light from darkness," Way dismissed well-meaning friends and relatives who tried to lift her spirits by minimizing the loss of vision in an otherwise healthy woman. "There may indeed be those who view it in a different light, those who think the loss of sight inconsiderable, provided they enjoy every other gratification," she conceded. But they knew "nothing of the pleasure—the inexpressible, the inexhaustible delight" that was once hers. Seeing and painting constituted the "pleasures that wove the charm that bound me to existence." "I feel all the horrors of my situation most sensibly—deep and heavy at my heart," she wrote.[64] Losing her sight, she lost her self. But Way, like her sister and her niece, understood the value of sight long before she stood in danger of losing it. Simultaneously transforming the objects in view and the subject who perceived them, a cultivated eye promised access to a new and better world. After all, no less an authority than William Joseph Williams had taught Way that only those with a full knowledge of color theory were equipped to discern the "beauty and harmony" of nature.

Just as a painter's training enhanced her appreciation of natural beauty, so, too, did it enhance her view of society. As portrait painters, the three women were most apt to read social realities in the faces and forms of friends and acquaintances, family, and clients. They described those they encountered with a level of pictorial detail unusual even by the standards of the day, noting the snowy white of a shawl, the glint of an eye, the faint flush of a cheek, the curl of a lip. They were more concerned with accuracy than with kindness. Painter and art teacher John Rubens Smith was "Neutral-Tint," except on those occasions when he was unlucky enough to be "Natural-Squint." One especially ruddy young man earned the moniker "Lobster" while another, of indeterminate appearance or affliction, was known only as "Skunk-eyes."[65] Way was more than willing to turn a sharp eye on her niece, insisting that the girl literally embody the taste and sensibility expected of a painter. She reminded Eliza how her form had been transformed during an extended visit to New York City: A "certain girl" had come to town, she wrote, a "great overblown fat clumsey country girl." This poor specimen could barely fit into her gown; she was "big as ever the pudding bag would let it be—tight!—strained to death—stiff, awkward, ignorant." Way took Eliza in hand, dosed her with laxatives, restricted her to "light fare," and thereby "reduced the cumbersome load of mortality that hung upon the vast dementions of her unweildy figure to something like a reasonable size." Even in New London, the same regimen would guarantee that Champlain remained "easy, genteel, refined, and tonish—Yorkish, if you please."[66]

Such descriptions of face and form owed much to the conventions of the belletristic literature that all three women enjoyed. But the precision of the women's observations and the conclusions they drew from them also derived from their conviction that bodies in general and faces in particular served as indexes of character, indexes that would be legible to the trained eye. Many individuals in the early republic expressed some degree of faith in some sort of physiognomy, but artists were among physiognomy's most enthusiastic adherents. The women in the Way Champlain family were no exceptions. Glimpsing Rembrandt Peale at an exhibition of his *Court of Death*, Eliza wrote that she "looked with all my might to see if I could discover those traits of genius and talents in the countenance of the artist which were so conspicuous in every stroke of his pencil." She was disappointed. Save for a "very penetrating blue eye," the great man was "quite plain." As a fledgling painter, Eliza conceded that she was not yet equipped to discern the genius in Peale's face, though she could recognize it in his canvas. The fault lay not with the man but with the girl: Peale's "genius was too mighty for the eye of the vulgar."[67]

Her aunt's eye was keener. When Charlotte Waite, an affluent young woman in Way's New York City circle, ditched one beau for another, she arranged for Mary to paint the new suitor. The young woman was less interested in a representation of his face than in a close reading of his character. As Way explained to her niece, Waite "wished me to examin him thoroughly, consider him in every point of view. . . . [And] when I had criticized, scrutinized and connoisseur'd him well, tell her my opinion and if it was worthwhile for her to set her cap for him." As it turned out, the young man's predecessor, who had been portrayed as a man of sense by miniaturist Samuel Waldo, turned out to be a "fool"; his portrait was "no likeness" but rather a deception that had "flattered [him] to death." Waite hoped to be better served the second time. On the appointed day, Way conferred approval on Waite's new "Yankee beau," a man whose "fine black eyes" and "intelligent countenance" revealed him as "smart and sensible" and who had recently spent time in New London, where he had hired none other than Betsey Champlain to take a likeness.[68]

New York City and its environs afforded plenty of opportunities for the women to leverage their cultivated eyes as a form of social capital, testing their mettle as connoisseurs. Mary Way and Eliza Champlain regularly lambasted ordinary mortals who attempted to appropriate the painter's powers of perception. A surgeon-dentist who was also a client once tried to impress Way with his knowledge of color theory, describing a lady he had seen on Broadway. Her beautiful complexion was neither real nor natural, he observed, but rather the reflection cast by the pink silk lining of her bonnet. Way recounted the story to her sister and niece in order to dismiss the man as the "greatest fool nature ever formed." Eliza entertained her family with a similar story about a Mrs. Keys, Charles Brockden Brown's sister-in-law, whom she encountered while visiting friends in the countryside. When the party walked up a hill to take in the view, poor Mrs. Keys blundered through "a most sentimental harangue on the beauty of the surrounding landscape" while the connoisseurs, Eliza included, listened in "mute astonishment at her folly."[69]

Among themselves, the Way Champlain women tacitly agreed that there were connoisseurs and connoisseurs: Mary Way tartly observed that Eliza was not yet prepared to appreciate a "sublime" view of Niagara Falls, telling the girl that "it would not please you as it does connoisseurs."[70] Way's brush skills and access to New York City's exhibitions and auctions clearly guaranteed that her connoisseurship would always exceed that of her sister. Yet both women agreed that, at least in New London, Betsey could safely assume the authority of a connoisseur, if only because there were no real connoisseurs to be had there. Tellingly, in one early literary effort, Champlain made a futile attempt to instruct a "buxom country dutchess" in the finer points of art appreciation. Offering to trade a likeness for the "dutchess's" fresh butter, "I endeavoured with all the skill I was mistress of to make her understand the design" of the ivory miniatures on the painting desk, Champlain wrote, "but found my labour in vain." On the one hand, the experiment demonstrated that there was no common ground between a woman who sold paintings and one who sold butter. On the other hand, besting a farmer's wife, who was as "coarse as three threads to an armful" and whose hand alone "would outweigh a common shoulder of mutton," hardly credentialed one as an authority on matters of taste.[71]

Of course, it was one thing to declare oneself a connoisseur within the family circle or to a milkmaid, another thing altogether to proclaim it to painters or patrons whose educated eyes and cultivated tastes were beyond reproach. Other connoisseurs were simultaneously potential allies who might affirm the women's talents and tastes and enemies poised to reveal their humiliating deficiencies of learning or skill. To court approbation, avoid embarrassment, and ease anxiety, the women studied the habits and opinions of confirmed connoisseurs. They angled to learn what the cognoscenti knew, to go where they went, and to see what they saw. Then they reported their experiences back to one another. Mary Way, in particular, never passed up an opportunity to tell her sister and niece about her career among New York's connoisseurs. The high point surely came in 1817, when James Monroe visited New York City. Way attended many of the festivities held to honor the president, including an art exhibition at City Hall. There, she managed to meet Daniel D. Tomkins, the vice president and a former governor of New York, who was "said to be the most polite man in the United States." As she explained to Eliza, Tomkins approached her because he had been told that "I was an artist, and soon let me know he was a connoisseur, and favor'd me with his remarks and observations upon the painting."[72] In a gallery packed with sightseers and politicians, the two art lovers—the two connoisseurs—managed to single each other out. For Mary Way, this flash of recognition and affirmation must have been as delicious in the recounting as it had been in the moment.

Mastering the Market

Connoisseurship might level the playing field between "the most polite man in the United States" and a female miniaturist at a gala exhibition, but it did not pay the bills. Artists remained every bit as dependent on the vagaries of the market as the artisans and mechanics they tried to distance themselves from. The early decades of the nineteenth century presented painters, especially, with far more opportunities than Copley or Peale had encountered a half century earlier. Anglo-American patrons still exhibited an annoying preference for portraits over, say, landscape and genre paintings. Yet the market for portraits in multiple media was accelerating. No longer the special preserve of an urban mercantile, clerical, or political elite, likenesses had come to figure as badges of respectability and refinement, as announcements of middle-class aspiration as well as middle-class status. The eighteenth century's solemn, ceremonial pendants pairing husband and wife gave way to a more inclusive, more expansive range of subjects. Entire families, posed together in groups or depicted individually, might sit to artists. Loving parents began to commission several miniature portraits over the course of a child's lifetime. Whether painted in miniature on ivory or rendered bust size on canvas or wood, likenesses were one part of an expansive consumer market for objects signaling taste and gentility.[73]

Growing demand, however, did not necessarily make it easier for an artist to earn a living. For one thing, artists of all stripes competed in an increasingly crowded labor market, in which more people supplied more images at more price points. In cities, the rising demand for art always seemed to lag behind the growing numbers of painters, engravers, and silhouette cutters who clogged the labor market. In the hinterland, even the most polished provincial towns could not generate enough patronage to support an individual for very long. When William Dunlap returned to New York City in 1787, he regarded Joseph Wright as his only competition. Thirty years later, Eliza Champlain complained that "this city is so overrun with artists that it is impossible I should ever get business enough." City directories bear out these assessments. The number of individuals in New York City who identified themselves as professional portrait painters working in any media roughly doubled every decade, increasing at a rate that outpaced the rise in population. Similar patterns appeared in Philadelphia, Baltimore, and Boston.[74] Some of this increase can be attributed to the ambitions of individuals like Mary Way and Chester Harding, who gravitated to cities in order to improve their technique, expand their roster of patrons, and burnish their reputations. But the increasingly crowded rolls of artists selling services in eastern cities also reflects the trajectories of European artists who migrated to the United States, mostly from Britain but also from Italy and, especially in the wake of revolution, France. While men like Antonio Meucci, John Francis Eugene Prud'homme, Louis Simond, or John Marras could add to a city's cachet, they threatened to take food out of the mouths of native-born painters. "Anything that comes from abroad is all the rage," Eliza Champlain grumbled, "while native talent is supposed to live and die in obscurity."[75]

Crowded and competitive in the best of times, the art market turned treacherous in hard times. Despite their growing popularity, portraits, which dominated all commissions, remained luxuries. And when middling and affluent households retrenched, portraits were among the first expenditures to go. Minor economic fluctuations might disrupt a painter's supply of patrons but full-blown financial crises, like the Panic of 1819, could devastate even the most established artists. Miniaturist Anson Dickinson, for example, had built a solid clientele in New York City. Between 1812 and 1820, he painted nearly three hundred likenesses; on the eve of the Panic of 1819, he averaged one commission a week. When the brunt of the panic hit, he was lucky to get one commission a month. Samuel F. B. Morse, who shined for three seasons in Charleston, weathered the initial stages of the financial crisis with his business intact. "The city fairly swarms with painters," he boasted, but "I am the only one who has as much as he can do." But when crop failures and collapsing cotton prices propelled the initial panic into a full-blown economic collapse, Morse found himself scrambling alongside everybody else. He had "no new commissions" and could wring only "cold procrastinating answers" from people who had once promised him work. Even after he dropped his fee from $80 to $60, he failed to attract sitters and was forced to live in his studio to save on rent.[76]

For painters who were more marginally situated than Dickinson or Morse, the Panic of 1819 proved catastrophic. Between October 1819 and April 1820, Betsey Way Champlain "had but two likenesses on ivory and one two-dollar one" from her New London clients. That meager business was not enough to support Champlain and her husband, who was dying of consumption. They survived the winter on a "five dollar bill" donated by a concerned friend and money sent by a son who sold his gun and watch to help them. Things were little better for Mary Way and Eliza Champlain on the other end of the Long Island Sound in New York City. Faced with mounting debts and dwindling commissions, the two were forced to give up their rented rooms and move in with friends. They briefly considered moving back to New London, hoping to save money by sharing quarters with Betsey. But the attractions of New London's low cost of living were offset by its depressed economy, which all but guaranteed that the two women would never earn enough to pay off their New York creditors.[77]

In good times and bad, the structure of the early national art market pushed painters toward entrepreneurship. They pursued a variety of strategies to generate new business, compensate for growing numbers of competitors, generate something approximating a steady income, and generally insulate themselves from economic fluctuations. Most obviously, artists worked to expand their markets, putting likenesses within the reach of people whose geographic location or social status would have precluded their access to portraits in the eighteenth century. At the same time, they worked to expand Americans' appetite for art, spectatorship, and taste more generally.[78]

Itinerancy was the most common of these strategies. Mobility was useful for fledgling painters, who traveled to earn money while mastering their craft. One young painter was told to head west, to the "country towns," and charge "so low that the cost of [the] picture need not stand in the way" of attracting sitters. But established portraitists also incorporated itinerancy into their business strategies. Harding, for one, maintained a strenuous travel schedule over the course of his entire career; on their twenty-fourth wedding anniversary, his wife calculated that he had spent only a decade at home.[79] Artists often selected one or two cities as sites for satellite studios where they painted for months at a time every year. An annual trip to Charleston, Richmond, or Washington, D.C., made sound business sense; it enabled a successful painter to develop a more or less national reputation while exploiting an underserved market. In flush times, the proceeds from these junkets more than compensated for the overhead of maintaining a second studio and residence. Samuel Morse cleared $3,000 a season in Charleston before the economy collapsed; Harding made enough in one extended trip to Baltimore and Washington, D.C., to offset the debt from his purchase of a four-story townhouse on Boston's Beacon Hill the year before. In a depressed economy, however, this stately progress from one city to the next accelerated into a mad dash through the hinterland. The goal was to locate anyone with cash to spare for a likeness before some other painter snatched him up: Morse was dismayed when he charged into Concord, New Hampshire, in 1819 only to discover that "the Quacks have been here before me," gobbling up all the available commissions.[80]

At least in theory, single-painting exhibitions presented another way to compensate for market constraints. Banking on the hope that people who could not afford to purchase a painting might pay admission to view one, the most ambitious U.S. artists staged public shows. Inspired partly by John Singleton Copley's success with similar ventures in eighteenth-century England and partly by the near collapse of the contemporary portrait market following the Panic of 1819, Rembrandt Peale, John Vanderlyn, William Dunlap, Thomas Sully, and Samuel F. B. Morse all created historical or allegorical paintings boasting complicated compositions, massive proportions, and technical virtuosity.[81] Trying to turn these triumphs into cash, painters developed new business skills that they plied in distant and unfamiliar markets. Once a picture was completed, the artist had to arrange transportation for a canvas weighing six hundred pounds or more. He had to locate exhibition spaces large enough to house and display it. Gallery space could be secured for a price in cities like Boston, New York, or Philadelphia. In the hinterland, however, an artist had to make do with whatever "public buildings, courthouses, and churches" were available.[82] In order to persuade an untried public to turn out for the viewing, the artist had to launch a complicated advertising campaign in local newspapers. Hired agents, who traveled with the paintings and handled daily logistics, could free painters from the burden of managing their exhibitions, but their salaries cut into profits.

Labor intensive at every step of the way, traveling exhibitions rarely generated consistent, much less considerable, profit. Rembrandt Peale's *Court of Death* was the signal success. Based on a well-known poem, the 12-by-24-foot painting used twenty-two allegorical figures representing qualities like Pleasure, Want, and Virtue to drive home the moral that "Death has no terror in the eyes of Virtuous Old Age, and Innocence, Faith, and Hope."[83] In its first year alone, *Court of Death* attracted 32,000 visitors and generated thousands of dollars in income; it continued to draw crowds for decades. Peale's success proved exceptional. Dunlap could boast that the public's response to his quartet of biblical paintings, which together covered more than a thousand square feet of canvas, was "honourable to me and my countrymen." Yet he counted his profits, when he could count them at all, in the hundreds rather than the thousands of dollars. Morse's *The House of Representatives* aimed to remind viewers of the virtues of political deference and vices of untrammeled democracy at a time when they were casting off the last vestiges of deference. Of course, it lost money everywhere it went. And then there was the exceptionally unlucky John Vanderlyn, who designed and built a rotunda across from New York's City Hall in order to display his enormous panorama of Versailles. When the rotunda's opening coincided with the onset of the Panic of 1819, the venture bankrupted him.[84]

Some painters moved beyond studios and galleries, marketing their training as artists and their authority as connoisseurs in new ways. Museum keeping, for example, offered an obvious and potentially lucrative form of diversification. Building on the skills developed to display and sell paintings, artists-turned-museum-keepers exhibited a range of objects that included paintings but that extended well beyond them in order to increase patrons and profits. Thus it is not surprising that a roster of early national museum keepers included not only the Peale family, but also Edward Savage, Joseph Steward, and Ethan Allen Greenwood.

Greenwood's museums provide a better model of aesthetic entrepreneurship than either Charles Willson Peale's famous and famously didactic Philadelphia Museum or the satellite museums that Peale's sons opened in Baltimore and New York City. Unlike Charles Willson Peale, Greenwood did not dwell on the potential contradictions between republican enlightenment and popular entertainment. And unlike Rembrandt and Rubens Peale, who sold shares in their museums with disastrous consequences, Greenwood became the New England Museum's sole proprietor almost two years after he purchased it. He retained full control of it and the two satellite museums he opened in Providence and Portland until 1839, when he sold the entire enterprise and retired to the country as a man of property and standing.[85]

Greenwood's success depended on his ability to juggle art, entertainment, and commerce. He viewed his museums as vehicles for taste and museum keeping as an extension of his work as a painter. He himself executed any number of the paintings that covered the museums' walls, and he played an active role in organizing and decorating the spaces. He ran his Gallery of the Fine Arts at a loss for two years "in the hopes that public taste would presently improve" before he conceded defeat and stored it. His aesthetic sensibilities were matched by his business sense. Greenwood controlled his cash expenditures by "paying for everything with either season or single tickets to the Museum," a former employee recalled. He bought up the contents of local and regional museums, even inferior ones, with an eye toward forestalling competition. As he noted when he purchased most of the Boston Museum at an 1822 auction, "My object . . . was as much to break up the establishment, as to obtain the contents."[86] After opening franchises in Providence and Portland, he rotated his collections: When Boston audiences tired of a curiosity or spectacle, it was dispatched to another Greenwood museum, where it continued to attract customers and generate profits.

Greenwood worked tirelessly to maximize attendance, especially in Boston. He lost no opportunity to tie his business to political and civic occasions. An ardent Federalist, he went out of his way to court the patronage of his party's elites when the legislature was in session. And when the Marquis de Lafayette returned to Boston in 1825 Greenwood hosted a reception at the museum, "handsomely" filling "the rooms with the beauty, taste, & fashion of the town." Yet he hardly limited himself to the city's elite. Instead, he catered to multiple markets, promoting a fluid definition of tasteful entertainment. Singing dwarves and pandrometers; two-headed calves and Thomas Sully's *Passage of the Delaware*; Maxcy the celebrated bugle player and medical lectures—all found at least a temporary home in the New England Museum. Greenwood may have railed against the "ridiculous," "infernal" circus, whose "nonsense and buffoonery" debased public taste and cut his "receipts in half," but he was not above purchasing dying circus animals and repurposing them as taxidermied zoological specimens.[87] By 1839, when he sold his museums, Greenwood had parlayed eye and entrepreneurship into financial security.

A Gendered Art Market

As business strategies, itinerancy, exhibitions, and diversification may have been uncertain, even risky. But they were all but closed to the steadily increasing numbers of women who had acquired some training in the arts and who sought, by choice or necessity, to turn avocations into vocations. The travel conditions and business strategies demanded by itinerancy, for example, flew in the face of polite gender conventions. Itinerants traveled alone, secured lodging on the fly, and advertised promiscuously. Working outside of established and familiar patronage networks, they solicited business from strangers. A woman who chose to travel with her brush removed herself from the social safety net that enabled her to simultaneously maintain her respectability and ply her trade. Thus when Susanna Paine, a self-taught painter who moved between Massachusetts, Maine, and Rhode Island, arrived in a new town, her first order of business was to secure her respectability: "No pecuniary straits had ever yet induced me to take any situation, however profitable—involving the least impropriety," she wrote. On the contrary. Paine "always determined to respect myself and to take no step that prudence and delicacy would not approve." Indeed, her memoir recounts her career as a constant struggle to secure the lodgings, painting rooms, sitters, and clothes that would confirm her respectability.[88] A turn as an itinerant was not beyond the realm of possibility, as Paine's career demonstrates. But it was surely beyond the realm of probability, especially for women who came to painting courtesy of academy educations that located them among the genteel.

More important than restrictions on where and how women could ply their trade were restrictions on the kind of artwork deemed suitable for women to create. Women were excluded from practices that were tied most closely to the trades—engraving, architecture, even sign and carriage painting—by craft traditions that cast the artisan's shop as a locus of masculine authority. The province of painting was no better. Heroic historical and allegorical paintings were interventions intended to shape the public sphere, so they remained the special preserve of men. So, too, did the traveling shows that aimed to turn those interventions into profit. Women were confined to portraits, the smaller the better. For the most part, female portraitists worked in miniature or with pastels and crayons. As historian David Jaffee has observed, these media were especially suited to women's domestic obligations; they required tools that could be picked up or put away on short notice. And neither miniatures nor pastels required the workspace necessary to execute full-length portraits.[89]

This specialization may have made portrait painting convenient. But it also confined women artists to the least lucrative corners of the art market. When Mary Way moved to New York City, she advertised her skills as a painter of likenesses, landscapes, or "views of country seats." She quickly discovered that most buyers wanted likenesses and that *her* buyers wanted miniatures. At the height of her career as a miniaturist, she charged $10 for paintings that took a week and $20 for those she "worked upon for a fortnight, steadily"; in September 1816, she reported that during the preceding summer, she had completed one of each.[90] As a point of comparison, at roughly the same time, Chester Harding, still a "backwoodsman" in Paris, Kentucky, could charge a provincial patron $25 for a bust-sized portrait. Female miniaturists less experienced and less skilled than Way commanded far less. Eliza Way Champlain typically charged around $6 per likeness; the completion of a $10 head in 1825 was a signal occasion. When she was in especially dire straits, the young painter happily collected $2 to make a minia-ture version of a portrait completed by a different woman artist. When por-trait commissions were especially meager, women might look to the growing market for small, ephemeral decorative arts. Eliza Champlain resorted to painting watch-papers: small, circular cutouts that decorated the inside of watchcases. On the one hand, demand was brisk; the number of men carrying pocket watches was on the rise, and the papers themselves were frequently replaced. On the other hand, these tiny paintings—with their feminized alle-gories and their close association with the culture of amateur female accom-plishment—were often bestowed as gifts from ladies to gentlemen. When even professionals like Champlain gave away watch-papers to friends and acquain-tances, it was difficult to drum up a paying clientele. And those who were willing to pay paid little indeed. Champlain was thrilled when a male friend distributed her watch-papers among some New York jewelers he knew; the sale of twelve of these "much admired" paintings netted $7.[91]

The most realistic, most reliable way for a woman to augment her income as a painter was to teach and, more precisely, to teach drawing and painting as an accomplishment suitable for young women and children. Teaching was the last resort for Mary Way and Betsey and Eliza Champlain, and for good reason. The hours were long; the pay was poor; and the students were rarely gifted. When Eliza Champlain's New York City friends organized a painting school for her in 1822, she quickly confirmed the limits of a career as a ladies' art teacher. She met her students thrice weekly for three-hour classes. The remainder of her time was consumed by "drawing and colouring patterns" for her students to copy. To underbid the city's other female teachers, she charged each of her sixteen students $5 in tuition rather than the $10 that she and her friends thought she deserved; her net profit would have been reduced by the cost of renting a schoolroom and purchasing supplies. And while she delighted in the work of her best students, she was saddled with "one most intolerable fool" whose "last piece" was "worse than the first" and who cast a pall on the whole enterprise. Although "I don't find teaching so very disagreeable as I expected," she concluded, "still it is an amusement I should never choose."[92] And that was precisely the problem with the whole range of women's artistic pursuits: choice. The same constructions of genteel femininity that pushed women to art fore-closed their ability to choose the kind of art they might produce and the paths they could pursue to profit from it.

And what of the patrons? Of the ladies and gentlemen whose appetite for images in general and likenesses in particular made it possible for a Mary Way or a

Chester Harding to become an aesthetic entrepreneur in the first place? Patrons seem to have understood that an artist's eye could contribute substantially to the success or failure of the representation. Thus, many of the sitters who hired one or another of the Way and Champlain family allowed the painter to select the clothes they would wear for the sitting. Eliza, for example, wrote that she herself had selected the dress that the imposing and "most elegant" Mrs. Shearman would wear for her sitting: a "heavenly sky-blue crape," chosen after a careful review of the woman's wardrobe because "she looks much better in it than in any of her other dresses." The matron trumped her painter in wealth, polish, and position but the painter had a better eye and, at least in Eliza's telling, the matron stood to benefit from it.[93]

The investment in the trope of the artist's eye was a knife that cut both ways. Just as a tractable sitter benefited from the artist's eye, one who was stubborn or tasteless could undermine a painter's work. Dunlap recounted that even a painter as prestigious as Gilbert Stuart could be "tortured by the want of taste in the decoration of the sitter." When a Boston "mantua-maker" won the lottery, she hired Stuart to paint her "with all the choice trumpery of her own shop, [and] the glittering gewgaws of the jewellers." Torn between his obligations to his creditors and his art, Stuart chose the former. The result was, in Stuart's words, "what I have all my painting life been endeavoring to avoid,— vanity and bad taste."[94]

Patrons were both courted and constructed by the aesthetic entrepreneurs they hired. Portraits provided sitters with likenesses and signaled their status as measured by participation in the market for taste. But the paintings did more: They allowed sitters to see themselves—literally—as sensible subjects, as creatures of feeling, taste, and virtue. They saw themselves, in other words, as men and women qualified for membership in the republic of taste. Just as important, sitters could observe others observing precisely those qualities in their portraits and, by extension, in themselves. Artists, in turn, stood to benefit from patrons' dependence on and endorsement of their taste. Notwithstanding the hazards of the market, the reciprocal relationship between artists and painters promised mutual benefit.

Some years after hiring Connecticut painter and wax sculptor Reuben Moulthrop to paint his portrait, the Reverend Ammi Robbins commissioned seven more portraits of himself and his kin. After five years, including a seven-week stint during which Moulthrop moved into the Robbins home and set up a studio in the minister's study, the work was complete. Robbins was delighted with the final products and relieved to reclaim his study. As much as he enjoyed the portraits, he found that he also enjoyed watching other people scrutinize them. He opened his house to accommodate the viewers, writing that "our p[eo]ple came in plenty day after day as into a Museum." It must have been a satisfying moment. Robbins simultaneously saw himself and his family rendered as objects of aesthetic pleasure and witnessed his community exercise their taste on those objects. Like the young Ethan Allen Greenwood, who had launched his career with an exhibition in his Dartmouth College lodgings, the reverend learned that paintings, along with the aesthetic entrepreneurs who created them, could confer new kinds of visibility.[95]

CHAPTER THREE

Picturing Race

Two women—one black, the other white—meet our gaze. The black woman is recessed into the picture plane, as though she has taken a step back, away from us. With a tilt of her chin, the white woman appears to project herself off of the ivory support and into our space. The painting of the black woman is finished and framed: Her likeness has moved into the networks of affiliation that sustain and are sustained by portraiture. The painting of the white woman is unfinished. It never served as a surrogate for the sitter in its own time, although it does fulfill that purpose in ours. At first glance, the two paintings might seem conventional: They are immediately recognizable as miniature portraits, painted with watercolors on thin sheets of ivory. In the first half of the nineteenth century, such likenesses were ubiquitous among affluent and middling Americans. Today, they are ubiquitous at historical societies and museums, in antiques shops, and on eBay. Yet while the genre is familiar these particular paintings are not. Portraits of nineteenth-century African American women are rare, portraits on ivory all the more so. Unfinished miniature portraits from any period are also unusual. But perhaps the most remarkable thing about these particular portraits is that, unlike the majority of extant miniatures, they survive embedded in their stories. They are enriched by stories about sitters, artists, and viewers; by stories about personal significance and cultural resonance of miniatures; and by stories about the relationship between aesthetics and authority.

The painting of the African American woman depicts Elizabeth Freeman, a Massachusetts slave who claimed her liberty in 1781. According to one story, after hearing the Declaration of Independence read aloud in a Sheffield church, she successfully sued for freedom in a case that challenged the constitutionality of slavery in Massachusetts. Freeman never learned to read or write. But even as a slave, she had been widely respected for her courage, integrity, and judgment. After gaining her freedom, she went to work in the household of Theodore Sedgwick, the attorney who had represented her. There, she was cook, housekeeper, nurse, and more. Sedgwick's first wife, Pamela Dwight Sedgwick, was regularly incapacitated, both physically and emotionally. Elizabeth Freeman stepped into the vacuum left first by her mistress's frailty and finally by her death in 1807. Freeman left the Sedgwick household a year later, when Theodore remarried: According to Sedgwick family lore, she balked at conceding her cherished authority to the new mistress. Instead, she retired to the small home she had purchased with her savings, worked as a nurse, and devoted herself to her grown child, grandchildren, and great-grandchildren. But she never cut her ties to the Sedgwick family circle. Instead, she returned at regular intervals to care for the family when she was especially needed. Indeed, it may well have been one of these visits—part sociability, part support—that occasioned Freeman's portrait, painted in 1811 by Susan Anne Livingston Ridley Sedgwick, the daughter-in-law of Freeman's former attorney and employer. Elizabeth Freeman died in 1829. Despite her own fondness for fine dress and what one contemporary described as the "reckless consumption" of her kin, she left not "a single debt" to encumber an estate that amounted to nearly $1,000.[1]

The subject of the second painting is Elizabeth (Betsey) Way Champlain, the Connecticut painter whose career we explored in Chapter 2. She began this self-portrait in 1818 and never completed it. Champlain was born into a middling mercantile family in New London just before the Revolution. It isn't clear when or how she learned to paint, but by the time she was in her twenties, she had begun to paint miniature portraits of neighbors and kin. Her 1794 marriage to a ship captain, George Champlain, and the births of their four children did not end her career. On the contrary. She continued to paint and teach throughout her marriage, perhaps to help stabilize the family's erratic income. From her husband's death in 1820 until her own, she lived mostly by her brush. Betsey Way Champlain worked diligently at her craft, learning when and where she could. Yet it would be a mistake to cast her merely as an earnest craftswoman, for she was an irrepressible culture vulture. Never mind that her adult years unfolded along a path that distanced her from the nicely appointed parlors and the comforting financial security boasted by her patrons; never mind that she worked for her bread and for the roof over her head. Champlain eagerly embraced every form of aesthetic pleasure that came her way. She wrote sketches and especially poems on themes like "Viewing a Comet," "Flattery," "the Muse," and "Fancy." She associated herself with a coterie of *very* minor poets who circulated between New York City and New London, Connecticut. She played guitar and the "flaggellett." In her forties she took up dancing, mastering the "five positions" of ballet, and waltzing her husband—clutching at his cane—around their parlor. This exuberant life came to an end in 1825, when Betsey Way Champlain died unexpectedly after a brief illness.[2]

Like the women they depict, the two miniatures make for odd pendants. Although Freeman and Champlain were more or less contemporaries, their paths never crossed. Their biographies diverge in all the predictable ways as a consequence of the women's differing legal status, class, and race. Yet, placed alongside of one another, these images and their stories have a great deal to tell us about the relationship between aesthetics and authority in the early republic. By the time they were created, ivory miniatures had become the likeness of choice for individuals who claimed, or hoped to claim, membership in a growing middle class. Portable, personal, and relatively affordable, miniatures were well suited to serve as symbols of the domestic intimacy and sentimental privacy that would become the hallmarks of bourgeois culture. Portraits were equal parts aspiration and representation, and these particular likenesses illuminate the kinds of visibility that patrons and painters believed a miniature could provide as well as the kinds of social and affective ties they hoped it would cement. But there was more to the appeal of this extraordinarily popular medium than its ability to pull on viewers' heartstrings. Celebrated largely for its capacity to conjure translucent complexion, an ivory miniature conformed to aesthetic principles that worked to visualize and thus enforce any number of social distinctions, especially those predicated on skin color. The portraits of Freeman and Champlain thus alert us to the construction of racial identities and prod us to consider how race was elaborated not in the public realms of commerce and politics, where historians usually seek it, but in the putatively private sphere.

Family Pictures

We cannot hope to understand the portraits of Freeman and Champlain until we understand how and why they were created. As the products of women artists, both likenesses have roots in the culture of female accomplishment that flourished in early national academies. They were created in contexts informed directly, albeit differently, by the gendered dynamics of the art market and the persistence of class distinctions within the republic of taste. Notwithstanding the differences in the lives of the sitters, both images were created to symbolize and nurture family ties and family love. Both paintings were intended to bind artists, sitters, and viewers together over time, space, and the passing of generations.

Let us start with the artists. We can say nothing for certain about how, when, or why either Susan Ridley Sedgwick or Betsey Way Champlain learned to paint, much less how they acquired the special skills necessary to paint in miniature on ivory. But it seems likely that both were introduced to the rudiments of watercolor painting as part of their acquisition of the accomplishments. Accomplishments were aimed at inculcating taste, as we have seen; watercolor landscapes, embroidered pictures, and bouquets of worsted flowers stood as the training's by-products rather than its end. That said, advocates of the accomplishments also pointed out that the ornamental skills had market value. In a pinch, a woman might turn her accomplishments into self-support. As one writer put it, the "fine arts or the sciences" that single women pursued for their "amusement or instruction" could become necessities depending on the "inactivity, folly, or death of a husband."[3]

For Sedgwick, the daughter of one prosperous man and the wife of another, painting remained an avocation, one of many accomplishments cultivated at elite schools in Boston and Albany, New York. She set enough store on her own talent that she mastered the painstaking technique demanded by a watercolor ivory miniature; she set enough store on art that she supported the efforts of her daughter, another gifted amateur artist who filled up her chapbooks with sketches copied from drawing manuals. But painting and drawing were only two of her many accomplishments. Like Betsey Champlain, Susan Ridley Sedgwick also enjoyed writing, a creative outlet and form of cultural production that offered distinct advantages over painting. For one thing, as a fledgling writer, she enjoyed the enthusiastic encouragement of her dear friend and sister-in-law, the renowned novelist Catharine Maria Sedgwick. For another, a writer could produce and sell her work from the privacy of her own home, shrouded in decorous anonymity. A portrait painter by necessity ventured into the public to secure sitters. Once she had a paying sitter, a painter was perforce compelled to study the subject, thus violating etiquette that admonished polite ladies and gentlemen never to stare at another "as if you were taking his picture" and that especially cautioned women that a bold or brazen look could be "interpreted in the worst sense." In the nineteenth century, it was far easier to be a scribbling woman than a painting one. Personal connections and social conventions all but guaranteed that when Susan Ridley Sedgwick entered the cultural marketplace in the late 1820s, her aim was not to sell portraits but to publish didactic children's literature.[4]

Pushed by desperation and pulled by a love of art, Betsey Way Champlain turned her accomplishment into a salable skill. This was no mean feat, for earning steady money as a female painter was far more difficult than pundits touting the marketability of the accomplishments had promised. In reality, it "required the greatest exertions to make both ends meet," as Champlain complained in 1822. More than once, she admitted that a "suppression of business" resulted in an "attack of hypochondriac," or a bout of what would today be called clinical depression. Confronted by fluctuating demand and slim profits, Champlain displayed enormous energy, resilience, and ingenuity. She painted kin, neighbors, and local notables. In the 1810s, she capitalized on the increasing sentimentality of mourning by taking likenesses of corpses. When portrait commissions were few and far between, she gave lessons to young women, a contingency plan she detested. All told, she painted enough of New London that some fifty years after her death a local historian declared that her portraits of "ladies," with their "delicacy of treatment and purity of sentiment," stood for the best of "old time" society. Despite her eventual status as New London's painter of record, Champlain always deplored her spotty training. She and her family were always certain that her artistic and financial progress was hobbled by her ignorance of theory and the lack of guidance that formal studio training could provide. The limits of training grounded in the ornamentals registered in the likeness she painted and the prices she could charge for them.[5]

If personal family histories and particular family fortunes account for the contexts in which Sedgwick and Champlain painted, the ascendance of the bourgeois family accounted for their subject matter. As art historian Robin Jaffee Frank has suggested, by the early nineteenth century, the growing importance of affection as a family value increased the popularity of ivory miniatures. Small and private, viewed and sometimes worn close to the owner's body, miniatures used physical proximity as a bid for emotional proximity. The sentiments symbolized by these paintings were also manifested by their disposition, for they were typically commissioned as gifts, sometimes bestowed singly, sometimes as part of a mutual exchange. Miniatures thus operated differently from oil portraits, which were retained by patrons until death, when they passed to the next generation. If oil portraits commemorated lineages, reminding viewers how a particular family had been developed and maintained over time, miniature portraits helped a family to create and reinforce networks within a single generation.[6]

As gifts, miniatures reified and realized the feelings that united sitter and recipient. Initially, affluent eighteenth-century Anglo-Americans exchanged them to mark betrothals and celebrate weddings. Given the price of high-style miniatures like the ones painted by Edward Malbone or Benjamin Trott, which could rival the cost of bust-sized oil portraits, it is not surprising that there was often something distinctly dynastic about the unions these portraits commemorated. However loving such marriages may have been, they were also political, social, and economic alliances between powerful families. Over the first quarter of the nineteenth century, however, the relationships represented and preserved by miniatures began to extend beyond the marital couple—dynastic and otherwise—to encompass wide-ranging networks of kin and friends. This shift surely reflected the growing influence of child-centered family ideals and the emergent culture of sentiment. But it also reflected the increasing availability and affordability of ivory portrait miniatures.

Cheap labor, much of it women's labor, helped create an expansive art market in the first decades of the nineteenth century. Women artists charged a fraction of the commissions demanded by their male competitors.[7] Especially in urban areas, middle-class families took advantage of the crowded, competitive, and gendered labor market to amass multiple representations of multiple kin. Miniatures depicting children, parents, siblings, cousins—even the deceased—heightened the genre's broadly domestic (as opposed to its narrowly conjugal) associations. So, too, did the growing numbers of women who commissioned paintings. The high cost of oil paintings placed them beyond the reach of most women buyers. But miniatures, cheap ones at least, were attainable for middle-class women.[8] Thus by the early nineteenth century, ivory miniatures had become affordable luxuries, mementos that could be purchased at any number of junctures in a family's life course.

The portraits of Elizabeth Freeman and Betsey Way Champlain operated in precisely this way. They commemorated and cemented relations among kin, real and fictive. They also captured the mixture of intimacy and interiority that had begun to distinguish middle-class families on both sides of the Atlantic. Depicting single sitters, they were family portraits in the broadest sense of the term.

Champlain, for example, began her self-portrait at the request of and as a gift for her sister, Mary Way, who had moved to New York City to further her own artistic ambitions. After more than seven years apart, Way had an "unconquerable desire" to see Champlain. In particular, she wanted to see her sister decked out in the costume she had only read about: a "sun-flower uniform" made of a "yellow turban, yellow gown and black apron with the row of flat-irons across the bosom." Once she had her sister's likeness in hand, Way promised, she would return the favor. The portrait exchange would have served as a surrogate visit, supplementing the sisters' letters and providing each with what Way termed an "ocular demonstration" of the other's unfolding life. And just as their letters often did, the portraits would have idealized that "demonstration," tempering the vicissitudes of fortune and the depredations of age with the literary and pictorial conventions of sentiment. As professionals whose work routinely naturalized those conventions, Way and Champlain were explicit about the role of idealization, even artifice, in representation. Champlain's self-portrait was no exception. Way instructed her sister: "You may flatter [your appearance] as much as you like provided you don't flatter away all the likeness

. . . just keep probability in view."[9] Although unfinished, the portrait seems to do just that. Forty-seven years old at the time that she began her self-portrait, Way Champlain depicted herself poised in an indeterminate spot between youth and old age. Unlined, full, and firm, her painted face resists our attempts to fix her age, much less the contours of her life history. It defies biography, belying the passage of time itself.

Betsey Way Champlain never sent the portrait to her sister. In any event, by 1818, Mary Way's failing eyesight would have made it difficult for her to see her sister's face reduced onto an ivory the size of a small child's hand. Although the sisters never exchanged likenesses, Champlain's unfinished self-portrait did play a part in cementing family bonds. Along with the sisters' voluminous correspondence, it was passed mother to daughter over three generations, helping to create family tradition and consolidate family identity.[10]

Freeman's portrait was painted by the daughter-in-law of a former employer whose entire family claimed the African American woman as close kin. Freeman's name among the Sedgwicks, "Mumbet," was a double diminutive, collapsing "Mammy," "Mother," and "Mah" (variously) into "Bett." "Mumbet" was more than a nickname. It enshrined Freeman as an ersatz mother to the youngest Sedgwick children, especially Catharine. Catharine Maria Sedgwick had been a lonely child, unable to count on her parents' physical or emotional presence. Her father, Theodore, a committed Federalist, devoted his energies to building a thirty-year career in politics and public service; stints in the Massachusetts House and Senate and in the U.S. House and Senate, as well as a seat on the Massachusetts Supreme Court, pulled him away from home for at least six months every year. Her mother, Pamela Dwight Sedgwick, suffered from poor health and crippling depression that confined her to bed for months at a time. Her father's career and her mother's incapacity left Freeman to serve as the "main pillar of our household," Catharine recalled. Accordingly, the little girl gave the servant something like the love reserved for a mother. Indeed, near the end of Freeman's life, Catharine praised her as " 'Mother'—my nurse—my faithful friend—she who first received me into her arms" and a "necessary link in the family chain." She remembered how as a child she "clung" to Freeman with "instinctive love and faith." She described herself as Freeman's "particular treasure."[11]

The family ties outlived the servant. Freeman's gravestone, purchased and inscribed by the Sedgwicks, memorialized her as their "Good Mother." Freeman herself was buried in the section of the Stockbridge, Massachusetts, cemetery reserved for the Sedgwick clan. And several years after Freeman's death, Henry Dwight Sedgwick, one of Catharine's brothers, wrote an abolitionist lecture around his memories of and deep love for "Mah Bett"; he confessed to his audience that he knew her "as familiarly as I knew either of my parents."[12] We will return to the peculiar family relations that obtained between Freeman and two generations of Sedgwicks. But for now, it is enough to observe that contemporary writers and scholars endorse the Sedgwick family story. For the most part, the likeness serves as a rare life portrait of an African American woman and as an illustration for books and essays recounting Freeman's 1783 lawsuit. Where the painting *is* discussed, it signifies an unproblematic gesture of familial affection.[13] Like the tombstone, then, the ivory miniature substantiates Freeman's special place in the Sedgwick clan, blurring multiple boundaries between real and fictive kin.

Susan Ridley Sedgwick's painting surely honors Freeman's special relationship with her former employers. But it may have been intended to deepen a different set of ties—ties among those who were born Sedgwicks and those who married them. It is not clear for whom the portrait was painted; the voluminous Sedgwick papers are silent on this point. Still, it is easy to imagine Sedgwick painting it as a gift for Catharine, her beloved sister-in-law, or for Theodore Sedgwick II, her husband. Whoever the original recipient was, the painting surely belonged to the Sedgwicks and not the Freemans, for it was donated to the Massachusetts Historical Society in 1884 by Maria Banyer Sedgwick, the artist's daughter.

Picturing Race

Placed alongside each other, the portraits of Elizabeth Freeman and Betsey Way Champlain compel us to think about the pictorial representation of race. The contrast in the sitters' lives is recapitulated in the stark contrast of painted flesh—one black, the other ivory. It is hard not to notice Freeman's blackness. To achieve it, Sedgwick had to violate the fundamental conventions that governed portraiture in general and ivory miniatures in particular. The gentle delineation of features that characterize ivory miniatures is replaced by bold definition. Thick, heavy lines articulate Freeman's brows, nose, and mouth, drawing attention to her most "African" features. Her solid form is without grace. Asymmetrical breasts hang heavy, unsupported by muscle or stays. Fabric strains around the girth of laboring arms. Delicate touches—the ruffled cap, the gold beads—suggest that Freeman possessed both feminine sensibility and genteel aspiration. But these small, fine details are overpowered by both the scale and the shape of Freeman's form. And then, of course, there is her skin. Sedgwick layered washes of a single color, probably Cologne Brown, to outline Freeman's features and to model the planes of her face. The same color is repeated behind her, in defiance of pictorial conventions that dictated an unobtrusive, complementary background. Freeman's black face is framed by the bold white of her cap and chemise; her body is anchored by the clear blue of her dress. Indeed, without her cap and dress, the sitter would literally disappear into the picture plane. The effect is flat, graphic, and black. Brow, nose, lips, breasts, and skin: Susan Ridley Sedgwick represented Elizabeth Freeman as a catalog of racial signifiers.[14]

Some twenty years after Sedgwick painted Freeman, Frederick Douglass, a man who was both deeply aware of his own appearance and acutely sensitive to the politics of representation, pondered the conundrums posed by "negro portraits." "Negroes can never have impartial portraits at the hands of white artists," he complained. Artists, like white people more generally, were oblivious to the enormous "variety of form and feature among us." Both groups had "adopted a theory respecting the distinctive features of negro physiognomy." Once impressed on an artist's mind, the theory "exercises a powerful influence over his pencil and very naturally leads him to distort and exaggerate" the sitter's supposedly African features. Notwithstanding technical skills or good intentions, white artists could not help but succumb to the "temptation to make the likeness of the negro rather than the man." By the time that Douglass wrote, the rise of racial science, with its emphasis on physiognomy, on the physical structure of different races, meant that the likeness of "the negro" was signaled primarily by conventions in form and shape. "High cheekbones, distended nostril, depressed nose, thick lips, and retreating forehead," rather than by skin color, signaled African descent.[15] But for an earlier generation, complexion rivaled physiognomy as a primary index of racial difference. Sedgwick's contemporaries would have recognized Freeman's likeness as a "negro portrait" not simply because of her features, but because of her skin, because of the monotonous washes of dark brown paint that define her.

The portrait's disconcerting blackness is not the effect of the media, of the difficulties posed by capturing nuanced dark tones with watercolor on an ivory support. Consider the miniature portraits that Pierre Toussaint commissioned of his family at around the same time that Sedgwick painted Freeman. Toussaint had been brought to New York City as a youth when his owners, wealthy French landowners and sugar planters, fled the uprising on Saint Domingue. To provide him with a trade that was marketable in an urban economy, his master and mistress apprenticed him to a hairdresser. Toussaint used this trade to support his mistress, to whom he was apparently devoted, and two of her husbands. After he had been granted his freedom, he turned his skill as hairdresser to the advantage of his own family. Over the course of a decade, his skill, charm, and discretion enabled him to build a business that generated a substantial income as well as a certain visibility among the city's elite. As Toussaint's friend and biographer, Hannah Lee, put it, by the 1820s, he was the city's "fashionable coiffeur," having attracted "all of the custom and patronage of the French families in New York" along with "many of the most distinguished ladies of the city." Some of his professional contacts joined his large collection of intimate friends. His house was "an abode of hospitality, and many *pale faces* visited there," Lee recalled.[16]

When Italian miniaturist Antonio Meucci visited New York in 1825–1826, Toussaint hired him to paint portraits of himself; his wife, Juliette; and his adopted niece, Euphemia. It was an unconventional choice. Judging by the extant evidence, those few antebellum African Americans who commissioned portraits chose bust-sized oil paintings, paintings that announced their status—their respectability, their prosperity, and their personhood—to the public at large. And, given the implicit publicity of these paintings, it is not surprising that so many represent men: African-descended ministers, activists, barbers, and men of affairs, men who were assuming positions of leadership within the North's free black communities. It is not clear why Toussaint, a public-minded man who was deeply involved in a variety of philanthropic efforts, diverged from this pattern by choosing to represent himself, much less his entire family, in a genre so closely associated with domestic intimacy. Perhaps he associated miniatures with the gentility and refinement of his wealthy clientele. Perhaps he was attracted to the genre's familial associations. Toussaint was, after all, a man who prized family, who expended great effort to preserve family ties against overwhelming odds; after moving to New York, he had tried repeatedly and unsuccessfully to recover family members who had been lost during the Haitian Revolution. Or perhaps miniatures recalled a pivotal moment in his own life, a moment that fused gentility, familial intimacy, and freedom, for when Toussaint's mistress was on her deathbed, she bequeathed him her miniature portrait along with his freedom papers.[17]

Whatever the rationale behind this unusual commission, Meucci's portraits allow us to see representative possibilities that are foreclosed in Sedgwick's portrayal of Freeman. Meucci's paintings of the Toussaints adhered to the conventions that governed portraiture, miniature and otherwise, in the 1820s. As a group, the images commemorate the economic security and refinement that the family acquired in New York City as well as its origins in Saint Domingue.

Pierre is dressed as the prosperous businessman he has become, wearing a starched shirt, plush coat, satin vest, and jeweled cravat pin. Euphemia, depicted in a delicately trimmed linen dress, pearls, tortoiseshell comb and holding a flower basket, could be any one of the city's demure young ladies.[18] If Pierre and his niece figure the Toussaints' New York present, it falls to Juliette to anchor the family's Caribbean history. Her lace-trimmed dress and coral jewelry testify to her husband's savvy as a provider capable of negotiating New York's dynamic economy. Her headdress, however, recalls the style favored by women of color on Saint Domingue, who adopted the madras headscarf in the eighteenth century. The scarves were a response to a French sumptuary law that prohibited women of color from wearing silk or leaving their heads uncovered. The law was aimed at aimed at enforcing distinctions between blacks and whites in general and eliminating black women from competition with white women for the sexual attention of white men in particular. But the strategy backfired, for the scarf itself became a focus of attention. It was reinvented by black women as a point of pride rather than as a badge of shame. It was regarded by European observers as a bid for allure, as yet another symbol of black women's hypersexuality. And, to some extent, Meucci's portrait reflects those associations. Juliette's low-cut dress nearly exposes her full breasts, which press up out of her bodice. The strands of coral that wind around her neck drop down into her cleavage, further articulating the shape of her breasts and drawing the viewer's eye back to the bust. If she is a refined ornament honoring her husband's skill, hard work, and determination, she is also exoticized and eroticized.[19]

Whether the sitters referenced bourgeois aspiration or Caribbean heritage, Meucci took pains to depict their complexions to accord with the genre's conventions. Conforming to early nineteenth-century gender norms, Pierre's skin is darker and more deeply colored than that of his wife or niece. Meucci stippled on multiple colors to model the planes of all three subjects' faces. He deployed the ivory support to serve as highlights on noses, lips, and brows. The ivory also contributes to the luminousness of each image. Compared to the vast majority of sitters, the Toussaints are strikingly dark. But like the vast majority of sitters, they are also strikingly delicate.

The differences that separate Meucci's portraits of the Toussaints from Sedgwick's portrait of Freeman reflect more than a difference in skill and technique, more than the distance that separated the cosmopolitan professional from the enthusiastic amateur. For one thing, the painting's execution suggests that Sedgwick possessed considerable brush skills: She could paint and shadow each tiny gold bead in Freeman's necklace, articulate the tight gray curls peeking out from beneath the ruffle on her cap, trace the tension in the fabric of her dress. She understood enough color theory to apprehend how and where light hit her sitter's body, and she was able to translate what she saw into the highlights and shadows depicted on the ivory support. The problem, then, is not that Sedgwick could not paint in watercolor in ivory but rather *how* she painted racial difference in general and skin in particular. Sedgwick was not alone. When the most accomplished early national American painters turned to nonwhite sitters, they encountered complexion as a problem of representation, as the object of fascination, as the reification of a hardening racial ideology.

Two canonical oil portraits, completed around the same time as the Sedgwick's miniature, suggest just how vexed the representation of non-European skin could be. Even artists whose technique was beyond question stumbled over the portrayal of nonwhite skin, effectively turning the paintings into "negro portraits." Charles Willson Peale's famous painting of Yarrow Mamout, a former slave who lived in Georgetown, Virginia, is beautifully executed and superbly colored. Mamout's multiple coats and knitted hat are richly rendered. His face is alert and expressive. But his flesh is arresting. In no other portrait is Peale so fascinated with the color and texture of human flesh. He seems to have reveled in his sitter's skin, stretched tight over the bones of the skull. Wrinkles—deep across the brow, tissuey around the eyes—are precisely delineated and colored. Multiple highlights give the face shape and dimension; Mamout's face emerges from the rhythmic movement of light across his forehead and brow, around his eye sockets, down his nose and lips. The effect is leathery and hard, even shellacked.

There is an almost scientific precision in Peale's depiction of Mamout's flesh, which is fitting, given that the painting likely wound up in Peale's Philadelphia Museum. There, it would have illustrated any number of different forms of curiosity and difference: advanced age (Mamout was reportedly more than 130 years old when he sat to Peale); religious faith (he was a devout Muslim); and race (he was African, probably Guinean). Peale's fascination with Mamout's skin reflects his broader interest in human variety, especially as it manifested in complexion. A self-taught naturalist and member of the American Philosophical Society, Peale had published a description of a man known only as James, "a very dark MULATTO, turning WHITE," which was widely reprinted. Peale explained that patches of James's black skin became a "reddish brown color by degrees" before becoming white. And not only was James white, he was "a clear wholesome white, fair, and what would be called a better skin, than any of the number of white people, who were present" when Peale examined him.[20] So fascinated was Peale by this specimen that he later painted him for display in the museum. Enlightened Philadelphians, Peale included, remained captivated by individuals like James and his more famous successor, Henry Moss, well into the nineteenth century. Peale's fascination with complexion as a register of difference informs Yarrow Mamout's likeness. More than any other element in the painting, this preoccupation with Mamout's skin turns the portrait into a specimen, suitable for display alongside stuffed birds, mastodons, and native costumes from the South Seas.[21]

This overdetermined depiction of complexion was not limited to representations of African Americans. Charles Bird King, who studied under Edward Savage and Benjamin West, became famous for his portraits of the Native Americans who visited Washington, D.C., on diplomatic missions between 1821 and 1837. Commissioned to hang in the War Department's Indian Gallery, the paintings were predicated on the notion that Indians were disappearing. King's work was intended to preserve a final glimpse of a vanishing people. As one guidebook put it in 1830, "But for this gallery, our posterity would ask in vain—'what sort of a looking being was the red man of this country?'" The "red man" depicted by King was distinguished by his dignity and his gravity, qualities equally suited to diplomats and representatives of dying cultures.

The "red man" depicted by King was also very often literally red. When King was just launching his American career, one of King's London associates remarked that his "greatest excellence is in his colouring of flesh."[22] King turned that "excellence" to good use in his early, romantic portraits of Pawnee delegates. His portrait of Pawnee chief Petalesharo is awash in red. The planes of the sitter's face and the musculature of his bare shoulder and chest are defined with a deep, rosy red. His complexion is reinforced by his costume. The feathers in his war bonnet are tinged with red, and the ribbons that tie the bonnet and hold the peace medal given him by President Monroe are red. Even more striking is King's famous 1821 group portrait of five Pawnee warriors, painted for display in his own studio and gallery. *Young Omahaw, War Eagle, Little Missouri, and Pawnees* drew from the Old Masters, especially Van Dyck's triple portrait of Charles I, in its composition and from King's own portraits of Petalesharo and Peskelchaco in the particular faces represented. Again, the sitters have reddish complexions. And, again, the red in the flesh is extended through their costume—the brilliant red feathers in their hair, the red face paint that adorns several sitters, the red ribbons holding peace medals, and the red war axe. Even the shadows cast along their necks and shoulders and by their jaws are bright red. King's paintings reify the racial shorthand—red man—that had become the catchall identifier for Native Americans by the early nineteenth century. Their "redness" is no longer merely a metaphor for their exoticism or their savagery. It is visible, palpable, an emanation from their flesh.[23]

From this perspective, Sedgwick's portrait of Freeman is hardly an outlier, a painting defined primarily by its unconventional medium or its amateur aesthetic. Like Peale and King, Sedgwick painted race and racial difference. And like Peale and King, she deployed complexion as a primary marker of that difference.

It would be a mistake to confine our discussion of race to the portraits of nonwhites painted by Susan Ridley Sedgwick or her professional contemporaries. The fashion for ivory miniatures, which spurred the renaissance in miniature painting in mid-eighteenth-century England and its emergence in late eighteenth-century Anglo-America, coincided with the transatlantic elaboration of racial ideologies and identities. Just as ivory miniatures played a role in the simultaneous expansion of polite society and the rise of the affectional family, so, too, did they play a role in the construction and representation of whiteness. English portrait miniatures, which emerged in the Tudor courts and spread to the gentry and middling classes by the seventeenth century, were originally watercolor-on-vellum or, less frequently, oil-on-copper. The densely colored paintings established the associations that would characterize the genre for more than two hundred years: intensely private images that might become public at the owner's discretion; tiny subjects who draw the viewer forward, into an intimacy born of proximity; the suggestion that possession of the picture signaled possession of the sitter. By the beginning of the eighteenth century, however, the miniature was in decline. Its popularity was restored first by the substitution of ivory for vellum and then by the adoption of a subdued palette that exploited the color, translucence, and texture of ivory.[24]

These shifts were neither obvious nor easy. Ivory does not welcome watercolors. Before the would-be miniaturist wrestled with the standard technical questions about creating a convincing representation, she first had to manage to get the paint to adhere to the support. This demanded the painstaking preparation of each component of the painting. The slippery sheet of ivory had to be degreased, bleached, and ground with pumice powder. The paint—pigment, water, and some kind of binder (gum arabic and sometimes sugar candy)—had to be mixed in precise proportions if it was to show in the correct way. As late as the 1820s, after the introduction of high-quality, commercially manufactured paint cakes, some miniaturists still opted to regrind the pigments to obtain the desired "fineness of texture." Even with properly prepared support and paints, applying watercolor onto ivory demanded a deft, dexterous touch. The painter first lightly traced the outline of the sitter. Less assured artists were encouraged to draw the outline to scale on a sheet of paper, which could then be placed beneath the ivory where, as one instructor observed, the support's "transparency will enable you to trace it very distinctly." Next, the painter colored in the shadowed areas of the face and background with a relatively dark "dead color" before washing solid colors onto the background and sitter's body, moving gradually from darker to lighter colors. To control the intensity of color, novice painters were encouraged to turn the picture upside down when they painted in the face's "general" color, which provided its foundation. By beginning with the chin and working down toward the forehead, the brush would become "exhausted" and "naturally make the forehead the lightest part" of the face.

Draperies and flesh required different paint mixtures and different application methods. Except for the filmiest empire dresses, clothing required opaque colors that were "floated" onto the ivory by laying the picture "horizontally," to allow the paint to "become perfectly flat from its fluidity." The features and planes of the face were added to the ivory (now turned upright) through layers of cross-hatching and stippling. The paint used for flesh was as translucent as the painter could manage to mix it, for sheer layers of delicate color allowed the translucent ivory to glow through the paint. The face's highlights were rendered by leaving the ivory bare or by gently removing paint with the tip of a lancet. By exposing the support in this way, the painter conferred upon the sitter a complexion that was literally ivory.[25]

By the end of the eighteenth century, American miniaturists, following a style established some thirty years earlier by English artists, had learned to exploit watercolor and ivory alike to create gently colored portraits of luminous ladies and gentlemen.[26] This distinctly English style of miniature portrait (epitomized on one side of the Atlantic by Richard Cosway and on the other by Edward Greene Malbone) was well suited for the aesthetic ideal of the late eighteenth and early nineteenth centuries, with its emphasis on restrained colors and elegant forms. But ivories also resonated with an Anglo-American social aesthetic that fused gentility, sensibility, and whiteness. On both sides of the Atlantic, artists and patrons prized ivories because they were luminous, transparent, delicate, and softly harmonious—politically freighted terms that confirmed the sitters' sensibility and located both artifacts and sitters squarely within the republic of taste.[27]

The transatlantic valorization of sensibility that encouraged the market for ivory miniatures was bound up with race as well as with class and gender: Sensibility was simultaneously confirmed by the visible register of emotion on pale skin, challenged by the cruel traffic in black bodies, and complicated by centuries of colonial encounter and conquest. The feeling and discernment that characterized men and women of sense may have originated in their hearts and minds. But those same qualities were most immediately apprehended on their bodies—in their posture and gait, through their expressive repertoire, and especially on their skin. Indeed, precisely because European skin registered "every passion by greater or less suffusions of colour," in Thomas Jefferson's words, it revealed an individual's character.[28] Like the scrim on a theater stage, white skin's opacity was an illusion; its fundamental transparency was revealed to sensible observers by the rise of feeling and the play of color.

This combination of mutability and transparency was predicated on and validated by scientific explanations of human character and variety. Broadly speaking, Anglo-Americans had two vocabularies for making sense of skin color: one based on ancient ideas about the humors, the other on anatomical science. Humoral theory posited that complexion, which included temperament and mental and physical capacity along with skin color, resulted from the interaction of climate and body. Because complexion was the product of ongoing, dynamic interaction, it was also mutable; it responded to changes in age, geography, and living conditions. Anatomical theory, on the other hand, fixed skin color within the physical structure of the body; scholars variously associated skin color with the topmost layer of the epidermis or with a thin membrane lying immediately beneath it. As literary historian Roxann Wheeler has demonstrated, humoral and anatomical models persisted side by side and in combination well into the nineteenth century. Taken together, they worked against the straightforward reduction of skin color to race.[29] Notwithstanding the significance of emergent racial ideologies, eighteenth-century and early nineteenth-century natural scientists viewed "white" skin as more than the opposite of or the negation of black.

In fact, even American commentators who were explicitly preoccupied with the elaboration of race along a black-white axis agreed that European whiteness was not a single color but a compendium of them. Samuel Stanhope Smith, the president of Princeton University and author of the influential *Essay on the Causes of the Variety of Complexion*, argued that climate accounted not only for, say, differences between Europeans and Asians. It also accounted for color differences among Europeans. As he explained, "White may be regarded as the colourless state of skin, and all the shades of the dark colours as different stains inserted into its substance." But Europeans were not white per se: "In Britain and Germany they are fair, brown in France and in Turkey, swarthy in Portugal and Spain." And in Anglo-America, Smith detected a "certain paleness of countenance." Generally speaking, the "American complexion does not exhibit so clear a red and white as the British, or the German. And there is a tinge of sallowness spread over it which indicated the tendency of the climate to generate bile." Complexions differed among classes as well as nations. Smith observed that "the poor and laboring part of the community in every country are usually more dark in their complexion"; exposure and privation left these unfortunates bereft of "the delicate tints of colour" that marked the higher classes. Happily, in the United States, he reported, republican society and the widespread distribution of property eliminated these class-based differences in complexion, except between field and house slaves.[30]

Even those who were not persuaded that climate was the sole determinant of skin color accepted the mutability and variety of European skin. In an 1814 essay refuting Smith, one writer observed that "the infants of Europeans, when newly born, are almost as remote from their parental fairness of complexion, as the infants of Africans are from their hereditary blackness." Nature "bleached" the skin, "complet[ing] the European complexion" "through the agency of the *cutaneous absorbents*," which removed the "superfluous matter which obstructs its transparency, and sullies its fairness."[31] Would-be experts encouraged arm-chair physiognomists to read skin color along with facial structure as a register of character. An 1809 essay on physiognomy, for example, insisted that "who-ever has reflected on the principles of our nature, well knows, that fluids as they circulate through the organized matter with which our bodies are composed, tinge the very outsides of the channels through which they flow, with their predominant colour." The skin's transparency, along with the "incessant return of those same fluids to the same places," created the complexion and revealed an individual's "passions." These varieties of mood and character registered in "hues as varied as their motions . . . some are red, others of a leaden cast; some are yellow, others green and even black."[32]

However much they may have differed on the origin and significance of black skin, American theorists agreed with Oliver Goldsmith on the implica-tions of white skin. In Goldsmith's words, "Of all the colours by which mankind is diversified, it is easy to perceive that ours is not only the most beautiful to the eye, but the most advantageous. The fair complexion seems, if I may so express it, as a transparent covering to the soul; all the variations of the passions, every expression of joy or sorrow, flows to the cheek, and, without language marks the mind."[33] It was this delicately colored transparency, celebrated in polite culture and belles lettres and validated by natural science, that ivory min-iatures promised to capture.

It was also what patrons hoped to acquire when they commissioned a minia-ture. A sitter might embody the seven deadly sins, but he did not want to pay good money to have that fact announced in a portrait. Portraits were negotiated likenesses, mediated by the market. Turning ordinary mortals into the ethereal creatures who graced miniatures was a tricky business, and one that Betsey Champlain explored in "Flattery," a 155-line poem that describes (among other things) the attempts of two aging, dissolute members of New London's gentry to control her depiction of them.[34] Champlain understood that she had not been hired to paint what she saw: "The task is mine," she wrote, to "palliate" the "up-start chin," the "nose's hook," and the "unmeaning eye"; in that way, she would "intelegence let speak."

The poem's subjects, a long-married couple named Frederick and Jane, proved a challenge even for someone as experienced as Champlain. Their advanced years and vices registered on their faces, especially on their skin. The woman was freckled, tan, and coarse; her husband boasted an oozing sore on his chin. Appearance portended behavior. During their sitting, a stream of bickering revealed a marriage based on years of infidelity, bad faith, worse temper, and boundless vanity. Imploring Champlain to depict them as they wished to be rather than as they were, they focused on their complexions as markers of character. The transparently tinted skin that the couple hoped to see on ivory, if not in the mirror, signaled their capacity for sentiment and revealed the delicate calibrations of their feelings to knowing observers. And, of course, it was this telling transparency that an ivory miniature was especially suited to capture. Casting herself as the beleaguered innocent, Champlain had little choice but to comply with this bit of self-fashioning. The sitters might "beat the bugs for vanity," but "they the cash detain, were nothing feigned." Champlain's poem poked fun at her patrons' exploitation of the conventions of sensibility just as she acknowledged that it was precisely this market for sensibility that allowed her to earn a living, however precarious. Transparency could be had for a price.[35]

Painting manuals, published mostly in London but circulated on both sides of the Atlantic, provide another index of the multiple layers of meaning that painters, patrons, and viewers associated with both ivory portrait miniature portraits and with complexion. By the early nineteenth century, the growing popularity of ivory miniatures created a demand for books that claimed to offer readers "An Introduction to Perspective, Practical Geometry, Drawing and Painting" along with "practical directions for Miniature, Crayon, and Oil Painting" or a systematic study of the "Art of Painting in Miniature on Ivory in the Manner at Present Practised by the Most Eminent Artists in the Profession."[36] Authors of books like these catered to a dual market. Some writers sought to capitalize on miniatures' promise as commodities, as salable objects that could provide reliable income for an artist who mastered the requisite skills. Other writers took advantage of painting's status as an accomplishment and pitched their books at genteel youth, paying special attention to young ladies. Many manuals emphasized miniatures' association with gentility, sensibility, and family. Virtually all of them sited luminous, transparent flesh as the genre's defining feature.

Even manuals aimed at amateurs included no shortage of technical data. Readers could expect to glean specifics about brush selection, color choice, and paint application, all tailored for a painting's disparate components, including a sitter's flesh, hair, clothing, and background. A reader might also learn how to prepare the ivory support for painting or how to grind pigment, although this sort of information waned as urban merchants began to sell pretreated ivory and premixed paints. Manuals that cast miniature painting as a youthful accomplishment also took pains to situate both the reader-cum-painter and the product within a social and cultural milieu of aestheticized gentility. Some authors punctuated their treatises with references to "Lionardo de Vinci," Titian, or Isabey (Cosway's French contemporary)—a sort of name-dropping that signaled the shared cosmopolitanism of writer and reader. Most authors echoed the emphasis on emulation that prevailed at academies, encouraging their readers to study and copy the paintings of great masters and local art teachers alike. They assured aspiring painters that success was within reach, so long as the novice practiced the proper "application and research" and, of course, hewed close to the instructions in the manual at hand.[37] They affirmed that success would manifest itself in the polish of both the painter as well as the painting; it would be measured and validated by tasteful family and friends.

A few books moved beyond precept and instruction to create fictional student painters whose adventures and relationships grounded the sentiments associated with miniatures in narrative and dialogue. *Conversations on the Art of Miniature Painting*, by British miniaturist Emma Kendrick, and *Letters Upon the Art of Miniature Painting*, by French miniaturist L. Mansion, unfolded as stories in which the heroine's progress as a painter, specifically as a miniaturist, unfolded apace with her progress as a young lady. Both books were structured as exchanges—one verbal, the other written—between a teacher and a pupil. Both texts linked painting and miniature portraits with a genteel sensibility, one that was exemplified by women and nurtured within the family.

Ellen Howard, Mansion's fictional English pupil, grew up to become the sort of ideal woman who "encourages genius, adds grace to wit, [and] strengthens thought." In her instructor's mind, the heroine's development as a female paralleled her "astonishing progress" as a miniaturist. Born with an "intuitive taste," Ellen had been "transported" by music and "captivated" by painting and sculpture since she was a child. On the cusp of womanhood, she commits herself to mastering the art of the miniature and asks her teacher, Mr. Deville, to "aid me with . . . advice and trace for me the path I must pursue." Ellen pursues that path doggedly through nearly two hundred pages of mind-numbing advice on drawing, color, and the particular difficulties posed by painting linen dresses and shirts. When the novelized manual ends, she has graduated from Deville's charge: She is an accomplished painter, and she is married to a man who saved her from an attacking bull. (Withal, Ellen's artistic trajectory was more convincing than her matrimonial one.) She commemorates her love for her husband

and her gratitude to Deville with a self-portrait so beautifully executed that it is "beyond all praise." On the back, she writes that the painting is a "pledge of my love for [her husband] and Mr. Deville's friendship for me."[38]

And Deville? As a critic, he champions the Old Masters; as a painter, he excels at the miniature portrait. To teach Ellen, he must turn his attention away from magisterial masterworks to focus on a more intimate, less commanding art form. As Ellen puts it, "You will put aside your Raphaels, your Michel Angelos, your Rembrandts, your Vandykes; and tell me what the Isabeys, the Augustins, and the Guerins have done to arrive at the height of perfection in drawing, taste, and colouring." To teach Ellen, then, Deville must attend to a form that signaled privacy rather than publicity, loving ties rather than universal truths, femininity rather than masculinity.[39]

If the culmination of Ellen's training inscribes her as a devoted student and loving wife, the masterpiece in Kendrick's *Conversations upon the Art of Miniature Painting* testifies to a daughter's love for her mother. The instructor, Miss K., was a thinly veiled stand-in for Kendrick herself, a noted miniaturist who had tutored Princess Georgianna. Her fictional pupil is a young girl who, like Mansion's heroine, is named Ellen. Embarking on her first portrait, Ellen chooses to paint her mother. "Let Mamma's portrait be your example in all you tell me," Ellen tells Miss K., "for I shall understand what you say twice as well, if you take that for your theme." Alas, the novice painter is unable to capture her mother. To be sure, as Miss K. pointed out, the face was "well proportioned" and bore "some resemblance" to the sitter. The color, however, was another matter altogether. The obedient Ellen followed her teacher's instructions and used purple madder and sepia for "sketching in" the sitter's face. But she mixed the paints dark when they needed to be pale; she applied them with a heavy hand when they needed to be "softly and slightly touched." The disconcerting, disappointing result? A sitter who was "delicately fair" wound up with features that were "hard," "strong," and "quite black." As Miss K. pointed out, "no one could possibly suppose, from this sketch, that your Mamma had so beautiful a complexion as she possesses." Or, in Ellen's words, the painting of her mother was "more hideous than a negress."[40]

Step by step, in the conversations that follow, Miss K. schools Ellen in the techniques that will allow her to capture her mother's delicate complexion. Ellen learns to observe the precise shadings of her mother's eyes and nose; she understands which colors work for foreheads and ears. By the fifth conversation, Ellen has created a fine portrait of her mother. Never mind that Miss K. thinks that the new portrait makes Mamma look solemn and "dull" rather than smiling and "bright"; at least Mamma is no longer as dark as a "negress." With her teacher's encouragement, Ellen shows the painting to friends and family, who serve as arbiters of her taste and technique. Display might be nerve-racking, but, as Miss K. observed, "the advantage to be reaped by submitting your productions to the judgment of others, is, that by this plan your eyes are often opened to deficiencies which you would not otherwise have remarked." Happily, there are no serious deficiencies: Ellen's audience likes the painting so much that they all ask to sit to her, especially her brother Dudley, who has just received a "a commission in the Guards" and who is "so vain of his red coat" that he wants to be immortalized on ivory. News of Dudley's impending sitting prompts a whole new series of instructions from Miss K., who cautions that even though the lines in a man's face must be "expressed more strongly" than those in a woman's, Ellen must not make her brother as "black as [her] first sketch" of her mother. (For her part, Ellen cannot bear to think back on that failed attempt and what it did to her mother.) By the close of the conversations, Ellen has become a promising miniaturist. And by gaining the skills required for miniature painting, Ellen gains new visibility within her circle. The skill that mattered most was a mastery of color.[41]

This preoccupation with color extended to the advice aimed at aspiring professionals as well as accomplished amateurs. Because of the cultural resonance of complexion, and because it ranked high on the list of things that patrons hoped to secure when they commissioned an ivory miniature, the depiction of skin was the subject of enormous technical discussion and instruction among Anglo-American artists. After all, it was easier to see transparency than to make it. Accordingly, manuals of all stripes devoted pages and pages to the exact mix and application of colors necessary to conjure luminous "white" flesh.

The first step was to learn to observe with a precision that escaped even sensitive viewers, for, as Peter Cooper explained, when "observing the colour of the human face, the uneducated eye sees nothing more than the general or local colour, making no nice distinctions between shadows, 'demi tints,' 'pearls,' or 'grey tints.'"[42] Once the artist learned to recognize the components of complexion, he or she could begin to notice that they shifted with a sitter's mood. As one manual explained, the excitement of the first sitting would render a subject flushed; the subsequent return of composure revealed the "ordinary complexion"; the effort required by an extended sitting changed the complexion yet again. Realizing this, the painter could make an informed decision about how to represent the subject: "The natural complexion, somewhat heightened, may be the best colour to be applied to the picture."[43]

Painting that complexion, heightened or otherwise, demanded that a painter identify and replicate the multiple shades that composed it. This was no simple process. In an 1821 manual, J. Dougall warned that "the colours of carnations

. . . or of those parts of the human body which appear uncovered . . . are so various that no rules can be laid down." Instead, he advanced a set of "broad principles" about the colors of men, women, and children.[44] But other writers were far more explicit, listing the various combinations of paint required by particular features. The key lay in the careful combination of minute bits of different colors. As one writer explained, even though Venetian red mixed with a little Indian yellow offered "the nearest approach to the general colour of "flesh," it could not begin to capture the tonal complexity of the white face.[45] And so a 1788 manual specified that "Vermillion and Carmine" be applied with "strongest Touches at the Corners of the Eyes, next the Nose, under the Nose, the Ears and Under the Chin." The shadows of temples and neck were to be "blueish Teints with Indigo" and the parts of the face that "rise and come forward to the Sight" should be in "Yellow Teints . . . composed of Oker and Vermillion." Finally, the artist should "dot . . . over the Shadows with green Teints."[46] Another writer preferred Indian red and indigo for the dead color with ultramarine blue and "the madder lakes" to add a finer touch to the flesh. Then the "lights and shades" of the complexion could be created out of "light red, pink madder, well ground vermillion, and raw terra de sienna."[47]

The *Course of Lectures on Drawing, Painting, and Engraving* stipulated the order for applying shadow tints: Begin with those that are a mixture of "carmine, gamboge, and Indian Ink" before proceeding with the "blue and grey tints," which were to be inserted "at the edges of the first shadows"; add the reddish shadows last. Then, at a second sitting, a "general colour" (either carmine and gamboge or Venetian red and gamboge) could be painted to "cover . . . the whole face," except, of course, for the highlighted areas, which required yet another sitting, color scheme, and application pattern.[48] Even J. Dougall, the self-proclaimed champion of "broad principle," took pains to stipulate the precise combinations of colors demanded by the lights and shadows of the "carnations" by dividing skin into color zones for the nose, chin, forehead, hands, fingertips, and joints. He also included detailed instructions for the whites of the eyes, the orbs of the eyes, the eyelids, and the lips.[49] Painting white flesh successfully was more than a paint-by-numbers proposition but it also demanded a level of premeditation and precision that no aspiring artist could afford to ignore.

Tracing the connections between these kinds of instructions and the literally thousands of extant ivories painted by metropolitan and provincial artists in late eighteenth- and early nineteenth-century America is no easy task. Letters written among Betsey Champlain, Mary Way, and Eliza Way Champlain, miniaturists all, afford a glimpse of their attempts to acquire the color theory and technique necessary to paint translucent white flesh, thereby realizing the style prescribed in art manuals and hailed by critics and connoisseurs. Throughout the correspondence, Betsey Champlain depended on her sister and later her daughter to supply high-quality ivory and particular colors that were not to be had in New London. But she also relied on them to share information that only more accomplished painters might provide, information available in New York City only. And most of what they passed along pertained to the vexing issue of color in general and flesh in particular.

Several years after moving to New York, Mary Way summarized what she had learned for the benefit of her sister. She relayed the wisdom of "connoisseurs" like William Joseph Williams, John Jarvis, and Joseph Wood, who were her contemporaries if not precisely her competitors. She also quoted liberally from a book that Wood had loaned her, John Payne's *Art of Painting in Miniature, on Ivory*. In effect, she offered her sister a crash course on the techniques and conventions of the eighteenth-century ivory miniature. Way explained that "transparent colours only must be used for the flesh, and for draperies, opaque or body colours, as they set off each other [making] the flesh tints appear to more advantage." The color of that flesh depended on the "force, strength, and disposition, or situation of the colours, in point of light, that are placed near it." And though faces required a "thousand different tints" too tedious to recount, Betsey should remember that "the most natural shades for the face are purples, blues, and greys, especially for a delicate complexion. These, however, should be warm'd, more or less . . . with red browns and yellows, such as burnt umber, burnt terra sienna, . . . or gamboge mixed with a little carmine." In order to pick out these tints in the face of a sitter, lighting was critical: Arrange one highlight that "strikes with most force upon the temple," creating a "delicate shade tint" along the cheekbone under the eye. As Way pointed out in a later letter, a painter who mastered these techniques could dispense with tricks like backing the support with foil or a daub of white paint to increase the luminosity. Ivory, she pronounced, was "handsomer, without [them], than any mortal complexion."[50]

Letters scattered over the next decade reveal Betsey Champlain working to improve her depiction of sitters' faces by focusing on their complexions. In 1824, after struggling with six recent front faces, she realized that she had "never fixed my room properly for the purpose." "Better late than never," she hung blinds and shutters that "shut or open at pleasure." One shutter was fitted with a door "divided into two—the upper to admit as much light upon the patient as will produce this rich gold shade I have before mentioned." It was, after all, easier to paint a luminous face when the sitter was lit to create the desired glow. In her refurbished room, Champlain happily reported, "You see before you what you are to copy, without laying more upon Fancy than she is able to bear or crowding her delicate stomach with too solid food for her digestive properties."[51]

Champlain also emulated fine paintings to hone her color perception and brush skills. She was particularly moved by one patron's snuffbox, which was decorated with the "likeness of a French king who is said to have reign'd in the 16th century." Fascinated by the way that the crimson turban "left a rich reflection upon forehead and ear," she badgered the client and his friends until she learned the name of the New York City merchant who sold the marvel. She then asked her daughter to call at the store immediately to peruse the snuffbox assortment "and see if there is any you think will answer as a modle for a painter." In the best of all worlds, she preferred a "front face, dark and richly shaded," or a "female, with ringlets."[52] Five years later, she obtained a far better "modle" by copying a miniature painted by Nathaniel Rogers, a noted miniaturist who helped found the National Academy of Design. The result was the "highest style of shading, and looks as if it would speak." The thrill was in the colors: "a white merino shawl, shaded to resemble black, and pencil colour'd ermine, the white draper very dingy." The face was "drawn upon the deepest yellow ivory" possible, which was exploited for the "harmonizing tints between the light and shade" and the highlights, which Champlain left "naked . . . natural as life." Her son William confirmed Champlain's achievement: The deeply shaded background set off the face of the sitter; the contrast between the two "gives life, ay being, to the peice."[53]

Like most of Betsey Champlain's paintings, this masterpiece has long since disappeared. Her work survives only in the shadow form of letters, making it difficult to see exactly how and when she refined her technique over the course of her career. Nevertheless, she brought at least some of her hard-won lessons to bear on an unfinished portrait of an unidentified sitter. The young woman's dotted dress graces her body but doesn't do battle with it. The unfinished lace collar draws our eyes up to the sitter's face, which is crowned by a heavy, black turban. As Mary Way's authorities promised, the dark, flat black of the turban intensifies the delicate stippled tints that Champlain had begun to apply to contour the young woman's face. A deep, brownish vermillion shades the nose while a fainter version defines the chin and jaw. A mixture of yellowish red brings the blush to her cheeks. Minuscule blue and gray dots mark the shadows around the eyes and beneath the mouth. It is precisely this delicately fashioned transparency that we see in the subtle reds, browns, yellows, and pinks of Champlain's unfinished self-portrait. Race was thus inscribed not only in the shocking blackness of Elizabeth Freeman's likeness, but also in the painstakingly crafted whiteness of Betsey Champlain's.

Seeing the racial ideology and the racialized aesthetic at work in the portraits of Elizabeth Freeman and Betsey Way Champlain, we can return to the familial contexts in which these images, and thousands like them, were produced, circulated, and viewed. We can situate the representations at the intersection of race, family, and sentiment. Freeman's portrait and the stories that swirl around it serve as a forceful reminder that federal-era New England was neither absolutely white nor absolutely free.[54] It directs our attention to the ambiguous boundaries that separated the various legal categories of dependency—economic and familial—that obtained in the early republic. Freeman was born a slave and died a wage earner. Throughout, she was also a family member. The will she dictated shortly before her death in 1829 enumerates her own family: A daughter, a granddaughter, and four great-grandchildren survived her to inherit an estate that included real property, furniture, clothing, and jewelry. Of the possessions she bequeathed to her daughter, two had special significance: a "short gown that was my mother's" and a black silk gown that was "rec'd of my father." Passed across the generations, the clothing registered Freeman's identity as a daughter and mother. It tethered Freeman's daughter, also named Elizabeth, to a family that stretched back to include grandparents. With the legal transmission of her property, Freeman claimed the lineal family that slavery had denied her.[55]

At the same time that Freeman was intent on preserving and extending her own lineal family, she was also included as a member of the Sedgwick family. To incorporate Freeman into *their* family imaginary, the Sedgwicks discursively severed her from her own. Neither Henry Dwight Sedgwick nor Catharine Maria Sedgwick acknowledged Freeman's regard for her father and mother, whose memories she preserved in the clothing they had given her. Henry Sedgwick's published account of Freeman's life acknowledged that she was once married, her husband a casualty of the Revolutionary War. He likewise mentioned her surviving child and her "large family of grand-children and great-grand-children." Although he mentioned Freeman's descendants, he did not dwell on the damage that their mother's enslavement must have inflicted on her children, an interesting departure from the conventions of abolitionist rhetoric that sought to move northern audiences by reminding them of the ways in which slavery violated the sanctity of black families. Instead, he chose to memorialize Freeman as a servant "who knew her station and perfectly observed its decorum" with none of the "submissive or subdued character" that so often resulted from slavery. Catharine Maria Sedgwick, who never mentioned Freeman's husband, acknowledged her surviving family only to dismiss them as "riotous and ruinous descendants" given to "reckless consumption." Such remarks recapitulate predictable stereotypes about African Americans' suitability for domestic service and their irresponsibility, fiscal and otherwise. But they also register a plaintive enviousness. "Mumbet" may have been the "main pillar" of the Sedgwick household (in Catharine's terms); she may also have been a servant "whose fidelity to her employers was such as has never been surpassed" (in Henry's).[56] Yet the fact remains that Freeman left that household and those employers in 1808, choosing to support her own household and serve her own family. Memoirs and fantasies notwithstanding, Freeman's family priorities diverged from those of the Sedgwicks.

What, then, were the conditions under which Sedgwick painted Freeman in 1811? Did Freeman even sit for the portrait? How was the miniature displayed, and to whom? Who claimed ownership of the likeness, of "Mumbet"? Here, it is suggestive to consider the possibility that the painting was a gift, passed from one Sedgwick to another. That symbolic exchange would have recalled a literal one. As children, Elizabeth Freeman and her sister had been gifts, given by their owner, Pieter Hogeboom, to his daughter, Annetje, to celebrate her wedding.[57] Freeman entered the household of Captain John Ashley, the man whom she would later sue for freedom, as dowry, as a gift exchanged between white kin to symbolize status, obligation, and love. Freeman's portrait may well have served the same symbolic role for a different white family. Withal, it is hard not to read Sedgwick's portrait of Freeman as a stunning act of appropriation, in which the possession signaled by an ivory miniature stood in for the possession of an African American woman, a former slave, a "mother." This appropriation depended on the strikingly racialized representation of "Mumbet." But it also depended on a set of historically specific social relations, on the murky distinctions between "slave," "servant," and "family" that survived the abolition of slavery in Massachusetts for several decades.

Betsey Way Champlain's self-portrait allows us to glimpse the tangle of race, family, and sentiment from a different perspective. Her likeness is governed by an aesthetic that is as deeply racialized as the conventions governing the likeness of Freeman. The delicately stippled complexion reminds us that as both an ideology of race and a system of visual signifiers, nineteenth-century "whiteness" emerged not only in a distinctly American opposition to "blackness" (or, for that matter, "redness") but also out of transatlantic discourses on aesthetics, gentility, and natural science. Considered alongside thousands of similar miniatures produced in the early republic, Champlain's painting suggests that the visual codes of whiteness were elaborated and disseminated not only in "public," in the realm of politics and work, but also in "private," in the bosom of the affectionate family.[58]

Champlain's self-portrait should also caution us against underestimating the complexity of those family affections. Like so many other nineteenth-century ivory miniatures, the painting was undertaken as a gift. Although it never reached its intended recipient, Mary Way, it was eventually passed to the artist's daughter, Eliza Way Champlain, who in turn gave the painting to her own daughter. Rather than reinforcing familial bonds within a single generation, it reinforced them across several generations. In the end, the painting realized its purpose: It became a symbol of family, of love.

The undelivered gift was also a symbol of unrealized aspiration. Betsey Way Champlain could never have scraped up the cash to commission such a painting. Most of the time, she barely managed to make her rent. It was only her skill, her labor, that made the gift possible. Just as the image flattered her likeness—"keeping probability in view" while erasing the marks of time and care—it flattered her rank and her income. Her gift surely recalled the gifts that circulated among her neighbors and friends, from the miniatures that she herself had painted for her patrons to bestow upon others to the exquisite portrait painted by Nathaniel Rogers that she used as a "modle" for her own masterpiece. The sisters' unrealized exchange recalled exchanges witnessed from a distance, a distance defined by fortune and gender. On ivory, if not in life, Betsey Way Champlain could claim more than gentility—she could claim the security that went with it. Like the painting of Freeman, Champlain's self-portrait testifies to the power of love, to the persistence of family mythologies, to the magic of portraiture. And like Freeman's portrait, Champlain's reminds us that love—like the gifts that concretize it—is always a creature of history and of history's contradictions.

CHAPTER FOUR

Looking Past Loyalism

When you visit The Woodlands, William Hamilton's Philadelphia estate, it is hard not to meditate on the passage of time. What was once the scene of lively hospitality, a sociable bachelor's paradise, is now a cemetery. A mansion that was celebrated in the early nineteenth century as the pride of Philadelphia has fallen into serious disrepair, a casualty of chronic urban underfunding. The exquisite furniture and objets d'art that made the house seem like a jewel box are long gone, replaced by a few rickety desks and dozens of cardboard file boxes. Formerly the darling of landscape painters, picturesque poets, and cultured tourists, The Woodlands has long since been overshadowed by the carefully restored mansions that line Fairmount Park.[1]

But if The Woodlands compels us to think about the relation between the eighteenth and twenty-first centuries, it also invites us to consider the relation between the colonial past and the early national present. Constructed and reconstructed between 1770 and 1789, Hamilton's estate almost immediately assumed pride of place as the early republic's preeminent country seat. It was admired and emulated by revolutionary luminaries including George Washington and Thomas Jefferson. Together, its gardens and buildings provided countless visitors with a vehicle for exercising the linked processes of looking, reading, and writing upon which the American republic of taste was grounded. By the first decades of the nineteenth century, its fame spread well beyond Philadelphia, for it was depicted in paintings, prints, poetry, and prose that circulated as far as Kentucky. The estate attracted attention precisely because it offered citizens who measured civilization in the progress of culture and the arts and who worried that the New World would always trail the Old World in these

Figure 13. William Hamilton's Adam-style home, The Woodlands, Philadelphia, PA, 1786–1789. Photographed by Joseph Elliott, 2002, for the Historic American Building Survey, Library of Congress, Washington, DC.

regards with a resounding affirmation of the nation's prospects. Yet The Woodlands was also the lifework of a confirmed loyalist and passionate Anglophile. During the war, Hamilton was twice tried for treason; after it, his enthusiasm for all things English continued unabashed. How, then, did his estate come to occupy a distinctive space in the national imaginary, in the republic of taste?

The answer to this question is rooted both in the decades preceding the Revolution, which witnessed the rising fortunes of the Hamilton family, and in the war itself, which witnessed the political misfortunes of William Hamilton. Ironically, the estate assumed its prominence as a symbol of republican taste not in spite of Hamilton's history but because of it. He engineered his return to Philadelphia society by using strategies he had cultivated in postwar London to ingratiate himself to influential Americans who had championed the patriot cause and now served as envoys of the republic. On both sides of the Atlantic, he made shrewd use of sociability to deflect attention away from his political past. Especially at The Woodlands, Hamilton elaborated a sociability grounded in the exercise of taste, in the shared appreciation of art, architecture, and landscape gardening. He thus succeeded in pushing politics into the far background even as he surrounded himself with politicians and political power brokers. Hamilton's emphatic silence on all things political opened the door for others— writers, artists, politicians, and tourists—to generate their own stories about the significance of his estate, a task that many of them took up with gusto.

Yet for all their attempts to cast The Woodlands as an American triumph, early national Americans never completely effaced either the estate's English origins or Hamilton's place on the wrong side of the war for independence. Like an unwelcome weed that keeps pushing up through a garden's ground cover, the past was hard to uproot. A close examination of the interlocking histories of William Hamilton, The Woodlands, and the meanings that observers attached to the estate offers insight into one spectacularly visible attempt to weed out the past or, failing that, to conceal it. Just as important, it illuminates the fundamental contradictions that dogged attempts to define a distinctly American aesthetic and forge an autonomous national taste.

William Hamilton

Any explanation of the fate of The Woodlands in the early republic must begin before the war, with William Hamilton and his kin.[2] The scion of a wealthy and powerful family, Hamilton had been positioned for prominence from his birth in 1745. He owed this enviable position to the financial, political, and social striving of the two preceding generations. By the middle of the eighteenth century, the Hamilton family had amassed economic, political, and cultural capital that was almost unparalleled in Pennsylvania. William's grandfather, Andrew Hamilton, was a Scottish emigrant of nondescript origins who moved to Philadelphia in 1714 following stints in Virginia and Maryland. He arrived in the city equipped with property and personal connections, which he parlayed into economic and political clout. By the time of his death in 1741, he claimed more than twenty thousand acres in the Delaware River Valley, forty lots in Philadelphia, and ten houses in Delaware and Philadelphia. Andrew Hamilton's political fortunes kept pace with his financial gains: At one point or another, he served as Pennsylvania's attorney general, a vice admiralty court judge, and provincial councilor. He was a primary mover behind the construction of the Pennsylvania State House, now known as Independence Hall. His place in history was assured by his successful defense of Peter Zenger, the New York printer charged with seditious libel against New York's corrupt royal governor, in a trial credited with helping to establish freedom of the press in the British colonies. At the end of his life, Andrew Hamilton built Bush Hill, a country manor so grand that it would eventually serve as John Adams's vice presidential mansion and so large that it could be repurposed as a hospital during the yellow fever epidemics of 1793 and 1795.

Andrew Hamilton's children—Margaret, Andrew Jr., and James—did their part to consolidate the family's position within the proprietary gentry, a group of non-Quaker elites allied with the Pennsylvania proprietors. Margaret married the spectacularly wealthy William Allen. Andrew Jr., William Hamilton's father, married well and used his wife's resources along with the waterfront properties he had inherited to expand his interests in shipping and commerce. James, the youngest, outshone them both. His many political offices included one term as mayor of Philadelphia and two as the colony's lieutenant governor. His business ventures added considerably to the wealth he had inherited. He used his money to create a supremely stylish life at Bush Hill, where he resided year-round. His mansion housed one of the first and finest art collections in the colonies as well as a considerable library. A lifelong bachelor, James entertained often and well. His economic, political, and social rank garnered him positions of prominence in virtually every one of the institutions that composed civil society in Philadelphia, from the Philosophical Society and the College of Philadelphia to the Dancing Assembly and the Mt. Regale Fishing Company.[3]

William Hamilton benefited enormously from all of these triumphs. When his father, Andrew Jr., died in 1747, William received a sizable estate, including a 350-acre tract of land along the Schuylkill River that would become the site of The Woodlands; this inheritance was later enlarged by a substantial inheritance from his maternal grandfather. Economic capital was supplemented by cultural capital, mostly courtesy of his Uncle James, who served as William's guardian and ensured that the boy received top-flight educations both in and out of school. A "Baccalaureatus" degree from Pennsylvania Academy and College (later the University of Pennsylvania) secured William a place among a tiny minority of elite Anglo-Americans. His formal schooling was surely enhanced by access to Philadelphia's rich cultural resources. Splitting his time between his mother's townhouse and his uncle's estate at Bush Hill, William could make use of the city's libraries as well as his uncle's extensive art and book collections. Given William's early and passionate interest in art and architecture, it seems likely that James took an interest in encouraging and educating his taste.

As he entered adulthood, William was thus poised to do his part in advancing the Hamilton family's fortunes through another generation, but he had other plans. Rather than busying himself by making money or managing colonial bureaucracies, he chose to use his resources to adopt the life of a leisured, landed gentleman, renting and selling the property he inherited to generate income. After coming into his inheritance in 1766, he settled on his riverfront acreage, determined to create his own rural estate. He began by building a house, which he positioned on a hill overlooking a sharp bend in the Schuylkill River. It is impossible to know, now, how the interior space of the original house was laid out. But at least from the outside, the building was grandly innovative. It boasted a two-story, tetrastyle portico flanked by bays stretching to the east and west. Although open porticos would become familiar by the antebellum period, in the eighteenth century they were decidedly avant-garde, as architectural historian James A. Jacobs has observed. The rubble and stone walls were covered with white stucco, mimicking the appearance of ashlar stone. And William positioned his home so that this imposing portico—and the white mansion it announced—would be visible to anyone traveling on the river or crossing the busy ferry below. He may also have begun work on the grounds during these early years.[4]

Whatever statement William intended his house to make, whatever future he envisioned for himself as the master of The Woodlands, was rudely disrupted by the American Revolution. When Philadelphia emerged in 1775 as an epicenter of rebellion, William and his Uncle James, by then an old man in poor health, were forced into a delicate dance of allegiances. The family was predisposed to align itself with the British Empire—hardly surprising, given that the Hamiltons owed their political and financial clout to their connections with Pennsylvania's proprietors and to the imperial power structure that class represented. Andrew Hamiltron's upward mobility had accelerated sharply in 1713, after he was hired to represent the Penn family's proprietary rights in Delaware; James Hamilton's political career was founded on serving the Crown's interests; and all the Hamilton men had profited from their connection to the Penns and to the proprietary gentry. The Hamiltons were thus inclined to count themselves among Philadelphia's loyalists.

As Philadelphia passed back and forth between American and British armies, even a predisposition to loyalism could create problems. While revolutionary Whigs controlled Philadelphia, James and William—like so many other Philadelphians who were less than enthusiastic about American independence—faced intense pressure to commit themselves and their resources to the Revolution. During the British occupation of the city, that pressure abated. And in 1778, when the Whigs regained control of a city all but ruined by the departing British army, there was hell to pay.

Throughout, James Hamilton took the path of the prudent Tory. As he put it, although he had "not actually joined [him]self" to the revolutionary "party," he had given it "no just cause for offence." In 1777 he was arrested, paroled, and given permission to move from Philadelphia to Easton, Pennsylvania, with his property intact. The following spring, with Philadelphia once again under Whig

control, he was released from parole and granted permission to return to Philadelphia and his home at Bush Hill so long as he swore allegiance to the Com-
monwealth of Pennsylvania, on pain of forfeiting his property. This last was a
gesture required of all former officers of the Crown. Rather than taking the oath
that would have allowed him to return to his beloved home, the elderly Hamilton slipped through British lines and settled in New York City, where he died
in 1783.[5]

William Hamilton lacked his uncle's political savvy. Initially, he seems to
have harbored some sympathy for colonial grievances, for he helped raise a
regiment for the Continental Army from his neighbors around The Woodlands. But he was apparently willing to push the colonies' grievances only so
far. When rebellion morphed into revolution, he resigned from military service. The exact tenor of his politics at the beginning of the war is unclear.
Loyalism, like republicanism, included multiple perspectives and levels of
commitment, and he left no indication of his views on the evolving legal and
constitutional disputes. Yet given his uncle's arrest and removal to Easton and
later New York, it is hard to imagine that he retained much affection for the
radical Whigs. And he must have been sensitive to his precarious position as
the favored nephew of a high-profile Tory. Whatever his sentiments, he kept
them to himself. But as the war ground on, and Pennsylvania's radical Whigs
demonstrated less and less appreciation for the sort of prudence exercised by
men like the Hamiltons, William's alienation from the patriot cause increased
proportionately.

William Hamilton ran afoul of the patriots twice during the Revolution.
Both episodes occurred when Whigs' anger at the British, their frustration with
the war's progress, and their resentment of war's privation reached a flash point.
And both instances point to his deepening commitment to the loyalist cause.

Hamilton was first arrested in 1778, when the Continental Army regained
control of Philadelphia. That summer, Whigs were keen both to retaliate against
the devastating destruction of property at the hands of the British and to crack
down on the city's significant loyalist population. The press hounded "Traitors"
and "Tories," urging them to hang their heads and "*not stare down* your betters
with *angry faces.*"[6] Those who had been particularly prominent or outspoken
were threatened by mobs. After a group of more than 150 Whigs formed an
association called the "Patriotic Society," aimed at "disclosing and bringing to
justice all Tories," even the most reticent loyalists must have felt vulnerable.[7] In
September, Hamilton found himself among fifteen other civilians charged with
high treason. Although he was acquitted after a twelve-hour trial, there is some
evidence that Hamilton actually had put his political sentiments into practice
and offered assistance to the British army. Following Hamilton's acquittal, New

York's loyalist judge, Isaac Ogden, wrote to Joseph Galloway, the most prominent American loyalist in London, reporting that he had run into a man who had attended the trial. "Billy Hamilton" was set free only because the most incriminating portion of a letter from the Lord Cornwallis—the corner of the paper that reportedly contained explicit directions for Hamilton—had been destroyed. This "defect of proof" made for "a narrow escape."[8] A narrow and sobering escape indeed, considering that two of the men who had been arrested along with Hamilton were hanged. Certainly the affair did nothing to endear revolutionary Philadelphia to Hamilton. Writing to a friend in the spring of 1779, Hamilton complained about an uninterrupted view of Philadelphia he had created before the war by clearing strategic sections of his property. To be sure, the view from The Woodlands was "most commanding" and, under different circumstances, this "peep at the Town" would be an object of admiration. But having grown to "cordially hate" the city, Hamilton now found the sight "absolutely disgusting." "Judge by this what must be the frame of my Mind," he brooded.[9]

Six months after registering his cordial hatred of the city, Hamilton was again arrested on suspicion of corresponding illegally with the British in New York. This time, the authorities were able to take advantage of harsh new attainder laws that greatly expanded the Supreme Executive Council's capacity to combat the state's loyalist population by sanctioning punishment without trial. After serving a brief stint in prison, Hamilton was declared "inimical to the American cause" and released on the condition that he pay a £200,000 security and "go within enemy lines" for the duration of the war. Shortly afterward, he was granted permission to immigrate to the Caribbean island of St. Eustatius. At the last minute, Hamilton opted to stay put. His aim was to wait out the war as close to home as possible in order to protect his property from Pennsylvania's revolutionary government, which had become increasingly aggressive in its pursuit of enemy assets. For almost three years, he shuttled back and forth between incarceration, banishment to western Pennsylvania, and confinement at The Woodlands. He and his family filed petition after petition, stalling for time. Hamilton was an obvious target surrounded by enemies, as his friend John Cadwalader, a general in the Continental Army, pointed out. No precaution was too great to ensure the safety of his person and his property. "Snares will undoubtedly be laid for you and therefore you cannot be too cautious as your deemed disaffected," Cadwalader warned. "Persons will no doubt be employed who may affect a behavior to put you off your guard." In such a climate the general urged his old friend "never even to speak upon the subject" of politics. Sound advice indeed. But, as Hamilton could have told the general, exercising caution in revolutionary Pennsylvania proved no simple matter. It was an impossible situation: Because of his property, he was not free to leave Philadelphia; because of his politics, he was not safe to remain there.[10]

When peace was finally concluded, Hamilton set sail for London. The journey had multiple agendas. Most pressing was the need to sort out finances related to his inheritance from his Uncle James, for the war had played havoc with transatlantic fortunes. There were other incentives. William's older brother, Andrew, had just died, leaving him to serve as guardian to seven children; the trip afforded an opportunity to check on two nephews who had been sent to England for schooling and to introduce his favorite niece, Ann, to cosmopolitan London. For his own part, Hamilton hoped to use Britain as the base from which he could launch a Grand Tour of the continent. In the meantime, he expected to immerse himself in the finer aspects of English culture. Perhaps he also welcomed the chance to put some distance between himself and Philadelphia's victorious Whigs.

Arriving in London, however, Hamilton ran up against the social and financial limitations that had dogged aspiring Anglo-American visitors for more than a century, limitations that had been compounded by the Revolution. For one thing, Hamilton was, by definition, a provincial. Even the spectacularly elegant Philadelphia socialite Anne Willing Bingham was not immune to Londoners' preconceptions about Americans. When Bingham hit town, Abigail Adams reported, admirers repeatedly asked, "Is she an American? Is she an American?" before they were "*obliged* to *confess* that she was truly an elegant woman" despite her origins. Never mind that Hamilton was a wealthy loyalist and an unapologetic Anglophile; he was shunted to the periphery of London's polite society. Although members of the aristocracy and gentry made occasional appearances on Hamilton's social radar and in his letters, he doesn't seem to have registered on theirs. Shortly after arriving in the city, for example, Hamilton made arrangements to have a portrait shipped from Philadelphia as a compliment to a Lady Cremorne. But the gift failed to serve as a springboard for a more intimate friendship. When Lord and Lady Cremorne invited Hamilton's loyalist cousin Andrew Allen to the spas at Tunbridge, they left William behind in London.[11]

Hamilton's Pennsylvania pedigree *did* ensure him access to the elite Americans congregating in London. Some sort of expatriate camaraderie was almost guaranteed, given the large numbers of Americans who passed through the city following the American Revolution. Some, like William Pepperell, were loyalists who had fled to the city during the war. Some, like the Adamses, were patriots in town on state business. Many more were there for reasons that had little to do with politics per se; they were trying to settle finances, to continue educations, and to restore family ties that had been disrupted by the war. American sociability offered a hedge against loneliness, as it surely did for Hamilton, who wrote that without the comforting presence of Benjamin Chew, another Philadelphia loyalist, he "should indeed be sadly off." But such encounters could also be fraught with political tension, for in the aftermath of war, Anglo-Americans carried political baggage to the metropole. They recognized one another not simply as fellow Americans, or as colonials visiting the metropole, but as Tories and patriots. Abigail Adams discovered ample acrimony on both sides. "The Refugees are very desperate bitter and venomous," she wrote, likening them to "Wolves" who "would devour us yet if they could." Ardent patriots scrutinized one another's dealings with Tories, ever on the lookout for signs of backsliding. Even Abigail Adams, whose republican credentials were impeccable, was not above suspicion. She declined to rekindle relations with relatives who had fled Massachusetts as Tories, fearing that because she was a "publick Character," she was vulnerable to the gossip of "persons who will belie one, and say things which were never meant or thought of."[12]

Rapprochement may have been easier to engineer when sociability obtained between the children of political antagonists. While in London, the Adamses' daughter Abigail, nicknamed Nabby, attended the theater, danced at balls, exchanged visits, and cultivated relationships with the children of prominent Tory families. It is likely that all parties involved believed that these encounters would help ease the reintegration of loyalists into American life, an immediate political problem that John Adams, for one, was keen to solve. It is also likely that such friendships both evidenced and validated widespread republican faith in the political importance of society. That said, this particular iteration of society depended on enormous discretion, carefully calibrated performances, and occasional dissemblance. In the winter of 1786, the Adamses' circle included twenty-eight-year-old Sarah Masters, a Philadelphia heiress who was connected to the Penn family through marriage. No doubt Masters was on her best behavior while dining with the Adamses. But in other settings she was not shy about her antipathy toward the American cause. William Hamilton, who had "seen the lady but once" in his first four months in London, could nevertheless report with confidence, "I am told she detests America most cordially." Indeed, Hamilton correctly predicted that Masters's hatred of all things American would squelch her romance with Benjamin Chew, who had every intention of returning to Philadelphia, notwithstanding his Tory politics.[13] Political differences might be set aside in London, but they did not disappear.

William Hamilton did his best to leverage his position among the city's preeminent American residents, patriots included. He started at the top, with John Adams, the U.S. ambassador to the Court of St. James and arguably the most important American in the city. He took his teenaged niece, Ann, to call on the Adamses, who had arrived in London shortly after the Hamiltons. Ann Hamilton provided the perfect entrée into their world. She was lovely and charming and made an immediate impression on both Abigail and Nabby. Notwithstanding the Hamilton family's political convictions, in the eyes of the Adams women, Ann embodied a distinctly *republican* beauty. While in London, mother and daughter relentlessly compared English and American women, deploying the transatlantic trope that cast female beauty as a register of national character. Not surprisingly, they decided that English ladies came up short: Abigail reported that the Duchess of Devonshire was "Masculine in her appearance"; Princess Elizabeth was a "short clumsy Miss" inclined to corpulence; and although Lady Salsbury was "small and genteel," she had bad skin. Americans of a loyalist bent fared no better. Nabby found Mary Masters Penn, the wife of Pennsylvania's former lieutenant governor, to be "ugly, Masculine and withot one trait of amiable femal Character." She damned Mrs. Penn's sister, Sarah Masters (she who "cordially hated America"), as "a fine bold beauty two ideas that in my mind are incompatible" and as the kind of woman whose "borrowed blushes" were the "result of an artfull die." Ann served as the Adamses' foil of choice, a delightful counter with which to affirm republican virtue. Ann, both women insisted, was everything that English and Tory women were not. Nabby thought that she possessed a "deli[cate] softness and sweetness of unconscious beauty." Abigail proclaimed her "one of the lovelyest Girls in the World," whose face was animated by the "Sparkling Eye of sensibility." Indeed, when Anne Willing Bingham's ostentation and ambition began to grate, Abigail went so far as to suggest that Ann Hamilton would prove the superior of the two American beauties. The young girl had a "finer face than Mrs. Bingham" and was already her equal in "person and mind."[14]

Ann created an opening that her uncle assiduously nurtured. Among the Adamses, William Hamilton pushed his own motives for visiting England—his political disaffection and his financial entanglements—into the background. Instead, he diverted their attention to his niece and to his role as her doting, dutiful guardian. As Abigail explained to her son after her first encounter with the Hamiltons, "[William] has brought his Neice over to this Country to give her an education, suitable to a fortune which he intends to give her." Hamilton humbly "requested [Abigail's] protection" for the girl, explaining that Ann would benefit from mature female guidance.[15]

The gambit worked. For the duration of the Hamiltons' time in England, the Adams women championed William Hamilton as a family man. Nabby noted that he displayed the "affection of a Parent," treating Ann "in every respect as his own Daughter." "He almost worships her," her mother effused, and he has "shewn her the world under his own Eye, and preserved her from

CHAPTER FOUR

growing giddy at the view." As uncle and niece, the Hamiltons quickly became fixtures in the Adamses' social life: Ann became one of Nabby's closest London friends. John Adams presented William Hamilton at Court. Hamilton reciprocated by giving Abigail and Nabby seats in his Covent Garden theater box, a treat that had hitherto been beyond their reach.[16] Hamilton's social persona—made of one part polite refinement and one part family drama—combined with his niece's good looks and winning manner to eclipse his wartime history and his politics. The bitter Tory became a benevolent and apolitical uncle, a man whose social graces and family position mandated an introduction to the king of England. Small beer that Hamilton's presentation had been arranged by the official representative of a government he loathed; at least he had made it to Court.

The social dilemmas were more easily resolved than the financial ones. William's most pressing mission in England had been financial: If he was ever to benefit from the estate he had inherited from his Uncle James, he first had to clear it of debt. At the same time, although William had managed to keep his own property safe from confiscation, the war had sorely disrupted his income at home. He thus arrived in England in 1784 with less cash than he might otherwise have, only to find that London was ruinously expensive. "I had as I thought formed a pretty good Idea of the expences in this country," he confessed to his agent back home, "but am sorry to say I was under the mark."[17] He had no idea just how far under the mark he fell.

The scramble for cash never stopped. Hamilton constantly cast about for ways to wrest funds from his American resources. He considered investing in "the trade of Basket making" and thereby turning free riverbank willows into commodities, for he had learned that in England they were "turn[ed] to wonderful account." He instructed his agent, Thomas Parke, in Pennsylvania to negotiate down the "extravagant interest" on past-due payments for debts he had incurred when he had been "confined" by the radical Whigs in 1780. He jockeyed to find buyers for property he had inherited in New Jersey. Hamilton's letters to Parke are punctuated with requests for "remittances" and, failing that, for assurances that "remittances" were on their way, for the fashionable life that he and his family wanted did not come cheap. His problems were compounded by the extended family he supported. Requesting £1,200, a sum that "will Dare say make you think me extravagant," he insisted. "Half an hours conversation would convince you of the contrary." "My own expenses are considerable, those for Jemmy Hamilton [a nephew who was in school] amount to upwards of 50 pr annum & Anns last quarter alone came to £600 Sterling exclusive of her clothing & other matters." Even the prospect of returning home to The Woodlands was expensive. London was full of "carriages, furniture & many matters of different kinds" that were in "better taste" than could be had in America and, at least in the off season, much cheaper. But without "command of money," Hamilton was thwarted in the pursuit of luxury "purchased at less than half its value."[18]

Unable to calibrate his ambitions and his resources, Hamilton was reduced to borrowing. By March of 1786 he had borrowed so much and repaid so little that his creditors, the Barclays, cut him off. When he asked them for an advance of £700, after making a payment of £250, the Barclays responded that "it will not suit them to advance more money." Instead, they came up with a counteroffer: "to accommodate their friend WH he may draw for 25 guineas if his occasions require it." Under other circumstances, this would have been humiliating. But by then, Hamilton admitted, "25 guineas (small as was that sum) was very acceptable to me having had no other money since the beginning of January."[19]

The consequences of being cash poor were driven home during Hamilton's one and only English summer, when he found himself confined to off-season London. Forget the Grand Tour of the continent he had fantasized about; he barely managed a garden tour of the English countryside. He spent most of the season walking the city. "I make nothing of 10 miles before dinner," he reported. All those pedestrian miles served as a reproach that Hamilton was not and never would be a member of English society. "London in the Summer season is a mere desert," Abigail Adams concluded, for "no body of consequence resides in it."[20] Stranded in an empty city, Hamilton had nothing to do but study the grand homes whose residents had decamped for more fashionable accommodations elsewhere. The summer of 1785 was "mortifying." After less than a year, he was forced to conclude that England was an ideal that lay beyond his reach. Lacking the resources to live well in England, he wrote, "My most ardent desire therefore is to get Home as soon as I can."[21]

This realization did not translate into enthusiasm for returning to the American republic. In his estimation, "the government in America" was not "equal to its gifts from nature," namely, its climate. England, on the other hand, was an "Elysium" with a "good fixed government." "Could I pack up my alls and transport them without material injury where I pleased," he wrote, "I should have little Difficulty in determining the place of my future residence."[22] Under the circumstances, though, he had no choice but to return to Pennsylvania armed with plans to improve The Woodlands along the lines of the English homes he so admired. When he returned to Philadelphia in 1786, he accelerated the renovation process he had initiated from London. Working with what he already had—a large, beautifully situated property; the core of a Georgian house; and the foundation of a fine art collection—Hamilton set about creating an Anglicized country estate in the belly of the republican beast.

The Woodlands

William Hamilton is best known now for his interest in horticulture and land-scape gardening. He transformed twelve acres of the land immediately surrounding his house into America's first large-scale garden in the English style. His achievement testified both to the pervasive Anglo-American investment in gardens as badges of gentility and to his own spectacular ambition and talent. By the time that Hamilton came into his majority and claimed The Woodlands, Philadelphia boasted a rich gardening history. William Penn had ensured that the city itself was dotted with gardens, for both ornamental and practical value. As the city developed, an enthusiastic interest in gardening became obligatory among its wealthy townsmen, including William's Uncle James. A handful of Philadelphians, John Bartram most notably, became distinguished botanists who participated in a transatlantic exchange of seeds, plants, and information. Hamilton grew up surrounded by serious gardens and serious gardeners. That said, the garden he devised and developed was in a class of its own.[23]

Even before Hamilton's trip to England in 1784, he planned to transform The Woodlands' grounds into some approximation of an English estate. It helped that the land he inherited, perched on a bluff overlooking a ninety-degree bend in the river, was what American and European visitors routinely hailed as "the most beautiful site in the area surrounding Philadelphia." But this magnificent setting was only a starting point. The year before he was tried for treason, he spent a princely £1,500 to manure his lawn, which stretched from the porch south toward the Schuylkill River. He surmounted wartime conditions—a "scarcity of Fence Nails, High prices, and Difficulty of getting Labourers"—to enclose one hundred acres at the rear of his house. His aim, he explained to a friend, was to give his "Hill & Dale" property a "parkish Look." These preliminary components served as the foundation of a recognizably English landscape garden.[24]

The months Hamilton spent in England afforded him the opportunity to study firsthand the picturesque garden style that epitomized eighteenth-century English landscape architecture. Championed by writers like Alexander Pope and Joseph Addison, codified by writers like Thomas Whately and William Gilpin, and exemplified by estates like Stowe and the Leasowes, picturesque gardens favored irregular lines and shapes, abandoning the strict geometry of an older, continental style. These carefully contrived "naturalistic" landscapes, often inspired by landscape paintings, organized plants, rocks, and water in order to create sight lines that guided viewers' eyes from the foreground to the distant background. They frequently incorporated ornamental buildings, statuary, or ruins to engage the intellect and prod the imagination. They could also afford a distinctly nationalist form of satisfaction; many English garden enthusiasts insisted that the picturesque testified to the superiority of English taste measured against the grotesque artifice of baroque continental design.[25]

Hamilton launched plans to immerse himself in the theory and praxis of the picturesque while he was in England before he left Philadelphia. He purchased a copy of Whately's 1770 *Observations on Modern Gardening* (then the definitive treatise on the modern English garden) and carried it with him across the Atlantic. Unfortunately for modern scholars, he never recorded which of England's rural estates he saw. But surviving records indicate that he visited a spate of counties famed for their landscape gardens, including Wiltshire and Buckinghamshire, which put him within reach of the celebrated gardens at Stourhead and Stowe. Whatever he saw on his tours of the countryside inspired him to ramp up his plans for The Woodlands. As his return to Philadelphia drew near, he shipped hundreds of plants home and roughed out further plans for his gardens and park.[26]

Transporting an idealized English landscape to the United States was no small matter. The task demanded capital and, characteristically, Hamilton seems to have spared no expense. Most obviously, he used his money to secure a jaw-dropping number and variety of plants, for there was little that was natural about the artless style that was the cornerstone of the picturesque. Authorities placed a premium on the play between multiple colors, shapes, and textures. To achieve the requisite range, gardeners needed to look beyond the species immediately at hand. Like his British counterparts, Hamilton mixed native plantings with imports. His taste was capacious. Writing from London in 1785, he urged his Philadelphia secretary to "take time by the forelock" and establish a "good nursery" for "large quantities" of domestic plants ranging from flowering locusts, sweet birch, and dogwoods, to honeysuckle and grapevines, to peonies, narcissus, and hollyhocks. He supplemented this native bounty with plants from around the world, importing literally hundreds of trees from England, including different varieties of firs, laurels, and myrtles. He introduced the ginkgo, the Lombardy poplar, and the Norway maple to North America. He built a massive greenhouse, flanked by several hothouses and covered in flowering vines, to house a collection that eventually grew to include some five thousand varieties of exotic plants from locations ranging from the Cape of Good Hope to Botany Bay to Japan.[27]

Hamilton bought more than stock. He used his fortune to secure both the expertise and labor demanded by an estate of this caliber. To acquire the expertise, he hired a series of exceptional gardeners, including John McArran, who went on to design the gardens at Philadelphia's Lemon Hill mansion; John Lyon, who became a noted seed and plant collector; Frederick Pursh, who would later write *Flora Americae Septentrionalis*, the second North American flora; and George Hilton, an African American who had traveled to London with Hamilton as an indentured servant and had returned to the estate as a paid gardener. To acquire the labor, he employed field hands who shuttled back and forth between The Woodlands and Bush Hill.[28]

Together, material, expertise, labor, and Hamilton's own exquisite aesthetic combined to create what one European visitor called "the Villa Borghese of Philad[elphia]."[29] Without extant plans, it is impossible to reconstruct the site with much precision. But judging from visitors' comments, the sum was more impressive than the already considerable parts. Hamilton took full advantage of his position above the river. Visitors entered the estate almost a mile north of the house, along a road that crossed a stream, passed by a cluster of stylish, neoclassical dependencies, and wound through groves of trees before it deposited them at Hamilton's door. A mile-long path from the portico on the opposite side of the house looped clockwise through the landscape park. He designed the path so as to structure visitors' sensory experiences as well as their promenades. Shady glens opened suddenly onto brilliant, expansive views of the river below. Seats placed beneath "arbours of the wild grape" and clusters of large trees offered a reprieve from summertime heat and humidity. Along the way, statues, urns, and memorials (including a tribute to the English poet-gardener William Shenstone) invited viewers to pause, reflect, and converse. When they finally reached the Schuylkill, they found a "natural walk" lined with grapes whose perfumed scent edged out the natural smell of the river during summer. They passed by a shell-lined grotto that Hamilton carved into the riverside. Heading back up the hill through more gardens, viewers found themselves in front of the massive greenhouse, covered with "the most flourishing jessamine and honeysuckle."[30] Small wonder that by the turn of the century, Hamilton had established himself as one of the nation's foremost gentlemen gardeners.

Hamilton's house was as remarkable as the gardens that surrounded it. He hired an unknown English architect to help transform the original structure into the late-Georgian style of Robert Adam. Adam, a Scottish architect, together with his brother, James, had dominated English domestic architecture in the two decades preceding Hamilton's visit; Adam's influence persisted through the end of the eighteenth century. Adam's distinctly English aesthetic, to say nothing of his cachet among English tastemakers, was calculated to capture the eye of an Anglophile like William Hamilton. With a loosely neoclassical feel, Adam's work was less concerned with reproducing the forms and aesthetic of the ancient world than with creating what he called movement, which he defined as the "rise and fall, the advance and recess" and the "diversity of form" in multiple parts of the building. Movement, he declared in a 1773 manifesto,

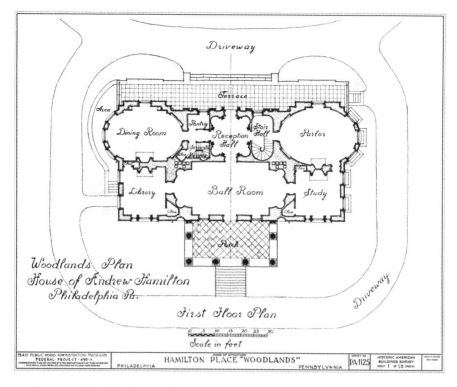

Figure 14. The Woodlands, first-floor plan. Historic American Building Survey, Library of Congress, Washington, DC. The 1940 floor plan, created through the Public Works Administration Program, mistakenly identifies the house as belonging to Andrew Hamilton.

"add[ed] greatly to the picturesque" of the building.[31] This penchant for movement, especially in a building's interior design, endeared Adam to the wealthy Englishmen who were overhauling their villas' grounds in accord with the complementary precepts of picturesque landscape architecture.

De rigueur for England's country houses, the Adam style was positively avant-garde in the United States. Eighteenth-century mansions, including the one Hamilton had initially constructed at The Woodlands, were typically organized as a series of rectangular rooms. In large houses, four rooms generally flanked a center hall; in Hamilton's original house, the two rooms that comprised the first floor seem to have been neatly divided by an east-west wall. Not so the renovated Woodlands. The new design, clearly the product of a close collaboration between Hamilton and the anonymous English architect, completely dissolved the footprint of the 1770 structure into a stunning, and stunningly original, space that marked a departure from even the most fashionable American homes. Hamilton retained the two-story portico that looked out toward the river and added matching columns and a temple façade to the building's northern front. But the small bays that had initially extended out from the sides of the house were swallowed up by substantial wings that nearly tripled the size of the house. The enlarged structure was then covered with lime (or perhaps stucco) to conjure a white, neoclassical temple rising above the banks of the Schuylkill.

Imposing as the house may have been to visitors who approached it from the entry road or the pleasure garden, the real marvel lay inside. A visitor entering the house for the first time would have expected to step into a long center hall. Instead, he would have found himself standing in a round vestibule whose walls were punctuated with niches for vases and statuary and whose ceiling opened up into a dome. Rather than guiding visitors in a single direction, the vestibule opened off in all directions: to parlor and library, to the grand saloon straight ahead, and to the expansive portico and beautiful grounds beyond that. The rooms beyond the entry were noteworthy in their own right. The dining room and parlor were oval, echoing the oval flowerbeds on the lawn surrounding the house. The rectangular saloon ended in domed, semicircular alcoves, whose niches recalled the ones in the vestibule. The alcoves led, in turn, to two small rooms called "cabinets." Although the second-floor bedrooms open off a traditional central hallway, the rooms echo the unusual shapes found on the first floor. The two largest bedrooms, including Hamilton's, were oval; angled walls and alcoves disrupt the right angles that one might expect to find in the smaller rooms. Upstairs and down, windows stretching from the floor almost to the ceiling provided stunning views of the grounds.

The dramatic floor plan provided a fit setting for the exquisite furnishings Hamilton assembled. Like most affluent Philadelphians, he looked abroad for furniture and tableware, wallpaper and fabrics. Before Hamilton left for England, he sold most of his furniture and when he was preparing to return home, he announced his intention to ship home "carriages, furniture, and many other matter of different kinds which cannot be done without and which may be & may be had in a better taste & some of them cheaper than in America." He also demanded that his old plate, probably inherited from his Uncle James, be sold not to pay off his London creditors but rather to purchase new plate "in the present taste." The inherited silver (and the cash it might generate) were "sacred" to the memory of his dead "Friend," he explained; "no incitement" except the promise of "new plate" could ever bring him to part with it.[32]

As Hamilton never failed to remind Parke, taste—his taste—would reign supreme at The Woodlands. Without detailed probate records or extant examples, it is difficult to speak with much precision about how that taste manifested itself, what it looked like. A handful of contemporary accounts and the mansion

Figure 15. The Woodlands' curvilinear vestibule, identified in the 1940 floor plan as the reception hall. Photographed by Joseph Elliott, 2002, for the Historic American Building Survey, Library of Congress, Washington, DC.

itself provide a few clues. Hamilton's taste in furniture seems to have departed from the light Federal style favored by people like the Binghams. Joshua Francis Fisher, who visited The Woodlands as a boy shortly before Hamilton's death, recalled the furniture as "Louis Quatorze" and later advanced the dubious claim that it had come from Versailles; by the late nineteenth century, it was being remembered as "old and massive."[33] We know more about the building's interior surfaces, thanks largely to the efforts of preservationists. The vestibule was painted in whites and ivories to create a faux marble finish. The drawing room walls were papered in a light blue and gray English panel print à la Robert Adam, while the brightly colored papers in the dining room and one of the oval bedrooms were distinctly French.[34]

The wallpaper was upstaged by the mirrors that Hamilton installed throughout the ground floor. The window shutters in these very public rooms were lined with mirrors, as were the double doors leading from the saloon into the vestibule. Columns of mirror were inserted between the windows along the curved walls of the dining and drawing rooms. Additional framed mirrors—looking glasses—hung on the walls.[35] The mirrors served a number of purposes.

CHAPTER FOUR

On the most pragmatic level, they brightened the rooms by reflecting both natural and artificial light; one visitor remarked in 1806 that because of the mirrors alongside the dining room windows, "the whole cemicircle seems light." And at a time when slightly more than half of households along the mid-Atlantic could claim a looking glass, Hamilton's sheets of mirror screamed "luxe." The mirrors also created a series of illusions. When the shutters were open, the mirrored panels lined the sides of the Venetian windows and reflected the grounds beyond, effectively dissolving the boundary between interior and exterior space. When they were closed, the mirrors functioned in much the same way that nineteenth- and twentieth-century department-store mirrors functioned: They expanded the exquisite space into a series of receding reflections with no clear starting and stopping points and multiplied the number of treasures that the house contained. The effect was not lost on guests. As one early visitor reported, the open shutters "repeat the [outside] landscape," transforming it into a "fairy scene." When closed, they worked their magic on the interior: "When you are at one end of the house & look through them, you not only see the whole length but <u>that</u> being reflected by these glass doors gives you an idea of its being twice the extent."[36] The reflections afforded a two-fold pleasure: one created by illusion itself and the other by the observer's recognition of the way the illusion was created.

We know much more about the art that graced The Woodlands because Hamilton's dazzling collection was what visitors remembered most about its interior. He had acquired a sizable number of paintings from his uncle, Pennsylvania's premier patron of the arts.[37] As an adult, Hamilton added to the collection he inherited. By the time The Woodlands was complete, he was able to fill it with art. He arranged statuary in the vestibule. The large niches in the saloon accommodated a marble Antinous and a bronze group depicting Apollo's pursuit of Daphne. He lined the dining room walls with family portraits, including two full-length portraits painted in London by Benjamin West, one depicting his Uncle James and another depicting him and his niece, Ann. The two small "cabinets" off the parlor and dining room, marked as a "library" and "study" on the floor plan, were given over to the floor-to-ceiling display of art. One visitor recalled years later that the walls of these rooms were almost entirely covered with pictures, "a large part of them of the Dutch and Flemish School." Another visitor described the spaces as "cabinets of gems."[38] Upstairs, Hamilton hung Peale's "large as life" copy of Titian's *Venus of Urbino* and a smaller copy of Adolf Ulrik Wertmüller's *Danaë Receiving Jupiter in a Shower of Gold*. The reclining nudes were discreetly covered with draperies to protect innocent eyes. (Twenty-year-old Harriet Manigault peeked and was horrified by what she saw: the *Venus* might have been a "fine painting," but it was also "a most *disgusting* looking thing" and "impudent"; the *Danaë*'s attitude as she received the shower of gold was nothing less than "frightful.")[39]

The estate was as notable for what visitors did not see—or did not see easily—as it was for the gardens, architecture, and décor. Like the builders of other picturesque estates, Hamilton took pains to control visitors' fields of vision. A good deal of that control focused on negation. Throughout the grounds, he used ha-has (narrow ditches) to contain animals without the visual disruption of a fence. Wooden fences separating lawn and garden disappeared between juniper hedges. The path leading from the house to the stable was sunk beneath the grade, much like a ha-ha; when it surfaced, it was concealed by "loose hedges" that left the unrefined sights, sounds, and smells of the "Stable Yard" "perfectly concealed," as one visitor marveled. Indeed, the only portions of the stable visible from the house or the driveway were Adamesque architectural elements—decorative niches and arches. When Hamilton's picturesque vista was sullied by the construction of a mill on the opposite side of the Schuylkill, he offered to buy it for £5,000; when that failed, he "entirely shut it out" with plantings. Within the house itself, he relegated the servants' work areas—the kitchen and storerooms—to the basement. Layers of hay and plaster inserted between the cellar ceiling and the first floor insulated Hamilton and his guests from the sounds and smells of work. The service areas were connected to the public portions of the house by enclosed staircases that opened into the main rooms via discreet jib doors. These smooth, sliding doors, bereft of any molding or trim, offered eighteenth-century builders a way to disguise servants' access points. They opened flat against the wall without intruding into the room and disappeared into the wall when closed. Patterned wallpaper further camouflaged the jib doors in the dining room. Dr. Charles Drayton, a houseguest, recounted their silent, seamless operations: Following one notable meal, "a formal pompous gentleman . . . stalked slowly" to the main door to usher the party out. But "when he turned, no body was to be seen, the company having passed thro the concealed door."[40]

The Woodlands was never really completed. Like all great estates, it was as much process as product. It represented an ongoing collaboration between wealth and learning, hired labor and personal vision, careful designer and astute observers. From the saloon to the grounds, from the stables to the kitchen, The Woodlands was Hamilton's lifework, and he spared no expense or effort in cultivating and embellishing it. The result was a grand, and grandly English, estate. Ironically, this very English estate would pave the way for Hamilton's return to society in very republican Philadelphia.

When Hamilton left Pennsylvania for England, politics had been his problem. When he returned, The Woodlands was his solution. Hamilton doubtless gained considerable personal pleasure from the time and money he invested in the estate. Yet he was also at pains to ensure that his investment paid political and social dividends by easing his return to Philadelphia and securing relations with a new cadre of political elites who passed through the city. A splendid vehicle for the pursuit of both sociability and horticulture, it provided Hamilton with a vehicle for reestablishing and reinventing himself.

Even before renovations on The Woodlands enabled him to resume living there, Hamilton used sociability to situate himself outside the political conflicts and commitments that branded him as a Tory, a loyalist, a traitor. In 1787, for example, he invited more than one hundred guests, including George Washington, to Bush Hill (where he waited out the construction) for a "superb entertainment" honoring delegates to the Constitutional Convention. The following July, he permitted some 17,000 Philadelphians to picnic on the grounds of Bush Hill after the Grand Federal Procession terminated at its edge.[41]

Once Hamilton became the live-in master of The Woodlands in 1789, he distinguished himself as a host, presiding over gatherings large and small. References to an evening at The Woodlands or an outing on its grounds are threaded through accounts of federal-era Philadelphia's high society. Thomas Twining, an agent of the East India Company, who was visiting Philadelphia on his return to England in 1795, noted in his diary that he had been invited to a "large party at dinner" made up "principally [of] members of Congress" at The Woodlands. Almost a decade later, a wealthy Philadelphia merchant, Thomas Cope, recorded a "family visit to the elegant seat of William Hamilton." Rufus Wilmot Griswold, celebrating the sociability of the republican court from the vantage point of the 1850s, memorialized Hamilton's table as "the frequent resort of artists and *bon vivants* of different sorts."[42] For the elite men who regularly congregated at Hamilton's estate—and Hamilton's guests were mostly men—sociability could serve both as a vehicle for politicking and a respite from it. At The Woodlands, it seems to have figured largely as the latter, for Hamilton cultivated his estate as a place where men's shared taste for art, gardening, botany, and Madeira wine eclipsed differences over policy. Sociability sans politics was not unusual in and of itself. The republican courts of Washington and Adams were, after all, calculated to provide precisely that.[43] The difference was that for other affluent, connected men (and their wives), sociability ultimately returned to politics. For Hamilton, in contrast, sociability served both as the process through which he could efface his political history and as confirmation that the erasure was complete.

Hamilton's passion for horticulture was similarly yoked to the dual projects of political effacement and social reintegration. Many of the politicians congregating in federal-era Philadelphia shared his interests in gardening and landscape architecture. Notable among them were Thomas Jefferson and George Washington, Virginians who famously lavished attention on their plantations as simultaneous registers of republican virtue and landed gentility. As an avid and affluent collector, Hamilton was well positioned to distribute plants and advice to both founders. In 1792, for example, he promised to send Washington "whatever . . . kinds of plants you desire," packed and ready for shipment to Mount Vernon. True to his word, he directed a servant to deliver more than 130 specimens, including four different varieties of willow, lilacs, junipers, "manna ash from Italy," and "paper mulberry of Japan." When Washington retired to Mount Vernon at the end of his second term as president, Hamilton sent him a "Clod of grass" for his lawn together with half of the Persian grass seeds held over from the previous season—all told, a "valuable acquisition" for an English-style estate. For Martha Washington, he selected an "upright Italian Myrtle & one of the Box leaved Myrtle" as a parting gift.[44]

Hamilton developed a far closer relationship with Jefferson, whose enthusiasms for gardening, collecting, and estate building rivaled his own. It is not clear how or when the two men met, but Hamilton's overtures increased when the Virginian was elected president. He invited Jefferson to "confer a favor" by "naming any seeds or plants he may wish to have from The Woodlands collection."[45] Jefferson was not shy in granting the favor. Indeed, throughout his presidency, he requested a steady stream of seeds and specimens, especially as his retirement to Monticello grew near. In addition to filling the president's orders, Hamilton also sent gifts of his own selection, including sweet acacia, gingkos, paper mulberry trees, a China varnish tree, and seeds for a "silk tree of Constantinople," which had been "collected from the Caspian sea." Lacking Hamilton's financial resources, Jefferson reciprocated on a less frequent, less lavish scale. In return for exotic ornamentals, he sent seeds for "winter melon from malta" and "quarantine corn" for use in Hamilton's kitchen garden. He also used political influence to secure what cash could not: Jefferson designated Hamilton as one of two recipients of the seeds collected by Lewis and Clark as they trekked across the continent.[46]

These exchanges paved the way for more expansive requests, in which Jefferson acknowledged the scale of Hamilton's accomplishments at The Woodlands. When Jefferson began to gear up plans to renovate the grounds at Monticello halfway through his second term in office, he turned to Hamilton for advice about making over a Virginia hilltop in the style of an English park. It was Hamilton's "taste," after all, that made "The Woodlands the only rival which I have known in America to what may be seen in England," and "thither without doubt we are to go for models in this art." With Hamilton's expertise in mind, the famously hospitable Jefferson extended an open invitation to visit and review the progress being made on his plantation grounds. He also recommended Hamilton's eye and expertise to others. When Jefferson's grandson Thomas Randolph was in Philadelphia studying botany with the naturalist Benjamin Smith Barton, Jefferson took pains to make sure that the young man had ample opportunity to view The Woodlands. Barton already took his classes to study at The Woodlands, but Jefferson requested "permission of occasional entrance" for Randolph so that the young man could devote his "vacant hours" to the kind of focused attention afforded by solitude. The education was meant to be aesthetic as well as scientific—he wanted the young man to "study well the style" of Hamilton's "pleasure grounds," for they formed "the chastest model of gardening I have ever seen outside of England."[47]

In all of these transactions, William Hamilton figured as a gardener and estate builder tout court. His relationships with Washington and Jefferson developed and operated within carefully delineated boundaries, boundaries defined by and contained within The Woodlands. Only Hamilton's greenhouse, his grounds, and his home drew him into their illustrious orbit. To be sure, the correspondence is punctuated by the period's conventional affirmations of warm affection and mutual esteem: George Washington "beg[ged]" Hamilton to "be assured" of his "sincere esteem & affectionate regard" while Thomas Jefferson extended "every wish" for Hamilton's "better health & happiness"; in return, Hamilton offered "perfect respect & sincerest regard" and "the most respectful consideration."[48] This "esteem" and "regard" did not, however, extend beyond a shared interest in the materials and techniques of gardening. Nor did it circulate among equals.

Throughout his correspondence with both men, Hamilton assumed a posture of deference. He was eager to please, to give, to send; Washington and Jefferson were happy to ask and content to receive. As early as 1784, for example, Washington remembered some of the cement work at Bush Hill and solicited Hamilton's thoughts on using cement to create a faux flagstone floor for the gallery at Mount Vernon. He wanted to know about its appearance, utility, and cost. He also requested detailed information about how, exactly, the stuff was mixed and where, specifically, the ingredients could be sourced. Abandoning the conventional apology or even a simple thanks, he concluded his letter by announcing "I will make no apology for the liberty I take by this request, as I persuade myself you will not think it much trouble to comply with it."[49] For his part, Jefferson never missed an opportunity to lodge a request with Hamilton. When he misplaced mimosa seeds that Hamilton had sent earlier, he simply wrote for another batch. When the name of a plant that Hamilton had offered to share "entirely escaped" him, he hoped that Hamilton would be able to recall it, for "this I would ask for next spring." Even when encouraging Hamilton to try the warm springs at Augusta to relieve his gout, he couldn't resist suggesting that the older man add on a visit to Monticello so that he could provide "lessons for the improvement" of its grounds.[50] In all cases, Hamilton's eager acquiescence to Washington's and Jefferson's requests was as deferential as it was gracious.

Yet the circumstances made for a curious form of deference. While early national elites continued to set great store by manners in general and politeness in particular, they had begun to deemphasize deference in favor of more egalitarian modes of courtesy, at least in their relations with one another. More to the point, in this particular set of exchanges, Hamilton was invariably the one dispensing the treasures. It was *his* greenhouse, *his* garden, *his* home that Washington and Jefferson sought to emulate. It was *his* expertise that was in demand. This interplay of deference and entitlement signals more than presidential prerogative. It gestures toward a broader set of political realities. For Washington and Jefferson, estates served as putative retreats from the burdensome world of public service. In fact, the worlds they created at Mount Vernon and Monticello were corollaries to their exercise of political power. The taste manifested in homes and gardens was one more register of virtuous discernment, one more register of political capacity. Their very need to retreat was itself a sign of virtue. Hamilton's estate was not his retreat from the world; it *was* his world. He exercised taste sans political aspiration. In other words, Washington and Jefferson were on a different footing than Hamilton not simply because they were politically powerful, but because they exercised power in a political realm in which Hamilton had no place. Their realm was the one that mattered, and Hamilton staked no claims to it.

Hamilton's radically depoliticized postrevolutionary persona is figured in the portrait that he commissioned of himself and his niece, Ann, from Benjamin West while they were in London. West did not complete the portrait until 1813, after Ann had died. When the finished painting finally arrived at The Woodlands, William hung it in the dining room, close to Wertmüller's portrait of his grandfather, Andrew Hamilton, and directly across the room from a portrait West had painted of James Hamilton in the 1760s. West's full-length paintings depict three generations of Hamiltons in the fantastic realm of grand manner glory. But there the similarities end.

West's portrait of James deployed the pictorial conventions of masculine command to signal Hamilton's political and economic clout. Here is a man accustomed to wielding power. His is the presentation of countless male sitters on both sides of the Atlantic in the eighteenth century. Like those other men, James stands alone. Unlike the vast majority of them, his singularity within the picture frame replicates his status as a lifelong bachelor, a *homme sole*. His expression is stern, even a bit belligerent. His wide stance, barrel chest, and ample stomach fully inhabit the middle of the canvas. His bearing telegraphs a message about male power that is amplified and extended by the props that surround him. The table that he fingers bequeaths him a proprietary air. The fluted column in the background and sword by his side confirm the very public nature of his authority. He is disconnected from his imaginary setting, which looks more like a collection of symbols than any real place. Nothing in the painting gestures toward Hamilton's keen interest in art, architecture, or litera-ture. He is a politician, not a connoisseur. At the height of his career, James Hamilton, a deeply cultured man celebrated for his eye, his patronage of the arts, and the rich material life he created for himself, chose to commemorate public power rather than private taste.[51]

If James Hamilton's portrait is about power, William and Ann's dual por-trait is about taste. Because West took so long to complete the painting, he ultimately repainted everything save the sitters' faces, making it impossible to know now exactly what William had in mind when he commissioned the paint-ing. Yet a drawing completed for the original composition suggests that West did very little to change the painting's central elements: Ann, William, and the book-covered chest on which William leans. In the finished painting, the two figures are fully imbricated in an extraordinarily rich material world. They are embraced by draperies—by the curtain that cascades behind them, the heavy red cloth covering the chest that William lounges against, the silk shawl tossed over the neoclassical chair. In the distant background we glimpse a picturesque landscape—a reference, perhaps, to the garden Hamilton planned to create at The Woodlands. West's 1785 drawing reveals that the sheets of paper in Hamil-ton's hand are a size more appropriate for plans and drawings than writing. Given Hamilton's intentions for The Woodlands, it is easy to imagine that they are meant to convey an architect's plan or a map of the estate. Unlike his uncle, William is portrayed as a connoisseur, as a man of taste.

In keeping with late eighteenth-century dual and group portraits on both sides of the Atlantic, the finished portrait is intimate, even domestic. Standing alongside his niece, *this* lifelong bachelor is pictured as a family man as well as a connoisseur. Ann reaches toward her uncle with both hands, a rare posture among West's sitters, and gazes toward his books, eager to learn from him. It is her bid for consideration, her need for guidance, that conspires to draw William away from the books and art that have hitherto absorbed his attention. With

Figure 16. Benjamin West, portrait of James Hamilton (ca. 1710–1783), from life, 1767.
Oil on canvas. Courtesy of Independence National Historical Park.

Figure 17. Benjamin West, sketch of William Hamilton and his niece Anna Hamilton of Philadelphia, 1785. Chalk on paper. © Trustees of the British Museum.

her brilliant white dress and shimmering gold wrap, she literally outshines her uncle. She becomes the immediate object of viewers' attention, precisely replicating Ann's role in William's polite performances with the Adamses while the two were in London. Indeed, it falls to Ann to embody the classical world that provided revolutionary and early national Americans with so many of the metaphors and symbols of virtuous publicity. In her empire gown, she serves as a kind of human column, countering the neoclassical column that symbolizes political power in James Hamilton's portrait. William, captivated by culture on the one hand and his niece on the other, relinquishes any claim to public power.[52] In art as in life, culture served as William Hamilton's bulwark against politics.

The Public Life of a Private Estate

William Hamilton's hospitality and horticulture begat publicity. Publicity gave the estate a life of its own. His roster of invited guests expanded early on to include American tourists and European notables. Thomas Cope took out-of-town guests on "excursions in the neighborhood," including The Woodlands, which provoked more "powerful attractions" than any other site. Rebecca Stoddert, the wife of the Secretary of the Navy, who was visiting Philadelphia from Annapolis, Maryland, declared that she was "determined to go to his House" and "see all that is worth seeing." A few years later, the botanist François André Michaux visited Philadelphia. "The absence of Mr. W. Hamilton deprived me of the pleasure of seeing him," he wrote. Undaunted, Michaux helped himself to a tour of the "magnificent garden," which had been the real aim of his visit all along. A decade after that, the ex-king Joseph Bonaparte made sure that his Philadelphia itinerary included The Woodlands. A visit to The Woodlands became de rigueur, so much so that when the twentieth-century antiquarian Harold Donaldson Eberlein wrote an early national travel diary as a hoax, he made sure his imaginary diarist spent time at Hamilton's estate.[53]

If word of mouth drew some visitors, others must have been attracted by the paintings, prints, written descriptions, and poetry that celebrated the estate almost from the time of its renovation in the late 1780s. Through the 1810s, The Woodlands was a popular subject for professional artists trying to drum up a U.S. market for landscapes similar to the market that flourished in England. Armed with aesthetic standards borrowed directly from the English picturesque canon, they were understandably attracted to The Woodlands, the closest approximation to an English picturesque estate in the United States. As a result, Hamilton's estate was featured in some of the earliest attempts to capture an American landscape. James Peller Malcolm, born in Pennsylvania and trained in England, painted the estate in watercolor in 1792 in order to include it as one of three country seats in a series of engraved prints devoted to Philadelphia. The next year, the English landscape artist William Groombridge (one of the central antagonists in the quarrels that ripped the Columbianum apart) depicted it in oil from a slightly different vantage point.[54] Despite this early notice, it fell to William Russell Birch to seal the estate's national reputation by including it among his engravings of villas. Birch's *Country Seats of the United States* imbued rural estates with civic significance by casting them as the perfect marriage of art and nature. Rural retirement, he wrote, afforded the physical and psychological space necessary to "form the National character favourable to the civilization of this young country, and establish that respectability which will add to its strength." The book's title page, which depicted not a residence but the unfinished U.S. Capitol dwarfed by a massive eagle clutching the national shield, drove the point home: The American country seat was a republican country seat. Birch assured his readers that where American country seats were concerned, money mattered less than taste; the benefits "consist more in the beauty of the situation," he wrote, "than in the massy magnitude of the edifice." The American environment, with its "Precipes and Crags," "Cataracts and Rivers," provided raw materials that could be refined by almost anyone with an eye for landscape. And indeed, in the pages that followed, Birch praised the nation's estate builders for their ability to seize upon "elegant," "pastoral," "sylvan," "handsome," even "visionary" sites when they constructed their estates.

Of the eighteen villas he selected for his collection, only The Woodlands was as notable for art as it was for nature. Certainly, the estate was "charmingly situated," with "superb" water views. But that was not the half of it. The estate grounds were "laid out in good taste"; the hothouse and greenhouse were "perhaps unequalled in the United States"; "Paintings &c. of the first master" embellished the interior. The Woodlands seamlessly combined "the beauties of art and the rarities of nature," bringing "credit to Mr. Wm. Hamilton, as a man of refined taste." *The Country Seats of the United States* never attained the success of Birch's previous print collection, *The City of Philadelphia*. Perhaps, as some art historians have suggested, the topic smacked of an elitism that was hard to market to middle-class buyers. Perhaps the problem was that American buyers had not yet developed a taste for landscape art. But even as Birch's book died a slow death, his depiction of The Woodlands gained a new lease on life in the 1820s, when it was transferred onto Staffordshire pottery and porcelain vases commemorating Philadelphia's historic homes.[55]

Around the same time that artists were calling attention to The Woodlands, it began to figure in the period's literary culture, courtesy of writers attracted to

Figure 18. William Groombridge (British, 1748–1811), *The Woodlands, the Seat of William Hamilton, Esq.*, 1793. Oil on canvas. Santa Barbara Museum of Art, Gift of Mrs. Sterling Morton for the Preston Morton Collection 1960.58.

Figure 19. Detail, *The Woodlands, the Seat of William Hamilton, Esq.*, depicting Hamilton's villa.

Woodlands *the Seat of* Mr. Wm. Hamilton *Pennsylv.a*

Drawn, Engraved & Published by W. Birch, Springland near Bristol, Pennsylvan.a

Figure 20. "Woodlands, the seat of Mr. Wm. Hamilton." From William Russell Birch, *The Country Seats of the United States of North America* (Springland, PA: designed and published by W. Birch, 1808–1809). Courtesy, The Winterthur Library: Printed Book and Periodical Collection.

its picturesque aesthetic. The year after Birch began to publish his views, the *Port Folio* published accounts of The Woodlands in verse and prose. In "The Woodlands," a poet who signed herself "Laura" described passing through the "gay confusion" and the "profusely scattered" treasures that "gladden'd" her eye. Then, "Led on by Fancy's secret, magic call" she entered the house, where her eyes were "raptur'd" by the "charms" and "beauties" Hamilton had assembled. She imagined that the art-filled interior was a "living canvas" whose very walls could speak.[56] Later that year, editor Joseph Dennie gave readers his own extended description of the estate. Warning that any "adequate" account of The Woodlands demanded that the "powers of genius should be united with the ardour of enthusiasm," he cataloged the "excellent," "exquisite," "masterly," and "admirable" highlights of Hamilton's art collection. He escorted his armchair tourists to the saloon, to look out over the "verdant mead" toward the Schuylkill, with its "waves here checked by the projecting rock, there overshadowed by luxurious trees."[57] More than a decade later, after removing to the "wilds" of Kentucky, the poet and landscape painter George Beck wistfully recalled The Woodlands, which he had painted at Hamilton's request in the

Figure 21. Vase depicting The Woodlands. Made by Tucker Factory, Philadelphia, ca. 1827. Glazed porcelain with enamel and gilt decoration, 8½ × 8¼ in. Philadelphia Museum of Art: Gift of Miss Mary Lea Perot, 1958.

1810s. Beck's landscape has long since disappeared. But his memory of the estate survives in verse. Transporting himself back to the Schuylkill, he conjured "those domes so dear to every feeling muse/What tears of joy my streaming eyes suffuse!" Like "Laura" and Dennie before him, the narrator ascends the hill and enters the house, where he is overcome by the "bright gems" that "round the mansion blaze!" The picturesque aesthetic of the estate's vistas, which frame "hills, dales, streams, and undulating lines," is replicated within the grounds. Art and nature invite the "wanderer" to lose himself, turning "round and round" as he makes his way through the "labyrinth" carved out by the paths.[58]

It was no accident that artists' depictions of The Woodlands generally included spectators or that poets invited their readers to "see" the estate through their words. The Woodlands was a vehicle for a particular kind of looking, one designed to turn perception into pleasure. The winding paths, the clustered trees and shrubs, the movement from shady enclosure to dazzling sunlight were calculated to evoke the physical and psychological responses associated with the picturesque. Inside the house, the curving walls and the angled passageways created a sense of movement. Niches filled with statuary and walls covered in paintings suggested that the house itself was constructed out of art. The mirrors played with light and perception. Stacks of botanical drawings depicted the plants in the greenhouse, allowing comparisons and inviting consideration of the accuracy, aesthetics, and aims of representation. The enormous windows, which opened onto the gardens and grounds from all sides of the house, connected the beauty of art to the beauty of nature. The Woodlands was a monument to the fascination with the power and limits of visual perception that marked the long eighteenth century on both sides of the Atlantic.[59]

It was also a testament to the connections between the visual and the textual. Strolling the grounds, visitors and tourists found themselves in the same picturesque landscape that had been popularized by print culture.[60] They knew its stylistic conventions from essays like "On a Taste for the Picturesque" and the "Distinction Between the Beautiful and the Picturesque"; they understood something about its emotional resonance from the novels of Sir Walter Scott and Charles Brockden Brown, from travel narratives like "Sketch of a Summer Passage up the Ohio," and from poems like "Temple of the Muses."[61] As they studied Hamilton's dazzling art collection, the same women and men exercised their taste, exploring their responses to various styles and genres. This was exactly as promised by the authors of essays like "On Criticism and Genius," or "General Reflections on Taste," or the "Influence of Taste upon Manners."[62] At least some of these visitors experienced the collection as a vehicle for connoisseurship, for apprehending the stylistic differences between, say, the German and Italian schools of painting or for reflecting on the particular merits of a West or a Wertmüller. This connoisseurship, itself a form of recognition, may have been grounded in exposure to paintings and prints, but it was also facilitated by published essays exploring precisely these topics.[63]

Art and architectural historians have suggested that novelty and scale accounted for The Woodlands' prominence in the early republic. But contemporary accounts hardly reel from the shock of the new. Instead, they smack of recognition; they suggest the satisfaction of the familiar. And why not? The many women and men who visited the estate had been primed for the pleasures of looking by an expansive print culture and by the increasing circulation of prints and paintings, although the latter is far more difficult to document with any precision.

The pleasures afforded in the linked processes of looking and reading were recapitulated in writing and in the far more elusive process of imagining. Consider a letter written by a young woman we know only as L.G., intended for her sister, following a visit to The Woodlands. She described the landscape in the language that echoed picturesque precepts for organizing landscape. Touring the house, she noticed that "the prospect from every room is enchanting." Looking out from the piazza, she understood how her view had been structured to move from the "windings of the Schuylkill" to the "blue mist of the Jersey shore." Walking through the grounds, she recognized that the Lombardy poplars enclosing the path were punctuated "here & there" by openings "to give you a view of some fine trees or beautiful prospect beyond." Exploring the estate in full daylight, she realized that the appearance of everything she saw would shift as the sun and moon moved across the sky. "It would take several days" of observing the "various beauties" at "different hours of the day and particularly at moon-light" to really know the place, she wrote. Retracing her progress through the grounds and house and describing all that she had seen, L.G. conceded that she had only glimpsed The Woodlands. Nevertheless, she wrote, "Such [knowledge] as I have I will venture to give to you & though you may not be able from my description to form an exact picture of [the estate], still you will have room to exercise your imagination & supply the deficiencies." For L.G. and her sister, The Woodlands was remarkable not because it was big or because it was unique, but because it mobilized the myriad associations that embedded looking, recalling, writing, and reading in subjectivity.[64] The estate encouraged the habits of looking and writing, reading and imagining, that offered some Americans the chance to transform themselves into the aesthetic subjects posited by philosophers like Lord Kames or David Hume and critics like Joseph Addison. In return, those aesthetic subjects granted The Woodlands a place in national culture.

Requiem for a Loyalist

Through the alchemy of reproduction and re-circulation—in text and image, in print and in private—The Woodlands emerged as an exemplar of republican taste credited with, in Birch's words, "form[ing] the National character" demanded by American "civilization." Eventually, it became the sort of historic house that located the nation's origins in old families and genteel traditions.[65] That alchemy worked some of its magic on Hamilton, too. When he died in 1813, newspapers in Philadelphia, New York, and Boston celebrated him as a man of good taste, affable manners, frank hospitality, and a "very general knowledge of botany."[66] He may not have been hailed as a patriot or even as a citizen, but his loyalist past had all but disappeared. The Anglo-American politics of taste had papered over the acid politics of Revolution.

Or had they?

In the spring of 1800, William Hamilton had had an especially awkward conversation with Thomas Jefferson. Hamilton gently reminded him of a snub he had suffered at Jefferson's hands several years earlier. Ever deferential, he tried to make amends for whatever he had once done to offend the newly elected president. In the moment, standing next to Hamilton at Hamilton's estate, Jefferson could not—perhaps would not—understand the reference. But safely ensconced back at John Francis's Hotel, where he was staying before moving to Washington City, Jefferson's memory refreshed itself.

The letter he wrote to assuage Hamilton's anxiety is revealing. The "appearance of neglect" took place in 1797, Jefferson recalled. He had been in Philadelphia serving as John Adams's vice president, no easy task given their political differences. To negotiate the treacherous sociability engendered by partisan feuding, Jefferson opted to stand on the ceremony of the first visit "to sift out those who chose a separation" from him and his party; he refrained, in other words, from calling on individuals until they had favored him with a call. Hamilton apparently failed to venture into the city to see Jefferson. As a consequence, Jefferson failed to visit The Woodlands or to acknowledge Hamilton in any way. This, he assured Hamilton, was political business rather than personal inclination. Hamilton had not offended him in 1797 or at any point since. No fences needed mending because none had been broken. More than that: Jefferson volunteered that *he* never took personally the "differences of opinion" that culminated in the Revolution. "During the whole of the last war," Jefferson insisted, "I never deserted a friend because he had taken the opposite side; and those of my state who joined the British government can attest my unremitting zeal in saving their property." Indeed, the two estate builders shared "so many agreeable points in which" they were "in perfect unison" that Jefferson was "at no loss to find of justification" of his "constant esteem" for Hamilton. To demonstrate once and for all that nothing had changed between them, Jefferson concluded the letter by asking if Hamilton's botanical collection included a *Dionaea muscipula*, a Venus flytrap. If it did, and if the specimen produced seeds, Jefferson wrote, "I should be very much disposed to trespass on your liberality so far as to ask a few seeds of that."[67] Presumably the request for a carnivorous plant signaled the return to business as usual between the two gentlemen gardeners.

If this was how loyalism figured as late as 1800—only half forgotten, still half visible—we would do well to return to the language that guests, tourists, and writers used again and again to describe the visual pleasures that could be obtained at The Woodlands: "Entranced" and "bewildered" eyes struggle to make terms of the "gay confusion." Circuitous paths pull wanderers "round and round" until they are "lost." Mirrors trick the mind, blurring the boundary between interior and exterior or extending interior space into infinity. Small cabinets hold treasures that may or may not be revealed. Shocking paintings hide behind curtains. At The Woodlands, visitors encountered deception, concealment, and disclosure. This logic of perception and misperception—a logic that structured visuality at The Woodlands, a logic that structured so much of early national literary culture—mirrored the social and cultural experiences of loyalist subjects who became republican citizens. It also mirrored the ways that early national citizens obscured the political choices that divided Anglo-Americans in the revolutionary period in order to foster the myth of republican unanimity. Jefferson's letter reminds us, as it surely reminded Hamilton, that loyalism might recede into the deep background but—like the proverbial elephant in the room—it never really disappeared.

Certainly Hamilton's political past was no secret to the Europeans who traveled through the United States in the decades following the Revolution and who published accounts of what they saw. The Polish patriot Julian Ursyn Niemcewicz, who had described The Woodlands as the "villa Borghese," tartly remarked that "in the time of the Revolution" Hamilton "took the side of the English. He narrowly missed being hung for this fine loyalty." The enlightened French aristocrat François Alexandre Frédéric, duc de La Rochefoucauld-Liancourt, who praised Hamilton as a "chearful man, a most excellent companion" and "in every respect the gentleman," also casually observed that "during the war" he had trouble collecting his rents because "Mr. Hamilton, along with the family of the Penns, belong[ed] to the Tory party."[68] European observers like Rochefoucauld-Liancourt and Niemcewicz had no reason to suppress Hamilton's Tory history. Neither they nor their continental readers had any stakes in the dusty political pasts of the influential citizens they met during their travels.

Those influential citizens, in contrast, had every reason to suppress this dimension of their collective history, regardless of their former allegiances.[69] Tories who chose to remain in the United States following the war were understandably careful not to trumpet their antirevolutionary commitments—they were on the losing side of a long and bloody war. Violence during the Revolution itself had been endemic; violent retributions against Tories in the immediate postwar period were hardly uncommon. Many loyalists suffered property confiscation during the war and after. Many more believed their property to be at risk as state governments decided how to handle loyalist populations.[70] To be sure, any number of loyalists fought successfully for their property rights in the courts in the decades following the Revolution. Still, discretion must have seemed the better part of wisdom while they rebuilt their lives cheek by jowl with their one-time enemies. William Hamilton, for one, worked hard to bury his political past. And small wonder. His place in Philadelphia society—his status as a gentleman—depended on the willingness of men like Washington and Jefferson to accept him back into the charmed circle of cosmopolitan elites. But wealthy and politically powerful patriots also had good reason to welcome men like Hamilton back into the fold. For one thing, the United States could not afford to squander the wealth and expertise of educated, wealthy Tories any more than it could afford to squander its economic relationship with Great Britain. Then, too, the United States' reputation as an honorable nation depended on the states' compliance with the Treaty of Paris, which sought to protect the political and economic rights of former loyalists. Finally, republican ideology still carried with it the imperative of unanimity and the fear of faction. Rapid reintegration facilitated the fiction that Anglo-Americans had been united in their patriotism.[71] There was, in other words, enormous incentive for Jefferson and Hamilton to push their "differences of opinion" into the background in the service of what historians glibly term "reintegration."

To say that reintegration benefited both patriots and loyalists is not to say that it was easy. Hamilton's reintegration demanded equal parts willed blindness and mindful effacement. His exchange with Jefferson in 1800, suffused as it was with anxiety and overcompensation, suggests something about the energy required to maintain that balance. William Hamilton is surely a poor candidate for a loyalist everyman. But he nonetheless provides an opportunity to consider both the range of strategies available to loyalists who chose to remain in the United States after the war and also the psychic costs exacted by successful reintegration.[72]

Judging by the near invisibility of Hamilton's loyalism in the historical record, his was a successful reintegration indeed. His unfortunate political commitments were obviously the object of Philadelphia gossip into the 1790s and beyond, for how else would European travelers have known about his indiscretions? But Hamilton's peers stopped short of writing down the history they whispered to foreigners. The William Hamilton who is refracted in the letters, diaries, and memoirs of Philadelphia's first families in the years following his return from England is merely a host, a gardener, a gentleman of unsurpassed taste. He is not a former Tory. He is, instead, the connoisseur captured on canvas by Benjamin West. Following the lead of early national Philadelphians, the scholars who have written about Hamilton and The Woodlands have likewise marginalized his loyalism. In their telling, revolutionary politics is incidental to estate building.[73]

And what of that estate itself? The Woodlands was unequivocally and unapologetically English. Having declared "England as a country" to be an "Elysium," Hamilton pledged to "give The Woodlands some resemblance of it." If "god grants me a safe return to my own country," he vowed in 1785, he would "endeavour to make [The Woodlands] smile in the same useful & beautiful manner" as England.[74] It is hard not to read a rebuke in Hamilton's unabashed Anglophilia. His estate's triumphant Englishness would serve as an object lesson to the rebellious Pennsylvanians who had threatened his family, his property, and his life during the war. Surely the resentment and hard feelings of 1786 eased in the years that followed, softened and perhaps dissolved by the pleasures of gardening, art, conversation, and Madeira. Regardless of Hamilton's reintegration into the American republic and his reinstatement to Philadelphia's beau monde, there is no reason to think that he wavered in his passion for a distinctly *English* rural retirement. On the contrary. He devoted his life to realizing it both inside the house and out.

Not so the many visitors who flocked to The Woodlands during the early national period. They looked for ways to cast the estate as an *American* triumph, as the product of American independence. Birch was not the only admirer to link the estate to "National character." Jefferson also sought to place The Woodlands at the center of a nationalist narrative. Although he admired it enormously, he wrestled with its Englishness in ways that recapitulated Anglo-Americans' postrevolutionary attempts to distinguish themselves from England by valorizing their culture at British expense. In 1806, for example, he praised Hamilton's "taste" for making The Woodlands "the only rival which I have known in America to what may be seen in England," conceding that "thither without doubt we are to go for models in this art." At the same time, it offered assurance that America's aesthetic subordination was neither natural nor eternal. By casting the estate as a "rival," as a competitor on a world stage, Jefferson echoed assumptions that had undergirded a nationalist vision of culture at least since Philip Freneau and Hugh Henry Brackenridge penned "The Rising Glory of America."[75] This was not an isolated remark. Several years later, Jefferson hailed The Woodlands as "the chastest model of gardening I have ever seen outside of England." It was a freighted adjective. By 1809, "chaste" was a word that had acquired impeccable republican credentials. During the Revolution, patriots appropriated it from the eighteenth-century British aesthetic lexicon and invested it with explicitly republican significance. For them, "chaste" meant more than stylistic purity; it signaled the virtuous purity of the republican aesthetic and the republican project more generally. Through the federal era, the word "chaste" made regular appearances in the correspondence of the founders, where it continued to signify in a distinctly republican mode. Jefferson himself invoked it to describe everything from oratory to architecture to parliamentary procedure to the reduction of military expenditures to carriage decoration. In describing The Woodlands as "chaste," then, Jefferson situated the estate within an eighteenth-century rhetoric that pitted haughty aristocrat against earnest republican, decadent luxury against virtuous simplicity.[76]

However fictive, such oppositions were central to the postrevolutionary attempt to imagine an explicitly American republic of taste and to define an explicitly American culture. Brought to bear on manners and materiel, they encouraged affluent and even middling Americans to endorse certain objects, styles, and forms of consumption as extensions of individual virtue and markers of national progress. This neat trick resolved the contradiction between the imperatives of republicanism and the temptations of refinement, as Richard Bushman has argued. But celebrating a constellation of objects as manifestations of virtue also deflected attention away from their status as commodities. More to the point, it deflected attention away from their status as commodities that were, more often than not, imported from Great Britain. Such was the case with Hamilton's estate. Indoors and out, The Woodlands was fabricated from British commodities. It was not merely patterned after English gardens. It was full of English plants and trees. It had been nurtured and maintained by the expertise of British gardeners. And although Jefferson kept pointedly silent on Hamilton's house, the "chaste" garden and grounds were designed as a deliberate complement to the Adamesque mansion and its opulent, imported furnishings.[77]

Far from being incidental to The Woodlands, politics—the cultural politics of the Revolution—was central to its creation and to its reception. Where Hamilton aspired to a "resemblance" that would pull his home closer to an English ideal that war and fortune had placed beyond his reach, Jefferson imagined a nationalist "rivalry" among gardens, a contest in which a virtuous young challenger might unseat an old and weary champion. Where Hamilton reveled in the estate's exuberant, imported-from-England materiality, Jefferson idealized it as a manifestation of abstract principles. These perspectives surely speak to the differences between the two men's ideological commitments and aesthetic inclinations, to say nothing of their political histories. But the differences also suggest something about the persistence of the English past into an American present and about the problems that plagued attempts to fashion an American republic of taste.

It was not for nothing that Birch, extolling The Woodlands as the kind of place that should "form National character," described it as a "noble demesne." The curious formulation that casts a "noble demesne" as the cradle of republican culture gestures toward the multiplicity of political and cultural perspectives that obtained in the unsettled decades following the Revolution. Historians of the early republic have become accustomed to looking for that multiplicity between political factions, or among people whose race, gender, and class excluded them from the full benefits of American independence, which is to say that they have become accustomed to looking for it in terms that validate and valorize the process of nation making. Withal, they have been far less interested in considering the sort of multiplicity suggested by The Woodlands, an estate built after the Revolution that served both as a monument to one man's Anglophilia and as a vehicle for effacing his loyalist past, an estate that was celebrated precisely because it spelled American taste and national refinement. But The Woodlands reminds us that loyalists were not expelled from the nation's borders when the Treaty of Paris was signed. It reminds us of the persistence of Anglophilia and Anglicization into the early national era. As an estate—a collection of buildings, gardens, and artifacts—it testifies to a narrative of contingent nationalism that is largely absent from local letters and diaries. Just as important, The Woodlands, together with the relationships it engendered and the images and texts it inspired, helps us recover the dialectic of remembering and forgetting upon which the nation depended.

CHAPTER FOUR

CHAPTER FIVE

Waxing Political

Imagine that you are in the center of a large room. High ceilings. Tall windows. In front of you sits John Adams, the second president of the United States, double chin resting gently on his collar. Nearby, stately George Washington stands head and shoulders above two young women dressed as personifications of Peace and Plenty. It isn't clear what they are doing here. Perhaps they have come to socialize, for nearby there is a small tea party under way. Three fashionable young ladies, attended by a slave, sip from delicate china cups. But before you can learn whether the presidents are planning to join the party, you are distracted by a terrible sight on the opposite side of the room. The king of France is preparing to die. His wife and children are beset with grief. The Dauphin clings to his father, unwilling to release him to the glinting blade of the guillotine. You turn away from this scene only to confront an Indian warrior advancing toward you, brandishing a tomahawk and a scalp still wet with blood. Behind him is an old woman whipping a small black boy who is powerless to protect himself from the lash. A handful of beautiful women, dressed in the finest silk fashions, smile flirtatiously at the boy and his mistress. Or maybe they are hoping to attract the attention of two bare-chested boxers who circle one another, fists raised.

What dreamscape have you entered? What strange amalgam of history and hallucination appears before you? The year is 1798. You are in Boston's Columbian Museum, surrounded by wax statues.[1]

Figures like the ones you have just conjured were prominent features of the early republic's most distinguished museums and its most obscure traveling shows. They afforded paying spectators "very exact" representations of the nation's founders and statesmen, "large as life" and "elegantly drest." Sometimes these men stood alone; sometimes they appeared in tableaux. Withal, they embodied the nation's brief history, its singular virtues, and its providential destiny. But as this imaginary tour suggests, the figures assumed their roles in a complex visual and spatial field. The usual suspects in the republican pantheon stood cheek and jowl with exotics and curiosities. They were accompanied by Indians, dwarfs, and "beauties," by Chinese "mandarins," English boxers, and beheaded criminals.

With the exception of the attention that has been lavished on Charles Willson Peale's famous Philadelphia Museum, scholars have been slow to explore early national museums like the ones founded by Gardiner Baker, Joseph Steward, and Daniel Bowen in the late eighteenth century or by Ethan Allan Greenwood some twenty years later.[2] They have all but ignored the wax figures that formed such a prominent part of those collections. The invisibility of wax figures surely owes much to their transience. For obvious reasons, they lack the shelf life of other museum artifacts, like paintings, arrowheads, fossils, and even stuffed birds.[3] They appear only in shadow form, in the written record: newspaper accounts, advertisements, museum ledgers, the letters and memoirs of wax sculptors and museum owners, and, very occasionally, the comments of spectators. But these statues are also invisible to contemporary eyes because they have no analogue in our art galleries and natural history museums; they suggest the kitsch and carnival of Madame Tussaud's rather than the stuff of serious criticism and sustained inquiry.[4] Just as important, displays that embedded emblems of decorous nationalism in illustrations of savagery and sensationalism have little place in our understanding of early national political culture or the republican project more generally.

However ephemeral they may have been and however incongruous they may now seem, waxworks *were* intended to further the republican project, especially when they were displayed in museums. Museums represented taste and knowledge, bound together by reason. Heirs to the enlightenment science of the eighteenth century, which had not yet segregated human from nonhuman sciences, they displayed both the man-made world and the natural one.[5] On both sides of the Atlantic, the mindfully assembled, painstakingly cataloged collections of images, objects, and artifacts they contained promised to enlighten and improve an extensive public, eager for knowledge. In the early American republic, especially, museums were touted for fostering particular modes of dispassionate and systematic observation; these modes of seeing were, in turn, closely connected to equally dispassionate and systematic modes of reading. As institutions that connected the right kind of looking to the right kind of reading, museums promised to create an educated and rational citizenry, to nurture the precise form of subjectivity demanded by a republic. Not surprisingly, perhaps, these ambitions were extraordinarily difficult to realize; they were regularly undermined by factors ranging from spatial constraints to the public's desire for novelty. Translating philosophical abstractions into particular objects and experience proved to be no mean feat. What early national museums failed to accomplish, however, is far less revealing than what they did accomplish. The great majority of actual museums, in distinction to idealized ones, ultimately demanded forms of looking and reading that flew in the face of republican protocols. They encouraged forms of subjectivity and gestured toward a political imaginary that undermined republican pieties as often as they reinforced them.

The Republic in Miniature

In theory, museums were calculated to play an obvious and straightforward role in the early republic. The fictional character Lucy Sumner, the virtuous foil for the infamous coquette Eliza Wharton, never tired of the "rational and refined amusement" she enjoyed at Daniel Bowen's Columbian Museum. In *The Coquette*, the nation's first best-selling novel, she famously summed up its salutary effects in this way: "The eye is gratified, imagination charmed, and the understanding improved."[6] Sumner's visits to the museum served as an alternative, and a reproach, to the more dissipated entertainments that helped lead her friend astray. Far from compromising virtue, they inculcated it.

Early national museum proprietors were quick to capitalize on this kind of sentiment, emphasizing the significance of their enterprises in broadly political terms and, especially, by tethering knowledge to nationalism. Throughout the early national period, they provided special entertainments to commemorate Independence Day, George Washington's birthday, and, after 1799, his death. Daniel Bowen, for example, marked Washington's birthday and later his death with specially penned orations at the Columbian Museum; on July 4th, he kept the museum elegantly illuminated and introduced patriotic statues like a female personification of Liberty. In New York City, the American Museum marked the "glorious anniversary" of independence with music and special, "splendidly illuminated" evening hours. Proprietors went out of their way to encourage the patronage of prominent citizens, elected officials, and visiting dignitaries.[7] Always attractive, this kind of patronage became even more desirable when it coincided with a civic holiday. Thus Ethan Allen Greenwood spent much of February 1822 coaxing Massachusetts politicians to his gala for Washington's birthday. He was gratified to see that "the Gov'r, Lt. Gov'r & many members of both branches of the Legislature" were counted among the eight hundred who turned out. By publicizing their involvement with nationalist celebrations and their popularity with leading citizens in the press, proprietors sought to imbue their museums with civic importance in the eyes of the public at large. The strategy seems to have worked: The "fullest house" Greenwood attracted during his first year in business came on July 4th, when he kept the museum open at night to show off illuminated transparencies of U.S. naval victories.[8]

The conviction that museums served the republic was more than proprietors' puffery. Just as they offered limited assistance to academies, state and local governments (at least in the North) often helped museums secure some form of subvention. To be sure, American museums never approached the level of patronage attained by comparable European institutions, a fact that Peale, for one, never tired of rehearsing. Nevertheless, local and state governments agreed that museums served and promoted the public interest. Although they did not provide cash outright, they often granted proprietors prominent exhibition space at reduced rates. Consider, for example, the striking number of museums that were housed within state buildings. New York City's American Museum, founded by the Society of St. Tammany and operated and later owned by Gardiner Baker, was granted space for a library and exhibition room in the Old City Hall that became available after Congress relocated to Philadelphia. In Philadelphia, the Supreme Executive Council provided Robert Edge Pine with a large room in the State House for the exhibition of his portraits. Joseph Steward's Hartford Museum was housed in the Connecticut State House for its first ten years; when Steward outgrew his State House quarters, he moved into a building that had once served as the governor's mansion.[9] And then, of course, there was Peale's Philadelphia Museum. Peale never received congressional funding; indeed, Peale was denied much of the "proper pecuniary aid" he sought. But in 1802, the Pennsylvania legislature granted him the use of Independence Hall in return for maintaining the building and grounds.[10] Precisely because early national museums were located in prominent public buildings acquired with government aid and because they so often served as the focal points of nationalist celebrations, they could assume an air of public importance. Site and spectacle helped underscore their role in the creation of an enlightened citizenry.

Reconstructing the broadly political agendas of museum proprietors is one thing; reconstructing museum visitors' responses is another. We know very little about how early national spectators viewed the contents of museums, especially the inevitable waxworks.[11] We can begin to recover their perspectives by situating the wax figures in a series of visual and cultural fields, exploring the constellation of associations that eighteenth- and early nineteenth-century viewers would have carried with them as they encountered the waxworks. Most obviously, wax displays resonated both with America's British heritage and history and with the political trajectory that culminated in independence. Like so many of the objects and texts that were eventually repurposed to symbolize the United States' political and cultural autonomy, waxworks were embedded in English culture: They numbered among the entertainments that fostered what English essayist Joseph Addison called the "pleasures of the imagination"; they played a role in the gentlemanly expansion of the natural sciences; and they figured in political spectacles ranging from the royal to the rough.[12]

Although it is not clear exactly when or how the enthusiasm for wax displays—much less the statues themselves—crossed the Atlantic, it makes sense to consider Americans' growing taste for waxworks as part of the Anglicization of colonial culture during the mid-eighteenth century. As early as the 1740s, accounts of English waxworks began to appear in colonial newspapers and magazines. Readers of Boston's *Evening Post*, for example, learned that the "Effigy of her late Majesty Queen Anne," eventually installed in Westminster Abbey, had been endorsed by a "great Number of the Nobility" as the "completest piece of the kind ever seen in Europe."[13] Aimed at giving far-flung provincials a sense of connection to metropolitan culture, these snippets effectively implied that waxworks were a notable part of that culture. Perhaps that is why Anglo-Americans traveling abroad made room for waxworks on their London itineraries. Katherine Greene Amory, a wealthy Bostonian, toured a "Wax Work in the Strand" in 1775 as part of a day-long expedition that included a visit to the Queen's elephants and dinner at the Swan. A decade later, while serving as minister to the Court of St. James, John Adams escorted his wife, Abigail, to the gallery operated by American émigré Patience Wright.[14] Like a stroll through Covent Garden or a trip to the theater, a visit to the waxworks was one more bit of British culture to be checked off a tour agenda.

Around the same time that colonial newspapers began taking note of British waxworks, impresarios began to bring traveling wax exhibitions through colonial cities. In 1756, Philadelphians lined up to view wax automatons that operated a clock; thirteen years later, they saw "the judgment of Paris on Mount Ida, when he assigned the golden apple to Venus," all modeled in wax. Visitors to New York City's Vauxhall Garden in 1770 were treated to seventy miniature wax figures depicting biblical and literary characters. The scattered advertisements for such entertainments have very little to say about who operated or attended them; it is all but impossible to do more than speculate on the various publics that these exhibitions created and catered to. That said, the waxworks that appeared in eighteenth-century America occupy one point along a cultural continuum that included itinerant theater companies and portrait painters. They served as one more register of the expansive appetite for markers of metropolitan culture that enticed entrepreneurial actors and artists to cross the Atlantic.[15]

Like plays and portraits, waxworks proved popular enough that a few Anglo-Americans began to consider sculpture and display as a viable source of financial support. Sisters Rachel Lovell Wells and Patience Lovell Wright provide the obvious examples. Almost nothing is known about their early lives. Patience later recounted that they learned the skills they would use as wax modelers by making figures out of bread dough. Certainly, their family connection to painter Robert Feke, a cousin by marriage, might have given them a far greater exposure to images and image making than they would otherwise have received. Whatever artistic aspirations the girls harbored were preempted by their marriages, Rachel to a Philadelphia shipwright and Patience to a Bordenton farmer. But by 1769 both sisters found themselves widowed—Patience with five children to support—and facing a precarious future. Perhaps inspired by Rachel's success making anatomical models for the Philadelphia Hospital, the middle-aged women launched careers as itinerant sculptors of wax portraits, moving up and down the eastern seaboard. They never managed to drum up a market for portraits of living adults or dead children, the subjects they deemed best suited for wax. Their touring exhibition, however, proved so successful that it ultimately supported two permanent exhibits. Wells's Philadelphia gallery specialized in biblical genre scenes like "the treachery of Delilah to Samson"; Wright's New York establishment, the precursor to her London gallery, was devoted to models of public figures such as George Whitefield and John Dickinson.[16]

Colonial waxworks served as more than mere entertainment. Wax anatomical models had much to offer Anglo-Americans who were intent on allying themselves with cosmopolitan medical and scientific practices. Modern anatomy had established itself as a "science of observation," dependent on its practitioners' close examination of the human body. But fresh cadavers, suitable for dissection, were not easy to come by, and rotting flesh was not pleasant to work with. Wax anatomical models provided anatomists and medical students with an alternative. The figures were placid, static, and richly aestheticized. They shielded viewers' sensibilities from the messy realities of death and decay. And the best of them bore an uncanny resemblance to fresh flesh. Indeed, as historian Joan B. Landes has observed, eighteenth-century anatomical mannequins, ornamented with human hair, glass eyes, and carefully tinted flesh, invited viewers to fantasize that they were peering into living bodies rather than carving up dead ones.[17]

By the 1770s, these models (often copied directly from British examples) were on regular display in Philadelphia, helping connect that city's forward-thinking men of letters to transatlantic, transnational communities dedicated to the pursuit of scientific knowledge. Dr. William Shippen Jr., generally credited with modernizing American anatomical education, supplemented his lectures

Figure 22. Patience Wright, life-size wax effigy of William Pitt, Earl of Chatham, 1779. Westminster Abbey. © The Dean and Chapter of Westminster.

and occasional dissections with drawings and wax figures imported from Europe. He also hired Rachel Wells, whom he regarded as "a great tho unimproved genius," to copy conjoined twins he had "preserved in spirits" as a gift for London's Royal Society.[18] Shippen's collection was exhibited for an exclusive public: medical students, university students, and men of affairs.

It fell to Abraham Chovet, however, to exploit wax models in demonstrations that fused science and spectacle for a paying public. An English surgeon who migrated to Jamaica and then fled to Philadelphia to escape a slave insurrection, Chovet was a founding member of Philadelphia's College of Physicians. He had relied on wax models of his own devising for academic lectures on both sides of the Atlantic, but in Philadelphia he also exhibited them commercially. Chovet's Anatomical Museum included any number of "physical rarities" and "curiosities," ranging from preserved cadavers, to diseased livers and lungs "preserved in wine of spirit," to a real skull filled with a wax brain. The biggest draw by far was a life-sized couple sculpted in wax. As one visitor explained in 1781, these marvels were "open in the middle," allowing a clear view of the organs and muscles. The viscera could be removed from the bodies for closer inspection. The woman was especially striking, for she was "8 months pregnant." He marveled at the "child in its natural position, with the umbilical cord twice wound round the neck." Probably modeled on the famous Venus figure at Florence's La Specola, Chovet's pregnant woman produced a "certain shock." It also produced a steady stream of customers, including the political leaders whose business drew them to Philadelphia. John Adams visited the museum while serving in the Continental Congress. A decade later, during the Constitutional Convention, George Washington took advantage of a July 4th recess to view "Doctr. Shovats Anatomical figures."[19]

If wax statues displayed in early national museums resonated with a century of Anglophilic cultural and scientific aspirations, they must also have recalled both the visual and material culture of Anglo-American politics. Wax statues of George Washington, Benjamin Franklin, and Ezra Stiles were the direct descendants of British royal effigies, which were in turn the distant descendants of ancient Roman funerary effigies. Initially, effigies of English kings and queens represented the deceased at their funerals. They simultaneously affirmed the ruler's power and confirmed his or her death for the populace. The figures gained some of their symbolic power and their compelling, unsettling verisimilitude from their proximity to royal bodies: The faces were often copied from death masks, the bodies were usually clothed in garments worn by the deceased, and the completed figures were positioned atop coffins during funeral processions. An effigy's ritual significance during the funeral was transformed into commercial opportunity afterward: Once the royal corpse was interred at

Westminster Abbey, its effigy remained on display to a paying public for an indefinite amount of time. Even after effigies lost their places in state-sponsored funerals, they retained a notable position in the public's experience of royal death. By the turn of the eighteenth century, the thoroughly commercialized manufacture and display of royal effigies were part and parcel of a trade in souvenirs and shows that flourished whenever a member of the royal family died.[20]

In the Anglo-American colonies, royal effigies played a different role, one that had less to do with marking the legitimate transition of royal power from one person to another than with affirming the vitality of royal power writ large. Indebted to (and dependent on) a Protestant monarchy that promised protection from the twin threats posed by Catholicism and the French, colonists developed a deep affection for the Crown, particularly after the ascension of the Hanoverian line. This warm, and warmly personal, attachment was encouraged by the effigies of the royal family that began to appear in colonial cities like Boston, New York, and Charleston in the mid-eighteenth century. Like the formal and officially sanctioned monarchical portraits that hung in public buildings, these wax kings and queens reinforced the royalization of colonial politics. Wax figures "exactly as big as Life" and "dressed in Royal Robes, in the same Manner as when sitting in the Parliament House," encouraged colonists to imagine that imperial politics was structured by personal relationships and loving identification, deepening what historian Brendan McConville has aptly called the "passions of empire."[21]

During and immediately after the Revolution, rebellious colonists put English rituals that personified political animosities and loyalties to new ends. In England, rude effigies of unpopular figures had long figured in popular politics; reportage about protests that included effigies regularly turned up in Anglo-American newspapers. For their part, colonists had routinely mocked and destroyed effigies of the Pope to celebrate Pope's Day. As the Imperial Crisis intensified, some colonists shifted the focus of their hostility away from the Pope toward individuals who embodied the worst evils of the British Empire: stamp collectors, colonial administrators, royal advisors (George Grenville and Lord Bute were special favorites), and finally the king himself. Like earlier effigies on both sides of the Atlantic, these villains were insulted and abused, hanged and beheaded. And like effigies of the Pope, they were sometimes paired with the devil. But where effigies of the Pope seem to have been comically grotesque, effigies of at least some Tories bore an unnerving resemblance to the originals. Especially when the original remained in the vicinity, the goal was intimidation and terror on an immediate and local level. John Mein, bookseller and publisher of the *Boston Chronicle*, famously fled Boston when locals substituted his effigy, clearly identified as such, for the traditional Pope on Pope's Day in 1769. In Philadelphia, Peale reported seeing an effigy whose "face was a well-made mask which was generally believed to resemble" its target, so much so that the subject "left town Secretly."[22]

A Republican Pantheon in Wax

The wax Washingtons, Adamses, and Franklins that appeared in galleries and museums in the years following the Revolution were thus local variations on a long and complicated transatlantic theme. Embedded in a specific Anglo-American history, they simultaneously harkened back to state-sponsored and state-sanctioned representations of royalty and to the personification of politics that galvanized patriot fervor during the Revolution. Yet waxworks also took on a new and explicitly republican significance in the early republic. Commemorating worthies who had either helped secure American independence or who embodied American virtue, they pursued the same aims as countless pantheons that appeared around the same time.

Early national pantheons took multiple forms, as art historian Brandon Brame Fortune has demonstrated. Some, like Joel Barlow's epic poem "Columbiad," which embedded cameos of exemplary Americans in a paean to America's millennial destiny, were constructed of words alone. Others, like Joseph Delaplaine's beautifully illustrated *Repository of the Lives and Portraits of Distinguished Americans*, used engraved portraits to illustrate biographical sketches. Many more were explicitly pictorial. The best known of these pictorial pantheons—Charles Willson Peale's Gallery of Distinguished Personages in Philadelphia or John Trumbull's portrait series for City Hall in New York and City Hall Council Chamber in Charleston—were designed to be mounted and viewed in public spaces. Others—notably Edward Savage's mezzotint portrait series—were meant for private consumption. Regardless of the form they took, republican pantheons inevitably included tributes to revolutionary heroes George Washington, Thomas Jefferson, John Adams, and Benjamin Franklin, along with a range of lesser characters ranging from generals to intellectuals.[23]

Whether they were assembled out of words, images, or both, republican pantheons gathered together men who were conspicuous for their talent, accomplishments, and virtue and enshrined them within the Temple of Fame, a conceit that invoked the iconography and architecture of both the classical world and Georgian England. These collective portraits provided the nation's most distinguished citizens with a form of honor that did not smack of overweening ambition. They also offered posterity a picture of the "characters and actions" that founded the nation. Most important, they provided ordinary citizens with models for emulation. As one writer enthused, to attain the "dignities of America" and "command the admiration of a world," a youth need only "look to a FRANKLIN, an ADAMS, and a long list of worthies." Like biographies, likenesses could serve as a spark for emulation. Charles Willson Peale was explicit on this point: His Gallery of Distinguished Personages would benefit the republic by "instruct[ing] the mind and sow[ing] the seed of virtue." Hence the importance of the pantheon's publicity. Although some collections—like Thomas Jefferson's "principal American characters"—were privately assembled and displayed, most were created in order to render history and virtue legible for public edification. Simultaneously representing men as individuals and as types, pantheons thus commemorated "republican character" in both senses of the term: They documented the accomplishments of republican "characters" like statesmen, intellectuals, generals, and divines, and they provided ordinary citizens with examples of republican "character," of intellect and morality.[24]

Modelers and museum operators took great care to align the iconographic conventions associated with and elaborated by the republican pantheon with their wax founders. Likenesses were identifiable as particular characters because of their resemblance to their originals (or, more accurately, to portraits of their originals). They further communicated the aspects of republican character they were meant to represent through stock iconographic accoutrements. Daniel Bowen, for example, positioned John Adams in the Temple of Fame, flanked by Liberty, complete with staff and cap, and by Justice, holding sword and scales. His Washington stood with Peace and Plenty. Bowen's rendition of Peace carried an olive branch; his Plenty held the requisite cornucopia. This visual vocabulary, borrowed directly from classical and European traditions, was initially popularized through engraved prints. Well before the turn of the nineteenth century, it was thoroughly conventionalized in multiple media. Its motifs worked their way onto crockery, textiles, and countless other commodities manufactured on both sides of the Atlantic; the same emblems also decorated images and objects manufactured within households for private consumption. Taken together, ceramic pitchers, damask bed hangings, and schoolgirl samplers promised to graft the lofty ideals of the Revolution and the elevated symbols of the pantheon onto everyday life.[25] When women and men viewed a wax Washington or Franklin, then, they encountered a familiar, two-dimensional representation stripped off of china, canvas, or paper and reconstituted in three dimensions. Museum waxworks thus served as one more declaration of republican virtue, one more assertion of national character in a crowded field.

Figure 23. Apotheosis of Franklin and Washington printed bed curtain, 1785. It was made in Britain and used in America. Linen and cotton, plate printed. The Colonial Williamsburg Foundation. Museum Purchase.

The Medium and the Messages

Yet in spite of everything that museum operators and wax sculptors did to incorporate their figures into the republican pantheon, the fit was always a bit awkward. In all kinds of ways, wax was not well suited for figuring an emissary from the Temple of Fame. For one thing, the very qualities that made wax distinctive—its singularly fleshlike appearance and texture—could summon multiple and contradictory associations, distracting viewers from the individuals, ideas, or narratives the statues were intended to convey. Certainly, Anglo-American aesthetic theory, which cast such a long shadow over American political theory, had nothing good to say about waxworks.[26] No matter the props and emblems that museum operators attached to their statues; where wax was concerned, the medium too often trumped the message.

More than a few viewers found they could not get past the realization that wax flesh suggested dead flesh. John Adams, for one, was deeply disturbed by his 1777 visit to Rebecca Wells's Philadelphia waxwork. There was no denying the sculptor's talent: The tableaux of Old Testament scenes and a gallery of Whig worthies, including Benjamin Franklin, William Pitt, and Catharine Maccauley, revealed that Wells possessed "genius as well as taste and art." Still, Adams could not shake the feeling of death. "I seemed to be walking among a group of corpses, standing, sitting, and walking, laughing, singing, crying, and weeping," he recalled in a letter to Abigail. It was for that reason that Adams far preferred Chovet's anatomical models to Wells's genre scenes. In his mind, "wax is much fitter to represent dead bodies than living ones."[27] The sentiment was not Adams's alone. Twenty-two-year-old Benjamin Silliman was both fascinated and repulsed by the many "beauties" he saw at Bowen's Columbian Museum in 1801. Of the "great multitude of curious things" the museum contained, the wax women were the objects that stuck in his imagination, for they inspired a disconcerting fusion of desire and repulsion. "I am so little of a connoisseur," he wrote, that "these same wax figures freeze me; they have the coldness of death." He confessed to his father, "I had rather spend half an hour with Miss————than a whole year with these wax beauties." The models were not soon forgotten. Five years later, traveling in Europe, the young scientist invoked Bowen's "beauties" to summarize and categorize the beauty of the women he encountered in Holland. Although "Dutch women have very fine complexions, probably the finest in the world," he decided, they generally "fail in expression and resemble fine wax work."[28] Given Silliman's view of "fine wax work," this was damning with faint praise indeed. As one authority intoned in an 1833 encyclopedia, it was the "ghastly fixedness" of these otherwise lifelike models that could make an Adams or a Silliman "shudder" by confronting him with a "petrified picture" of his "earthly part."[29]

Wax could summon to mind more than mortality. Like ivory, the period's other fashionable medium, wax absorbs light; the subject modeled in wax, like the sitter painted on ivory, can appear to glow from within. When delicately painted and tinted, wax flesh could call to mind the subtle gradations in complexion that were associated with whiteness. The waxlike complexions that Silliman enjoyed in Holland were, in his words, also "of a very pure and beautiful white, with less redundancy in rouge than the English women possess." His remarks register the preoccupation with human variety that characterized so much of natural science in the long eighteenth century. But they also registered yet another possible aesthetic association. In fact, wax figures, like ivory miniatures, set a standard for the ideal complexion, especially the ideal white female complexion. In one of Aphra Behn's tales a character named Iris is graced with an "infinitely fine" complexion; she had "skin soft and smooth as polish'd Wax, or Ivory, extremely white and clear." Samuel Richardson's Lovelace took pains to describe Clarissa's "wax-like flesh," whose "delicacy and firmness" testified that she was healthy as well as beautiful. And in the nineteenth century, novelists created countless heroines whose skin "literally [had] the delicacy of wax" or whose complexions were "like wax, delicately tinted with white and red."[30] No matter that wax could be molded to depict criminals as well as heroines or that it could be painted to represent Indian warriors or Chinese mandarins. Wax served as a metaphor for a feminized, aestheticized whiteness for some viewers, just as it suggested death to others. Hardly a neutral media, it thus came freighted with layers of association that could complicate or disrupt the message that a pantheon intended to convey.

Then there were the completed statues. Early national American painting remained indebted to a British aesthetic tradition that ranked portraiture well below history paintings and that set out clear standards for its execution. Good portraits did more than capture the likeness of a particular man or woman. Instead, as Sir Joshua Reynolds had explained in the *Discourses* he delivered to the Royal Academy, a portrait ought to distill the sitter's essence on canvas without fixating on the changeable details. It was only by transcending the merely particular, by gesturing toward the universal, that portraiture might fulfill its didactic promise and serve a larger social good.[31] U.S. sitters, painters, and viewers generally shared the British conviction that likenesses ought to elevate the transcendent above the specific. Indeed, it was precisely this connection to the transcendent that confirmed the civic importance of art.

To be sure, painters, sculptors, printmakers, and wax modelers were all preoccupied with the accuracy of their likenesses. But the meaning of and standards for accuracy varied from one discipline to another. Accuracy depended on not only the relation between the representation and the original but also the mimetic capacity of a particular medium. An accurate marble bust, for example, represents differently than an equally accurate oil painting. At the waxwork, accuracy triumphed over transcendence only to collapse into verisimilitude.

It was, in fact, that very exactness that had pushed wax modeling out of the realm of art and genius, at least for Reynolds. The genius of the artist resided in his ability to transcend the petty particulars of representation, he insisted; too close a copy could be "disagreeable." Waxwork provided a case in point. As Reynolds understood it, wax's potentially disagreeable verisimilitude was a function of the medium. The problem was that by using the "softness of wax" to express the "softness of flesh"—a strategy that was painfully obvious—artists deprived viewers of the "magic which is the prize and triumph of art." Although a good wax model was certainly "more exact in representation" than either a painting or sculpture, it failed to pack the right emotional punch. The most cursory visit to the waxworks proved that "the pleasures we receive from imitation is not increased merely in proportion as it approaches to minute and detailed reality," he declared.[32] It was not merely the physical properties of wax per se that banished it from the realm of high art. Wax statuary was mired in the local, the specific, the particular.

Modelers and exhibitors went out of their way to revel in the particulars so disdained by the British canon. The physical properties that made wax so suitable for true-to-life anatomical models that showed how living bodies functioned could also depict how they died or how they departed from the norm. Violent death, in all its grisly specificity, was a recurrent motif at waxworks. Advertisements for a life-sized group depicting the death of General Moreau, an ally-turned-enemy of Napoleon who had been hit in the leg by a cannonball at the Battle of Dresden, assured viewers that Moreau's thigh bone was "plainly to be seen together with the arteria Cruralis" and that his "countenance exhibit[ed] the pallid hue of death." When Reuben Moulthrop, a successful wax sculptor, re-created General Butler's death during the Battle of Wabash River, he advertised the pains he took to depict wounds to the subject's leg and breast.[33]

Although Moulthrop and his peers followed the example of academic artists in Britain like Benjamin West who had expanded the genre of history painting to include recent events of national significance, they also departed sharply from the conventions structuring that genre. West's famous, frequently reproduced depiction of the death of General James Wolfe at the Battle of Quebec, for example, has little to say about the injuries that felled the hero. Viewers would have known that Wolfe had been wounded three times over the course of the day—in the wrist, in the groin, and finally in the chest. West rendered bandages around the general's right arm and showed a doctor pressing a bandage against his torso; he delicately avoided any reference to a groin injury. Although the white bandages reference injury, nothing in the painting depicts the actual violation of Wolfe's body. In keeping with contemporary theories that insisted that an idealized representation was superior to a literal one, West's aestheticized depiction of Wolfe's death offers viewers a metaphor for patriotism and national glory, not the final minutes of a bleeding, convulsing, wheezing human body. Wax sculptors, in contrast, celebrated the corporeality and mortality of their subjects.

"Correct likenesses" of physical oddities were almost as appealing as depictions of fatal injuries. Statues of John Hutton, who lived for 108 years and four months, and of Mrs. Ann Moor, who managed to survive for three years without eating solid food, attracted audiences throughout the North for several decades. In 1800, the good citizens of New Haven turned out to see Job in his afflictions, "smitten with Biles." Tom Thumb and other less illustrious dwarves were fixtures throughout the early national era. The American Museum boasted a "correct personal likeness" of Daniel Lambert, "the English Mammoth," who "weighed 739 pounds"; "his body was 9 feet 4 inches in circumference, and his leg 3 feet 1 inch." Museum operators and audiences were not interested in the grotesque only. Their fascination with physical precision extended to less lurid, less spectacular subjects. Gardiner Baker's museum advertised "universally admired" models of New York siblings; "the boy is 4 ½ years of age, and the infant 5 ½ months," according to the advertisement. And in 1797, Daniel Bowen promised viewers that *his* Washington measured "6 feet and one inch in height, with exact proportion."[34]

The aesthetics of verisimilitude extended to the figures' hair, clothing, and accessories. Indeed, much of their special appeal depended on their ability to capture the most transient, least transcendent elements of self-presentation. Statues were adorned with appropriately coiffed human hair and wore specially made clothing. Advertisements promised that spectators could see Moreau (he of the shattered leg) "dressed in the magnificent uniform of the Russian General"; Christopher Columbus draped in "princely robes"; an American held captive in Algiers with the "dress he wore in his state of servitude"; or Chinese "Mandarines" costumed in the "modern stile of that country." And Baker's museum extended the dubious claim that its statues of Benjamin Franklin, John Hancock, the 108-year-old John Hutton, and assorted beauties were "all in suits of cloaths that they wore in their lifetimes."[35] As Baker's boast suggests, this focus on costume extended beyond belles and curiosities to political figures. George Washington, a fixture in waxworks throughout the country, was variously advertised as appearing in "his military Dress," in "full uniform," or "drest in an elegant suit of black."[36] If clothing contributed to the "life-like" appearance of all wax figures, it also sealed the identification between a real subject and his or her wax double.

For all these reasons, clothing the figures was an ongoing concern for museum proprietors, including Ethan Allen Greenwood, who operated museums in Boston; Providence, and Portland. He regularly contracted with a Mrs. Duchene to create, clean, mend, and refurbish the clothing worn by his figures.

Most of her work was devoted to maintenance. But sometimes she was hired to provide makeovers: to sew new garments for statues purchased from other area museums or to give "Princess Charlotte" a new dress for the 1823 Christmas season. Greenwood himself regularly shopped with an eye out for his figures, reporting that he bought twelve yards of silk "for dresses," selected a new hat for his "Dandy," and periodically acquired unspecified "articles" to embellish finished statues. Indeed, when would-be wit "Lemuel Catchpenny" lampooned the claims and aspirations of wax sculptors, he took aim at the attention they lavished on costume. Assuming the identity of a wax impresario, the pseudonymous writer boasted that before he turned Hagar out into the desert beautified with "golden trees and flowering shrubs," he bought her a silk bonnet and took her to a milliner's shop to "rig her out completely," for thus did the waxworks "promote the fine arts and improve public taste."[37]

For wax sculptors, costume was not just an integral part of the spectacle, it was an integral part of the likeness. As a Mr. Letton promised, his exhibition of "Elegant" individuals like Alexander Hamilton, Napoleon Bonaparte, Lord Nelson, and a Turkish ambassador would please visitors precisely *because* of the combination of "correct Likenesses and Elegant dresses."[38] The statues' costumes contributed to the visual spectacle of the waxwork just as guests' clothing contributed to the visual spectacle of a ball. The political resonances, however, were far different. In the early national imaginary, clothing in general and fashion in particular were suspect, serving as metaphors for social disguise. But at the waxwork, clothing created authenticity.[39]

Finally, wax statues lacked the fixity of painted likenesses or statues sculpted out of stone or metal. The bodies beneath the clothing were easily manipulated. Unlike a statue, carved from a single piece of marble, a wax model was assembled from discrete parts, much like today's department-store mannequins. Because museum proprietors regularly took shows on the road, and because they needed to change up stationary exhibits in order to attract repeat business, it made a great deal of sense to make statues that could be taken apart and reassembled relatively easily. This convenience lent the figures an air of malleability, even instability, that set them apart from paintings, prints, and stone and bronze sculptures. The wax Adams who sat in the Temple of Fame today might be standing next to Washington next week. Should Adams fall out of favor with the public and disappear from view, his arms, hands, legs, and feet might wind up attached to a Chinese mandarin or a Republican.

Spectators knew this. When Bowen transported a group of figures from Boston for an exhibition in Salem, a writer (likely Bowen himself) described the preparations in a brief essay titled "Demolition of the WAX-WORK," which was printed in newspapers in both cities. The writer depicted the "droll and humorous scene" as the statues were stripped of their clothing and piled into the wagon. The tableau simultaneously encouraged and undermined readers' expectations about the lifelike qualities of the statues: The Sleeping Fair was "waken'd from her dreams by having her head twisted off." Mrs. Platt and her children "were turned topsy turvy like different kinds of poultry in a market cart." The Boston Beauty was "deprived of her petticoats" while her legs were "crammed in with the Prince of Wales." As the writer described the bizarre scene, he erased the distance between the wax figures and the real persons they represented: The venerable Franklin was squeezed into a narrow box with the "RHODE ISLAND CHARMER." Alexander Hamilton—subjected to "an indignity not to be pardoned"—was "crammed in with the little NEGRO WENCH." The "Bishop Provost" snuggled into a tête-à-tête with the "Philadelphia nymph." The governor, "stripped of his new clothes, and neat wig," found himself "packed with the dirty old HERMIT." Only George Washington remained above the farce. Ever dignified, he traveled in the respectable company of Liberty and Plenty. Martha Washington was not so fortunate; she made the journey to Salem by lying with a friar. Piled on the street in broad daylight, the "heretofore elegant" waxwork now offered viewers and readers an object lesson in "the fall of human grandeur and the destruction of earthly pomp."[40] Maybe. But it also conjured visual fantasies that violated political and social propriety, fantasies that fused sex and violence, fantasies that conjoined the characters of the republican pantheon with characters from novels and genre paintings.

This tantalizing potential for transgression also attracted the attention of sculptor Hiram Powers. His first commission was the restoration of some "mutilated" wax figures that found their way into Joseph Dorfeuille's Western Museum in Cincinnati in the 1820s. Years later, he recalled seeing the severed heads scattered on the floor. Powers "could not help laughing" at the sight of Napoleon Bonaparte "kissing the bearded visage of Lorenzo Dow," General Washington whispering state secrets into a beggar's ear, and John Quincy Adams "breathing soft nonsense under the long tresses of Charlotte Temple," who did not seem to appreciate the favor.[41] Powers concluded that the spectacle was a "burlesque of sculpture." But more than art was being sent up. Like the anonymous author of "Demolition of the Wax-Work," Powers parodied the very notion of a pantheon. As vulnerable as they were malleable, the mutilated heads belied the fixed accomplishments and reputations of the founders.

Writing the Book of Nature

Wax models displayed in museums were set apart from the kinds of representative figures who typically filled the republican pantheon by more than their media, their costumes, or their malleability. They were further distinguished by the creatures that crowded around them and by the settings in which they appeared. The other objects, specimens, and images contained within museums created a densely crowded visual and spatial millieu that shaped viewers' perceptions of the wax figures just as it shaped their experiences of the museum. As physical and imaginative spaces, brick-and-mortar museums departed from the ideals that structured pantheons. The figures of most pantheons formed a self-contained circle of virtuous individuals; new figures might gain admission to the Temple of Fame, but only after they demonstrated their worthiness. Notwithstanding their didactic responsibilities to ordinary citizens, men like Washington and Franklin had been elevated to a realm of splendid isolation by their accomplishment. But in situ a wax statue of a man worthy of inclusion in the republican pantheon was isolated neither from the other figures in the waxworks nor from other displays in the museum. The meanings that any one wax figure generated depended at least partly on the constellation of meaning and knowledge generated within the museum as a whole. Just as important, those meanings were inextricably connected to the various forms of observation encouraged by the museum itself. To understand how women and men viewed waxworks, and how the waxwork figured into their political imaginary, we need to broaden our focus from the figures to the museums in which they were so often housed.

Scholarly accounts of early national museums generally begin and end with Peale's storied State House museum, which opened its doors in 1802. They are typically illustrated either by a watercolor depiction of the museum interior, painted by Peale and his son Titian Ramsay Peale, in 1822 or by Peale's self-portrait, *The Artist in His Museum*, commissioned by the museum's trustees the same year. Both the scholarly studies and the paintings focus our attention on Peale's hyper-Linnaean display space. Through the Long Room, the story goes, Peale established his bona fides as an enlightened man of science. He advanced his vision of a republic predicated on harmonious hierarchy and secured through rational instruction. His museum contains and literally embodies enlightened science and scientific learning in America. This reading surely captures Peale's aspirations for his museum and his legacy. But it also rests on a remarkably static view of the museum, one that eclipses the years before Peale secured the State House space and the years after 1822, when he turned management of the museum over to his son Rubens. The State House museum's Long Room and all that it symbolized bore little resemblance to earlier incarnations of Peale's museum or to the enlightened amusement provided by other American museums.[42]

As Peale himself admitted in his autobiography, the road to the iconic Long Room was fraught with trial and error. Just as his career as a museum operator

Figure 24. Charles Willson Peale, *The Long Room, Interior of Front Room in Peale's Museum*, 1822. Watercolor over graphite on paper. Detroit Institute of Arts, USA Founders Society Purchase, Director's Discretionary Fund. Bridgeman Images.

was grounded in his career as a painter, so, too, did his museum grow out of his studio space. In the 1780s, he built additions to his home studio to accommodate his portraits of revolutionary heroes and his ill-fated moving-picture exhibit. This combined exhibit space, measuring seventy-seven feet in length, housed portraits and paintings on one end and natural curiosities on the other. Although Peale clustered his American characters together within a sea of landscapes and history paintings, he made no attempt to impose any kind of classification scheme on his specimen collection beyond separating things that lived in water from those that lived on land and flew in the air. Instead, the "admirably preserved" creatures were displayed in a "most romantic and amusing manner," as Manasseh Cutler observed following a visit in 1787. Peale had constructed an artificial pond, set in a fanciful forested beach. On the pond's surface sat his stuffed fish and waterfowl. The surrounding landscape included "bear, deer, leopard, tiger, wild-cat, fox, raccoon, rabbit, squirrel, etc.," while the "boughs of the trees were loaded with birds, some of almost every species in America, and many exotics." Thinking back on what he had seen, Cutler, a clergyman and naturalist, realized that it was "not in my power to give any particular account of the numerous species of fossils and animals, but only their general arrangement" around the pond's painted surface. However taken he was with the prospect of the whole, Cutler could not fully grasp its discrete parts. All told, Peale's first stab at a museum looked less like a space for rational observation than a glimpse at "*Noah's Ark* into which was received every kind of beast and creeping thing in which there was life."[43]

When the museum moved first to Philosophical Hall in 1794 and then to the State House in 1802, Peale seized the chance to rethink the organization and display of his collection. Indeed, the desire to present the museum's contents in a properly Linnaean fashion was one cornerstone of his repeated pitches for public support.[44] The Philadelphia museum was to be a "great national magazine" of nature, an institution bent on "more generally diffusing an increase of knowledge in the works of the Creator." He tirelessly proclaimed that *his* "assemblage of nature" revealed not a collection of "*whimsical forms*" but rather a "great whole, combined together by unchangeable laws of infinite wisdom." Visitors to such a place would leave "carrying with them powerful lessons of morality." "How valuable must an institution such as a museum be to a republic?" he asked, certain that he had already supplied the answer.[45]

But it was one thing to construct an argument out of words about the importance of a museum for a republic dependent upon an educated and rational citizenry, another to realize it in real space with real objects. Once he was ensconced in Philosophical Hall, Peale began experimenting with various strategies for presenting his collection. Philosophical Hall afforded him the space to begin to sort specimens and artifacts into loose departments. But how best to display them all, especially his large bird collection? Glass cases differentiated one object from another (and protected all the artifacts from visitors who were tempted to poke, squeeze, and pet the specimens). Initially, Peale built custom glass-display cases to suit each individual specimen (an "endless, and expensive labor") before seizing on standardized case sizes. This was more than convenience; it also created an "appearance uniform and agreeable," a visual aesthetic that resonated with his view of nature. The Philosophical Hall quarters marked a significant improvement over the studio space on Lombard Street. (Peale, who regretted that moving the museum out of his house cut into his profits, was also certain that the "removal" gave the museum "more importance" in the eyes of the public.)[46] But even the Philosophical Hall configuration was not universally heralded as a success. Joseph Dennie, writing in the *Port Folio*, dismissed it as an "overrated . . . show for the amusement of children." The problem was not the contents, which were "sufficiently" delightful, but rather their display, which revealed "a deplorable want of scientific arrangement."[47] It was not until Peale acquired the upper floors of Philadelphia's State House in 1802 that he was able to fashion the "great national magazine" he had promised Philadelphians and national politicians since the 1790s. In its State House incarnation, the Philadelphia Museum finally gave shape to Peale's ambition to create an American rival to the great museums of Europe and his "determination to order and represent both the social and natural world."[48]

Peale's achievement owed much to his well-documented vision of the republic. But it also depended on access to a large exhibition space, one that accommodated the orderly display and mindful segregation of artifacts. The new State House quarters, in combination with the rooms he retained in Philosophical Hall, gave him exactly that. Displays devoted to art and antiquity remained in Philosophical Hall. Across the yard, the State House space was large enough to partition. Peale built separate rooms to house his collection of quadrupeds and marine life, although he later sacrificed the marine room to make way for the mammoth. He created cases for ethnographic display, although these eventually followed the marine exhibit back across the yard to Philosophical Hall.

The heart of the new museum was the Long Room, Peale's primary exhibition space. Extending for one hundred feet—the entire length of the building's Chestnut Street front—the Long Room embodied Peale's ambitions for the museum as a whole. Nature's peaceful regularity was revealed through the Linnaean classification system made manifest along its walls. The Great Chain of Being, with its ascending life forms, was suggested by the vertical displays of species, crowned by man. On the left side of the room, stuffed birds, posed in front of painted habitats, were arranged in orderly glass cases rising twelve feet from the floor. Above the cases, Peale ran two rows of portraits depicting "distinguished personages" and "characters of distinguished eminence." On the right side of the room, projecting cases between the windows created alcoves devoted to the display of thousands of insects, minerals, and fossils.[49] To be sure, the museum's layout was always a work in progress; Peale and his sons tinkered constantly with the details. But the radically increased floor space did afford Peale the opportunity to create a Linnaean "world in miniature."

This studiously controlled vision, unfolding across multiple buildings and floors, was perpetually challenged by the acquisition of new specimens. In Peale's view, no artifact was in and of itself worthy of the public's attention. Unless an object was "systematically displayed," it degenerated into "mere show."[50] The problem was that Peale's tightly organized displays did not easily accommodate the new artifacts that he was constantly soliciting from patrons, fellow collectors, and travelers. Only a few years after moving into the State House, Peale complained about the "difficulties which are daily increasing for want of Room." New objects must be "put in their proper places—and I am determined not to exhibit any thing which shall not be nearly in classical arrangement." This "classical arrangement," which rendered nature and society legible, was after all the point of the museum. On at least one occasion, Peale discarded museum holdings because of spatial constraints. When he moved to the State House, he destroyed several of his ethnographic wax figures "for want of room to keep them." As he explained, "I neglect many little contrivances which might serve to catch the Eye of the gaping multitude;—and thus give me some quarter dollars." Instead, he subscribed to a "steady perseverance," pursuing "improvements of a Scientific cast" in order to influence "those who come to study the subjects of the Museum."[51]

As these last remarks suggest, Peale expected that his museum would do more than communicate a particular picture of the natural and human world. He also intended it to foster a particular set of observational practices. The multitudes were not to gape. His museum was not the place for slack-jawed staring. Nor were patrons to glance, letting their eyes slide promiscuously from one curiosity to another. Instead, they were to observe, to exercise the kind of steady, attentive looking that had become the hallmark of Enlightenment scientific practice. By the end of the eighteenth century, as historian Lorraine Daston has suggested, this kind of observation was valorized for its own sake. If it delivered better studies of natural phenomena, it also exercised a salutary effect on observers themselves. Peale claimed that his museum actually enforced this kind of scientific looking: "I have seen young men in a rattling manner enter the rooms," he boasted, only to have their "view" gripped by the kind of "pious and reverential tendency" that could only be called forth by the "wonderful variety of animals" contained within a "well stored museum." In an instant, the visitors' "mad career" gave way to "serious reflection."[52]

These observational practices, so obviously calibrated to meet the needs of a republic by cultivating a rational and dispassionate citizenry, were embedded in and reinforced by textual practices and in texts themselves. Peale routinely likened the museum to a "great Book that every human being may read." A sign outside the museum's exhibition space reminded visitors that they were about to enter the "book of Nature open" and tickets granting admission literally spelled out "NATURE" across the open pages of a book. For Peale and for other naturalists, reading was an integral component of observation, not merely a metaphor for it.

Peale's carefully written display guides reminded visitors of the close relationship between looking and reading. All of the artifacts were labeled. The birds and quadrupeds were identified by their Linnaean genera as well as their specific names, which were translated into English, French, and Latin; a chart showing the Linnaean system of birds was displayed at the entrance to the Long Room. Across the Long Room from the portraits, Peale displayed "a short history of the memorable events of each" man. All of these labels—these "important append-ages," in Peale's words—were set in gilt frames, behind glass, prominent remind-ers that visitors should attend to texts as well as artifacts.

Then there was the *Scientific and Descriptive Catalogue*, a serial subscription he planned to publish with the assistance of French émigré and naturalist A. M. F. J. Palisot de Beauvois. Although the project was mostly directed at natural history scholars and the influential men who made up the museum's board of visitors, Peale also hoped that it would serve a wider public. Copies would be located throughout the museum, thus "putting into the hands of the visitor an accurate description of the object of his attention" and guiding his eyes from case to case.[53] Like so many ambitious publishing ventures in the early republic, the *Catalogue* foundered long before it was complete. Peale's unrealized aspirations appear in *The Artist in His Museum*. In the background, a father and son work their way through the ornithological display with the aid of a book, possibly a guide to the collections. Their steady, sustained gazes are grounded by the knowledge contained in the book.

The Artist in His Museum left little doubt that Peale had come a long way from the "most amusing and romantic" collection he had cobbled together behind his house on Lombard Street. But he had also come a long way from other museums, whose proprietors were more than happy to accommodate the "gaping multitudes" Peale so disdained. Even large museums, like the ones operated by Bowen, Baker, Steward, or Greenwood, struggled constantly with spatial constraints. Proprietors faced continuous pressure to expand their col-lections, for new objects and attractions tempted old customers to return. But the need to house and display a perpetually expanding collection could crowd the largest spaces and provide indiscriminate audiences with an equally indis-criminate mix of art and nature.

Daniel Bowen's Columbian Museum was one such venture. In 1796, Bowen moved his collection into new quarters on Boston's Mall, on what is now Trem-ont Street. The museum interior measured ninety by twenty feet. This seems like a considerable space, especially by the standards of eighteenth-century Bos-ton, until one accounts for all that Bowen had to cram inside it: more than a hundred "elegant paintings," some measuring eight by ten feet; more than fifty life-sized wax statues; eight "concert clocks," which featured large automatons playing harpsichords, organs, and clarinets and a mechanical butcher who killed his ox at the appointed hour; a variety of tapestries; a "large collection of natural and artificial curiosities" that included assorted birds, beasts, and reptiles (among them a peacock whose plumage spanned fifteen feet and a "monstrous serpent" that extended fifteen feet); and a Grande Forte piano played by a blind man.[54] Nearly ten years later, after a fire destroyed the original Columbian

Figure 25. Charles Willson Peale, *The Artist in His Museum*, 1822. Oil on canvas, 103³/₄ × 79⁷/₈ in. Image courtesy of the Pennsylvania Academy of the Fine Arts, Philadelphia. Gift of Mrs. Sarah Harrison (The Joseph Harrison, Jr. Collection).

Museum, Bowen acquired a new partner, a new location on Tremont Street, and a new museum. Built in a "style of finished elegance, never surpassed" in Boston, his new Columbian encompassed an upper and lower hall, almost doubling the size of the original. Judging from broadsides and newspaper stories, even this cavernous space was filled up with "art and nature." By the time the new franchise opened, Bowen seems to have come close to replicating the range of holdings lost to fire. To those, he added more of everything and then some. The new Columbian boasted more wax figures, more paintings, and more prints, now arranged into a "novel and pleasing" gallery. It contained a "beautiful" glass fountain, which stood in front of a large painting of the "celebrated Fountain at Versailles" and which was surrounded by "upwards of 100 Figures of French Fashion and taste." It displayed more natural curiosities, including an African lion, an exact replica of Peale's mastodon, and a "mammoth" oyster shell from India weighing 495 pounds. It sponsored new amusements, including the deceptions the "Magic Temple" and the "Invisible Lady" and a room-sized "Phantasmagoria" with "a great variety of transparent moving figures."[55]

Unlike Peale, who was willing to reduce the number of items on display to accommodate the kind of rational presentation that fostered focused observation, the vast majority of museum proprietors had no room for—and no interest in—highly specialized spaces. They had no investment in the observational practices that such spaces supposedly encouraged.[56] At most, museum operators seem to have sorted artifacts into broadly generic categories: Paintings and prints tended to hang in designated "galleries"; animals and "natural curiosities" might appear alongside each other; and wax figures of all sorts were housed together. Order counted for less than spectacle.

This was certainly true of Ethan Allen Greenwood's museums. From the beginning, he was sensitive to questions of site. Immediately after acquiring his first museum, he repainted the building's interior and refurbished its cases. Within a year he moved the organ, dismantled the "Great Alcove," installed a "monkey room," ripped out three interior doors to "give a free passage around," embellished the performance stage with columns and arches, created two forests, and built a "large apartment for Wax figures." Many of his figures were displayed in cases that presumably lined the walls of the "apartment." But some appeared in theatrical dioramas, posed against specially painted scenery and accompanied by props. Still others were displayed outside the wax room when the occasion arose. Greenwood's wax men and women moved into and out of the forest; they posed in front of the panoramas he periodically exhibited. Even within their designated "apartment," lined up behind glass, characters of all kinds must have occupied close quarters, given that the museum contained more than one hundred of them.[57] It is difficult to see how the most diligent

Plate 1. Jacob Marling (American, 1774–1833), *The May Queen* (*The Crowning of Flora*), 1816. Oil on canvas, 30 1/8 × 39 1/8 in. Chrysler Museum of Art, Norfolk, VA. Gift of Edgar William and Bernice Chrysler Gabisch. 80.181.20.

Plate 2. Susan Anne Livingston, portrait of Elizabeth "Mumbet" Freeman (ca. 1742–1829), 1811. Watercolor on ivory. © Massachusetts Historical Society, Boston, MA. Bridgeman Images.

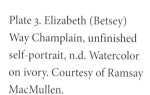

Plate 3. Elizabeth (Betsey) Way Champlain, unfinished self-portrait, n.d. Watercolor on ivory. Courtesy of Ramsay MacMullen.

Plate 4. Anthony Meucci, *Pierre Toussaint*, ca. 1825, miniature. Watercolor on ivory, 3 1/4 × 2 5/8 in. Negative #2841. Object #1920.4. New-York Historical Society.

Plate 5. Anthony Meucci, *Mrs. Pierre Toussaint* [Juliette Noel Toussaint], 1825. Watercolor on ivory, 3 1/4 × 2 5/8 in. Negative #2842. Object #1920.5. New-York Historical Society.

Plate 6. Charles Willson Peale, *Yarrow Mamout*, 1819. Oil on canvas. Philadelphia Museum of Art, Philadelphia, PA. Bridgeman Images.

Plate 7. Charles Bird King,
Young Omahaw, War Eagle,
Little Missouri, and Pawnees,
1821. Oil on canvas,
28 × 36 1/8 in. Smithsonian
American Art Museum.
Gift of Miss Helen Barlow.
1985.66.384,222.

Plate 8. Edward Greene
Malbone, portrait of Mrs.
Richard Sullivan (Sarah
Russell) (1786–1831), 1804.
Watercolor on ivory. Yale
University Art Gallery, Lelia
A. and John Hill Morgan,
B.A. 189. LL.B. 1896, M.A.
(Hon.) 1929, collection.

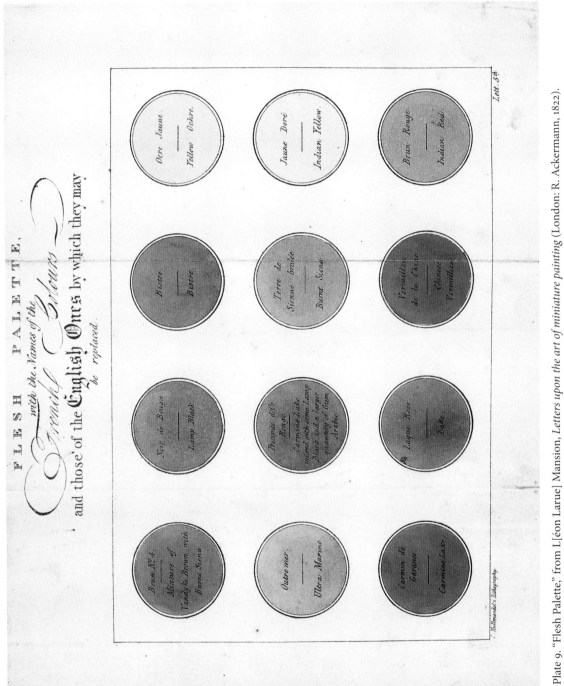

FLESH PALETTE,
with the Names of the
French Colours
and those of the **English Ones** by which they may
be replaced.

Ocre Jaune. — Yellow Ochre.	Bistre. — Bistre.	Noir de Bougie. — Lamp Black.	Brun N.º 4. — Mixture of Vandyke Brown with Burnt Sienna.
Jaune Doré. — Indian Yellow.	Terre de Sienne brulée. — Burnt Sienna.	Peignoir d'Or Rouge. — Carmine Lake mixed with some Lamp Black and a larger quantity of Gum Arabic.	Outre mer. — Ultra Marine.
Brun Rouge. — Indian Red.	Vermillon de la Chine. — Chinese Vermillion.	Laque Rose. — Lake.	Carmin de Garance. — Carmine Lake.

J. Netherclift's Lithography.

Lett. 5.th

Plate 9. "Flesh Palette," from L[éon Larue] Mansion, *Letters upon the art of miniature painting* (London: R. Ackermann, 1822).
Courtesy, The Winterthur Library: Printed Book and Periodical Collection. Winterthur Museum and Library.

Plate 10. Elizabeth (Betsey) Way Champlain, unfinished portrait of an unidentified sitter, n.d. Watercolor on ivory. Courtesy of Ramsay MacMullen.

Plate 11. Benjamin West, *Portrait of William Hamilton and Ann Hamilton Lyle*, 1785–1810. DAMS #231. Historical Society of Pennsylvania Collection.

visitor could practice the observational skills demanded by both science and republican society in such a space.

In the absence of images or detailed descriptions of museum interiors other than that of the Philadelphia Museum, advertisements suggest the diverging aims of the collections.[58] The aesthetics of display and the logic of observation were recapitulated in the prints, which told audiences what they would see and how they would see it. Consider, for example, Peale's 1799 advertisement for an "Ourang Outang" (orangutan), recently arrived at his museum. The advertisement is dominated by a striking woodcut. But this "wild man of the woods" was no mere curiosity. On the contrary, Peale instructed readers, this specimen was "so nearly approaching the human species as to occasion some Philosophers to doubt whether it is not allied to mankind." Although the orangutan was the main attraction, visitors to the "useful repository" were also promised the opportunity to examine quadrupeds, amphibious animals, fishes, birds, insects, fossils, and wax models. Like the museum's specimens, which stood in for larger zoological categories, the eleven wax figures represented "persons of various savage nations, all in their proper habits and surrounded by their implements of war, husbandry, etc." Withal, Peale's exhibitions allowed spectators to ponder the relationship of one life form to another and to grasp the harmonious hierarchy that structured creation.

A few years later, when Bowen deployed art and nature to entice patrons into the Columbian, he offered up a very different catalog of the "world in miniature." His broadside announced curiosities, animals (live and taxidermied), wax figures, and paintings. Like Peale, Bowen boasted a variety of animals. Unlike Peale, he listed them individually and in random order, without regard to species, origin, or size. This disregard for the conventions of natural history is illustrated by the woodcuts decorating the broadside. Animals are figured without regard to proportion. The bear and porcupine are about the same size; they both tower above the lion. The human world represented at Bowen's museum mirrors the jumble of the animal one. Among his wax figures, Bowen lists three life-sized tableaux depicting the execution of the French royal family; President John Adams; and George Washington, the last attended by personifications of Justice, Peace, and Plenty. But this conventional assortment of politicos is followed by (among many) Franklin; Stiles; sixteen "maidens" representing each state in the union; a 108-year-old-man; Siamese twins; assorted literary characters, including Charlotte weeping at Werther's tomb; two Greenwich pensioners; a handful of Indian warriors (one brandishing a real scalp); an unnamed guillotine victim; a "Negro boy" under the lash; a pair of Chinese Mandarins; and Tom Thumb—the last advertised "small . . . as life." If Peale's museum was an encyclopedia, Bowen's was a miscellany.

Figure 26. "The Ourang Outang, or Wild Man of the Woods," advertisement for Peale's Museum. *Claypoole's American Daily Advertiser*, Apr. 13, 1799. Library Company of Philadelphia.

Certainly, cosmopolitan visitors, whose expectations had been primed by the categories that structured natural science, commented on the "miscellany" they encountered at museums. Europeans were predictably snooty. One German prince dismissed U.S. museums ("except, perhaps, the Peale Museum, at Philadelphia") as mere "accumulations" of curiosities. Greenwood's Boston museum was especially vexing. The collection was housed in a maze of "narrow rooms, passages, and closets" connected by "many flights of steps." The confusion of the space mirrored the collection: "stiff, awkward wax figures," "bad

Figure 27. "Columbian Museum, near the Mall, Boston: The Columbian Museum contains a very extensive collection of artificial and natural curiosities," broadside ([Boston]: Printed at D. Bowen's ornamental printing office, under the Columbian Museum, where hand-bills, shop-bills, cards, blanks, &c. is done with neatness, on reasonable terms, [1799]). 1 sheet ([1] p.): ill.; 60 × 46 cm. Collection of the Massachusetts Historical Society.

paintings and engravings," fashion plates ripped out of European magazines, and specimens of natural history "hung without any order." Visitors were forced to navigate this confusing visual field "without any ticket or further direction" to guide them.[59] British naval officer and novelist Frederick Marryat was more contemptuous still. The "most interesting and valuable specimens" were placed "side by side" with the "greatest puerilities and absurdities in the world," not least of which was the obligatory collection of "execrable wax-work." Characterized by a "want of taste," "discrimination," and "correct feel-ing," American museums, he carped, "remind you of American society—a cha-otic mass, in which you occasionally met what is valuable and interesting, but of which the larger proportion is pretence."[60]

Even sympathetic Americans, those who credited museums' contributions to republican society, echoed the frustration expressed by Europeans. The Rev-erend William Bentley, the indefatigable diarist and collector from Salem, Mas-sachusetts, regularly visited Bowen's Columbian Museum, which he proclaimed a "wonderful beginning to our country." But the methodical, scientifically minded preacher was by turns confused, overwhelmed, and put off by the riot of images, objects, sights, and sounds he encountered there. "The arrangement by no means met my wishes," he wrote after a visit in 1798. Two years later, he was back. This time, he concluded that despite the interest of particular objects, the "whole effect is lessened by the want of arrangement, by the monstrous effect of wax figures, & the absurd appearance of the whole in one view."[61]

Waxing Political

What are we to make of these miscellanies and, especially, their "monstrous," "execrable," "awkward" wax figures? It is too easy to dismiss them either as false starts on a trajectory that would ultimately culminate in the Smithsonian or as outright failures. Rather than focusing on the stories these museums did not tell, the truths they did not communicate, we would do well to look closely at the ones they did, for the human menageries at the waxworks gesture toward a very different political imaginary than the one idealized in the republican pantheon.

The most obvious messages conveyed by wax displays underscore the salience of race to the cultural politics and imperial ambitions of the early republic. Far from appearing in the rarified isolation of the pantheon, assorted founders appeared in museum settings that explicitly referenced a multiplicity of cultures and races. Figures representing Native Americans, Africans, Asians, and Pacific Islanders simultaneously evoked "the savage" or, at best, "the primi-tive" and located Europeans and Euro-Americans at the apex of civilization. In museums of all calibers, formal displays of nonwhites elaborated difference in order to demonstrate hierarchy.[62]

In the Philadelphia Museum, oil portraits of the "Distinguished Personages" who had forged the republic crowned the Long Room; wax models depicting nonwhites were grouped together in the Model Room. Representing North America, the Caribbean, the South Pacific, Siberia, Africa, and China, Peale's ethnographic statues recapitulated the stock racial types that occupied the attention of natural historians like Oliver Goldsmith and Samuel Stanhope Smith.

Only two of Peale's wax figures represented specific individuals: the Shawnee chiefs Blue Jacket and Red Pole. Both fought against U.S. General Anthony Wayne in the Northwest Territory and then signed the 1795 Treaty at Greenville; both later helped broker an accord among Native American enemies. From Peale's perspective, Blue Jacket and Red Pole were exemplary Indian leaders, men who embodied the promise of peace and the inevitability of U.S. territorial expansion. But despite all that these two men accomplished and all they symbolized, they did not warrant space in the museum's portrait gallery. Instead, Blue Jacket and Red Pole were modeled in wax and situated alongside representatives from the rest of the "savage" nations.[63]

Other museums went much further than Peale's in reducing nonwhites to types. However many Native American warriors they displayed, museum proprietors never identified the figures as members of specific tribes, much less as particular individuals. These undifferentiated Indians were disconnected from the political struggles and diplomatic dilemmas that loomed so large in early national politics. Their costumes, tomahawks, and scalps owed less to ethnographic exposition than to the spectacle of violence. Americans of African descent fared worse. Unlike Indians or "Mandarins," they never stood alone as examples of ethnographic types. Instead, they were confined to tableaux shared with tea-sipping, whip-wielding whites. And although scenes depicting the "rustic discipline" of African Americans may have been calculated to evoke sympathy, they could just as easily evoke vicarious feelings of sadistic pleasure in a distinctly racialized pain. Either way, displays that featured "Negro wenches" and "black boys" simultaneously transported troubling questions about the status of African Americans out of the realm of politics and into the realm of sensation and sealed the association between skin color and servitude.[64]

Such representations contributed to the construction of the United States as a white republic, and they did so in ways that scholars now take for granted.[65] That said, wax displays invited comparisons that cut in multiple directions. The same exhibits that reinforced some hierarchies undermined others. A wax George Washington may have been juxtaposed against Indian chiefs, "negro wenches," and "Chinese mandarins," but he also bumped up against assorted

AMERICAN.   NEGRO.   HOTTENTOT.   LAPLANDER.   CHINESE.

Figure 28. Frontispiece depicting "The Five Varieties of the Human Race," from Oliver Goldsmith, *An history of the earth, and animated nature, Vol. I* (Philadelphia: Printed for Mathew Carey, 1795). Courtesy of the American Antiquarian Society.

criminals, victims, rustics, and freaks. For all we know, he stood his ground alongside the calf with eight legs and the dog with two heads. Wax displays turned the nation's founders and its most prominent statesmen into curiosities who could be integrated into or dissociated from nationalist narratives according to viewers' whims.

In fact, the great majority of U.S. museums made no attempt to present a systematic picture of universal truth. Instead, the eclectic, freewheeling collections they housed emphasized the eccentricity and serendipity of acquisition and encouraged the equally eccentric, equally serendipitous assessments of audiences. The overwhelming number and variety of artifacts, the unruly logic of their presentation, and the absence of texts to anchor the eye worked against causal connections and overarching narratives. Never mind the conviction, shared by museum proprietors, government officials, and educated and influential citizens, that museums furthered the republican project by spreading universal knowledge among the citizenry. The material conditions that obtained in early national museums invited viewers to integrate the objects of display and the process of viewing itself into insistently individual, even idiosyncratic, experiences.[66]

It was precisely this idiosyncratic quality that so disarmed Bentley on his trips to the Columbian. Bentley was, among other things, a scholar, an amateur naturalist, and an avid collector; his personal cabinet eventually formed the core of the collection at Salem's Marine Society Museum. He was, in other words, a man experienced in the linked skills of observing, categorizing, and assessing. But the Columbian enforced a different kind of looking. "I found many things to give me pleasure," he admitted after his 1798 visit. But what kind of pleasure *was* that? Thinking back on the "extensive waxwork," Bentley could "pronounce nothing." The tapestries "obliged [his] attention." "The painting, Death of Lewis [Louis XVI], from which the wax work of the same name is taken, was good, but the resignation of Washington interested" him. Upon reflection, "many portraits" interested Bentley. The mechanisms of the musical clocks were "ingenious," but it was the sound they made, which resembled "Organ & Clarinets," that he found captivating. In the menagerie, he looked at a sleeping bear, which demonstrated "insolent contempt for every visitor." He looked at the "Babboon" who seemed "fond of entertaining his guests. He looked at an "affronted" porcupine. He looked at two owls, who gave him "no share of their notice." No longer the passive objects of scientific scrutiny, the anthropomorphized animals seemed to size Bentley up, only to find him wanting. At the Columbian, the systematic, systematizing gaze of the enlightened man of letters had become a series of flickering glances that passed back and forth between the observer and the observed.[67]

If Bentley is any example, women and men experienced a tour through the museum as a visual picaresque, in which eye, imagination, and conversation floated from object to object. They glanced and they gaped, with no regard for the spectatorial protocols that Europeans expected and that Peale worked so hard to foster. This meandering obviously bore little resemblance to an orderly exploration of the "book of nature" at the Philadelphia Museum. But it was also a far cry from a trip to the Temple of Fame, where serious-minded citizens focused their eyes and their minds on a very select group of men whose deeds and character they sought to emulate.

These undisciplined habits of observation were encouraged by the mutable, potentially deceptive objects under consideration. At Bowen's museum and many others like it, wax statues unsettled the orthodox representations of prominent statesmen that obtained in paintings, prints, and statuary. After all, those like-nesses were calculated to bolster the political and cultural authority of the sitter by rendering his face as a physiognomic map of republican virtue, by framing him with the heroic trappings of nation building, or both. There was little ambiguity in Gilbert Stuart's magisterial Lansdowne portrait, for example. But a wax Washing-ton? That was another matter. A wax Washington was authenticated as much by the superficial details of costume—the full uniform or elegant black suit—as by its physiognomy and the character revealed there. It was not a seamless whole but was composed of discrete parts, many of which could be exchanged with the figures surrounding it. The same qualities that seemed to bring it to life—skin, hair, complexion—could be implicated in deception. Think, for example, of the common waxworks joke, almost as clichéd in the eighteenth century as it is today, in which innocent spectators mistake mannequins for men.[68]

Objects and observation alike were anticipated by the print culture that pulled patrons into the museums. Newspaper advertisements and broadsides prepared patrons to see statesmen as curiosities, as objects of spectacle rather than emulation. The exuberant promiscuity suggested in print was made mani-fest in the museums proper, with their fantastic settings, their indifference to epistemological categories, their elastic notion of what, exactly, constituted a figure of interest. Standing beside Charlotte Temple, Baron von Trenck, and the Belle of Philadelphia, a wax Washington narrowed the gap between the exem-plary characters of the pantheon and the characters that filled the pages of romances, novels, and plays or the characters that inhabited genre paintings and prints. At the museum, Washington became a character that could be fea-tured in an infinite number of tableaux and narratives, political and otherwise.

This imaginary defies the possibilities and imperatives that generally struc-ture historians' understanding of early national political culture. Waxworks nei-ther enshrined nor undermined deference. They side-stepped the compulsions of party. In this, they resembled the "lounger" essays that appeared in Joseph Dennie's *Port Folio* between 1801 and 1809. Although the *Port Folio* reflected Dennie's ardent Federalism, it never reduced to it. Instead, as Laura Rigal has argued, the magazine was a "faux aristocratic bric-a-brac," a "cabinet of curiosities rather than a Linnaean museum." The *Port Folio's* "miscellaneous ethos" obtained not only in the range of its contents but also in the perspectives afforded by "Samuel Saunter," "Meander," and "Charles Chameleon," among others, in essays on manners and morals. These commentaries on contemporary life cannot be contained within any particular ideological perspective, as Rigal observes. Confounding the divisions of party politics, Dennie's loungers model the discontinuous, "idle viewing" of the consumer whose eye flits from commodity to commodity.[69] The *Port Folio*, which cost $5 a year and which trumpeted its remove from the workaday lives of ordinary women and men, cast the lounger's perspective as a privilege extended only to the elite few. Museums and waxworks extended this affluent lounger's perspective to anyone who could spare the twenty-five cents needed to walk through the front door.

There is no reason to believe that museum proprietors set out to create this complex, contradictory visual field, that they planned to assemble pantheons only to poke fun at them, or that they aimed to open up an alternative imaginary. Like the fictional Lucy Sumner who relished the rational amusement at Bowen's museum, Ethan Allen Greenwood routinely assumed that his museums afforded visitors a far more elevating form of entertainment than that on display at, say, the circus. And like Sumner, he attributed the success of unsavory spectacles like the circus to audiences' lapsed taste and inexplicably poor judgment. "It is astonishing that any part of the public can be pleased with such nonsense," he fumed in 1823.[70] Museum proprietors' persistent efforts to link themselves to civic celebrations and commemorations suggest that they viewed their businesses as ventures that enhanced the public good. The degree of public support granted to museums suggests that others shared proprietors' assumptions. Inflecting knowledge and taste with nationalist importance, these institutions were crucial to the attempt to forge an explicitly American republic of taste.

Yet when these ideals and aspirations assumed physical form, when they materialized into real buildings stuffed with real objects, they inadvertently created spaces that all but guaranteed that the most straightforward ideological messages could be, and were, destabilized. This amounted to more than the inevitable gap between rhetoric and reality. The distance was exacerbated by the market, by the commercial contexts in which museums operated. Proprietors faced ongoing pressure to lure repeat business with new objects and novel attractions. If they aspired to educate the public taste, they soon learned that catering to multiple tastes was a precondition for keeping the doors open.

As a consequence, the wax figures that crowded into early national museums told Americans multiple, contested stories. They simultaneously reminded them of their English heritage and their republican future. They located Anglo-Americans atop a global, racialized hierarchy. Displays of wax figures thus embodied, however metaphorically, the narrative trajectory of American exceptionalism and American destiny. At the same time, however, they encouraged a political subjectivity that owed little to the rigid virtue, deferential ethos, and unified perspective of the republican ideal and still less to the disciplined commitment demanded by partisan politics. At the waxworks, spectators were invited to situate statesmen in an imaginary that was chaotic, crowded, and potentially transgressive.

Museums did boast a broadly political importance in the early republic. They diffused knowledge, to be sure, but they also served as sites where citizens were encouraged to construct political and national imaginaries. That these imaginaries could and sometimes did diverge from the straight and narrow path imagined by, say, Charles Willson Peale should direct our attention to the intersection of politics, culture, and markets in the years following the Revolution. Markets, and capitalism more generally, were connected to political life by more than policy, by more than tariffs, treaties, and Supreme Court rulings. The structures of thinking, feeling, and fantasizing that were central to the creation of political and national identities were powerfully shaped by the logic of the market.

CHAPTER SIX

Political Personae

From the moment he was elected president of the United States, George Washington was everywhere. Although the man incarnate may have spent most of his time in the nation's capitals or at home in Virginia, his face was far better traveled. The reproduction of Washington's face was as relentless as it was unprecedented. Congress, state governments, colleges, and European royalty commissioned portraits of "His Excellency." Multiple copies of these likenesses were subsequently sold to museums and collectors and purchased for exchange as gifts, especially among influential members of the Federalist Party. These official portraits spawned countless engraved prints, which were sold on both sides of the Atlantic. Indeed, figuring Washington became a cottage industry for a handful of the nation's most prominent artists and engravers. Even artists whose republican virtue led them to paint the president gratis for public institutions were happy to turn a profit by selling copies of their own originals. Charles Willson Peale, for example, painted Washington from life seven times and then copied several of those portraits for sale; Peale's portraits alone generated more than two hundred prints in the eighteenth and nineteenth centuries. Entrepreneurial painters and engravers who lacked access to precious face time with Washington marketed "fictitious" and unauthorized portraits. The intensity of public demand and the money to be made from satisfying it are suggested by a potentially apocryphal anecdote about Joseph Wright, who was said to have stolen Washington's likeness by painting a miniature of the president unawares while he sat in a New York City church.[1]

Washington did more than grace the walls of public buildings and genteel parlors. He literally loomed large at early national civic celebrations. Throughout the nation, he adorned transparencies: Extremely large portraits hung across the fronts of prominent buildings. At night, the building was lit at the windows behind the canvas to project a glowing likeness that floated far above the citizens on the street. And the most influential of those citizens were likely decked out with ribbons depicting the first president. Of course, not all of Washington's likenesses were as lofty as, say, Gilbert Stuart's Lansdowne portrait (1796) or as explicitly patriotic as a civic transparency hoisted on July 4th: Consider his appearance at the waxworks. But his face also appeared on the accoutrements of daily life. He graced almanacs and sheet music. He decorated mugs, plates, and tea sets. And after his death, when the production of Washingtoniana reached new highs, a mourning citizenry could comfort themselves with hand-kerchiefs depicting the great man on his deathbed.[2]

Stretching from the canonical to the ephemeral and encompassing every-thing in between, this catalog of Washingtons seems to confirm everything we know about his emergence as a national symbol. Visual and material culture worked in tandem with print culture to conflate the great man and the poten-tially great nation; the compulsive urge to depict him helped ease and obscure the profound tensions that followed the ratification of the Constitution. Withal, scholars working in a variety of fields—including history, literature, and art history—have stressed Washington's ability to transform himself into a symbol of national unity, a transformation that depended on his austere sincerity and daunting self-control. These were the qualities that constituted republican gen-tility, the qualities that distinguished his masterful performance as commander in chief, first president, and, finally, pater patriae.[3]

Much like museums, Washington's many likenesses were tasked with trans-lating the idealized republic of taste into visible reality. And much like museums, they tell a more complicated, more contradictory set of stories than scholars usu-ally acknowledge. Washington's portraits simultaneously reference revolutionary iconoclasm, royal diplomacy, republican virtue, and early national political cul-ture. They raise questions about how Anglo-Americans' fascination with the man's physical appearance shaped the visual politics of the early republic. The hyper-production of Washington's likeness directs us to the intersection of com-modification, consumption, and political culture in the early republic. By the early nineteenth century, depictions of Washington signaled authenticity and its opposite. Embellishing elaborate engravings and shoddy medals, sturdy mugs and flimsy almanacs, Washington's image referenced both love of country and love of commerce. An exploration of the multiple contexts in which Anglo-Americans and others produced and viewed these images underscores both the power of visual politics and the promise held out by the republic of taste in the early republic. Paradoxically, it also demonstrates the ways that those same images insistently undermined the very notion of a republic of taste.

Behold the King

It is impossible to understand how and why different audiences regarded Washington's appearance without considering British rule and, especially, representations of the English king. The king was the celebrated, symbolic linchpin of the hyper-British identity that distinguished Anglo-America by the mid-eighteenth century. Indeed, as historian Brendan McConville has argued, when most provincials conceptualized their connections to Britain, they conceptualized them vis-à-vis the king. They also imagined those relations as "passions that bound the empire together," based on an affection that was as reciprocal as it was abiding. Thus colonial newspapers published the names of those Anglo-Americans fortunate enough to kiss the monarch's hand. Gentlemen and plebes celebrated coronations and royal birthdays with toasts and bonfires. From Massachusetts to South Carolina, ministers venerated the king as God's chosen bulwark against popery. This increasingly effusive ceremonial and rhetorical culture was supplemented by a rich visual and material culture. After 1700, colonists could revere and even enjoy their king not simply by reading about him in the press, toasting him on his birthday, or praying for him on Sundays, but also by looking at him. By the eve of the Revolution, portraits of British rulers had become common elements in a colonial visual culture that extended from state houses to taverns to residences.[4]

Paintings of monarchs lent grandeur and authority to public buildings throughout the colonies. In some cases, these paintings arrived courtesy of provincial administrators, like the Massachusetts officials who commissioned full-length commemorative portraits of William and Mary in 1740, or Virginia's Royal Governor Lord Botetourt, who purchased copies of Allan Ramsay's magisterial *George III* and *Queen Charlotte* to flank the ballroom entrance at the governor's palace. More often, though, the likenesses were dispatched from the Crown as official emblems of royal authority. The surviving records, admittedly sketchy, suggest that these paintings began to cross the Atlantic around the turn of the eighteenth century. Over time, as one sovereign succeeded another, a province could amass a significant portrait collection. On the eve of the Revolution, for example, Boston's Town House boasted Charles II, James II, George II, and Queen Caroline in addition to William and Mary. A sprawling family tree in pictures, the likenesses affirmed a royal lineage that stretched from London to Hanover and back again. Staring down at their subjects, these kings and queens avowed that royal succession was natural, even orderly; they belied the plots, executions, wars, and frantic diplomacy upon which this particular succession depended.[5]

The official representations that lined the walls of the government buildings were imposing not simply because they linked seats of colonial power to a

Figure 29. *Their most Sacred Majesties George the IIId. and Queen Charlotte with His Royal Highness George Prince of Wales, Frederick Bishop of Osnaburg, Prince William Henry, Princess Charlotte Augusta Mattilda, Prince Edward and Princess Sophia Agust.*, engraved by Richard Earlom (1743–1822) after Johan Joseph Zoffany, London, 1771. Royal Collection Trust / © Her Majesty Queen Elizabeth II 2015. RCIN 604687.

divinely ordained succession, but also because so many of them were enormous. Although portraits had become increasingly popular among the colonial gentry, full-length portraits remained a rarity; one art historian estimates that fewer than twenty-five survive from the entire colonial era. A standard full-length portrait like Ramsay's *George III* measured around seven and a half feet tall and almost five feet wide—and that was before it was encased in a frame, which could easily add another eight inches all around. Never mind that only the very wealthiest families could afford a painting that large; only a handful of the very grandest Anglo-American homes could accommodate it. Scale helps to explain the awe that John Adams felt when he first encountered the full-length portraits of Charles II and James II, decked out in "royal ermine" and "long flowing robes," on display at the Massachusetts Supreme Court.[6]

Although large-scale portraits remained the preserve of public buildings, prints depicting British royalty enjoyed a far wider circulation. Explicitly

Figure 30. George III, William Pitt, and James Wolfe, engraved by Nathaniel Hurd, Boston, 1762. Courtesy of the American Antiquarian Society.

market-oriented, engravers catered to a variety of tastes and budgets, especially after the expansion of the print trade in the 1730s. The upper end of the market would have included prints like one engraved by Richard Earlom in 1771. Translating the elements of the Grand Style into mezzotint, it was about the same size as the standard bust-format oil portrait and would have warranted the same prominent display. Conspicuous display was clearly the aim of John Randolph, the wealthy planter and attorney general of Virginia Colony, when he purchased pendant prints of the king and queen on the eve of the Revolution. Simpler in composition than Earlom's family group, these prints were nevertheless imposing enough to claim pride of place in the dining room of Tazewell Hall, Randolph's Williamsburg mansion.[7]

Humbler likenesses, like the one published by Boston's silversmith-cum-engraver Nathaniel Hurd, clustered at the opposite end of the print market. Hurd arranged three miniature likenesses of George III, William Pitt, and James Wolfe around a simple plinth inscribed with the virtues of the "Best of KINGS." Bearing little relation to any individual, the figures are identified by their dress, props, and inscribed names. Moreover, Hurd had shaped and sized each of the faces to fit inside a watch cover, enabling buyers to choose between displaying them whole or cutting them into pieces. Although it is safe to say that Hurd's prints were probably not destined for the parlors of the wealthy and powerful, it is far more difficult to guess his intended buyers. Especially at its lower margins, the precise contours of the Anglo-American print market are elusive. Moreover, the logic of preservation—which dictates that the objects survive in direct proportion to their cost—makes it far more difficult to track the circulation of cheap prints than expensive ones. Still, the number of print sellers who advertised that their wares included prints of "smaller Quality: Cheap for Cash" suggests that a king and a queen could be had for little more than a song.[8]

Whether the likeness in question was a towering oil portrait or a crude profile, its meaning was at least partly political. Yet images of the monarch also registered meanings whose connection to the imperial project was far more attenuated, meanings that owed far less to the politics of empire per se than to the intersection of visual culture and the market. The same engraving of George III that testified to an owner's devotion to the Crown, for example, might simultaneously have composed part of a larger collection of exemplary print "heads." Distant cousins of the pantheons that would gain favor after the Revolution, these collections were popular on both sides of the Atlantic. Providing a picture of the world writ small, these collections created a systematic, pictorial survey of society's orders and ranks, including royalty but extending well beyond it. The interest in mapping society helps account for the variety of representative heads that found their way into North American shops, where kings and queens were displayed among the "Judges of England"; William Pitt; Marshal Keith, a Scottish Protestant mercenary; many "esteemed patrons of America"; and "Effigies of all the New-England Ministers ever done in Metzotinto." Alongside these stalwarts of the Protestant empire, collectors could find likenesses of Spanish and Prussian monarchs; "Mr. Gerrick, Actor"; "Mr Beard, Singer"; and "Ann Arnold, the Jersey Nanny," a black servant engraved by John Greenwood in 1748.[9] The English king may have taken precedence in this lineup, but he also served as one representative type in a series of representative types.

Just as the king might have figured as one head among many, he might have appeared as one picture among many. Eighteenth-century colonists sought a variety of objects embellished with some form of pictorial representation, including wallpaper, embroidered fire screens, ladies' fans, and ceramics as well as paintings and maps. Prints marked the most affordable point of entry into this world of pictures. To be sure, portraiture was, by a wide margin, the most popular genre among colonists who bought prints, just as it was among those who commissioned paintings. But if it was the most popular genre, it was hardly the only one. Colonists' appetite for images is suggested by the generic range of extant eighteenth-century prints: The same retailers who stocked the royals also hawked landscapes, pictures of Roman antiquities, views of elegant buildings from around the world, "Sea Pieces" and "Scripture Pieces," hunting scenes and fishing scenes, copies of Old Masters, and, especially, William Hogarth's conversation pieces, which were the pictorial equivalent of best sellers and remained in demand for years after his death.[10] Their appetite also registers in the language of merchants who announced the arrival of a "very choice Collection," "a choice Assortment," or "a parcel of Fine Missitinto Prints." When the Boston merchant Albert Dennie acquired the "greatest variety of most curious Pictures" in 1742, he invited the buying public to "pick & chuse for 6 *d* & 12 *d* a Piece."[11] This vague language suggests more than plentitude; it promises variety. Anyone with "6 *d* & 12 *d*" to spare could seize the opportunity to discover and indulge taste. Dennie and his competitors aimed to capitalize on customers' lively engagement with the consumer market rather than on their putative veneration of the Crown.

Iconoclasm

The passions that bound the British Empire together eventually gave way to the passions that ripped it apart. And in town after town, the moment when love surrendered to hate was marked by iconoclasm. Sometimes the drama of deposition was calculated to become the stuff of legend. The destruction of the massive equestrian statue of George III on New York City's Bowling Green in 1776 is the obvious case in point. The statue had been commissioned to demonstrate the colony's gratitude for the repeal of the Stamp Act and to soften the statement made by a statue of William Pitt commissioned at the same time. The monument consisted of a fifteen-foot marble pedestal supporting a larger-than-life, classically dressed George III on horseback, looking every inch the latter-day Marcus Aurelius. Although the sculpture had been a target of petty vandalism almost from its installation, it survived six years—until the night George Washington, commander in chief of the Continental Army, ordered that the Declaration of Independence be read aloud before an assembly of soldiers and civilians. Immediately afterward, a mob charged onto the Bowling Green, roped the statue, pulled it to the ground, and hacked it to pieces. Reduced to a pile of rubble, the gilded lead that once symbolized the subjects' "firm attachment and affection to his Majesty's person" was transformed into the rebelling army's cartridges. The impulse epitomized by the New York City mob recurred throughout the colonies. In public spectacles that might have been stage-managed by Tom Paine, patriots buried, burned, and defaced images of the English monarch.[12]

In the eighteenth-century imagination, these violations of canvas, paper, and gilded lead concretized and personalized the abstractions of political theory. They encapsulated the pivotal moment when Anglo-Americans were compelled to reinterpret more than a decade of political conflict, recasting their benevolent monarch as a ruthless tyrant. The political rupture symbolized by iconoclasm was paralleled and intensified by ruptures in the contexts and conventions of pictorial representation and reception. The expansion of revolutionary agitation abruptly narrowed both the range of meanings generated by royal likenesses and the contexts in which those likenesses could operate. As the first British Empire broke apart, a likeness of the king ceased to be one head, one picture, among many. After 1776, a portrait of George III was pointedly a portrait of the monarch.

This amounted to far more than a repoliticization of the images. It was also a reconfiguration of the interpretive field in which portraits could signify. Unlike effigies of stamp collectors, parliamentary ministers, and royalty—which were created specifically for ritualized abuse and destruction—portraits had been created as didactic objects of observation, intended to serve specific, and decidedly conservative, social and political ends. As Jonathan Richardson put it in his influential *Essay on the Theory of Painting* (1715), in the absence of the person depicted on canvas, the likeness was meant to "keep up those Sentiments" that might otherwise "languish," chief among them "Love, and Duty."[13] Through the craft of painter and printer, a person removed from the viewer by distance or even death could continue to instruct. Richardson was doubtless optimistic about viewers' attentiveness. But as he understood, regardless of how effectively portraits communicated, the flow of communication ran in one direction: It moved from the collaboration between artist and subject out to spectators.

The iconoclasm that marked the beginning of war reversed this flow, urging audiences to address images directly and emphatically. During the Continental Army's retreat from Cornwallis following the Battle of Cowpens, for example, General Nathanael Greene reportedly pulled a portrait of George III off the wall of Steele's Tavern and wrote "George, hide thy face and mourn" across the back. He then hung the frame backward, forcing the king to face the wall. The anecdote, which smacks of myth, quickly became part of North Carolina's revolutionary lore; the framed picture that Greene supposedly defaced has been preserved in a museum.[14] Apocryphal or not, the story—with its heady combination of text and gesture—suggests that iconoclasm was arresting not only because it allowed men and women to reject the king, but also because it allowed them to do so by "talking back" to representations and by extension to the king himself. In the moment of address, the distance between the likeness and the original narrowed, further eclipsing the multiple meanings that had accumulated around the portraits over the first half of the eighteenth century.

By collapsing the distance between the sitter and his representation, revolutionary iconoclasm reinvested portraits of statesmen with intense ideological significance. It encouraged viewers to use images as vehicles for mobilizing their own passions, political and otherwise. In all of these ways, the destruction of royal portraits paved the way for the reception of republican ones.

Royal Politics of Republican Representation

When the likenesses of James, Charles, Charlotte, and especially the Georges that had accumulated over almost a century were destroyed or discarded, portraits of George Washington frequently replaced them, often in straight-up trades. In 1783, Princeton College commissioned a portrait of Washington from Charles Willson Peale to replace a picture of the king that had been damaged by an American cannonball during the war. The owner of the Royal George Tavern in Alexandria, Virginia, reportedly ripped down the sign of the king and replaced it with one depicting the other, better George. In New York City's Bowling Green, a carved and painted wooden Washington was eventually erected on the same pedestal that once supported the unlucky equestrian statue of George III.[15]

By 1819, this kind of exchange had become more than shorthand for regime change; it had become a punch line. When Washington Irving's everyman, Rip Van Winkle, stumbles down from the Catskill Mountains after a twenty-year nap, the full realization that his village has changed comes when he spies the sign marking the inn. There, the "ruby face of King George" was "singularly metamorphosed." The man's red coat had turned blue; a sword replaced his scepter. And underneath the face, "GENERAL WASHINGTON" was painted in large letters.[16] Irving's joke plays out on two levels. Van Winkle knows nothing of the political and social revolutions that have "metamorphosed" his community. But neither does he understand that the sign symbolizing those revolutions continues to depict a head of state, continues, in fact, to depict a "George." Irving pokes fun at Van Winkle's ignorance of change and his ignorance of continuity.

By and large, scholars who have explored Washington's textual and pictorial representations catch the first joke and miss the second. They point out, for example, that, in life and in art, Washington eschewed the kind of "royal ermine and long flowing robes" that had once awed a young John Adams. Instead, he chose to represent himself first in a military uniform and then, during his presidency, in a black velvet suit. They have likewise noted that painters and engravers replaced English emblems with American ones. Thrones and scepters gave way to liberty poles and caps, eagles, and painted copies of the Declaration of

Independence or the Constitution. In their eagerness to celebrate Washington as the man who would not be king, scholars and curators tend to overlook the extent to which political and cultural change was accompanied by continuity.[17]

When Washington replaced the king, he generally did so in postures borrowed from monarchical portraits. To establish the gravitas of man, office, and nation, artists mined a vocabulary of poses and postures derived from continental traditions stretching back to the fifteenth century, which were in turn a reinterpretation of classical traditions. Gilbert Stuart's Lansdowne portrait, generally hailed as a quintessentially republican image, simultaneously anchors Washington in an especially rich collection of republican symbols and poses the president to mirror Ramsay's coronation portrait of George III, which was copied repeatedly for display in the English colonies. And when the Continental Congress voted in 1783 to erect an equestrian statue of Washington to mark its permanent home, it ordered up an exact duplicate of the Bowling Green statue that had been destroyed some seven years earlier. Like Marcus Aurelius and George III before him, Washington was to be "represented in Roman dress, holding a truncheon in his right hand" and crowned with a laurel wreath. The royal resonance of the proposed statue was reinforced by French sculptor Jean-Antoine Houdon, who campaigned for the commission. Houdon boasted to Jefferson that "being in Possession of the foundary at which was cast a fine equestrian Statue of Louis the 15th," he could deliver one "on Terms more Moderate than any other Artist in Paris." If some members of Congress balked at the monument's projected cost, none expressed reservations about a depiction of Washington modeled after not one but two European kings.[18]

The multiple convergences between republican and royal portraiture can be interpreted as a technical problem of pictorial representation. How could artists devise a visual grammar that depicted the break with Britain and the creation of a modern republic in ways that were intelligible to viewers whose associations were steeped in and structured by British culture? Even the use of classical motifs and themes, a gambit that aimed to sidestep recent history by suggesting that "antique precedent and contemporary incident were one," ultimately worked to align rather than differentiate American, British, and European art forms.[19] This should not be surprising, for in the eighteenth century, Americans perforce imported their classicism from Europe. Small wonder, then, that the line of descent that linked a statue of Washington to a statue of a Roman emperor ran straight through an English king.

The artist's problem was the diplomat's solution. Even before the war was over, Washington's portraits began to figure as components of diplomatic exchange, publicizing the American cause and facilitating international relationships and alliances. Precisely because his likenesses mediated between older

Figure 31. *George Washington Eqer. Général en Chef de l'Armée Anglo-Amériquaine, nommé Dictateur par Congrès en Fevrier 1777*, engraved by Esnauts et Rapilly, Paris, 178-. Library of Congress.

forms of encoding authority and attempts to establish new ones, they allowed European power brokers and princes to assimilate Washington and the republic he stood for into an international political imaginary. Indeed, his likenesses proved effective not because they varnished republican novelty over monarchical convention but because they encouraged foreign viewers to imagine the relationship between the two. For if the portraits gestured toward American ideological, political, and historic particularity, they also assimilated Anglo-America into a rubric of stylistic conventions and diplomatic performances associated with Europe's courts and its community of nations.

Portraits of Washington first circulated on the continent during the Revolutionary War. In some cases, these images—especially engraved prints—were clearly created and marketed with an eye toward capitalizing on world events.

Like German and French engravings that condemned the destruction of George III's statue on the Bowling Green, pictures of "General Washington" served as a pictorial extension of conversations about world events generated by the press. Accuracy counted for little. In many instances, the man on paper bore no connection to the real Washington. Instead, artists inserted the head of some other person—real or imagined, living or dead—onto an appropriately posed body set amid props borrowed from other images. Even the influential engraved portraits published in France by Esnauts and Rapilly arrange a catalog of allegorical and decorative motifs that came to symbolize and specify the American Revolution (cannons, banners, liberty pole and cap, palm and laurel branches) around a portrait bust of someone other than Washington.[20] The relative accuracy of these engravings counted for little in pictures that were rhetorical devices arguing for or against the viability of the revolutionary cause.

Especially when the engraving aimed to rally support for the rebelling colonies, its compositional and symbolic elements had to be legible to viewers who measured international affairs against standards set by monarchical European nations.[21] Washington's portraits thus served as political conversation pieces. As the confederation's unofficial charge d'affaires in Amsterdam explained as late as 1785, the addition of a Washington bust had turned his room into a "Sanctuary." There, he gushed, "are introduced your homagers, the friends of Civil Liberty, Equality, and true Greatness."[22] Hyperbole, to be sure. But regardless of their deepest political convictions, these friends of "civil liberty, equality, and true greatness" had been primed by a likeness of Washington who could fit comfortably into galleries lined with portraits of kings and princes.

Picturing Diplomacy

As the war for independence ground on and Europeans and Americans jockeyed for advantage with one eye on the immediate execution of the war and the other on the potential reconstruction of alliances afterward, portraiture assumed an increasingly prominent role in diplomatic exchanges. Likenesses were potent tools in a world where most diplomats acted on behalf of kings and their ministers and where much diplomatic work demanded an acute sensitivity to personalities and lineages. It was precisely this sensitivity that prompted French ambassador Conrad Alexandre Gérard to read a portrait as a renewed alliance. In 1779, relations between France and the United States had been severely strained by an alliance between France and Spain that had been forged independently of the United States. Congress spent much of the summer debating whether or not to ally themselves with the other two nations. In September, after months of heated argument, Congress asked Gérard to sit for a portrait. The seasoned diplomat correctly understood the request as a gesture of friendship and as a signal that the United States would ultimately align itself with France.[23]

Such an acutely personalized politics was consonant with eighteenth-century ideas about nationhood and international relations. As literary historian Martha Rojas has pointed out, the rhetoric and practice of eighteenth-century diplomacy personified the state and constructed treaties as agreements that "assume the addresses between personal friends."[24] It was in this milieu that portraits played a diplomatic role. A likeness of a king, his emissary, or even a revolutionary general provided a stand-in for the subject, who was in turn understood to stand for the nation as a whole. Diplomatic portraits simultaneously conjured both individual and national presence out of absence. Moreover, the process of exchange—the social mechanisms whereby portraits were requested, dispatched, and displayed—organized international relations as a series of carefully nurtured friendships among a small handful of men. In 1785, for example, Count Solm of Saxe wrote that he gave his just-arrived portrait of Washington "sufficient embellishment by Placing it between the King of Prussia & his Illustrious Brother Henry." Only a year earlier, the "Illustrious Brother Henry" himself had visited Paris, where he dined at the home of the Comte de Rochambeau, an aristocrat who had served in the Continental Army during the Revolution. There, Henry had seen Washington's "Picture with great pleasure," a fact that Rochambeau was careful to communicate to Washington. Long after it was bestowed upon a friend and potential ally, a portrait could generate correspondence reinforcing personal and political bonds.[25]

In practice, of course, nations—like friends—were not necessarily equals. Powerful nations dictated the ceremonial protocols for the performance of "friendship," and weak nations adjusted accordingly. This meant that, republican principles notwithstanding, the United States conducted much of its diplomacy in language and ceremony borrowed from and responsive to European courts. Especially where portraits were concerned, royal conventions trumped republican ones. Thus, the pursuit of diplomatic favor prompted the Continental Congress to write to "their great, faithful, and beloved friend and ally, Lewis the sixteenth, king of France and Navarre" in 1799 to express their pleasure that "Providence has been pleased to bless your nuptials with the birth of a princess" and convey their prayers that the "virtues and honors" of his "illustrious family" might be perpetuated in a worthy "race of descendents." In the same communication, they requested portraits of the king and his "royal consort" Marie Antoinette, which they promised to place in the Congress's council chamber so that the "representatives of these states may daily have before their eyes the first royal friends and patrons of their cause." Immediately after approving this letter, Congress drafted a second. This time, they asked "Lewis the sixteenth" to provide "necessary supplies" for the Board of War (totaling 505,792 pounds, 5 shillings, and 6 pence sterling) and for the Marine Committee (totaling 63,056 pounds, 11 shillings, and 2 farthings sterling).[26] The two nations may have been "great, faithful, and beloved" friends, but they were unevenly matched. The exigencies of power dictated that friendships commemorated by the paintings would play out in the tenor of the court, in flamboyant flattery and dynastic celebration.

The same dynamic applied to the countless portraits of Washington that were propelled abroad during and after the Revolution by American and European power brokers. Consider the North American career of Don Juan de Miralles, which joined patronage and portraits in the service of diplomatic maneuvering. Miralles was a Spanish-born merchant, based in Havana, who had parlayed his wife's money and connections into a fortune based on licit and illicit trade between Cuba and St. Augustine. When war broke out, Miralles was selected to be one of the "observers" dispatched by Spain to gather intelligence, cultivate relationships with rebel leaders, and pursue an agenda dear to the hearts of Spaniards and Cubans: reclaiming the Floridas and regaining control over the Mississippi River. Between his arrival in Philadelphia in 1778 and his death in 1780, Miralles successfully advanced the mutual interests of Spain and the United States. He served as the conduit for Spanish and Cuban resources and managed to secure a promise from Congress that if Charles III entered the war on the side of the colonies, he was free to try and reclaim the Floridas from Great Britain.[27]

On the American end of this negotiation, Miralles's influence depended on his ability to insinuate himself into networks of power, for he had no official status. After slipping into Charleston in 1778, he made his way to Philadelphia, where he immediately became a fixture of the city's social circuit and eventually a fixture of the nation's political scene. He used considerable personal charm and generous gifts to gain access to and nurture friendships with men of power, not least of whom was George Washington. He became a noted host, celebrated for dinner parties where he heaped flattery on the wives and daughters of congressmen. He forged lucrative partnerships with businessmen, including Robert Morris, the "financier of the revolution." He also served as a conspicuous patron of the arts; in revolutionary Philadelphia, that meant supporting Charles Willson Peale. In 1779, Peale presented engraved portraits of Washington to political luminaries, including Henry Laurens, who was then president of Congress; Tom Paine; Gérard; and Miralles. Miralles promptly ordered four dozen more—presumably to be sent abroad. The following year, Miralles commissioned five copies of Peale's *George Washington at Princeton*. He kept one for himself, where it would have been displayed for the benefit of his American friends. He sent one to the captain general of Cuba and another to Havana's

CHAPTER SIX

House of Eligio de la Puente, a primary Cuban supplier for the colonies, thereby ensuring that Cuba's political and mercantile power centers had likenesses of Washington. He shipped the other two to unspecified Spaniards. (Peale thereafter boasted, perhaps erroneously, that his paintings had made it as far as the Spanish Court.)[28] He also made certain that his purchases were well publicized not only through word of mouth but also in the Philadelphia press. Like the dinner parties, the compliments, the business deals, and the gifts, these commissions confirmed Miralles as a friend of the Revolution.

On the Spanish end of this negotiation, Miralles's success depended on his ability to champion the patriot cause in Cuba and, especially, in Madrid. This was no easy task. Spanish authorities detested the English. Yet their own holdings in the Americas made them skittish about endorsing colonial rebellion. Miralles needed to convince skeptical Spaniards that the Anglo-Americans were capable of holding up their share of a high-risk, high-stakes partnership. Toward that end, he wrote tirelessly and enthusiastically about American capacity, commitment, and leadership. Many of his communiqués included Peale's portraits of George Washington. Scholars have generally ascribed Miralles's purchases to his enthusiasm for the patriot cause, his veneration of Washington, even his affection for Peale. They have read his purchases, in other words, in ways that reify the culture of diplomatic "friendship" and placed the imprimatur of inevitability on American independence. In fact, those likenesses served dual strategic purposes: They were gifts aimed at wooing support within a far-flung Spanish bureaucracy and they were evidence testifying to the possibility of American victory.

It is worth reconsidering Miralles's purchases of *George Washington at Princeton* from the Spanish perspective. The original portrait had been commissioned by Pennsylvania's Supreme Executive Council "not only as a mark of the great respect which we bear to His Excellency, but that the contemplation of it may excite others to tread in the same glorious and disinterested steps." Peale selected the Battle of Princeton as the backdrop for a full-length military portrait. The painting situated Washington's achievement in relation to the specifics of military victory rather than the abstractions of republican character, as the art historian Lillian Miller has observed.[29] But notwithstanding its historic specificity, *George Washington at Princeton* closely resembled the fictitious military portraits of American officers that had been published across the Atlantic in the preceding years; indeed, Peale's Washington closely resembled countless portraits of European military heroes.[30] Precisely because it fit so neatly within the conventions of European military portraiture, because it was coded in martial rather than ideological symbols, the portrait appealed to Spain's absolutist monarch and his advisors as well as Pennsylvania's radical council.

Figure 32. Charles Willson Peale, *George Washington at Princeton*, 1779. Oil on canvas, 93 × 58½ in. Image courtesy of the Pennsylvania Academy of the Fine Arts, Philadelphia. Gift of Maria McKean Allen and Phebe Warren Downes through the bequest of their mother, Elizabeth Wharton McKean.

In royal courts, in the townhouses and country estates of sympathetic aristo-crats, and in the headquarters of foreign merchants who shipped materiel to North America, Washington's likeness—and, by extension, the republican project—was located in visual and social fields dominated by aristocrats, enlightened and otherwise. The aim of diplomatic portraits was to align the United States with European monarchies, not to distinguish it from them. In that context, royalism rather than republicanism set the standards for effective depiction.

The Republic Embodied

However Washington appeared abroad, within the United States he emphati-cally represented republican virtue, which was in fact an entire catalog of vir-tues. It encompassed sacrifice, disinterestedness, self-control, and resistance to the seductions of faction. Even before the colonies declared their independence, Washington struck some observers as a nearly perfect incarnation of the re-publican idea. By the end of his life, Americans reflexively theorized and elabo-rated virtue in relation to Washington. His credentials were based on his biography—on his transformation from adoring younger brother to family scion; on his storied bravery during the French and Indian War; on his valor as commander in chief of the Continental Army; on his selfless service as president of the United States; on his devotion to his plantation and his family; and on his lifelong struggle to master his volatile temper.

Long before his death, Washington's remarkably full life was well on its way to becoming a national fable in which republican virtue fused the exceptional-ism of man and nation. The fable's meaning was distilled in a series of emblem-atic scenes ranging from the danger and privation of colonial and revolutionary battlefields to the triumph of his first inauguration. It was confirmed in Wash-ington's multiple resignations, in those moments when, like Cincinnatus, he retired from military command and political office to return to his "own vine and fig tree."[31] In these exemplary scenes, as in the larger narrative they com-posed, Washington simultaneously typified the qualities that engendered revo-lutionary heroism and republican virtue and provided countless citizens with an object of emulation. "Let Our youth look up to This Man as a pattern to form themselves by," as Connecticut politician Silas Deane intoned in 1775.[32]

It was no coincidence that Deane's exhortation was predicated on the lan-guage of looking. For if citizens of the republic were to learn *about* George Washington, and more important, learn *from* George Washington, they needed to do more than read about him. They needed to see him, to grasp his greatness with their eyes. Looking, more than listening or even reading, created the ground for imaginative identification, for emulation. Even biographers invited readers to imagine that they were watching Washington rather than merely reading about him. Mason Locke Weems's best-selling biography claimed to offer young readers a peek "behind the curtain." With the parson's help, they would discover the real man "not in the glare of [the] public," under the watchful "eyes of millions," but "in the shade of private life." And when Weems's Washington finally succumbed to fever and ascended to heaven, the living observers who had peopled the preceding pages of his book were replaced by dead ones: Floating in the clouds, Washington was surrounded by fallen patriots, "martyred saints," who "devour[ed] him with eyes of love."[33] Sixty years later, George Washington Parke Custis published a memoir about his adoptive grandfather, describing the key moments of Washington's life as a "tableau vivant," a series of shifting "life pictures" in which Washington was always the central figure.[34]

On one level, of course, writers like Weems and Custis were simply making use of a long-standing literary trope that figured reading as a surrogate for looking. But this familiar device took on new meaning and new urgency in the early republic. From the 1780s onward, Americans insisted that Washington's character announced itself in his physical appearance. The national fixation on Washington's face and form was bolstered by physiognomy and its attendant fantasies of legibility. It was reinforced by the repeated assurances of art theorists and aesthetic entrepreneurs alike that the faces of eminent men—whether encountered firsthand or through portraits—might serve as the basis for a republican pantheon that could "instruct the mind" of the viewer and thereby "sow the seeds of Virtue," as Peale put it.[35] And, as we will see, U.S. audiences were capable of responding to exhortations to visualize Washington not least because of the many likenesses of the pater patriae that circulated through the republic; readers could imagine they were seeing Washington in battle or on the ballroom floor because his was already a familiar form. But this national fascination was fueled more immediately by Washington's carefully orchestrated, richly stylized public appearances during his presidency. Indeed, it was precisely this putative correspondence between Washington's inner and outer being, a correspondence that was reaffirmed whenever he appeared in public, that primed Americans to produce, circulate, and consume so many iterations of his image.

One of the most striking aspects of Washington's mystique, both in the early republic and in our own time, is the extent to which it coincides with his physicality, with his face and form. Recent years have witnessed a *National Geographic* television program that promised to show viewers what the real man looked like and the launch of an exhibit at Mount Vernon featuring three wax statues, created under the direction of a forensic anthropologist, that depict Washington "as an adventurous young surveyor and frontiersman, as the force-ful commander-in-chief of the Revolutionary War forces, and as the dynamic first president of the United States."[36] Washington's dentures are counted among the "treasures" collected at Mount Vernon and are prominently featured both in the museum and on its website. Contemporary biographers ranging from Joseph Ellis to Ron Chernow go out of their way to remind readers of Washington's face and his physique; Richard Brookhiser went so far as to quote a female body builder's assessment of Washington's "well developed thighs." ("*Nice* quads" was her conclusion.)[37] The assumption that Washington's body *matters*, that it communicates some otherwise ineffable truth, has become axio-matic, making it easy to forget that this was not always the case.

In fact, the association of Washington's sterling character with his vaunted physique was not the inevitable effect of the man's posture, his height, his pro-file, or his teeth. It was an artifact of war and nation making. It was the product of a particular history. Before the Imperial Crisis, the handful of detailed physi-cal descriptions of Washington allowed that he was tall, muscled, and possessed of "regular" features. But observers did not necessarily attach any larger mean-ing to this catalog of features. During the war, loyalists and Englishmen unsym-pathetic to the patriot cause were hardly dazzled by the general's physical presence. The Anglican minister Jonathan Boucher, for one, found Washington to be "shy, silent, and slow" and concluded that only the "interested representa-tions of party" could lead anyone to consider him a "great man." Bennett Allen, a minister and loyalist, dismissed him as a "mediocrity." Someone writing as an "Old Soldier," who offered a knowledgeable and largely favorable critique of Washington's abilities as a tactician, found him to be unfortunately "slow in parts."[38] Not surprisingly, the use of Washington's form as an indicator of his greatness seems to have originated among wartime patriots, who seized on his body as the embodiment of their cause. After meeting Washington for the first time, Abigail Adams famously borrowed from John Dryden to gush:

Mark his Majestick fabrick! he's a temple
Sacred by birth, and built by hands divine
His Souls the deity that lodges there.
Nor is the pile unworthy of the God.[39]

Marylander John Bell put Washington's body to explicitly political purposes in 1779. Promising European readers that Washington was a model of "candour, sincerity, affability, and simplicity," Bell directed their attention to Washing-ton's "person" (tall and "well-made" with features that were "manly and bold," albeit "marked with the small pox") because he was "convinced" that it "bears a great analogy to the qualifications of his mind." Anyone wanting proof that Washington represented the "perfect alliance of virtues of a philosopher with the talents of a general" need only look at his body.[40] For viewers like Adams and Bell, Washington's person delivered assurances about the patriot cause that could not necessarily be garnered from events on the ground.

After Washington assumed the presidency in 1789, paeans linking his mythic character to his arresting appearance became all but obligatory. Having watched the man in movement and repose, a British observer was struck in 1790 by the realization that "no man could be better formed for command." Almost a decade later, an American wrote that although Washington's "whole aspect pronounces him the Hero formed to rush fearless" through the "rude tempest of war," his "countenance" showed him to be "more supremely blest in the kindred sunshine of harmony and peace."[41] Around the same time, a man who once peeked through a window to catch a glimpse of Washington pronounced him "almost a different being" from the political elites who surrounded him and different "indeed from any other person ever reared in this country." By the turn of the nineteenth century, those lucky enough to have seen the man in the flesh insisted that even a chance sighting "inspired veneration."[42] Observations like these circulated on both sides of the Atlantic in manuscript and in print. Once the "letters," "dispatches," and "sketches" made their way into print in the United States, they were reprinted almost endlessly. Small wonder that when Custis sat down to record his *Recollections*, he felt compelled to include an entire chapter parsing Washington's "personal appearance."

Visual Politics

If regurgitated descriptions of Washington's looks owed much to the expansion of print in the decades following the Revolution, the preoccupation itself owed much more to the intersection of visual and political cultures that marked the early republic. During the war and after, political questions merged with aesthetic ones, not only at the level of philosophical abstraction but also in the material world. Eager, and sometimes desperate, to demonstrate that they had freed themselves from forms and fashions that smacked of empire and aristocracy, Americans self-consciously manufactured new ones. Civic celebrations, rituals, and symbols thus became crucial components of revolutionary and early national political cultures.[43] Almost without exception, these cultural gambits drew their power from their fundamental visuality. The iconographic and allegorical images that decorated teacups, textiles, and almanacs reminded citizens of the need for virtue. Parades and processions created visible symbols of polity and government at the same time that they served as vehicles to participate in both. Citizens found affirmation and encouragement both by observing the faces of other citizens and by knowing that they themselves were objects of observation. It was in this context that people homed in on Washington's body. In a world where patriotic sentiment was sustained and circulated visually, it is not surprising that citizens were exhorted to "look upon" the man as a "pattern."

This was precisely what happened during Washington's highly ritualized, much-ballyhooed public appearances. The most celebrated of these took place in 1789 when he traveled from Virginia to New York City to be sworn in as president and in 1789 and 1791 when he toured New England and the southern states. Each of these journeys unfolded as a series of carefully orchestrated spectacles calculated to project Washington as the embodiment of a nationalist, Federalist civic culture. A typical stop went something like this: Washington's arrival was announced to the massed spectators by cannon and artillery fire. He and his attendants promenaded through the town or city, followed by local notables, who were organized by profession and rank. At a designated point, Washington stopped, climbed onto a porch or balcony, and watched the remainder of the procession pass beneath him. After a formal welcome (delivered and accepted in front of the crowds), he was honored with a private dinner, which provided his hosts with the chance to make speeches and toasts. If the town was large enough or wealthy enough, dinner segued into a ball. Meanwhile, the people out of doors typically celebrated his presence with illuminations and transparencies. If he lingered more than a day, he and his entourage visited local sites that demonstrated the town's improving spirit before the evening ceremonies began again. This cycle was repeated day after day, in town after town.[44]

These were expressly visual events, aimed at drawing observers' attention to Washington himself. The emphasis was not on oratory, either as performed in real time or as circulated by the press in the days and weeks that followed. While politically ambitious hosts used the occasions to advance their own agendas through speeches and toasts, Washington merely expressed his gratitude for their efforts, communicated his satisfaction with everything that he saw, and assured spectators who turned out to see him that their presence excited his sensibility. At most, during his presidential tours, he affirmed his faith in the new federal government. His words were restricted in number and restrained in tone.

Not so the visual spectacle that surrounded him on these trips. In towns and cities from New Hampshire to Georgia, Washington's admirers and supporters created elaborate settings that framed and staged him. One of the most dramatic was engineered by Charles Willson Peale on the bridge at Gray's Ferry, just outside Philadelphia, for Washington's journey to his inauguration. At either end of the bridge, Peale built enormous Roman arches, wreathed with laurel and cedar and connected to each other by greenery lining the bridge's railings. Banners attached to the arches proclaimed "Behold the Rising Empire" and "May Commerce Flourish." Another banner with the motto "Don't Tread on Me" hung from a twenty-five-foot liberty pole. The pièce de résistance was a remarkable bit of theater: As Washington passed beneath the first arch and "the acclimations of an immense crowd of spectators rent the air," a crown of laurel floated down onto his head, courtesy of a pulley system operated by Peale's daughter, Angelica.[45]

Similar symbols and devices, minus the mechanical magic, appeared wherever Washington did. In order to communicate the importance of the man and all that he represented, private and public spaces were adorned with arches, garlands, flowers, paintings, and banners. When Washington greeted the citizens of Boston, he stood on a specially constructed colonnade that projected out above the street, the better to "exhibit in strong light '*The Man of the People.*'" During the week he spent in Charleston in 1791, the city's wealthy planters went all out. They erected triumphal arches in front of their doorways, created multicolored illuminations in their mansions, turned their gardens into nighttime promenades, and affixed arrangements of flowers, shrubbery, and the requisite laurel branches to the walls of virtually every room in which the president spent any amount of time. The venerable Exchange Building, the scene of several balls and banquets honoring the president, was the jewel in Charleston's crown. In addition to plastering the walls with greenery, the city fathers hung a miniature ship containing 136 lamps from the ceiling in lieu of a chandelier. They seated Washington beneath an enormous, specially commissioned "emblematical painting representing commerce distributing plenty over the globe." Even in towns that could not begin to afford a welcome like the ones offered by Boston or Charleston, citizens demonstrated their eagerness to impress Washington. They decorated their doors and street-facing windows and cleaned the streets in front of their houses. In Providence, the poor were issued candles to ensure that the city's illumination would provide a spectacle worthy of the president.[46]

Yet Washington was not the primary audience for the celebrations that his visits engendered. Like Peale's trick with the laurel crown, these events were designed to hold the eyes of the thousands of women and men who turned out to see the president. Judging by contemporary accounts, they succeeded. It is admittedly difficult to reconstruct individuals' affective response to Washington from a distance of more than two hundred years. But the scattered remarks of citizens who attended these celebrations suggest the extent to which they encountered Washington with their eyes. When Washington processed through New York on his way to be inaugurated, "the eye could not rove with freedom," according to the editor of the *Daily Advertiser*; "One great object engaged it and WASHINGTON arrested and fixed its gaze."[47]

This kind of language was more than newspaper hyperbole. Isaac Stockton Keith, a Presbyterian minister, narrated Washington's arrival in Charleston as a series of shifting sight lines that kept Washington squarely in view: Expansive vistas of the "clear and serene" harbor, the "gaily" dressed fleet of accompanying ships, and Washington's "elegant" barge, rowed by thirteen men sporting "beautiful sky blue silk jackets," gradually gave way to the focused perspective of a street scene as Washington and his welcoming party made their way from the wharf up Bay Street to the Exchange Building. When Washington mounted the steps of the Exchange Building and "took his station" on the porch, the street scene segued into a portrait that gave the entire procession the "opportunity of seeing and saluting the President" as they passed beneath him. Further north, in Delaware, young Elizabeth Montgomery aimed for a bird's-eye view when Washington passed through Wilmington. She and a friend climbed an apple tree atop Quaker Hill, which jutted out over the road Washington would travel. Looking down at the procession, she fantasized that they occupied the same spot where Washington had once watched the sunset during the war. The perch enabled her to see the president and to see the world through his eyes, to admire him as an object and to inhabit his subjectivity.[48]

This emphasis on looking was not limited to people like Montgomery, who had no choice but to peer at Washington from a distance. Citizens whose social position enabled them to get close to Washington, to speak with him, were just as moved by the sight of him. A woman who attended one of the Charleston balls wrote to a friend that the room was packed. "Almost everyone went to see him, eager to have sight" of him. And when Washington finally appeared before the assembly, "joy sparkled in every countenance." The guests' pleasure intensified when he "went all round the room and bowed to every lady—this gave particular satisfaction, as every one was anxious to have a good view of him." The letter writer felt the same way. "Tho I had seen him so often," she explained, she attended the ball "to have one more look."[49]

And why not? This kind of looking served as a primary vehicle for the experience and performance of virtuous patriotism. Consider Washington's reception by the "Ladies" of Trenton, New Jersey, in 1789, while en route to his inauguration. Trenton had been the scene of a significant victory for the Continental Army in 1776. To honor the battle and the president-elect, the women ordered the construction of a triumphal arch measuring some twenty feet high and twelve feet long, supported by thirteen columns and spanning the bridge into Trenton. The arch was decorated with evergreens, laurels, and artificial flowers made by the women themselves; it was crowned with a sunflower dome containing the battle's dates. It bore the gilt inscription "The DEFENDER of the MOTHERS will be the PROTECTOR of the DAUGHTERS" and it was lined with the white-gowned "Ladies" and their daughters. As Washington passed, the women serenaded him with a "Sonata of their own composition." Wiping a tear from his eye, Washington thanked the women for the "exquisite sentiments he experienced in that affecting moment" and for the "taste" with which they had decorated the bridge. Such teary moments (and there were many of them whenever Washington took to the road) served as occasions for the exhibition and exchange of sentiment. This sentiment was initiated in the moment when citizens beheld Washington and saw him looking back. The "exquisite sentiment" on display in Trenton captured the nation's imagination not because of the words participants exchanged but because of the images they conjured: a beautifully ornamented bridge; a cluster of lovely young women; a general's tear.[50]

The importance of looking at Washington was underscored by the multiple likenesses that inevitably accompanied his public appearances. During his inauguration, New York sported no fewer than three enormous transparencies depicting him, including one that pictured Fame descending to crown him with laurels. At a "very crowded and brilliant assembly" held to celebrate Washington's birthday in 1791, Congressman Theodore Sedgwick reported that the "one circumstance pleasing" among the overdressed women and boisterous gentlemen was the president. Washington was present in person and in a large military portrait, "procured for the occasion," that depicted the general "trampling under his feet a British standard, and lying in the ground before him the King of England's crown inverted." And the ladies who thronged to balls and levees that boasted Washington's presence often sported sashes, headbands, and fans decorated with his picture; judging from the number of miniature portraits that circulated during these years, some of them must also have worn jewelry bearing his image.[51]

Thus did Washington's body become both symbol and source of national unity, contributing to politics of both the nation-building and partisan varieties. By focusing attention on the great man's person, Washington and his supporters deflected it, however briefly, from the increasingly rancorous world of partisan politics that emerged during his first term in office. Unlike his material surroundings or equipage, the elements of Federalist political culture that attracted jibes about his monarchical pretensions, Washington's body was above reproach. Citizens looked to him, and looked at him, for inspiration and reassurance. Figured as an object of aesthetic admiration, as a work of art, Washington transcended debate. Citizens might approve or disapprove, but they could not quibble. Overwhelmingly, they registered their approval.[52]

Apotheosis of Washington

Most Americans, of course, never saw George Washington in the flesh. They were too far removed from the places in which he appeared; they were born too late. For these men and women, portraits stood in for the original. When the real Washington was out of reach, a burgeoning supply of painted and engraved portraits reminded Americans of their nation's history, confirmed its providential future, and spurred citizens to virtuous emulation. Well into the nineteenth century, some Americans continued to believe that an authentic portrait of Washington—be it an oil painting, a print, or a bust—had the power to reawaken and even create powerful sentiments about the founding father and, by extension, the republic itself.

The increasing number of "authentic" portraits—that is, paintings that Washington actually sat for or the paintings and prints that were copied from them—allowed countless people to "see the true likeness of that phenomenon among men," in the words of Benjamin West.[53] Yet the growing availability of these likenesses exacerbated concerns about authenticity, about the relation between pictorial representation and physical reality. This unease surfaced most regularly in relation to engraved prints, the most widely disseminated form of likenesses. After Washington's inauguration, artists and engravers generally dispensed with the military props that marked wartime likenesses. Instead, they relied on the painted or engraved face to perform the work of identification and authentication, to confirm that the sitter really was George Washington. This shifting emphasis coincided with a new, romantic style of portraiture. It reflected the economics of the art market: It was far less labor-intensive, and therefore less expensive, for a painter or engraver to render a head than to produce a full figure posed against an elaborate background. The simpler format also signaled the absence of an established set of presidential props; as the art historian Wendy Wick Reaves has observed, without a set of codified signatures for republican statesmen, engravers and printmakers could avoid the issue altogether by focusing on the bust.[54] Finally, the tight focus on Washington's face that dominated his portrayal during his presidency and after signaled the equation of character, person, and office celebrated in Washington's public appearances. More than that, it afforded ordinary citizens the close, intimate view that had once been the purview of elites.

Figure 33. *His Excel. G[eorge] Washington*, engraved by John Sartain in 1865, after a 1787 engraving by Charles Willson Peale. Published in Horace W. Smith, *Andreana* (Philadelphia, 1865). Courtesy of the Library Company of Philadelphia.

Presidential portrait prints thus raised the stakes for authenticity at the same time that they narrowed the locus of authenticity to Washington's face. But which face was that? Was Washington best represented by the distinctive oval heads painted and engraved by Peale? By Wright's aristocratic profile, with its aquiline nose, high cheekbones, and pointed chin? By the boxy forehead and squared-off jaw that distinguish Stuart's canonical images? However formulaic they may be in composition, these portraits vary considerably in their most critical element: Washington's face. And this vexing variety was only exacerbated by the growing market for portrait prints, which encouraged artists and engravers of varying tastes and abilities to produce copies of copies of copies. All Washingtons were not created equal.

Certainly that was the conclusion of Johann Caspar Lavater, the principal architect of "scientific" physiognomy. The 1789 English edition of his *Essays on Physiognomy* concluded with a discussion of Washington's character as revealed in portrait prints. The U.S. press was quick to reprint Lavater's analysis of Washington's likenesses. Analyzing a print based on Edward Savage's extremely

G.WASHINGTON.

Born Virginia Feb.[y] 11.th 1732.
General of the American Armies 1775.
Resign'd 1783.
President of the United States 1789.

Figure 34. *G. Washington*, engraved by James Manly after Joseph Wright, ca. 1790. Courtesy of the Library Company of Philadelphia.

popular face, Lavater detected "probity, wisdom, and goodness." But closer examination revealed that if the forehead demonstrated "uncommon luminousness of intellect," it lacked depth and excluded penetration. Worse, the eyes possessed "neither that benevolence, nor prudence, nor heroic force, which are inseparable from true greatness." He could only conclude that "if Washington is the Author of the revolution . . . the Designer has failed to catch some of the most prominent features of the Original." Far more promising, Lavater suggested, was a sketch based on one of John Trumbull's likenesses, which conveyed the qualities that Washington was most celebrated for: "valor . . . moderated by wisdom" and "modesty exempt from pretension."[55]

In an era when a likeness was not a more or less accurate representation of an individual face, but a map of character, getting Washington's face right was no small matter. Accordingly, artists and engravers competed not only to produce the most exact likeness but also to convince a buying public that they had

Figure 35. *Washington*, by an unidentified engraver after Gilbert Stuart, Philadelphia, mid-nineteenth century. Courtesy of the Library Company of Philadelphia.

done so. As early as 1787, for example, Charles Willson Peale advertised a mezzotint portrait of "His Excellency General Washington," deemed by unspecified authorities as the "best [likeness] that has been executed in a print." Several years later, advertisements for a medal based on Wright's profile described the product as a "strong and expressive likeness," "worthy of the attention of the citizens of the United States of America." The medal's quality was endorsed by four prominent citizens who vouched for the designer's skill. In 1800, an advertisement for a print based on Stuart's Lansdowne portrait quoted a magazine review to make the claim that "in point of resemblance, [the image is] said by those who have seen the General, to be uncommonly faithful." That same year, engraver David Edwin described a small, cheap copy of Stuart's

Athenaeum Portrait as the "best Likeness of the Celebrated Washington which has ever been published."[56]

No one worked harder to stake a claim for authenticity than Rembrandt Peale, the second surviving son of the artist, museum entrepreneur, and patriot Charles Willson Peale. Extravagantly ambitious, Rembrandt Peale saw himself as the scion of the nation's first family of art, and he believed that Washington's likeness was his patrimony. By the early 1820s, he had settled on a portrait of Washington as the vehicle most likely to stabilize his finances and secure his place in art history. While Peale intended that the original painting would be purchased by and displayed in Congress, he also anticipated selling painted and printed copies to an infinite number of individuals and institutions. The result was the magisterial *Patriae Pater* (1824), a composite likeness culled from the artist's assessment of extant life portraits and his own memories of the first president. (The president sat to the adolescent Peale as a favor to his more famous father.) Peale aspired to paint the definitive Washington, unseating Stuart's enormously popular Athenaeum Portrait in the process. The magnitude of his ambitions was suggested pictorially by the massive, trompe l'oeil stonework "porthole" that encases Washington's bust, giving it a monumental permanence. Peale's intentions were also announced by the twenty-page advertising brochure that publicized both the original portrait and the copies that he almost immediately began to paint, print, sell, and exhibit. Cataloging the strengths and weaknesses of one Washington or another and reminding readers that he was one of the few painters still living who had laid eyes on the great man, Peale relentlessly built a case for the superiority of his own rendition.[57]

Prospective buyers (in Congress and elsewhere) didn't have to take Peale's word. The pamphlet concluded with the testimony of eighteen nationally powerful men who had seen Washington incarnate. For men like John Marshall, Bushrod Washington, and Andrew Jackson, Peale's image served as a point of departure. It invited them to recall Washington in battlefields, state houses, and drawing rooms. It compelled them to reflect upon the character they saw in the man's features and expression. Almost to a one, they confessed that they knew little about art, although many reported seeking out multiple likenesses of Washington. Instead, each positioned himself as a connoisseur of Washington's face. They recognized the man portrayed on canvas because his features were permanently lodged not only in their minds but also in their hearts; Each recognized the president in the "porthole" because of the image's "effect upon my heart," because it inspired a "glow of enthusiasm that made my heart warm." If these remarks testified to the verisimilitude of Peale's portrait, they also lent credibility to Peale's claims about the sheer power of Washington's face. "Nothing can more powerfully carry back the mind to the glorious period which gave

Figure 36. Rembrandt Peale, *George Washington (Patriae Pater)*, 1824. Oil on canvas, 71.5 × 53.25 in. U.S. Senate Collection.

birth to this nation," he wrote, "nothing can be found more capable of exciting the noblest feelings of emulation and patriotism."[58]

Peale's brochure was more than one man's self-aggrandizement. Among artists who had painted Washington from life, the deep preoccupation with authenticity went well beyond a workmanlike desire to meet customary standards for "accurate and pleasing likenesses." Stuart so fetishized the authenticity of his canonical Athenaeum Portrait that although he copied it endlessly, he refused to complete it. As he explained to painter John Neagle, it would be "more valuable as it came from his hand in the presence of the sitter" than it would be if finished, "for by painting upon, it would be more or less altered." The unfinished canvas, to say nothing of its painted and printed copies, suggested the moment of painterly creation and the proximity of the sitter. Even the painter-cum-writer William Dunlap, who described his own copies of Washington's likeness as "cash," vividly remembered his first glimpse of the then-general. In his autobiography, he recalled the appearance of the man "whom all wished to see" and the electrifying moment when Washington set eyes on him: "It was a picture." The moment and the "picture" lingered at the edges of his mind, ready to be called forth by a "true" likeness of Washington; in his three-volume history of American art, Dunlap took pains to comment on the authenticity of every Washington produced by the many painters, engravers, sculptors, and wax modelers whose careers he chronicled. Like Peale, Stuart and Dunlap acknowledged the power that emanated from Washington's face even as they maneuvered to profit from it.[59]

The dialectic between Washington's "true" face and the vexing variety manifested in its many likenesses helped fuel the Cult of Washington by intensifying the desire for authenticity. An authentic likeness testified to its owner's discernment. It inspired heartfelt, heartwarming nationalist reveries. Both as the object of observation and as a prop in social performance, it provided a vehicle for the display of a deeply emotive, richly aestheticized patriotism. At the same time, the satisfactions afforded by a "true likeness" were heightened by the presence of so many vulgar copies. The hunger for authenticity was further exacerbated by its elusiveness, for every new portrait might render its predecessors obsolete.

Ultimately, the American public's yearning for an authentic Washington registered more than the collective desire to forge an immediate, heartfelt connection to the pater patriae himself. It registered the market. The Cult of Washington that depended on his many likenesses resembled nothing so much as the emerging culture of connoisseurship, which depended upon the nexus of aesthetics, consumption, and commodification. The multiple desires inspired by and fulfilled through Washington's likenesses were best satisfied through consumption. At least where the father of the country was concerned, the most direct route into the imagined community of the nation ran straight through the market.

Washingtoniana

Given the significance they attached to Washington's appearance, Americans of all ages and ranks were inspired to produce images of Washington from the Revolution onward. Many of these images were created more or less independently of the market, as keepsakes or gifts. Samuel Powel, who served as Philadelphia's mayor both before and during the Revolution, cut a silhouette of his good friend Washington. Conjuring physical proximity and social intimacy, the profile was framed, preserved, and passed down through generations of Powels along with more conventionally valuable forms of property. Schoolgirls incorporated his image into the elaborate, embroidered paintings that crowned an academy education. And any number of artistically inclined citizens must have devoted hours to copying engraved and painted portraits; in 1824, for example, Boston teenager Eliza Susan Quincy spent several days copying an engraved portrait of Washington that she wished to give to the Marquis de Lafayette as a gift.[60]

Around the turn of the nineteenth century, though, the production of this sort of amateur art, along with the painted and printed portraits from which it was borrowed, was outpaced by commercially produced likenesses rendered in various media and price ranges. The acceleration of Washingtoniana was fueled by the expansion of manufacturing and markets. But it was also fueled, as many scholars have recognized, by Washington's death, which allayed anxieties about his monarchical pretensions and rekindled republican affections.[61] In his lifetime, Washington decorated crockery, medals, and printed texts ranging from almanacs to sheet music. After his death, he graced all that and more. He became a familiar element of signage, jewelry, textiles, and primers. He appeared on maps of the United States and reproductions of the Declaration of Independence. A depiction of Washington on his deathbed, based on Tobias Lears's eyewitness account, even made its way onto a handkerchief that was marketed on both sides of the Atlantic. Indeed, it is difficult to imagine a surface that Washington had *not* decorated by the middle of the nineteenth century.[62]

Some of these artifacts conformed more or less closely to conventional aims of portraiture. That is, they employed a variety of materials as vehicles for depicting Washington. But many others incorporated Washington's likeness as a decorative motif to enhance an object whose primary purpose was not portraiture. As a result, men and women who owned Washington's face did more than look at him. They wore him, folded him, drank from him, wrote on him, and blew their noses and wiped their tears with him. Considering how flimsy and ephemeral many of these images and objects were even in their own time, many Americans also discarded him.[63]

This proliferation of Washingtoniana testified both to nationalism and to nostalgia for the Revolution, a fact that makes it easy to map the loftiest medal and the flimsiest almanac onto a familiar political narrative.[64] Yet the same objects that signaled politics and patriotism also reveal a hankering for fashion and novelty accompanied by an acute awareness of the price tag. In this regard, the range of associations that accompanied Washingtoniana resembles the range of associations that accompanied likenesses of George III on the eve of the Imperial Crisis. Washingtoniana signaled meanings generated by markets in general and commodification in particular. More to the point, they illuminate the ways in which consumption and commodification inflected early national political culture.

For the most part, the commodification of Washington operated much like the commodification of anything else. Entrepreneurially minded printers, jewelers, manufacturers, merchants, and showmen sought to provide a Washington to fit any budget. Portrait prints, for example, were sold with and without frames, in multiple sizes, and in differing levels of quality. In 1800 a large engraving taken from Stuart's Lansdowne might cost as much as $20 but small busts were available for $1 each. The endless processes of replication contributed to a trickle-down aesthetic, as each image moved from a more to a less expensive rendition. The progress of a Washington likeness from a live sitting to mass production is suggested by John Reich's 1806 commemorative medal. The original was commissioned by Joseph Sansom, a wealthy Philadelphian. One side featured Washington in civilian dress; the profile was said to be based on a drawing that Stuart "sketched on purpose" for the medal. On the reverse side was a monument assembled out of the symbols associated with Washington's resignations from the military and the presidency. The following year, cheaper copies were available in silver, bronze, or white metal. Other producers sought from the outset for the broadest possible market. In order to attract "every citizen throughout the United States" who possessed the "virtue to esteem" Washington or the "generosity to patronize the arts and manufactures of America," the engraver James Manly issued a medal with a "striking and approved likeness," available in three different metals, at prices ranging from $1 to $4.[65]

In an increasingly crowded market, survival—to say nothing of success—demanded that merchants and manufacturers work hard to capture the public's attention and to distinguish their product from those of their competitors. Toward that end, some entrepreneurs sharpened their pitches. To maintain public interest in his museum's wax Washington, Daniel Bowen hawked the statue from every imaginable angle. In April 1797, he warned patrons the likeness would be available "but a few days longer" before it went on tour in Philadelphia and Europe. Eight months later, when it was back in Boston for the foreseeable future, Bowen needed a new hook. This time, he highlighted the quality of his model, which he claimed was "universally avowed to the most perfect of any ever ordered to the public view." (Even then, he billed Washington beneath three automatons who danced to the music of a mechanical harpsichord, and a tableau depicting the king of France on his way to the guillotine.) Other entrepreneurs sought novel vehicles for Washington's likeness. John Smith of Philadelphia offered customers their choice of two Washingtons (in either military or presidential costume) painted on vitrified glass. Hung against a wall, the portraits impersonated "every fine oil painting." Set in a window, they looked like stained glass but better, for their "transparent brilliance exceeds every other manner of colouring." If beauty was not enough to motivate buyers, there was always the practical to consider: Unlike oil paintings or prints, Smith's paintings could be "cleaned with soap and water in a moment."[66] Scarcity and superiority; novelty and utility: The same enticements that fueled consumption writ large fueled the consumption of Washington.

Face Value

The market value of objects celebrating Washington, like the market value of objects celebrating other national figures, was connected to political capital. Washington was never exempted from criticism. Especially during his second administration, when conflicts over economic and foreign policy sharpened, he found himself the object of pointed and personal attacks. His critics overwhelmingly wielded words, whether spoken, published, or privately circulated, rather than images. Washington never inspired the political caricature that was published to denounce either John Adams or Thomas Jefferson, much less the displaced violence that was visited on effigies of popes, kings, and stamp collectors.[67] But that is not to suggest that the production of Washingtoniana traces an unwavering line of patriotic feeling through decades of political turbulence. Material culture registered Washington's fortune more obliquely, in the pace of production and in pricing. There was never a moment when the production of Washingtoniana ground to a halt; from the Revolution down to the present, someone somewhere was hawking some version of a Washington likeness. But when Washington's political capital increased—when he was inaugurated; when he resigned the presidency; and, especially, when he died—so, too, did the production of Washingtoniana.

Washington's value as a political symbol was also reflected in the price placed on his representations. Here, the exemplary case emerged during Jefferson's ill-fated embargo. In 1807, two print sellers had agreed to what at first appeared to be a mutually beneficial trade: Augustus Day of Philadelphia would provide fifty prints of Jefferson to John Jarvis of New York; in return, Jarvis agreed to send fifty prints of Washington to Day.[68] Both prints anchored a full-length figure in a magisterial setting symbolizing the subjects' accomplishments and their signal role in the nation's history. Day's Jefferson, which had been engraved by Cornelius Tiebout after a painting by Rembrandt Peale, was positioned between a bust of Franklin and a "philosophical apparatus," and Jefferson held a copy of the Declaration of Independence in one hand. In Day's

Figure 37. *Thomas Jefferson, President of the United States*, engraved by Cornelius Tiebout, Philadelphia, ca. 1801. Library of Congress.

GENERAL WASHINGTON.

Figure 38. *George Washington / painted by Gabriel [sic] Stuart 1797; engraved by James Heath Historical engraver to his Majesty, and to his Royal Highness the Prince of Wales.* London, 1800. Library of Congress.

words, the print proclaimed Jefferson's triumph as a "philosopher and states-man." The Washington likeness was the English engraver James Heath's copy of Stuart's already famous Lansdowne portrait.

However well matched the prints initially seemed, in the wake of the embargo Jefferson's popularity plummeted, taking with it the market value of his portrait. Although the Heath prints continued to command $6 each, the Tiebout prints sold for mere pennies. The Jeffersons "began to depreciate before they were dry from the press"; by the following year they "were now of *less value than waste paper*," Jarvis recalled. Accordingly, the New York printer decided that the fifty Jeffersons he had received from Philadelphia warranted only twenty-five Washingtons in exchange. Augustus Day countered by volun-teering to accept twenty-five prints of Alexander Hamilton in lieu of the missing Washingtons. (Given Hamilton's martyr status and the concomitant demand for his portraits among New York City's Federalist merchants, this was not much of a concession.) Jarvis refused even this; twenty-five portraits of Wash-ington were more than fair compensation for the devalued Jeffersons.

When the dispute finally reached court, Jarvis's attorney explained his cli-ent's position in language that erased the boundary between sitter and picture, in language that conflated politics, markets, and aesthetics. By the time that the Tiebout prints arrived from Philadelphia, he recalled, "'Jefferson' himself had already lost so much of his popularity, and was sinking so rapidly, that his likenesses (*which of course were depreciated with the original*) had already fallen to almost nothing." Jefferson's dismal political prospects did nothing to enhance the prints' value as long-term investments. Predicting—incorrectly, as it turned out—that "there was no chance of HIS [Jefferson's] ever being re-elected," the attorney argued that "there was no probability of THEIR [the prints' value] ever rising." Heath's Washington prints, on the other hand, were a sure thing. They "were always saleable and never fluctuated in value." More than that, they promised to appreciate; like Washington himself, he predicted, they were "*likely to rise in public estimation*." The incommensurability between the two presidents extended from the market for politics to the market for aesthetics. Whatever Peale and Tiebout aspired to, "the 'Jeffersons' were never considered matches for the 'Washingtons,' by any persons of the least taste or judgement." Indeed, Jarvis's attorney came prepared with a deposition demon-strating that when the Jeffersons "were submitted to the test of criticism," they came up short.[69] Artistic failures summed up political ones.

In response, Day and his attorney made no claims about the merits of the real Jefferson or the printed one. They insisted, instead, on the primacy of the initial contract and of the market itself. Day refused to "speculate upon the continuance of the popularity of his PRINT or its LIKENESS." As a businessman, "his object was, to turn the one to good account while the other was in public favour." If Jarvis had made a poor bargain, as everyone agreed he had, he had only himself to blame. Not surprisingly, the court ruled in favor of Day, awarding him $118.12.

For Augustus Day, John Jarvis, and their customers, the boundary separating political and market cultures was porous indeed. The surviving trial transcript depicts this boundary from the standpoint of producers and sellers. The consumer perspective appears only indirectly, refracted through wretched sales and falling prices. How did potential buyers experience the interpenetration of market and political cultures? It is notoriously difficult to map the universe of associations, assumptions, and aspirations that consumers bring to the marketplace, to pin down the meaning of any particular purchase, much less the meaning of consumption writ large. The capacity of objects and acquisitions to encompass multiple and contradictory meanings is, after all, one of the hallmarks of modern consumerism. That said, the opportunity to reject a Jefferson and, especially, to settle on the Washington of one's choice (on a medal or a mezzotint; depicted by Stuart or Peale) clearly enabled some Americans to affirm partisan allegiances and pay homage to their shared republican heritage at the same time that they indulged their personal taste.

What is less certain, and far more important, is the relationship between the allegiance to nation and party on the one hand, and the satisfaction of individual desire on the other. The proliferation of Washingtoniana after the 1790s raises questions about the extent to which shopping for a picture of a dead statesman resonated with the process of voting for a live one. The almost endless reproduction of Washingtoniana in particular and the commodification of political culture more generally may well have conditioned new forms of political behavior that shaped the transition from the deferential political culture of the eighteenth century to the mass-based, partisan politics that defined the nineteenth century. The broad outlines of this shift have been clear for a long time. In historian Andrew W. Robertson's succinct formulation, "Where the deferential political culture relied on personal relationships set within a localized, physical community, the participant political culture was sustained by a print community based on abstract relationships—ideology, interest, and common affiliation—among individuals." As Robertson suggests, one effect of this narrative has been to center analyses of the emergence of democratic politics around parties and the press. When vertical relationships are supplanted by putatively horizontal ones, candidates get pushed to the periphery. Yet this account of early national political culture would have been unrecognizable to its participants. For even as eighteenth-century election rituals like "spouting" (speechmaking that demonstrated erudition and avoided policy) and "courting" (flattering voters) gave way to the jostle of partisan politics, candidates, especially presidential candidates, continued to serve as symbols of an explicitly individuated, deeply personalized form of political affiliation.[70]

Notwithstanding the cult of the mute tribune, which dictated that presidential candidates could not campaign openly and which persisted well into the 1820s, candidates who could not speak on their own behalf and who did not receive direct votes from citizens nevertheless appealed to constituents through an alchemy of character, biography, and ideology.[71] Voters, in turn, drew upon the information (and misinformation) at hand in order to construct their own relationships to candidates. Those relationships were based on both ideological affinity and individual identification. They depended in equal measure on the calculation of interest and the cultivation of fantasy. The press, of course, played a key role in fostering connections between candidates and voters. Editors tirelessly expounded on their candidates' virtues while vilifying the opposition. Newspapers thus provided one site for mediating relationships between constituents and candidates.[72] The consumer market provided another. Like reportage, images and objects provided information about candidates and officeholders; the purchase of a medal or mug emblazoned with a politician's image, like the purchase of a newspaper, confirmed partisan loyalty. Things, like texts, could clarify and articulate feelings about potential officeholders, just as they clarified and articulated feelings about George Washington.

But the press explicitly aimed to induct voters into the disciplined ranks of the party faithful. Whether editors were reporting on internal improvements or holding forth on manners and morals, they kept partisan goals firmly in sight. The purveyors of portrait prints, medals, and mugs, by contrast, operated in a market that encouraged and even depended on more open-ended, ambiguous structures of meaning. Certainly, the sheer variety, the pervasiveness of images like the Tiebout and Heath prints created the sense that statesmen, including Washington, were both more familiar and more available than they had been in the years immediately following the ratification of the Constitution. It was one thing to glimpse a likeness of the founding father ensconced in a state house or hoisted as part of a civic ritual. It was another to be able to pull him out of your pocket, imprinted on your handkerchief. Familiarity may not breed contempt, but it rarely fosters deference.

At the same time, the multiplication of likenesses eroded the ability of political elites, including parties, to control the message that the images were meant to project. No one understood that better than Washington himself. At the dawn of his political career, Washington was quite willing—even eager—to see himself reproduced on canvas and paper, to encounter himself engraved in metal and transferred onto ceramics. As he famously joked in 1785, "I am so hackneyed now to the touches of the Painter's pencil, that I am now altogether at their beck, and sit like Patience on a monument, whilst they are delineating the lines of my face." But by the 1790s, he began to shy away from artists. He admitted that he had grown tired of posing. Even more important, he confessed, "These productions have in my estimation been made use of as a sort of tax on individuals, by being engraved, and that badly, and hawked about or advertised for sale."[73] It was one thing to become the focus of the people's admiring gaze, to figure as an object of emulation. It was another thing altogether to become a commodity, and a potentially shoddy one at that. Washington was painfully aware that his face had been transformed into a product whose fate was beyond his control.

It is significant that Washington focused his sense of unease on sellers rather than buyers. In his estimation, the problem lay with painters like Stuart, who referred to copies of the Athenaeum Portrait as "$100 bills"; with printers like Day and Jarvis, who calculated his face value down to the nickel; or, for that matter, with authors like Weems, who once crowed that there was "a great deal of money lying in the bones of old George" for those willing to "extract it."[74] Washington could imagine good economies that depended upon carefully calibrated balances between commerce, manufacturing, and agriculture. He could also imagine the destructive ambitions of stockjobbers turned demagogues. He could not imagine the public ascendance of taste that diverged from the conventions of gentility, conventions that he himself had fostered in his clothing, his public appearances, his equipage, and his plantation. In the end, what Washington could not imagine was the operation of individual taste divorced from the strictures of the republic of taste. His 1793 language is telling. Washington worried that his portrait prints functioned as a "tax," a form of expenditure enforced by external authority. Consumer taste and individual desire do not register in his account. The imaginative structures mobilized by the play of choice in a market that promised to satisfy individual desire through purchases large and small were simply beyond him.[75]

Had Washington been more prescient, he might have turned his attention to those individuals who perused the prints that engravers and merchants "hawked about or advertised." He might have wondered about consumers who saw in his face not only a symbol of the republic but also a commodity whose value rose and fell with the market. Washington might have wondered about the people courted by Joseph Delaplaine in 1814, when the latter began to solicit subscriptions for what would become the lavishly illustrated *Repository of the Lives and Portraits of Distinguished Americans*. Delaplaine acknowledged that there was widespread disagreement about which artist had captured the best likeness of George Washington, and so he graciously promised to include two portrait prints of the first president, one taken from Stuart's Athenaeum Portrait, the other from Houdon's bust. In this way, he purred, his *Repository* could "render universal satisfaction." Universal satisfaction, it seems, depended as much on the accommodation of particular taste as it did on explication of Washington's deeds and character.[76]

George Washington could not envision a world in which citizen-consumers would seize upon his likenesses, investing them with multiple meanings, political and otherwise. Ironically, representations of Washington, the president who feared that the dissent of faction would create "ill-founded jealousies," raise "false alarms," and destroy "Public Liberty," encouraged citizens to express patriotism as personal desire.[77] Enshrined in the metaphoric Temple of Fame as the quintessential citizen of the republic of taste, Washington could not grasp the difficulties of translating that controlled and orderly world into a nation conjured out of pictures, objects, and markets.

The Nation's Guest in the Republic of Taste

In the summer of 1824, sixty-seven-year-old Marie Joseph Paul Yves Roch Gilbert du Motier, the Marquis de Lafayette, famously returned to the United States, where he was famously welcomed by its citizens. Lafayette's arrival in New York City launched a thirteen-month spectacle that played out across all twenty-four of the states then composing the Union and that advanced the interests of all persons involved. For Lafayette, the tour announced him as a man who was universally beloved in the nation he had helped to create, if not the one into which he had been born. It confirmed his status as a hero who warranted inclusion in the pantheon, and it validated his moderate political commitments, which had proved too conservative for the Jacobins during the Terror and too liberal for the royalists who dominated French politics in the 1820s. As if honor and adulation were not enough, midway through his visit, Congress granted him $200,000 and 24,000 acres of land in and around what is now Tallahassee, Florida. Americans, for their part, seized on the presence of the last surviving revolutionary general. Through him, they could simultaneously celebrate the founding generation and cement their connections to it. Joining together to shower thanks and love on the "Nation's Guest," as he was called, they could rise above partisan quarrels and sectional wrangling. Lafayette afforded Americans nothing more and nothing less than the chance to prove themselves worthy of their republican patrimony. The crown jewel in a decade of commemorative celebrations, his visit had the feel of a last hurrah, marking the moment the Revolution became a thing of recorded history rather than lived memory.[1]

The tour hit all the right emotional notes: Lafayette inspired "ardent joy," the "deepest sensibility," and the "thrill of delight." His arrival brought "renewed vigor to patriotic feelings and national pride." He tapped "springs of gratitude" in the hearts of all who beheld him. Such sentiments obviously owed much to the national temper. Fifty years after the start of what would become a war for independence, citizens were keen to honor their history. But Lafayette's return resonated so powerfully because it used older forms of visual and material culture, older forms of ceremonial performance, to address contemporary concerns. It was not simply that the tour provided citizens with an occasion for expressing their freighted relationship to the past. It was also that Lafayette literally appeared in ways that telescoped the early national past into the Jacksonian present. In no small measure, Lafayette's tour triumphed precisely because of the way and the extent to which it played on the everyday aesthetics and the visual politics that Americans had cultivated in order to forge a republic of taste.[2]

Lafayette's trek explicitly recalled George Washington's journey to be sworn in as first president and his tours of New England and the southern states some thirty-five years before. There were speeches and toasts, to be sure. But Lafayette's tour, like Washington's before it, unfolded as a series of intensely visual performances. The aging general's entry into any particular town was organized into a series of shifting tableaux and sight lines organized for the benefit of the thousands of spectators who turned out in hopes that they might catch a glimpse of him. From the moment he first came into view, to his procession through the streets, to his appearance on a balcony or a raised porch, to his presence at balls and at levees, he was staged and framed, just as Washington had been. Hundreds of specially constructed arches, inscribed with republican imagery and mottos, marked his progress. Masses of greenery and enormous banners provided a backdrop, the better to show off his form, still tall and upright despite his years. Come nighttime, illuminations, transparencies, and fireworks transformed streets and skies, heightening citizens' perceptions of their surroundings.

From New York to New Orleans to St. Louis, citizens were at pains to show off evidence of their improvement, their progress along civilization's trajectory. And in town after town and state after state, that progress was manifested not only by factories or orphan asylums but also by institutions that had served as the cornerstones for the republic of taste. Thus Lafayette stopped at colleges and academies, where he impressed upon the rising generation the virtue of the founders and where that generation, in turn, impressed him with testimonials and odes rendered in fine penmanship and decorated with ornate calligraphy. He visited art galleries and museums, including the one operated by Charles Willson Peale's sons in Baltimore, where he showed special interest in portraits of the founders and in the specimens of the continent's distinctive flora and fauna. He was entertained in the nation's finest homes, hotels, and gardens. These already-elegant spaces were further fitted up with specially made furniture, likenesses of Washington, prints of battle scenes, and in one case the "elegant engraving of the Fac Similies of the hand writing and signatures of those worthies who signed the declaration of Independence," flourishes that were calculated to appeal to his taste and underscore his connection to the nation's founding. He was honored at balls that enabled ladies and gentlemen to show off physical and social grace alike. The beautifully appointed halls, fashionable clothing, and gracious manners served as a balm for political disagreements, contemporary and otherwise. At a ball in New York, for example, Lafayette mistook Miss Gertrude Ogden for the daughter of a veteran of the Continental Army. When Ogden gently corrected him, explaining that her father had been "loyal to king and country," he politely congratulated her on her loyalty to her father, and the fete continued in the spirit of comity and friendship.[3]

While the tour enabled Lafayette to take one last look at the United States, it also afforded Americans the chance to take one last look at him. He proved a riveting sight wherever he appeared. The moment he boarded a steamboat en route to Virginia was "precious" for passengers and crew alike; "every eye was fixed in a steady gaze upon his venerable figure" as he strolled the deck. In Troy, New York, the "grateful throngs" who gathered in the streets and at windows to "catch another and another look at the illustrious visitor" inspired the editor of the local *Sentinel* to spout Shakespeare: Likening Lafayette's triumphal return to Bullingbrook's, he wrote, "You would have thought the very windows spake/So many greedy looks of young and old,/through casements darted their desiring eyes/Upon his visage." And when the "females" in Providence, Rhode Island, peered out of upper-story windows to "view this distinguished personage," the paper reported that "many a fine eye was wet with the gush of a tear, which the rush of so many sublime and sympathetick emotions went warm from the heart." Women were not the only spectators to be moved by the sight of the aging hero. Celebrated astronomer Nathaniel Bowditch reported that "the moment he beheld Lafayette" parading through Cambridge, Massachusetts, he was "carried away by the enthusiasm of the moment." Losing "all self-command," he "recovered his senses" minutes later when he found himself cheek by jowl with the rest of the crowd that surged around Lafayette's carriage "huzzaing."[4]

Americans did not need an encounter as close as Bowditch's to see the Nation's Guest. Lafayette's likeness was ubiquitous, courtesy of the unstinting efforts of the nation's aesthetic entrepreneurs. In a little more than a year's time, Lafayette sat for nearly twenty life portraits, which were immediately copied in both painted and printed form. Throughout his visit, he passed through crowds of men, women, and children who wore ribbons, gloves, or hatbands that reflected his likeness back to him. He appeared on many objects (medallions, rings, and pocket watches) that were explicitly commemorative and others (ceramics, side chairs, sheet music) that were less so. Endlessly and insistently repetitive, these images were intended to honor Lafayette. But they were also intended to teach current and future generations a lesson. As the governor of Kentucky explained when he commissioned a life portrait, "every citizen" was "eager to look at Lafayette" because "in viewing him" they not only remembered "the principles of revolution," they also found themselves "improve[d]" and "strengthen[ed]" by the great man's example.[5]

These transporting moments and transformative lessons were extended to a broader public through the press, which encouraged readers to see Lafayette in their minds' eyes. Newspaper coverage of the tour was both dense and detailed. Editors scrambled to publish accounts of local visits in something resembling real time. In the days and weeks that followed, they extended their initial reportage with more comprehensive descriptions of the balls, illuminations, fireworks, and toasts that the city had sponsored. All of this local coverage was supplemented by similar stories that were culled from newspapers around the country and that appeared for weeks preceding and following the brief time Lafayette spent in town. Citizens who remained hungry for all things Lafayette and whose appetites were not satiated by the newspapers could relive the "thrill of delight" that the general inspired by purchasing retrospective pamphlets like two that were published in Lexington, Kentucky, following Lafayette's visits to Transylvania College and the Lafayette Academy or *Honour to the Brave; Merited Praise to the Disinterested*, which offered a blow-by-blow summary of a "grand fete" in New York City and described the event down to the table decorations, which featured a replica of the Erie Canal, complete with running water and bobbing boats.[6]

Throughout the year that Lafayette spent in the United States, commentators and observers reflexively correlated these visible displays of taste with republicanism, patriotism, and national identity. To be sure, newspapers regularly singled out women's roles in the aesthetic dimensions of the tour. From Maine to South Carolina to Cincinnati, "the Ladies" were credited for ensuring that the Nation's Guest ate at tables, socialized in ballrooms, and slept in bedrooms that had been tastefully embellished. Beauty, it seemed, was becoming women's work. But it was not only "the Ladies" who put their taste to the service of honoring Lafayette.

The massive triumphal arches, swooping banners, and illuminated buildings that transformed U.S. cities during Lafayette's tour were all emblems of Americans' collective capacity for taste. The gentlemen who opened up their houses and their halls to the masses eager to greet Lafayette were celebrated in the prints for their refined taste as much as for their selfless patriotism. New Yorkers boasted that the "fine taste and lavish expenditure" of the city's Castle Garden fete could best the competition not only in the rest of the republic but also in the rest of the world. The good people of Fairfield, Connecticut, who arranged themselves along the roadside to greet Lafayette as carefully as they arranged the decorations on his banquet table, believed that they had succeeded in displaying their taste before a national audience. Even explicitly military honors could be leavened with taste. Certainly that was the case with the obelisks that marked the site of Cornwallis's surrender at Yorktown; those monuments were executed with taste as well as zeal. Taken together, as one newspaper editor put it shortly before Lafayette returned home, the past year had provided Americans with ample opportunity to demonstrate their "taste and liberality" to themselves and the world. If published accounts of Lafayette's visit are any measure, by the mid-1820s, taste offered proof of national becoming.[7]

When Americans proclaimed the tastefulness of the welcome they gave Lafayette, they did more than confirm the aesthetic value of all those banners and medals, parades and paintings. They also tethered themselves more closely to a past that was just receding from view. Consider Lafayette's pass through Trenton, New Jersey, in the fall of 1824. Residents of the city and the surrounding countryside were acutely aware of Trenton's place in the nation's history. In 1776, it had been the scene of a significant and much-needed victory for the Continental Army, when General Washington routed the Hessians and began to reclaim New Jersey. Thirteen years after that, it had been the scene of a famous display of sensibility and taste, when Washington, the president-elect, exchanged compliments and tears with "the Ladies" as he passed beneath a floral arch en route to New York City to assume his new office.

Both elements of the city's history must have been on the minds of Trentonians as they prepared to welcome the Nation's Guest. Several thousand "gallant volunteers" rendezvoused in the city's center, sporting the "full dress and harness of the soldier." Together, they took pride of place in the mile-long parade that ushered Lafayette's barouche to the State House and provided an "unsurpassed" recollection of the Continental Army's valor. But it was the other element of Trenton's history that provided the "crowning feature" of its celebration. At the head of the avenue leading to the State House, city residents reerected the arch under which Washington had passed in 1789. "It had been carefully preserved from the delapidations of years," the local paper explained. Now—wreathed with evergreens and baytree boughs, covered in natural and artificial flowers, and inscribed "FIRST TO WASHINGTON.—THEN TO LAFAYETTE"—it was "destined to be the over arching canopy for another revolutionary hero." Twenty-four "beautiful young ladies," dressed in "purest white" and representing the states, flanked the arch. Just as their grandmothers had serenaded Washington as he passed beneath the arch, they, too, sang for Lafayette. Although Lafayette failed to shed a tear as Washington had, he reported that he was "greatly moved" by the "fairy scene." How could it have been otherwise? Together, the French general and Trentonians simultaneously reenacted history and fulfilled its promise.[8]

Yet for all that Lafayette's visit recalled Washington's eighteenth-century tours, it also illuminated how much the republic had changed in the intervening years. Most obviously, the nation was far larger and its sectional differences far more pronounced. The thirteen states that ratified the Constitution had been joined by eleven more. Notwithstanding the passage of the Missouri Compromise in 1820, slavery was becoming an increasingly visible, increasingly divisive source of national conflict. The politics of patriotism had shifted, too. By the middle of the 1820s, a far broader cross-section of the laboring classes secured roles in the civic celebrations that feted the Nation's Guest. Perhaps because Lafayette's personal and ideological inclinations were decidedly more democratic than Washington's had ever been, he made sure that his tour included formal meetings with Native Americans in western states and free African Americans in eastern cities.[9] Despite the repeated gestures that all participants made toward the founding generation, Lafayette's tour had a decidedly Jacksonian feel.

This was as true of the tour's aesthetic aspects as its political ones. The entertainments afforded Lafayette were more lavish in size and scope than anyone could have imagined thirty-five years earlier. If Lafayette passed beneath the same, storied arch that Trentonians built to honor Washington, he also passed beneath at least two additional arches, similarly sized and decorated, in his final approach to the New Jersey State House. Where one arch had been plenty to mark a hero's progress in 1789, three or more were requisite in 1824.

Scale may have been the most immediately visible difference, but it was hardly the most important. The celebrations honoring Lafayette were thoroughly and intensely commercialized. In an attempt to wring revenue from the Nation's Guest, artists and artisans of all stripes worked around the clock, splashing his face and name across any available surface. At the upper end of the market, he was depicted on commemorative jewelry and elegant mezzotint engravings; at the lower end, his name was spelled out in the bristles of a clothes brush.[10] Especially in larger cities, where total expenditures for entertainments could reach well into the thousands of dollars, aesthetic entrepreneurs scrambled to secure a piece of the action. In the months leading up to Lafayette's visit to Philadelphia, for example, the gentlemen who served on the official reception committee were inundated by bids and counterbids from artists, artisans, and tradesmen. Printers campaigned to get commissions for engraved invitations and commemorative ribbons while a French dancing master insisted that he alone possessed the qualifications to direct the civic ball. The caterer who was willing to provide one thousand citizens with a cold buffet for $600 began to haggle over who would assume responsibility for the inevitable breakage the moment he secured the contract.[11]

The Peale family outdid themselves and everyone else in Philadelphia in the attempt to turn a profit off the general's return. Rembrandt Peale grandly loaned his recently completed "porthole" portrait of Washington to decorate the reception hall, only to recall it so that he could exhibit it to paying customers in New York City. When the reception committee balked at the change in plans, Peale promised that he would bring the painting back to Philadelphia just ahead of Lafayette's arrival, on the condition that the interior of Independence Hall be rearranged so that his masterpiece could be shown to better effect. It was only when the reception committee threatened to replace the *Patriae Pater* with "an original" portrait of Washington painted by Peale's archrival "Stewart" that the ambitious artist relented in his demands. The moment that the reception committee settled its dispute with Rembrandt Peale, it confronted another with his younger brother. Franklin Peale, who was charged with managing the family's museum, petitioned the city for $250 to offset lost revenue. Because the museum would close for a day to accommodate Lafayette's reception, Peale explained, "I conscientiously think that this sum should be allowed to us."[12] Lafayette may have inspired veneration, patriotism, and gratitude, but he also ignited a rush toward the main chance.

From one perspective, of course, the differences between the public's receptions of Washington and Lafayette suggested progress. They testified both to what Philip Freneau had termed "the rising glory of America" and to what William Dunlap would call "the rise and progress of the arts of design in the United States." From another perspective, however, the contrast looked like the worst kind of declension. One student at Princeton's theological seminary was troubled by the grandeur of the welcome that Americans had extended to their guest. "Does not the conviction flash across your mind on sober reflection that this man has been idolized?" he asked his cousin. "Far be it from me to say that we ought collectively to have folded our arms on his approach," he added; nevertheless, he counted Americans' veneration of the French general as a "National sin." If the minister in training was in the minority, he was not alone. Fretting about the "present <u>Fayettomania</u>," one observer found Philadelphia's reception to be "extravagant, almost to idolatry." If Jesus Christ had been content to enter Jerusalem "seated on an Ass," he wondered, and even George

Washington had "declined" the kind of pomp and ceremony currently on display, who was Lafayette to embrace it?[13]

That both men cast their disapproval in religious terms is not surprising. Protestant Christianity, especially in its American iterations, had long registered concerns about the material manifestations of earthly ambition. And by the 1820s, many Americans were coming to feel an evangelical revival of the spirit that breathed new life and new urgency into these long-standing concerns. But the moral lapse displayed by both the American hosts and their guest was also an aesthetic one. It is significant that the Philadelphia observer framed his unease with an eye toward the trappings and props that surrounded Lafayette, juxtaposing them against both the unadorned tree boughs that welcomed Christ into Jerusalem and the austere classicism that accompanied Washington everywhere. Philadelphians' citywide fete was altogether too big, too grand, too enthusiastic. It defied the standards of taste exemplified by the first generation of Christians and by the first generation of U.S. citizens. American's "veneration" of Lafayette may have been a "National sin," but it was a sin born as much of bad taste as of false gods.

Of course, most Americans did not trouble themselves about such things. On the contrary. They embraced the chance to celebrate Lafayette. More than that, they reveled in the opportunity to mobilize the visual, material, and literary cultures that evidenced the nation's taste as a means of demonstrating their heartfelt connection to its founding. Together, these images, and objects, texts, and spectacles created a sense of seamless connection with the past. Small wonder, then, that when Americans sought to provide a welcome worthy of Lafayette, they sought to welcome him into a republic distinguished by its taste.

Taste proved to be such an effective mechanism for connecting past and present precisely because it had loomed large in virtually every dimension of Americans' attempts to forge a culture capable of sustaining the republic. A preoccupation with aesthetics and visuality broadly conceived had been central to the academy movement. The capacity for taste, as much as the capacity for reason, garnered several generations of academy students new visibility as exemplars of the republic. The importance of taste was underscored by writers and painters, printmakers and museum keepers, who insisted that they and their products belonged near the center of the republican project. These aesthetic entrepreneurs did much to extend the market for the kinds of images, objects, and spaces that registered taste even as they struggled to profit from that market. Taste had purchase in both the private and public spheres. The particular aesthetic practices and parameters that distinguished the early republic provided ordinary men and women with a means to see themselves and others. They provided politicians and power brokers with a means of representing legitimate political authority. Whether it took the form of an ivory portrait miniature, a gracefully penned letter, or an arch built for a president, taste seemed to confer the ability to consolidate, defend, or acquire cultural power. Just as aesthetics provided philosophers and founders with a vocabulary for articulating political differences, the attempt to realize taste in everyday practice fostered institutions, objects, and modes of interaction that promised to ease those differences. Taste bred harmony and virtue. More than that: It produced the objects, images, and subjectivities that would render the new nation legible to the broader world. A potent fusion of the textual, the visual, and the material, the American republic of taste promised women and men a new and better way of being in the world.

From the outset, however, this promise was constrained and compromised. Severing the intellectual underpinnings and material props of the American republic of taste from Europe in general and Britain in particular proved all but impossible. The attempt to demonstrate what, exactly, was American about the nation's displays of taste was at best an ongoing project. As the eighteenth century gave way to the nineteenth, the expansion of the market created new contradictions that threatened to erode the republic of taste from within. Both in its ideal form and in the attempts to realize it, the republic of taste was explicitly and intentionally exclusionary. It did not include all citizens or even most of them; that, in fact, had been precisely the point. But the growing availability of elegant and novel goods to suit every budget and please every taste threatened to drain taste of its power. It was not simply that the range of commodities that were available to growing numbers of buyers democratized gentility and extended the prerogatives of taste to women and men who were never meant to be its beneficiaries. It was also that commodification served to create more unstable imaginaries and open-ended structures of meaning. This was especially ominous when the goods in question were explicitly tied to national identity and national history. The interpenetration of market and political cultures did not augur well for the republic of taste. In the end, even the women and men who invested the aesthetics of everyday life with such importance never succeeded in fashioning a republic out of taste. But in the attempt, they went a long way toward forging the early American republic.

Notes

INTRODUCTION

1. Henry Cheever, diary, Jul. 5, 1829, Cheever-Wheeler Family Papers, American Antiquarian Society.

2. Hannah Webster Foster, *The Coquette*, ed. Cathy N. Davidson (New York: Oxford University Press, 1986), 113.

3. Personal conversation with Jonathan Burton, executive director, Philadelphia Landmarks, Inc. Multiple nineteenth-century histories contain references to both the Powel silhouette and the Argand lamp; see, e.g., William Spohn Baker, *Engraved Portraits of Washington* (Philadelphia: Lindsay and Baker, 1880), 186. The Powels' taste for fine furnishings lends credence to details about the Argand lamp, but the frequent assertion that Powel took the silhouette "in the last years of the Presidency" is erroneous, given Powel's 1793 death.

4. The scholarly literature on taste is as extensive today as the word "taste" was in eighteenth-century Britain and thus is far too large to be surveyed here. But consider the trajectory suggested by the following titles: Denise Gigante, *Taste: A Literary History* (New Haven, CT: Yale University Press, 2005), which explores connections between taste as a physical sensation and an aesthetic judgment; John Barrell, *The Political Theory of Painting from Reynolds to Hazlitt: "The Body of the Public"* (New Haven, CT: Yale University Press, 1986), which traces artists' attempts to justify painting and the fine arts more generally according to the precepts of civic humanism; Peter de Bolla, *The Education of the Eye: Painting, Landscape, and Architecture in Eighteenth-Century Britain* (Stanford, CA: Stanford University Press, 2003), which considers the contentious ramifications when access to the fine arts extends beyond the Royal Academy to a larger public; and John Styles and Amanda Vickery, eds., *Gender, Taste, and Material Culture in Britain and North America, 1700–1830* (New Haven, CT: Yale Center for British Art and the Paul Mellon Centre for Studies in British Art, 2006), which explores the operation of taste in genteel and working-class contexts in the British Atlantic.

5. Galvanized by the larger rehabilitation of aesthetics within literary studies, Early Americanists, especially literary scholars, have begun to recover the importance of taste and aesthetics in colonial and early national America. See, e.g., Jay Fliegelman, *Declaring Independence: Jefferson, Natural Language, and the Culture of Performance* (Stanford, CA: Stanford University Press, 1993); David S. Shields, *Civil Tongues and Polite Letters in British North America* (Chapel Hill: University of North Carolina Press for the Omohundro Institute of Early American History and Culture, 1997); Eric Slauter, *The State as a Work of Art: The Cultural Origins of the Constitution* (Chicago: University of Chicago Press, 2007); and Edward Cahill, *Liberty of the Imagination: Aesthetic Theory, Literary Form, and Politics in the Early United States* (Philadelphia: University of Pennsylvania Press, 2012).

6. Slauter, *State as a Work of Art*, 128, 132–133; Cahill, *Liberty of the Imagination*, 140–146.

7. See note 5.

8. Although most American historians now agree that the American Revolution promised greater economic, political, and social equality than it actually delivered, questions about how and to what extent class structures and class identities were (or were not) changed for diverse categories of citizens and noncitizens remain the focus of heated and productive debate. This literature is too

large to be cited in any detail, but the range of approaches and conclusions is suggested by the articles and responses in Cathy Matson, ed., "Connection, Contingency, and Class in the Early Republic's Economy," a special issue of the *Journal of the Early Republic* 26:4 (Winter 2006), 515–651; and "Symposium on Class in the Early American Republic," *Journal of the Early Republic* 25:4 (Winter 2005), 521–569.

9. For a succinct and insightful discussion about how historians might approach the connections between discursive constructions of taste, material culture, and lived experience, see John Styles and Amanda Vickery, "Introduction," in Styles and Vickery, *Gender, Taste, and Material Culture*, 1–31, esp. 14–20.

10. These words were not interchangeable synonyms; they referred to distinct if related qualities, as anxious intellectuals never ceased to remind their readers. Yet the frequency with which writers ranging from Joseph Addison to Archibald Alison to Blair invoked these distinctions suggests something about most readers' utter lack of interest in them.

11. Hugh Blair, *Lectures on Rhetoric and Belles Lettres*, ed. Linda Ferreira-Buckley and S. Michael Halloran (Carbondale: Southern Illinois University Press, 2005), 11; [Joseph Addison], "Spectator no. 411, Saturday, June 21, 1712," *Spectator*, ed. Donald F. Bond, 5 vols. (Oxford: Oxford University Press, 1965), 3:535; [Joseph Addison], "Spectator no. 225, Saturday, Nov. 17, 1711," in Bond, *Spectator*, 2:376.

12. "An Essay on Taste, from a New Work," *Boston Magazine*, Nov. 1783; "Taste, a Fragment," *Philadelphia Repository and Weekly Register*, Mar. 19, 1803; "Simplicity, the Attendant of Good Taste" (New Harmony, IN) *New-Harmony Gazette*, Mar. 21, 1827. The range of these publications suggests something about the prevalence of the discussions.

13. John Wales, addresses delivered at New Haven (Yale), 1801 and 1802, Patten and Wales Papers, 1768–1884, Collection 525, f. 2, American Antiquarian Society.

14. This is not to deny the importance of rhetoric to eighteenth-century aesthetics. The ubiquitous Blair, to take but one example, fell back on discussions of visual representation in order to help his readers sharpen their verbal representations. Yet even texts—the books and magazines that imparted or satisfied taste, the letters and commonplace books that simultaneously internalized and demonstrated it—were material objects. The aesthetic value of texts depended partly on the words they contained and partly on their material form, on the embellishments in a binding, on the engravings that illustrated a story, and on the regular and rhythmic slant of the penmanship.

15. A search of the National Archives' Founders Online project returns nearly two thousand iterations of "taste." The letters quoted are "To James Madison from Thomas Jefferson, 8 February 1786," Founders Online, National Archives (http://founders.archives.gov/documents/Madison/01-08-02-0254); "To James Madison from Thomas Jefferson, 14 February 1783 (second)," Founders Online, National Archives (http://founders.archives.gov/documents/Madison/01-06-02-0071); "Notes on a Tour of English Country Seats, &c., with Thomas Jefferson, 4–10? April 1786," Founders Online, National Archives (http://founders.archives.gov/documents/Adams/01-03-02-0005-0002-0001); and "From George Washington to Lafayette, 28 May 1788," Founders Online, National Archives (http://founders.archives.gov/documents/Washington/04-06-02-0264);

16. By way of comparison, a search of the National Archives' Founders Online project returns well under one hundred iterations of "connoisseur" and its variants; of these, fewer than thirty appear in documents created by or sent to Adams, Jefferson, and Washington. For quotes, see "From George Washington to Marie-Joseph-Paul-Yves-Roch-Gilbert du Motier, Marquis de Lafayette, 30 October 1783," Founders Online, National Archives (http://founders.archives.gov/documents/Washington/99-01-02-11991); "From George Washington to David Humphreys, 22 October 1786," Founders Online, National Archives (http://founders.archives.gov/documents/Washington/04-04-02-0272) ; and "From Thomas Jefferson to Maria Cosway, 24 April 1788," Founders Online, National Archives (http://founders.archives.gov/documents/Jefferson/01-13-02-0027).

17. See, e.g., "Fine Arts," *Port Folio*, Jan. 15, 1803; "Benjamin West, Esq.: President of the Royal Academy," *Port Folio*, Sept. 1811; "Fuseli's Lectures on Painting," *Atheneum; or, Spirit of the English Magazines*, Jul. 1, 1817.

18. See, e.g., advertisements in the (New York) *Mercantile Advertiser*, Oct. 28, 1803; (New York) *Morning Chronicle*, Mar. 8, 1803; (Baltimore) *American and Commercial Daily Advertiser*, Mar. 31,

1820; (New York) *National Advocate*, Jul. 3, 1822; (Charleston, SC) *City Gazette and Daily Advertiser*, May 14, 1819; and (Washington, D.C.) *Daily National Intelligencer*, Nov. 28, 1829.

19. Two Letters, upon the Lands, Settlements, &c. of the Western States and Territories," (New York) *Literary and Scientific Repository, and Critical Review*, Jun. 1, 1820; "Clermont Sheep Shearing," (Albany, NY) *Balance and State Journal*, Jun. 26, 1810; "Cheese Making," (Baltimore) *American Farmer*, Mar. 2, 1821; M. J. B. Vitalis, "Essay on the Nature of Sheeps' Dung, and on Its Use in Dyeing Cotton of a Turkey Red Colour," (Philadelphia) *Archives of Useful Knowledge, a Work Devoted to Commerce, Manufactures, Rural and Domestic Economy, Agriculture, and the Useful Arts*, Jul. 1, 1812.

20. Historians and literary critics have begun to disentangle and clarify the relation between U.S. political independence, on the one hand, and the relative cultural and economic autonomy of the United States vis-à-vis Britain, on the other. Exemplary recent studies include Sam W. Haynes, *Unfinished Business: The Early American Republic in a British World* (Charlottesville: University of Virginia Press, 2010); Jessica M. Lepler, *The Many Panics of 1837: People, Politics, and the Creation of a Transatlantic Financial Crisis* (New York: Cambridge University Press, 2013); Elisa Tamerkin, *Anglophilia: Deference, Devotion, and Antebellum America* (Chicago: University of Chicago Press, 2007); Leonard Tennenhouse, *The Importance of Feeling English: American Literature and the British Diaspora, 1750–1850* (Princeton, NJ: Princeton University Press, 2007); and Kariann Akemi Yokota, *Unbecoming British: How Revolutionary America Became a Postcolonial Nation* (New York: Oxford University Press, 2011).

While scholars have demonstrated increased interest in the circulation of ideas, capital, and individuals, they have paid far less attention to the circulation of commodities or, in other words, to trade. Although economic historians seem to agree that British trade resumed following 1783, they have been slow to provide a systematic, detailed analysis of imports, focusing instead on American exports. See Thomas M. Doerflinger, "Farmers and Dry Goods in the Philadelphia Market Area," in *The Economy of Early America: The Revolutionary Period, 1763–1790*, ed. Ronald Hoffman, John J. McCusker, Russell R. Menard, and Peter J. Albert (Charlottesville: University of Virginia Press for the U.S. Capitol Historical Society, 1988), 166–195; John J. McCusker and Russell R. Menard, *The Economy of British America, 1607–1789* (Chapel Hill: University of North Carolina Press for the Institute of Early American History and Culture, 1985), 351–378; Douglass C. North, *The Economic Growth of the United States, 1790–1860* (New York: W. W. Norton, 1966), 17–35; Anna C. Clauder, *American Commerce as Affected by the Wars of the French Revolution and Napoleon, 1793–1812* (Clifton, NJ: Augustus M. Kelley, 1932); and Emory R. Johnson, T. W. Van Metre, G. G. Huebner, and D. S. Hanchett, eds., *History of Domestic and Foreign Commerce of the United States*, 2 vols. (Washington, DC: Carnegie Institution of Washington, 1915), 1:125–126, 2:1–7. I am indebted to Cathy Matson for helping to make sense of the lacunae in this literature.

21. Cf. Richard L. Bushman, *The Refinement of America: Persons, Houses, Cities* (New York: Vintage, 1993), who argues for the steady and unidirectional diffusion of refinement from aristocratic courts to middle-class homes and farms; and T. H. Breen, *The Marketplace of Revolution: How Consumer Politics Shaped American Independence* (New York: Oxford University Press, 2004), who argues that the pursuit of pleasure through consumption culminated in a liberal, rights-based politics.

22. On images and especially objects as elements of status in the colonial period, see Kate Haulman, *The Politics of Fashion in Eighteenth-Century America* (Chapel Hill: University of North Carolina Press, 2011); Styles and Vickery, *Gender, Taste, and Material Culture*; Cary Carson, Ronald Hoffman, and Peter J. Albert, eds., *Of Consuming Interests: The Style of Life in the Eighteenth Century* (Charlottesville: University of Virginia Press for the U.S. Capitol Historical Society, 1994), esp. Carson's essay, "The Consumer Revolution in Colonial British America: Why Demand?"; Bushman, *Refinement of America*; Gordon S. Wood, "Inventing American Capitalism," *New York Review of Books*, Jun. 9, 1994.

23. The study of visual and material culture that occurred during this period was largely inaugurated by Bushman's *Refinement of America* and has been reenergized by publications in multiple disciplines. See, for example, Wendy Bellion, *Citizen Spectator: Art, Illusion, and Visual Perception in Early National America* (Chapel Hill: University of North Carolina Press for the Omohundro Institute of Early American History and Culture, 2011); David Jaffee, *A New Nation of Goods: The Material*

Culture of Early America (Philadelphia: University of Pennsylvania Press, 2010); Maurie D. McInnis and Louis P. Nelson, eds., *Shaping the Body Politic: Art and Social Formation in Early America* (Charlottesville: University of Virginia Press, 2011); Martha J. McNamara and Georgia B. Barnhill, eds., *New Views of New England: Studies in Material and Visual Culture, 1680–1830* (Boston: Colonial Society of Massachusetts, 2012); Slauter, *State as a Work of Art*; and Michael Zakim, *Ready Made Democracy: A History of Men's Dress in the Early Republic, 1760–1860* (Chicago: University of Chicago Press, 2003). Useful overviews of visual culture include Patricia Johnston, ed., *Seeing High and Low: Representing Social Conflict in American Visual Culture* (Berkeley: University of California Press, 2006); Nicholas Mirzoeff, *The Visual Culture Reader*, 2nd ed. (New York: Routledge, 2002); Vanessa R. Schwartz and Jeannene M. Przyblyski, eds., *The Nineteenth-Century Visual Culture Reader* (New York: Routledge, 2004); and Styles and Vickery, *Gender, Taste, and Material Culture*. Forthcoming work is equally promising. See, e.g., Linzy Brekke-Aloise, "Fashioning a Republic: Dress and Consumer Culture, 1783–1845" (book in progress); Zara Anishanslin, *Fashioning Empire: Hidden Histories of Labor, Landscape, and Luxury in the British Atlantic World* (New Haven, CT: Yale University Press, forthcoming); and Marla R. Miller, *Knowing Your Place: Landscapes of Labor in a Massachusetts Town* (Baltimore, MD: Johns Hopkins University Press, forthcoming). Studies that explore the visual and material culture of the early republic have appeared regularly in *Early American Literature*; *William and Mary Quarterly*; and *Common-place*. Symposia exploring the same would include *Fields of Vision: The Material and Visual Culture of New England, 1600–1800* (Nov. 2007); *The Cultural History of Eighteenth-Century America*, WMQ-EMSI Workshop (May 2007); *Made for Love: Selections from the Jane Katcher Collection of Americana* (Mar. 2007); Object Relations Workshop (May 2004); and "Gender, Taste, and the Long Eighteenth Century Symposium" (May 2004). On Bushman's influence, see Catherine E. Kelly, "Refinement of America: Persons, Houses, Cities," in "A Retrospective on the Career of Richard Bushman," *Dialogue: A Journal of Mormon Thought* 44:3 (2011), 19–28.

At the same time, the once moribund study of early national literary culture is now vibrant, and literary scholars are increasingly attentive to the materiality of texts. A by no means representative list of titles that contributes to our understanding of literature as simultaneously textual and material for this period would include Slauter, *State as a Work of Art*; Trish Loughran, *The Republic in Print: Print Culture in the Age of U.S. Nation Building* (New York: Columbia University Press, 2007); Heidi Brayman Hackel and Catherine E. Kelly, eds., *Reading Women: Literacy, Culture, and Authorship in the Atlantic World* (Philadelphia: University of Pennsylvania Press, 2009); Caroline Winterer, *The Mirror of Antiquity: American Women and the Classical Tradition, 1750–1900* (Ithaca, NY: Cornell University Press, 2007); Mary Kelley, *Learning to Stand and Speak: Women, Education, and Public Life in America's Republic* (Chapel Hill: University of North Carolina Press for the Omohundro Institute of Early American History and Culture, 2006); Susan M. Stabile, *Memory's Daughters: The Material Culture of Remembrance in Eighteenth-Century America* (Ithaca, NY: Cornell University Press, 2004); and Shields, *Civil Tongues and Polite Letters*.

24. The study of how visual and textual histories together can push the history of the senses has now moved past tired arguments about Marshall McLuhan's great divide (which equated the triumph of a monolithic print culture with the triumph of an equally monolithic visuality) and equally tired discussions about the relative importance of one sense vis-à-vis another in order to ask how a specific textual culture shaped a specific visual culture and vice versa. For a wide-ranging survey of literature on the history of the senses, which questions the great-divide thesis while tirelessly attacking the primacy of visuality in the same terms that McLuhan sets out, see Mark M. Smith, *Sensing the Past: Seeing, Hearing, Smelling, Tasting, and Touching in History* (Berkeley: University of California Press, 2007). Leigh Eric Schmidt's brilliant *Hearing Things: Religion, Illusion, and the American Enlightenment* (Cambridge, MA: Harvard University Press, 2000) provides a welcome example of the benefits of situating sensory history within print culture.

CHAPTER ONE

1. Caroline Chester's 1816 journal, reprinted in Emily Noyes Vanderpoel, comp., *More Chronicles of a Pioneer School from 1792 to 1833, Being Added History on the Litchfield Female Academy Kept by Miss Sarah Pierce and Her Nephew John Pierce Brace* (New York: Cadmus Bookshop, 1904), 193.

2. On the importance of sensibility in women's education, see Mary Kelley, *Learning to Stand and Speak: Women, Education, and Public Life in America's Republic* (Chapel Hill: University of North Carolina Press for the Omohundro Institute of Early American History and Culture, 2006), 18–19.

3. Caroline Chester, diary and commonplace book, 1815, in Vanderpoel, *Chronicles*, 193. Emphasis added.

4. Like colonial education itself, the scholarship documenting it is a patchwork affair. The best synthesis remains Lawrence A. Cremin, *American Education: The Colonial Experience, 1607–1783* (New York: Harper and Row, 1970). Regional and local studies that inform my discussion include Robert Middlekauff, *Ancients and Axioms: Secondary Education in Eighteenth-Century New England* (New Haven, CT: Yale University Press, 1963); Robert J. Vejnar III, "The State of Education in Colonial Virginia," *International Social Science Review* 77:1–2 (2002), 16–31; and James Mulhern, *A History of Secondary Education in Pennsylvania* (Philadelphia: Author, 1933). On venture schools, see Kim Tolley, "Mapping the Landscape of Higher Schooling, 1727–1850," in *Chartered Schools: Two Hundred Years of Independent Academies in the United States, 1727–1925*, ed. Nancy Beadie and Kim Tolley (New York: Routledge Falmer, 2002), 19–44.

5. Historians of education disagree over the relationship between venture schools and academies and even on the precise definition of an "academy." Some scholars have posited a linear narrative in which prerevolutionary venture schools give way to postrevolutionary academies. But numerous academies were established before the Revolution; many venture schools opened afterward; and some venture schools gained enough public support to incorporate as chartered academies. Moreover, while some scholars, notably Kim Tolley ("Mapping the Landscape") have advocated a narrow definition of academies, others like Lawrence Cremin (*American Education: The National Experience, 1783–1876* [New York: Harper and Row, 1980]), have encouraged an inclusive, elastic definition.

6. Cremin, *American Education: The National Experience*, 103. Rush quoted in Theodore R. Sizer, *The Age of the Academies* (New York: Teachers College, 1964), 13.

7. Although precise national figures are all but impossible to determine, state-based numbers are suggestive: Between 1780 and 1800, twenty academies were chartered in both Connecticut and Massachusetts. By 1817, New York had chartered forty. Three years later, Pennsylvania could claim fifty-seven. In Virginia, South Carolina, and North Carolina, the number of academies increased tenfold in the first half of the nineteenth century. If nonchartered schools were included in the tally, the numbers would soar. See Margaret A. Nash, *Women's Education in the United States, 1780–1840* (New York: Palgrave Macmillan, 2005), 40; Middlekauff, *Ancients and Axioms*, 151; Tolley, "Mapping the Landscape," 23; Joseph J. McCadden, *Education in Pennsylvania, 1801–1835 and Its Debt to Roberts Vaux* (New York: Arno, 1969), 18; Mulhern, *History of Secondary Education in Pennsylvania*, 252; Cynthia A. Kierner, *Beyond the Household: Women's Place in the Early South, 1700–1835* (Ithaca, NY: Cornell University Press, 1998), 265n45. Together, New Hampshire, Massachusetts, and Maine established thirty-four coeducational academies between 1783 and 1805. Of the more than thirty academies in Richmond, Virginia, that admitted women, five were coeducational. See Nash, *Women's Education*; Kierner, *Beyond the Household*, 158.

8. Nash, *Women's Education*, 38; Middlekauff, *Ancients and Axioms*, 146, 145; Mulhern, *History of Secondary Education in Pennsylvania*, 240. Although the Pennsylvania legislature stipulated that academies annually educate between four and ten poor children gratis in return for funding, it is not clear how many academies complied.

9. Mulhern, *History of Secondary Education in Pennsylvania*, 178.

10. On the politicization of debate over the classical curriculum, see Linda K. Kerber, *Federalists in Dissent: Imagery and Ideology in Jeffersonian America* (Ithaca, NY: Cornell University Press, 1970), 111–134. For one example of the common joke about the farmer's son who tackled Latin, see "Latin Scholars," *Rural Magazine and Farmer's Monthly Museum . . .* , May 1819.

11. Quoted in Kerber, *Federalists in Dissent*, 114, 121.

12. See Caroline Winterer, *The Culture of Classicism: Ancient Greece and Rome in American Intellectual Life, 1780–1910* (Baltimore, MD: Johns Hopkins University Press, 2002), 15–43.

13. On the academy curriculum, see Joseph F. Kett, *The Pursuit of Knowledge Under Difficulties: From Self-Improvement to Adult Education in America, 1750–1990* (Stanford, CA: Stanford University

Press, 1994), 90–95; Harriet Webster Marr, *The Old New England Academies Founded Before 1826* (New York: Comet Press Books, 1959), 168–245; Middlekauff, *Ancients and Axioms*, 154–171; Mulhern, *History of Secondary Education in Pennsylvania,* 242, 299–300, 328–329; Tolley, "Mapping the Landscape," 30–37; and Sizer, *Age of the Academies,* 9, 15, 28, 31. The choices that students and parents were offered, and the selections they made, were less driven by gender than we might imagine. In fact, the typical course of study pursued by males and females was more similar than it was different. Even Latin, long assumed to be an exclusively male preserve, was available to a significant percentage of female students. Indeed, the only truly gender-specific subjects seem to have been navigation and surveying (for males) and needlework (for females). See Nash, *Women's Education,* 41–49; Kelley, *Learning to Stand and Speak,* 67–111.

14. Simeon Doggett, *A discourse on education, delivered at the dedication and opening of the Bristol Academy* . . . (New Bedford, MA: John Spooner, 1797), 18.

15. It is impossible to offer even a rough approximation of the number of students who entered early national academies. For the most part, schools did not begin publishing catalogs of students until the 1830s. Unfortunately, extant school records from earlier decades are, at best, haphazard. On the difficulties in using school records to count students, see Marr, *Old New England Academies,* 87, 88. The earliest systematic count of academy students dates from 1855, when Henry Barnard counted 263,096 pupils; Barnard's research is discussed in Sizer, *Age of the Academies,* 12.

16. William C. Reichel, *A History of the Moravian Seminary for Young Ladies,* 4th ed. (Bethlehem, PA: Published for the Moravian Seminary, 1901), 339, 342; Lynne Templeton Brickley, "Sarah Pierce's Litchfield Female Academy, 1792–1833" (Ph.D. diss., Harvard University, 1985), 52–54, 606n13.

17. William C. Reichel, *Historical Sketch of Nazareth Hall from 1755 to 1869* (New York: Lippincott, 1869), 31; Brickley, "Sarah Pierce's Litchfield Female Academy," 54.

18. Edmund Quincy, *Life of Josiah Quincy of Massachusetts* (Boston: Ticknor and Fields, 1867), 23–24.

19. Marr, *Old New England Academies,* 93; "Thoughts on the establishment of academies in Pennsylvania," *American Museum, or Universal Magazine,* Sept. 1791. See also "On Education," *Boston Magazine,* Apr. 1784.

20. This figure, standard among historians of education, is based on Henry Barnard's 1856 estimates. See, e.g., Robert L. Church and Michael W. Sedlak, *Education in the United States: An Interpretive History* (New York: Free Press, 1976), 36–37.

21. John Swanwick, *Thoughts on Education, Addressed to the Visitors of the Young Ladies' Academy in Philadelphia, October 31, 1787* (Philadelphia: Thomas Dobson, 1787), 25; James Abercrombie D.D., *A charge delivered after a examination on Thursday, July 30, 1807 to the senior class of the Philadelphia Academy* (Philadelphia: Smith and Maxwell, 1807), 8–9. On the rationale for women's education, see Kelley, *Learning to Stand and Speak,* 34–65; Nash, *Women's Education,* 15–33.

22. On debates over content of female education, see esp. Nash, *Women's Education*; Kelley, *Learning to Stand and Speak*; and Linda K. Kerber, *Women of the Republic: Intellect and Ideology in Revolutionary America* (Chapel Hill: University of North Carolina Press, 1980).

23. John P. Brace, "Address at the Close of the School, Oct. 25, 1819" and "Address at the Close of the School, Oct. 26, 1816," in Vanderpoel, *More Chronicles,* 202, 210; Mary Magdalen M'Intosh, "Association of Ideas," in *School Exercises of the Lafayette Female Academy; Including Triumphs of Genius, a Poem, by Caroline Clifford Nephew, of Darien, Georgia* (Lexington, KY, 1826). On women's status and national character, see Mark L. Kamrath, "An 'Inconceivable Pleasure' and the *Philadelphia Minerva*: Erotic Liberalism, Oriental Tales, and the Female Subject in Periodicals of the Early Republic," *American Periodicals* 14 (2004), 3–34; Kerber, *Women of the Republic,* 19, 22; Nancy F. Cott, *Bonds of Womanhood: "Woman's Sphere in New England, 1780–1835* (New Haven, CT: Yale University Press, 1977), 130–131.

24. Sarah Pierce, "Address at the Close of School, Oct. 29, 1818," in Emily Noyes Vanderpoel, comp., *Chronicles of a Pioneer School from 1792 to 1833* (Cambridge, MA: University Press, 1903), 177–178.

25. Advertisement, (New York) *Independent Journal,* Sept. 11, 1784.

26. Hugh Blair, *Lectures on Rhetoric and Belles Lettres,* ed. Linda Ferreira-Buckley and S. Michael Halloran (Carbondale: Southern Illinois University Press, 2005), 8.

27. Caroline Chester, diary and commonplace book, 1815, in Vanderpoel, *Chronicles*, 153; Sara Gratz Moses, copybook, 1832, Doc. 821, Winterthur Library.

28. Blair, *Lectures*, 51; Henry Theodore Cheever, diary, Jul. 5, 1829, Cheever-Wheeler Family Papers, American Antiquarian Society; Mary Ann Bacon, diary, in Vanderpoel, *Chronicles*, 67.

29. "A Ride Through Part of Maryland & Virginia. In the Month of May 1803," in Hetty Anne Barton, diary, 1803, Historical Society of Pennsylvania.

30. Blair, *Lectures*, lectures IV and V. For Blair, Joseph Addison ("Pleasures of the Imagination," *Spectator*, Jun. 21, 1712) provides the point of departure. In Addison's terms, the pleasures of the imagination "arise from visible Objects, either when we have them actually in our View, or when we call up their Ideas into our Minds by paintings, Statues, Descriptions, or any the like Occasion."

31. James Milnor, "On Female Education," *Port Folio*, 3rd ser., May 1809, 391.

32. E. Jennifer Monaghan, "Literacy Instruction and Gender in Colonial New England," *American Quarterly* 40:1 (1988), 18–41; E. Jennifer Monaghan, "Readers Writing: The Curriculum of the Writing Schools of Eighteenth-Century Boston," *Visible Language* 21:2 (Spring 1987), 168–213; Tamara Plakins Thornton, *Handwriting in America: A Cultural History* (New Haven, CT: Yale University Press, 1996), 2–41; William Huntting Howell, *Against Self-Reliance: The Arts of Dependence in the Early United States* (Philadelphia: University of Pennsylvania Press, 2015), 85–114; William Huntting Howell, "A More Perfect Copy: David Rittenhouse and the Reproduction of Republican Virtue," *William and Mary Quarterly*, 3rd ser., 64:4 (Oct. 2007), 757–790.

33. *William C. Reichel, A History of the Rise, Progress, and Present Condition of the Bethlehem Female Seminary* (Philadelphia: J. B. Lippincott and Co., 1858), 116, 107. The epigrams are from Samuel Salisbury, penmanship book, 1780, vol. 5, Penmanship Collection, 1762–1856, American Antiquarian Society; "Specimens of Writing Made by the Scholars in Nazareth School for the Autumnal Examination, 1793," Nazareth Hall, Collection 212, Winterthur Library.

34. Longer transcriptions, like business letters, required the greater control of pen and ink as well as the ability to space letters and lines evenly, filling the page without crowding it. For a mock business letter, see Charles Schweiniz, in "Specimens of Writing."

35. Milnor, "On Female Education," 391; Elizabeth Salisbury to Stephen Salisbury II, n.d. [Sept. 1809], Salisbury Family Papers, box 14, folder 3, American Antiquarian Society; Henry Theodore, journal, Jun. 21, 1829, Cheever-Wheeler Family Papers, Box 54, American Antiquarian Society. On the impossibility of separating style from substance, see Jay Fliegelman, *Declaring Independence: Jefferson, Natural Language, and the Culture of Performance* (Stanford, CA: Stanford University Press, 1993).

36. Samuel Salisbury, copybook, 1780, vol. 5, Penmanship Collection, 1762–1856, American Antiquarian Society.

37. Mary Jane [Derby] Peabody, *A Letter for Auld Lang Syne* (privately printed, 1881), 15–16; Samuel May, copybook, 1822, vol. 18, Penmanship Collection, 1762–1856, American Antiquarian Society.

38. George Fisher, comp., *American Instructor, or, Young Man's Best Companion* (Philadelphia: printed by Benjamin Franklin, 1748), 28–29. Fisher's book went through ten editions between 1748 and 1794. See also Nathan Towne, *The Art of Writing Reduced to Its First Principles* (New York, 1812), 9–10.

39. On the importance of the body as a register of republican virtue, see esp. Richard Bushman, *The Refinement of America: Persons, Houses, Cities* (New York: Random House, 1992); Fliegelman, *Declaring Independence*; and Christopher Lukasik, *Discerning Characters: The Culture of Appearance in Early America* (Philadelphia: University of Pennsylvania Press, 2011).

40. Charles Latham Jr., *Episcopal Academy, 1785–1984* (Devon, PA: W. T. Cooke, 1984), 223; Vanderpoel, *Chronicles*, 147; Mary Ann Bacon, journal, 1802, in Vanderpoel, *Chronicles*, 75.

41. Lyman Powell, A.B., *The History of Education in Delaware* (Washington, DC: Government Printing Office, 1893), 43; Lucy Sheldon, diary, Jan. 2, 1802, in Vanderpoel, *Chronicles*, 46. See also Bushman, *Refinement of America*.

42. Mary Bacon, diary and composition and extract book, ca. 1820, in Vanderpoel, *Chronicles*, 73; Swanwick, *Thoughts on Education*, 10; "Notice for the Clermont Seminary, Philadelphia PA," *Port Folio*, 3rd ser., Oct. 1810, 387–389. See also *Prospectus, Rules and Regulations of Carre and Sanderson's*

Seminary (Philadelphia: Sanderson, 1816), 4; James Cosens Ogden, *An Address Delivered at the Opening of the Portsmouth Academy, on Easter Monday, AD 1791* (Portsmouth, NH: George Jerry Osborne, 1793), 22.

43. Hannah Webster Foster, *The Boarding School* (Boston: I. Thomas and E. T. Andrews, 1798), 42; Bacon, diary, ca. 1820, 73. Bacon's essay followed the argument and the language of "Letter IX" in Reverend John Bennett's *Letters to a Young Lady*, which went through seven American editions between 1796 and 1818 and was excerpted in numerous periodicals.

44. See, for example, Lucy Sheldon's diary, for 1801, in Vanderpoel, *Chronicles*, 48–49, 52; Charlotte Sheldon's diary in Vanderpoel, *Chronicles*, 10–17.

45. George Younglove Cutler, journal, Jul. 12, 1820, in Vanderpoel, *Chronicles*, 194.

46. "Rules for the School and Family," copied by Eliza Ann Mulford, 1814, in Vanderpoel, *Chronicles*, 146; Atkinson [NH] Academy Record Book (1803–1945), American Antiquarian Society; "Reminiscences of Leicester Academy, delivered by request of its Trustees, at Leicester, on the Annual Exhibition of the Students, August 10, 1847 by John Pierce, Pastor of the First Church in Brookline, Assistant Preceptor of the Academy From from July 1793 to July 1795," Bigelow Family Papers, box 1, folder 2, American Antiquarian SocietyA. At Litchfield, instruction in politeness was taken so seriously that some students received academic prizes for it; see, for example, "Extracts from the 'Private Journals of Mr. John P. Brace,'" Nov. 1, 1814, in Vanderpoel, comp., *More Chronicles*, 104. On manners and youth, see C. Dallett Hemphill, *Bowing to Neccessities: A History of Manners in America, 1620–1860* (New York: Oxford University Press, 1999), 87–103.

47. Atkinson Academy Record Book; Latham Jr., *Episcopal Academy*, 223; Reichel, *Rise and Progress of Bethlehem Seminary*, 33–35.

48. "Reminiscences of Miss Esther H. Thompson," in Vanderpoel, *Chronicles*, 297–298;. Charles Hammond, "Historical Discourse," *Discourses and speeches delivered at the semi-centennial of Monson Academy, Monson Mass, July 18th and 19th, 1854* (New York: John A. Gray, 1855), 25.

49. Edward D. Mansfield, "Personal Memories," in Vanderpoel, *Chronicles*, 42; "Extracts from the 'Private Journals of Mr. John P. Brace' for 1814 and 1815," in Vanderpoel, *More Chronicles*, 81–163; George Younglove Cutler, "His Journal, July–August 1820," in Vanderpoel, *More Chronicles*, 94, 195.

50. Caroline Chester, journal, 1816, in Vanderpoel, *More Chronicles*, 190–191.

51. Peter de Bolla, *The Education of the Eye: Painting, Landscape, and Architecture in Eighteenth-Century Britain* (Stanford, CA: Stanford University Press, 2003), 78.

52. The best single resource on this topic is Roy Jay Winkelman's exhaustive doctoral dissertation, "Art Education in the Non-Public Schools of Pennsylvania, 1720–1870" (Ph.D. diss., Pennsylvania State University, 1990).

53. On the Bethlehem Female Seminary, see Kathleen Eagen Johnson, "'To Expand the Mind and Embellish Society': The Educational Philosophy and Ornamental Arts of the Bethlehem Young Ladies Seminary, 1785–1840" (M.A. thesis, University of Delaware, 1978), 73; and Winkelman, "Art Education," 299–324. On the imprints of Leonardo da Vinci's *Treatise*, see Leonardo da Vinci, *Treatise on Painting [Codex Urbinas Latinus 1270]*, trans. A. Philip McMahon (Princeton, NJ: Princeton University Press, 1956), 362–367; on the *Treatise*'s circulation in America, see Janice G. Schimmelman, *A Checklist of European Treatises on Art and Essays on Aesthetics Available in America Through 1815* (Worcester, MA: American Antiquarian Society, 1983), 138–140.

54. R[ichard] Turner, *An abridgment of the arts and sciences: being a short, but comprehensive system, of useful and polite learning* (New York: James Oram, 1802); William Duane, *Epitome of the arts and sciences being a comprehensive system of the elementary parts of an useful and polite education, upon the plan of a similar work of R. Turner . . . augmented and improved, and adapted to the use of schools in the United States* (Philadelphia: William Duane, 1805). Both Duane and Turner went through multiple editions in the United States. Quotations are from Turner, *Abridgement*, 43–35. For the use of volumes like these for art instruction, see Winkelman, "Art Education," 243–260.

55. For the Dorchester Academy, see Jane C. Nylander, "Some Print Sources of New England School Girl Art," *Antiques*, Aug. 1976, 292–301; and Betty Ring, *Girlhood Embroidery: American Samplers and Pictorial Needlework, 1650–1850*, 2 vols. (New York: Alfred A. Knopf, 1993), 1:94–99. For Nazareth Hall, see the Nazareth Hall Collection Finding Air, Winterthur Library. On the Bethlehem Female Seminary and Germantown Academy, see Winkelman, "Art Education," 270, 454–456.

56. On Rollin and Pope, see Caroline Winterer, "The Female World of Classical Reading in Eighteenth-Century America," in *Reading Women: Literacy, Authorship, and Culture in the Atlantic World, 1500–1800*, ed. Heidi Brayman Hackel and Catherine E. Kelly (Philadelphia: University of Pennsylvania Press, 2007), 109–115; Charlotte Sheldon, diary, 1796, in Vanderpoel, *Chronicles*, 11; Peabody, *Letter for Auld Lang Syne*, 12; Mary Johnson, "Madame Rivardi's Seminary in the Gothic Mansion," *Pennsylvania Magazine of History and Biography* 104:1 (Jan. 1980), 21; Mary Wilbor, diary, 1822, in Vanderpoel, *Chronicles*, 234.

57. See esp. the arguments made by Linda K. Kerber in *Women of the Republic*, 139–261; Mary Beth Norton, *Liberty's Daughters: The Revolutionary Experience of American Women, 1750–1800* (New York: Little, Brown, 1980), 256–294; and Barbara Miller Solomon, *In the Company of Educated Women: A History of Women and Higher Education in America* (New Haven, CT: Yale University Press, 1985), 14–26.

58. Thomas Woody, *A History of Women's Education in the United States*, 2 vols. (New York: Octagon, 1974), 1:563–565. See also Winkelman, "Art Education," 439; Kelley, *Learning to Stand and Speak*, 69–71, 77–78; and Nash, *Women's Education*, 41–45.

59. "Clermont Seminary," *Port Folio*, Oct. 1810, 387; *Prospectus, Rules and Regulations of Carre and Sanderson's Seminary*, 4; "Intelligence," *Christian Spectator* (Jan. 1828), 46; John S. Bassett, "The Round Hill School," *Proceedings of the American Antiquarian Society*, new series (Apr. 1917), 57; Philip Freneau, "The Desolate Academy," *American Museum* (Jun. 1787), 567–568.

60. Peale is quoted in Edward J. Nygren, "Art Instruction in Philadelphia, 1795–1845" (M.A. thesis, University of Delaware, 1969), 3; James Cox, "Drawing and Painting Academy," *Poulson's Daily Advertiser*, Sept. 6, 1816. On drawing masters in the early national period, see Nygren, "Art Instruction," 25–27; Winkelman, "Art Education," 273–298; Carl W. Drepperd, *American Pioneer Art and Artists* (Springfield, MA: Pond-Ekberg, 1942); William Kelby, comp., *Notes on American Artists, 1754–1820, Copied from Advertisements Appearing in the Newspapers of the Day* (New York: New-York Historical Society, 1922); Alfred Coxe Prime, comp., *The Arts and Crafts of Philadelphia, Maryland, and South Carolina: Gleanings from Newspapers*, 2 vols. (Topsfield, MA: Walpole Society, 1929–1932).

61. Female students' commonplace books rarely conformed to the formal categories that marked classical commonplace books; instead, they were compiled by accretion, by mixing poetry, prose, records of daily experiences, and even artwork. Nevertheless, the point of keeping a commonplace book was the same as it had been for earlier generations of male students and men of letters: to cultivate taste and sensibility by emulating and internalizing the wisdom and judgment of other worthy minds. On the function of commonplace books in self-fashioning, see esp. Mary Thomas Crane, *Framing Authority: Sayings, Self, and Society in Sixteenth-Century England* (Princeton, NJ: Princeton University Press, 1993). For examples of students' commonplace books, see Vanderpoel, *Chronicles*; and Vanderpoel, *More Chronicles*.

62. See esp. Ring, *Girlhood Embroidery*, 1:16–17, 22, and passim. Teachers were so influential in shaping students' needlework that art historians can tell where girls and women attended school from examining their embroidery. See, for example, Ring's discussions of the style of the Misses Patten who taught needlework in Hartford, Connecticut (ibid., 202–210), or Abby Wright, who taught in South Hadley, Massachusetts (ibid., 159–165). On emulation and needlework, see Howell, *Against Self-Reliance*, 116–156; and "Spirits of Emulation: Readers, Samplers, and the Republican Girl, 1787–1810," *American Literature* 81:3 (Sept. 2009), 497–526. Student drawing and painting have attracted far less scholarly attention than needlework; for an example of teacher influence in those subjects, see a discussion of students who studied under Orra White at Deerfield Academy in Suzanne L. Flynt, *Ornamental and Useful Accomplishments: Schoolgirl Education and Deerfield Academy, 1800–1830* (Deerfield, MA: Pocumtuck Valley Memorial Association and Deerfield Academy, 1988).

63. Quoted in Johnson, "'To Expand the Mind and Embellish Society,'" 37.

64. These arguments are based on data presented in Ethel Stanwood Bolton and Eva Johnston Coe, *American Samplers* (Boston: Massachusetts Society of Colonial Dames, 1921), which contains an appendix listing all epigrams from all of the eighteenth- and nineteenth-century samplers that the Society of Colonial Dames had been able to locate by 1921. While art historians agree that Stanton and Coe's list of samplers is not exhaustive, they also agree that it is representative. For quotations,

see *American Samplers*, 265, 250, 268, 269. The Litchfield student Mary Bacon's 1802 "diary & composition & extract book," for example, contains poems and essays elaborating these themes; see Vanderpoel, *Chronicles*, 66–79.

65. Betty Ring has done more than any other scholar to trace the literary and print sources for schoolgirl needlework; my discussion here is greatly indebted to her scholarship. On Mary Beach's copy of Cornelia, Mother of the Gracchi, see Ring, *Girlhood Embroidery*, 1:96; on Nancy Lincoln's "Washington Family," see ibid., 87. On *The Seasons*, see Louise Stevenson, "The Transatlantic Travels of James Thomson's The Seasons and its Baggage of Material Culture," *Proceedings of the American Antiquarian Society* 116 (2006), 121–165. On schoolgirl needlework, see also John F. LaBranche and Rita F. Conant, *In Female Worth and Elegance: Sampler and Needlework Students and Teachers in Portsmouth, NH, 1741–1840* (Portsmouth, NH: Portsmouth Marine Society, 1996); Glee F. Krueger, *A Gallery of American Samplers: The Theodore H. Kapnek Collection* (New York: E. P. Dutton, 1978); Susan Burrows Swan, *Plain and Fancy: American Women and Their Needlework, 1700–1850* (New York: Holt, Rinehart and Winston, 1977); and Bolton and Coe, *American Samplers*. For general descriptions of the art made by female students, see Brickley, "Sarah Pierce's Litchfield Female Academy"; Catherine Keene Fields and Lisa C. Knightlinger, eds., *To Ornament Their Minds: Sarah Pierce's Litchfield Academy, 1792–1833* (Litchfield, CT: Litchfield Historical Society, 1993); Flynt, *Ornamental and Useful Accomplishments*; Nylander, "Some Print Sources of New England School Girl Art"; Betty Ring, *Let Virtue Be a Guide to Thee: Needlework in the Education of Rhode Island Women* (Providence: Rhode Island Historical Society, 1983); Ring, *Girlhood Embroidery*.

66. "Extract from a paper read May 4, 1896, before the Village Library Company of Farmington [CT], on 'Farmington Society One Hundred Years Ago,' by Julius Gray," in Vanderpoel, *More Chronicles*, 259. On the increasing numbers of frame makers, see Ring, *Girlhood Embroidery*, 1:22, 24. Families were willing to pay large sums to frame their daughters' work. For example, Caroline Stebbins's family paid $5.00 to frame the embroidered picture of Mt. Vernon that she completed as a student at Deerfield Academy in 1806–1807. For the cost of the frame, they could have purchased an additional half year's tuition for instruction in reading, writing, and grammar. See Flynt, *Ornamental and Useful Accomplishments*, 21.

67. Thomas Jefferson, *Early History of the University of Virginia: as contained in the letters of Thomas Jefferson and Joseph C. Cabell* . . . (Richmond, VA: J. W. Randolph, 1856), 387–389, 457, 471; W. H. Van Vleck, "Nazareth Hall, a Fragment," in *Historical Sketch of Nazareth Hall*, ed. Reichel, 9–10.

68. "Drawings by Students of Nazareth Hall," Collection 212, Nazareth Hall, Winterthur Library. It is not clear why male students began to produce completed, representational images in the 1810s; however, the shift seems to have coincided with the arrival of Charles F. Seidel as principal in 1809. See Reichel, *A History of Nazareth Hall*, 32–33.

69. Johann Daniel Preissler, *Die durch Theorie erfundene Practic* . . . , 3 vols. (Nurnberg: Bey ihme zu finden, 1744–1747). On the development of this approach to drawing, see Ann Bermingham's splendid *Learning to Draw: Studies in the Cultural History of a Polite and Useful Art* (New Haven, CT: Yale University Press for the Paul Mellon Centre for Studies in British Art, 2000), esp. 33–76. Cf. Fliegelman's analysis of silhouettes in *Declaring Independence*, 64.

70. Bermingham describes this as mastery of "visual taxonomy of stylistic attributes" in "Elegant Females and Gentlemen Connoisseurs: The Commerce in Culture and Self-Image in Eighteenth-Century England," in *The Consumption of Culture: Image, Object, Text*, ed. Ann Bermingham and John Brewer (London: Routledge, 1995), 489–513, the quote is on 504.

71. Michael Warner, *The Letters of the Republic: Publication and the Public Sphere in Eighteenth-Century America* (Cambridge, MA: Harvard University Press, 1990). Cf. Steven C. Bullock's discussion of the antithetical aims of Masonic art in "'Sensible Signs': The Emblematic Education of Post-Revolutionary Freemasonry," in *A Republic for the Ages: The United States Capitol and the Political Culture of the Early Republic*, ed. Donald R. Kennon (Charlottesville: U.S. Capitol Historical Society and the University of Virginia Press, 1999), 177–213.

72. William Bentley, *The Diary of William Bentley: Pastor of the East Church, Salem, Massachusetts* (Salem, MA: Essex Institute, 1905–1914), vols. 2–4. For Joseph Dennie on the Philadelphia Academy, see *Port Folio*, May 1809. On Litchfield's literati, see Vanderpoel, *Chronicles*, 182. For public

notices of exhibitions and examinations, see, among many, the broadsides advertising the Nichols Academy Examination, Nov. 20, 1822; the Gilmanton [NH] Academy Exhibition at Gilmanton Academy, Oct. 5, 1802; the Leicester Academy 1814 Order of Exercises for Exhibition; and the Leicester Academy 1816 Order of Exercises for Exhibition, in the Broadsides Collection, American Antiquarian Society. See also Vanderpoel, *Chronicles*; Vanderpoel, *More Chronicles*; and Reichel, *Bethlehem Souvenir* for accounts of exhibition programs at Litchfield Academy and Bethlehem Female Seminary.

73. Atkinson Academy Record Book, Aug. 29, 1821; Reichel, *Bethlehem Souvenir*, 109–111. Catharine Beecher described the stage in "true theater style" in Vanderpoel, *Chronicles*, 180. Dialogue titles are drawn from the broadsides for the Gilmanton [NH] Academy Exhibition at Gilmanton Academy, Oct. 5, 1802, and the Leicester Academy 1814 Order of Exercises for Exhibition, in the Broadsides Collection, American Antiquarian Society.

74. "Notice for the Clermont School, Philadelphia PA," *Port Folio*, 3rd ser., Oct. 1810, 389.

75. "Dialogue Spoken at the Autumnal Examination in the Year 1793, at Nazareth Hall, concerning Astronomy and the Use of the Globes: delivered by the scholars of the I class at that time eleven in number, written by B[enjamin] Mortimer," Nazareth Hall Collection, Winterthur Library. On the orrery as a metaphor for the United States, see Howell, *Against Self-Reliance*, 85–114; and Howell, "A More Perfect Copy." On gesture and oratory, see Carolyn Eastman, *A Nation of Speechifiers: Making an American Public After the Revolution* (Chicago: University of Chicago Press, 2009), 25–27, 35, 62–64.

76. This scrutiny was deemed so fundamental that, in 1814, two students at the Litchfield Academy forfeited the opportunity to receive academic prizes because they refused to submit their journals for public inspection. Vanderpoel, *More Chronicles*, 94.

77. Jane C. Giffen, "Susanna Rowson and Her Academy," *Antiques* (Sept. 1990), 436–440; Reichel, *Bethlehem Souvenir*, 76; Vanderpoel, *More Chronicles*, 22.

78. "May Day; or the Crowning of Flora," *New-York Weekly Museum*, Jun. 22, 1816, 122; "The Crowning of Flora in the United States," *Port Folio*, Jul. 1810, 31–32; Davida Deutsch, "The Crowning of Flora," *Luminary* 9:2 (1988).

79. Cf. work by the feminist art historians Anne Higonnet and Ann Bermingham: Bermingham, "Elegant Females and Gentlemen Connoisseurs"; Higonnet, "Secluded Visions: Images of Feminine Experience in Nineteenth-Century Europe," *Radical History Review* 38 (1987), 16–36. Both Higonnet and Bermingham have suggested that what most distinguished the amateur artistic productions of eighteenth- and nineteenth-century (European) women was the extent to which their work was shrouded in privacy and also the extent to which it was conceived, executed, and displayed within the domestic sphere.

CHAPTER TWO

1. On Greenwood's New York stay, see entries for Jan. and Feb. 1806; on the Hanover exhibition, see Apr. 11, 1806, in *Extracts from the Journals of Ethan A. Greenwood: Portrait Painter and Museum Proprietor*, ed. Georgia Brady Barnhill (Worcester, MA: American Antiquarian Society, 1993; hereafter cited as *Extracts*), 105, 106. On Greenwood's payments to Savage, see Georgia Brady Baumgardner, "The Early Career of Ethan Allen Greenwood," in *Itinerancy in New England and New York: Dublin Seminar for New England Folklife 1984*, ed. Peter Benes (Boston: Boston University, 1986), 216.

2. See *Extracts*, Jan. 1, 1813, 115; and Jul. 4, 1818, 138 and passim.

3. No scholar of the early republic has paid more attention to situating artists' products alongside their career trajectories than David Jaffee. See esp. his *A New Nation of Goods: The Material Culture of Early America* (Philadelphia: University of Pennsylvania Press, 2010); and "One of the Primitive Sort: Portrait Makers in the Rural North, 1760–1860," in *The Countryside in the Age of Capitalist Transformation*, ed. Steven Hahn and Jonathan Prude (Chapel Hill: University of North Carolina Press, 1985), 103–138. See also Paul J. Staiti, *Samuel F. B. Morse* (New York: Cambridge University Press, 1989).

4. Cf. Jaffee, "One of the Primitive Sort," who describes rural portrait painters as "artisan entrepreneurs."

5. Charles Willson Peale, *The Autobiography of Charles Willson Peale*, in *Selected Papers of Charles Willson Peale and His Family*, ed. Sidney Hart (New Haven, CT: Yale University Press for the National

Portrait Gallery and Smithsonian Institution, 2000), 5:41. Dunlap is quoted in Neil Harris, *Artist in American Society: The Formative Years* (New York: Simon and Schuster, 1966), 59. This approach owes much to David Jaffee's pathbreaking work on provincial artists, although it departs from his emphasis on provincial style. See Jaffee, "One of the Primitive Sort," and *New Nation of Goods.*

6. Scholars have suggested that early national men who looked to literary careers, including William Dunlap, were partly motivated by a desire to defend and advance a model of masculinity that was increasingly out of place in a society that saw politics and commerce as men's appropriate sphere of action. See, e.g., Catherine O'Donnell Kaplan, *Men of Letters in the Early Republic: Cultivating Forms of Citizenship* (Chapel Hill: University of North Carolina Press, 2008); and Bryan Waterman, *Republic of Intellect: The Friendly Club of New York City and the Making of American Literature* (Baltimore, MD: Johns Hopkins University Press, 2007). See also Martin Myrone, *Bodybuilding: Reforming Masculinities in British Art, 1750–1810* (New Haven, CT: Yale University Press for the Paul Mellon Centre for Studies in British Art, 2005).

7. John Trumbull, *The Autobiography of John Trumbull, Patriot-Artist, 1756–1843*, ed. Theodore Sizer (New Haven, CT: Yale University Press, 1953), 82. Emphasis in the original.

8. The preceding accounts appear in William Dunlap, *History of the Rise and Progress of the Arts of Design in the United States*, ed. Rita Weiss, 2 vols. (1834; repr., New York: Dover, 1969), vol. 2, pt. 1, 59, 104–105, 150, 97. Fathers' financial concerns about their sons' prospects were all too well grounded, as we will see. That said, the frequency with which painters recounted overcoming paternal reservations in order to chart new courses resonates with the period's antipatriarchal literary tropes and hints at the ways that literary culture could serve as a template for making sense of experience. Not all young men had to overcome paternal reservations in order to paint; a partial list of those whose fathers supported them would include Washington Allston, Samuel F. B. Morse, and William Dunlap. The best recent discussion of men's ability to choose careers is J. M. Opal, *Beyond the Farm: National Ambitions in Rural New England* (Philadelphia: University of Pennsylvania Press, 2008). See also Joyce Oldham Appleby, *Inheriting the Revolution: The First Generation of Americans* (Cambridge, MA: Belknap Press of Harvard University Press, 2000); and Joseph F. Kett, *Rites of Passage: Adolescence in America, 1790 to the Present* (New York: Basic, 1977).

9. Chester Harding, *A Sketch of Chester Harding, Artist, Drawn by His Own Hand*, ed. Margaret E. White (1929; repr., New York: Kennedy Galleries and Da Capo, 1970), 31.

10. See, e.g., the sketches of Anne Hall and Anne Leslie in Dunlap, *History*, vol. 2, pt. 2, 368–370, 398–399. Even the Way Champlain women, who talked at length about their lives after deciding to paint professionally, never discuss how or why they settled on painting as a vocation. On the problematic nature of a "professional woman artist" in the early republic, see Laura R. Prieto, *At Home in the Studio: The Professionalization of Women Artists in America* (Cambridge, MA: Harvard University Press, 2001), 12–40; and Anne Sue Hirshorn, "Anna Claypoole, Margaretta, and Sarah Miriam Peale: Modes of Accomplishment and Fortune," in *The Peale Family: Creation of a Legacy, 1770–1870*, ed. Lillian B. Miller (New York: Abbeville Press in association with the Trust for Museum Exhibitions and the National Portrait Gallery, Smithsonian Institution, 1996), 220–247. For similar discussions focusing on a slightly later time period, see April F. Masten, *Art Work: Women Artists and Democracy in Mid-Nineteenth-Century New York* (Philadelphia: University of Pennsylvania Press, 2008); and Kirsten Swinth, *Painting Professionals: Women Artists and the Development of Modern American Art, 1870–1930* (Chapel Hill: University of North Carolina Press, 2001). On the larger problem of female professional ambition in the early republic, see esp. Mary Kelley, *Learning to Stand and Speak: Women, Education, and Public Life in America's Republic* (Chapel Hill: University of North Carolina Press for the Omohundro Institute of Early American History and Culture, 2006); and *Private Woman, Public Stage: Literary Domesticity in Nineteenth-Century America* (New York: Oxford University Press, 1984).

11. The number of female artists who counted artists among their family members is striking. A partial list includes Patience Lovell Wright and her sister Rachel Lovell Wells, cousins of Robert Feke; Anna Claypoole Peale, Margaretta Peale, and Sarah Miriam Peale; Sarah Goodridge and Elizabeth Goodridge; and Mary Way, Elizabeth Way Champlain, and Eliza Champlain.

12. Trumbull, *Autobiography*, 10–13; Staiti, *Samuel F. B. Morse*, 8.

13. Dunlap, *History*, vol. 2, pt. 1, 258; Harding, *Sketches*, 3–17. On Harding's less successful brother, see Swannee Bennett and William B. Worthen, "The Harding Brothers," in *Arkansas Made: A Survey of the Decorative, Mechanical, and Fine Arts Produced in Arkansas, 1819–1870*, vol. 2, *Photography, Art* (Fayetteville: University of Arkansas Press, 1990), 148–150.

14. Dunlap, *History*, 1:417. Although Jarvis was referring specifically to the Philadelphia partnership of Paul, Pratt, Retter, and Clarke, his remarks are broadly applicable. See, e.g., Bettina A. Norton, "The Brothers Blyth: Salem in Its Heyday," in *Painting and Portrait Making in the American Northeast: Dublin Seminar for New England Folklife Annual Proceedings 1994*, ed. Peter Benes (Boston: Boston University, 1995), 46–63.

15. Thompson S. Harlow, "The Life and Trials of Joseph Steward," *Connecticut Historical Society Bulletin* 46:4 (Oct. 1981), 98–100; Dunlap, *History*, vol. 2, pt. 1, 231.

16. Dunlap, *History*, vol. 2, pt. 1, 31–33, and vol. 2, pt. 2, 348.

17. If scholars of eighteenth- and early nineteenth-century Anglo-American painting take the deficiencies of training as their starting point, they can draw very different conclusions from this fact. Cf. Harris, who, in *Artist in American Society*, emphasized the extent to which this hobbled the arts. See also Margaretta Lovell, "Bodies of Illusion: Portraits, People, and the Construction of Memory," in *Possible Pasts: Becoming Colonial in Early America*, ed. Robert Blair St. George (Ithaca, NY: Cornell University Press, 2000); and Jaffee, *New Nation of Goods*, which emphasize artists' and craftsmen's creativity in confronting the challenges.

18. Peale, *Autobiography*, 14–17, 21–31.

19. On the evolving struggle for technique, see Lance Mayer and Gay Myers, *American Painters on Technique: The Colonial Period to 1860* (Los Angeles: J. Paul Getty Trust, 2011). For a detailed overview of one painter's technical strategies, see Stephen H. Kornhauser, "Ralph Earl's Working Methods and Materials," in *Ralph Earl: The Face of the Young Republic*, ed. Elizabeth Mankin Kornhauser (New Haven, CT: Yale University Press, 1991), 85–91.

20. Carrie Rebora Barratt and Ellen Miles, *Gilbert Stuart* (New Haven, CT: Yale University Press for the Metropolitan Museum of Art, 2004), 291; Dorinda Evans, *The Genius of Gilbert Stuart* (Princeton, NJ: Princeton University Press, 1999), 114–118; Dunlap, *History*, vol. 2, pt. 1, 72–96.

21. Mayer and Myers, *American Painters on Technique*, 27; Mary Way to Betsey Way Champlain, 1814, in *Sisters of the Brush: Their Family, Art, Life, and Letters, 1797–1833*, ed. Ramsay MacMullen (New Haven, CT: Past Times, 1997), 25–32.

22. Dunlap, *History*, 1:268–270; Maura Lyons, *William Dunlap and the Construction of an American Art History* (Amherst: University of Massachusetts Press, 2005), 21–22.

23. Dunlap, *History*, 1:256, and vol. 2, pt. 1, 59.

24. Earlier plans to study in London were jettisoned by his mother, who pointed out that if he were to die before returning, he would leave his family in poverty. Harding, *Sketch*, 4–5, 30–36, 46.

25. Quoted in Hirshorn, "Anna Claypoole, Margaretta, and Sarah Miriam Peale," 229; *First Annual Exhibition of the Society of Artists of the United States* (Philadelphia: Thomas L. Plowman, 1811).

26. For Sarah Goodridge, see Agnes M. Dods, "Sarah Goodridge," *Magazine Antiques* 51 (May 1947), 328–329; Barbara N. Parker, "Goodridge, Sarah," in *Notable American Women*, vol. 2, *G–O*, ed. Edward T. James, Janet Wilson James, and Paul S. Boyer (Cambridge, MA: Harvard University Press, 1971), 63–64. For Anne Hall's training and subsequent career, see Dunlap, *History*, vol. 2, pt. 2, 368–370; William H. Gerdts, "Hall, Anne," in James et al., *Notable American Women*, 2:368–370. For general discussions of social barriers that limited women's access to training in the early republic, see Prieto, *At Home in the Studio*; Hirshorn, "Anna Claypoole, Margaretta, and Sarah Miriam Peale"; and Mirra Bank, *Anonymous Was a Woman* (New York: St. Martin's, 1979). Women's access to training and employment increased considerably by the mid-nineteenth century: see Masten, *Art Work*.

27. Elliot Bostwick Davis, "Training the Eye and the Hand: Drawing Books in Nineteenth Century America" (Ph.D. diss., Columbia University, 1992); Peter Marzio, *The Art Crusade: An Analysis of American Drawing Manuals, 1820–1860* (Washington, DC: Smithsonian Institution Press, 1976). See also Albert A. Anderson, comp., *Teaching America to Draw: Instructional Manuals and Ephemera,*

1794–1925: An Exhibition at the Grolier Club of New York, 17 May to 29 July 2006, and the Special Collections Library, the Pennsylvania State University Libraries, 29 September 2006 to 7 January 2007 (University Park: Pennsylvania State University Libraries, 2006); Edward J. Nygren, "Art Instruction in Philadelphia" (M.A. thesis, University of Delaware, 1969), 178–188; and Carl W. Drepperd, *American Drawing Books* (New York: New York Public Library, 1946). The most sophisticated analysis of drawing books to date is Anne Bermingham's exemplary *Learning to Draw: Studies in the Cultural History of a Polite and Useful Art* (New Haven, CT: Yale University Press for the Paul Mellon Centre for Studies in British Art, 2000).

28. Carington Bowles, *The Artist's Assistant in drawing, perspective, etching, engraving . . .* (Philadelphia: printed by Benjamin Johnson for Benjamin Davies, 1794), 9; Rembrandt Peale, *Graphics: A Manual of Drawing and Writing, for the Use of Schools and Families* (New York: J. P. Peaslee, 1835) and *Graphics: Second book of drawing. For the use of the public schools* (Philadelphia: E. C. & J. Biddle, 1845).

29. On Robertson's 1802 *Elements of the Graphic Arts*, see Megan Holloway Fort, "Archibald and Alexander Robertson and Their Schools, the Columbian Academy of Painting and the Academy of Painting and Drawing, New York, 1791–1835" (Ph.D. diss., City University of New York, 2006); Dunlap, *History*, 1:251. According to Janice G. Schimmelman (*A Checklist of European Treatises on Art and Essays on Aesthetics Available in America Through 1815* [Worcester, MA: American Antiquarian Society, 1983], 191), Williams's collection of art books also included Du Fresnoy's *The Art of Painting* and Richardson's *Essay on the Theory of Painting*. For a suggestive account of one professional artist's use of drawing books, see Elliott Bostwick Davis, "Drawing Books and Fitz Hugh Lane," in *The Cultivation of Artists in Nineteenth-Century America*, ed. Georgia Barnhill, Diana Korzenik, and Caroline F. Sloat (Worcester, MA: American Antiquarian Society, 1997).

30. Archibald Robertson, *Elements of the Graphic Arts, Vol. I* (New York: David Longworth, 1802), 3, 5. Scholars have tended to exaggerate the opposition between practical manuals, on the one hand, and theoretical treatises, on the other. While it is certainly true that drawing books shed much of their overt theorizing over the course of the nineteenth century, they never abandoned their claims to inculcate taste along with technique. See, e.g., John Gadsby Chapman, *The American Drawing Book: A Manual for the Amateur and Basis of Study for the Professional Artist* (New York: Redfield, 1847).

31. "Art," in Abraham Rees, *The Cyclopedia, or Universal Dictionary of Arts, Sciences, and Literature* (Philadelphia, 1805–1825), no pagination. Rees's definitions and distinctions turn up verbatim in the commonplace book and diary kept by Emmeline Moore while attending school in Cornwall, Connecticut, in the mid-1820s; see Emmeline Moore, diary, 1826–1828, Document 1046, Winterthur Library. The same distinctions appear in the earliest domestic drawing book in the collections at the American Antiquarian Society; see, e.g., *The Golden Cabinet, Being the Laboratory or Handmaid to the Arts* (Philadelphia: William Spotswood, 1793), 88–89; and Eliza Way Champlain to Betsey Champlain and Mary Way, May 1821, in MacMullen, *Sisters of the Brush*, 208. Significantly, at the end of the nineteenth century, Chester Harding's grandson wrote that Harding "was not always consistent in his drawing, which he seemed to regard as mechanical": Harding, *Sketch*, xii.

32. Greenwood's original journals no longer exist; Georgia Brady Barnhill speculates that their twentieth-century owner transcribed the journals, editing out personal information, and then destroyed the originals. Even in their abridged version, they provide insight into Greenwood's professional development. *Extracts*, 91–94.

33. In 1809, he recorded, for example, that he had painted eight portraits on a visit to Windsor and another five in Rockingham or writing at the close of 1812 that "I have painted about 70 portraits & did but little in Jan, Aug. & Sept."

34. *Extracts*, Oct. 12 and 20, 1801, 102; Jan.–Mar. 1806, 105–106; Aug. 28, 1809, 111; Dec. 31, 1812, 115; May 18 and 31, 1813, 116; Sept. 8, 1813, 117; Oct. 2, 1818, 139.

35. Ibid., May–Jun. 1813, 121; Feb. 21, 1815; Dec. 31, 1817, 136. It may be significant that Greenwood commenced his subscription to the *Port Folio*'s kinder and gentler second series, which retreated from the sharp, overtly partisan criticism of the first series. See Kaplan, *Men of Letters*, 216–230.

36. *Extracts*, Dec. 18, 1816, 128; Jul. 29, 1816, 124; Apr. 7, 1817, 134; Mar. 10, 1820, 146.

37. Ibid., Jun. 24, 1813, 116.

38. Ibid., Jun. 6, 1816, 123–124; May 23, 1818, 137.

39. Peregrinus, "Landing of the Fathers," *Palladium*, Mar. 14 and 17, 1815, reprinted in *Collections of the Massachusetts Historical Society* (Boston: John Eliot, 1815), 225–232; *Extracts*, May 9, 1815, 122.

40. "Dying Hercules," *Boston Daily Advertiser*, Jul. 25, 1815; *Extracts*, Jul. 29, 1815, 124; Staiti, *Samuel F. B. Morse*, 18–19, 37–38.

41. *Extracts*, Mar. 5, 1817, 132; Feb. 21, 1817, 130; Mar. 6, 1817, 131; Mar. 24, 1817, 133; and passim.

42. Ibid., Sept. 18, 1821, 151–152.

43. Ibid., Aug. 10–13, 1825, 178.

44. Ibid., Sept. 18, 1821, 151–152; Aug. 10, 1825, 178.

45. Dunlap, *History*, 1:17–18. On biographies and nation building in the early republic, see Scott E. Casper, *Constructing American Lives: Biography and Culture in Nineteenth-Century America* (Chapel Hill: University of North Carolina Press, 1999), 19–68. See also Brandon Brame Fortune, "Portraits of Virtue and Genius: Pantheons of Worthies and Public Portraiture in the Early American Republic, 1780–1820" (Ph.D. diss., University of North Carolina, Chapel Hill, 1987).

46. The only extended study of Dunlap as an artist and art historian is Lyons, *William Dunlap and the Construction of an American Art History*. For the most part, scholars have been most interested in Dunlap's theatrical career, but see Joseph J. Ellis, *After the Revolution: Profiles of Early American Culture* (New York: W. W. Norton, 1979), 113–158; Robert H. Canary, *William Dunlap* (New York: Twayne, 1970); and Oral Sumner Coad, *William Dunlap: A Study of His Life and Works and of His Place in Contemporary Culture* (New York: Dunlap Society, 1917). Dunlap chronicles his poor health and financial difficulties in William Dunlap, *Diary of William Dunlap, 1766–1839; the Memoirs of a Dramatist, Theatrical Manager, Painter, Critic, Novelist, and Historian*, Collections of the New-York Historical Society 1930 (New York: Benjamin Blom, 1930), 666–770, passim.

47. Dunlap, *History*, 1:243. Quotations from Dunlap's autobiography are cited within parentheses in the text.

48. Leah Lipton, *A Truthful Likeness: Chester Harding and His Portraits* (Washington, DC: National Portrait Gallery and the Smithsonian Institution, 1985), is the standard overview of Harding's career. See also Jaffee, *New Nation of Goods*, 235–237; Franklin Kelly et al., *American Paintings of the Nineteenth Century, Part 1* (New York: National Gallery of Art, 1996), 271–277.

49. Tellingly, Harding uses "genius" once in the first half of the *Egotistigraphy* in reference to his father's "inventive genius," which filled the attic with worthless machines and did nothing to support the impoverished family. Harding, *Sketches*, 4.

50. Ibid., 18.

51. For scholarly accounts of Harding that adhere to the *Egotistigraphy*, see Jaffee, *New Nation of Goods*, 227–238; and Joyce Oldham Appleby, *Recollections of the Early Republic: Selected Autobiographies* (Boston: Northeastern University Press, 1997).

52. Dunlap, *History*, vol. 2, pt. 2, 290–291.

53. Ibid. Emphasis added.

54. Ibid., 292.

55. Ibid., 293–294.

56. Harding, *Sketches*, 65–70, 88–97; Alan Fern, "Foreword," in Lipton, *Truthful Likeness*, 7.

57. Dunlap, *History*, vol. 2, pt. 2, 295.

58. On shifting ideals and representations of artists, see Harris, *Artist in American Society*, 218–254. By the end of the century, artists once again sought to distance themselves from associations with the market. See Sarah Burns, "The Price of Beauty: Art, Commerce, and the Late Nineteenth-Century Studio Interior," in *American Iconology*, ed. David C. Miller (New Haven, CT: Yale University Press, 1993), 209–238.

59. Cf. Paul Staiti's discussion of John Singleton Copley's social ambition. In mid-eighteenth-century Boston, Copley laid claim to gentility by aggressively styling himself as a gentleman in his appearance and housing. Staiti, "Character and Class," in *John Singleton Copley in America*, ed. Carrie Rebora and Paul Staiti et al. (New York: Metropolitan Museum of Art, 1996), 53–78.

60. This summary of the careers of the Way Champlain women's careers relies on Ramsay MacMullen's edited collection of their letters (*Sisters of the Brush*) and unpublished letters in the

Way Champlain collection at the American Antiquarian Society. Betsey Way Champlain's career is discussed at length in Chapter 3 of this book. See also Catherine E. Kelly, "Miniature Worlds," *Common-place* 3:2 (Jan. 2003); Jaffee, *New Nation of Goods*, 85–88; Robin Jaffee Frank, *Love and Loss: American Portrait and Mourning Miniatures* (New Haven, CT: Yale University Press, 2000); and William Lamson Warren, "Mary Way's Dressed Miniatures," *Magazine Antiques* (Oct. 1992), 540–549.

61. Way offers a detailed account of her acclimation to the New York City art world in Mary Way to Betsey Champlain, ca. 1814, in MacMullen, *Sisters of the Brush*, 25–32.

62. Ibid. John Payne's *Art of Painting in Miniature, on Ivory*, which Way borrowed from Joseph Wood, outlined both the aesthetics and the techniques that had come to characterize eighteenth-century English miniatures. Payne's principles structured Way's work and provided the criteria she used to assess others.

63. Mary Way to Eliza Way Champlain, Dec. 1820, in MacMullen, *Sisters of the Brush*, 167.

64. Mary Way to Eliza Way Chanplain, [Jul.] 1820, in ibid., 158–159.

65. Eliza Champlain to Betsey Way Champlain, Jan. 16, 1825, in ibid., 326; Mary Way to Eliza Champlain, Sept. 1816, in ibid., 56; and Anna Fitch to Eliza Champlain, Dec. 1821, in ibid., 221.

66. Mary Way to Eliza Champlain, Feb. 1820, in ibid., 114–116.

67. Eliza Champlain to Mary Way, Jan. 2, 1821, in ibid., 170.

68. When John Wesley Jarvis, a noted New York City painter who occasionally offered advice to Mary Way, met Henry Inman for the first time, he peered into the younger man's face with a "singular look of scrutiny," cried "By heavens, the very head for a painter!," and accepted Inman as his pupil. See Dunlap, *History*, vol. 2, pt. 2, 349; Eliza Champlain to Mary Way, Jan. 2, 1821, in MacMullen, *Sisters of the Brush*, 171; Mary Way to Eliza Way Champlain, Dec. 1816, in ibid., 58–59. On the importance of physiognomy in the early republic, see Christopher J. Lukasik, *Discerning Characters: The Culture of Appearance in Early America* (Philadelphia: University of Pennsylvania Press, 2011).

69. Mary Way to Eliza Champlain, ca. 1818–1819, in MacMullen, *Sisters of the Brush*, 116; and Eliza Way Champlain to Betsey Champlain, Sept. 24, 1822, in ibid., 260.

70. Mary Way to Eliza Champlain, Jun. 1817, in ibid., 88.

71. Betsey Way Champlain to Mary Way, Jun. or Jul. 1816, in ibid., 38.

72. Mary Way to Eliza Way Champlain, Jun. 1817, in ibid., 88.

73. Scholars have seized on changes in style and subject but have been less quick to note the increase in the sheer numbers of portraits. See, e.g., Margaretta M. Lovell, "Reading Portraits: Social Images and Self-Images in Eighteenth-Century American Family Portraits," *Winterthur Portfolio* 22:4 (1987), 46–71; Karin Calvert, "Children in American Family Portraiture, 1670 to 1810," *William and Mary Quarterly*, 3rd ser., 39:1 (Jan. 1982), 87–113. See also Jaffee, *New Nation of Goods*; Frank, *Love and Loss*; and Richard L. Bushman, *The Refinement of America: Persons, Houses, Cities* (New York: Vintage, 1992).

74. Cf., e.g., *Longworth's American almanac, New York Register, and city directory, for the forty-fourth year of American independence* (New York: Desnoues, published for Jona. Olmstead, 1819), which lists a dozen self-identified artists specializing in likenesses, in multiple media, and *Longworth's American almanacc, New York register, and city directory, for the thirty-fourth year of American independence* (New York: David Longworth, 1809), which lists four. Similar patterns obtain in Philadelphia (see John Paxton Adams, *The Philadelphia directory and register, for 1819* [Philadelphia: published by John Adams Paxton, printed by David Dickinson, 1819]; and James Robinson, *The Philadelphia directory, for 1810* [printed for the publisher, 1810]); Baltimore (see Edward Matchett, *The Baltimore directory and register, for the year 1816: containing the names, residence and occupation of the citizens . . . also a correct list of the courts . . .* [Baltimore, MD: printed and sold at the Wanderer Office, 1816]; *Matchett's Baltimore Director, corrected up to June 1831* [(Baltimore, MD: R. J. Matchett, 1831]); and Boston (*1800, the Boston Directory* [Boston: printed and sold by John Norman, 1800]; *The Boston Directory . . .* [Boston: Edward Cotton, 1810]; *The Annual Boston Advertiser . . .* [Boston: C. Stimpson Jr. and J. H. A. Frost, 1825]). City directories almost certainly underestimate the actual number of working painters at any given time (missing, e.g., itinerants, painters hovering at the border between

amateur and professional, and painters who moved back and forth between the fine and decorative arts), but they provide a reasonable metric of change over time.

75. Dunlap, *History*, 1:266; Eliza Champlain to George Oliver Champlain, Nov. 25, 1820, in MacMullen, *Sisters of the Brush*, 162.

76. Mona Leithiser Dearborn, *Anson Dickinson, the Celebrated Miniature Portrait Painter, 1779–1852* (Hartford: Connecticut Historical Society, 1982), 13; Staiti, *Samuel F. B. Morse*, 58–63; Harold E. Dickson, "The Artist's Profession in the Early Republic," *Art Quarterly* 8 (Autumn 1945), 261–280.

77. Betsey Way Champlain to Eliza Champlain, Spring 1820, in MacMullen, *Sisters of the Brush*, 145–146; Eliza Champlain to Betey Way Champlain, May 2, 1820, in ibid., 147–148.

78. We know most about the spread of portraiture into the New England hinterland. See, e.g., Jaffee, *New Nation of Goods*; Jaffee, "One of the Primitive Sort"; David Jaffee, "Peddlers of Progress and the Transformation of the Rural North, 1760–1860," *Journal of American History* 78:2 (Sept. 1991), 511–535; and Benes, *Itinerancy in New England and New York*.

79. Harding, *Sketches*, xvii.

80. Ibid., 136–138; Joyce Hill, "New England Itinerant Portraitists," in Benes, *Itinerancy in New England and New York*, 150–171; the quote from Morse is on 160.

81. Harold E. Dickson, "Artists as Showmen," *American Art Journal* 5:1 (May 1973), 4–17; Staiti, *Samuel F. B. Morse*; William Oedel, "The Rewards of Virtue: Rembrandt Peale and Social Reform," in Miller, *Peale Family*, 150–167; Lyons, *William Dunlap*, 25–32.

82. Dunlap, *History*, 1:291.

83. Oedel, "Rewards of Virtue," 157.

84. Dickson, "Artists as Showmen"; Dunlap, *History*, vol. 1; Staiti, *Samuel F. B. Morse*, 94–98; Oedel, "Rewards of Virtue," 155–156.

85. On Peale's museum as a business, see David C. Ward, "Democratic Culture: The Peale Museums, 1784–1850," in Miller, *Peale Family*, 270–274. On Greenwood's career, see *Extracts*, 92–101.

86. *Extracts*, Aug. 14, 1822, 156.

87. Ibid., Jun. 26, 1825, 176; Dec. 9–15, 1823, 163–164.

88. Susanna Paine, *Roses and Thorns: Or, Recollections of an Artist* (Providence, RI: B. T. Albro, 1854), 165–166. On women artists and the problem of respectability, see Prieto, *At Home in the Studio*; and Hirshorn, "Anna Claypoole, Margaretta, and Sarah Miriam Peale."

89. Jaffee, *New Nation of Goods*, 229–336.

90. Ibid., 87. See also Mary Way to Eliza Champlain, Sept. 1816, in MacMullen, *Sisters of the Brush*, 53.

91. Harding, *Sketches*, 23; Eliza Champlain to Betsey Way Champlain, May 18, 1825, in MacMullen, *Sisters of the Brush*, 47; Eliza Champlain to Betsey Champlain, Apr. 1821, in ibid., 203–205.

92. Anna Fitch to Mary Way, Jun. 1822, in MacMullen, *Sisters of the Brush*, 227; Eliza Champlain to Betsey Way Champlain, Apr. 1822, in ibid., 232.

93. Eliza Way Champlain to Mary Way, May 1821, in ibid., 208.

94. Dunlap, *History of Design*, 1:218. Dunlap measured his own shortcomings as a portraitist by the extent to which the final product depended on the qualities the sitter brought to the endeavor. Significantly, he concluded the "best head I painted was my friend John Joseph Holland who felt and sat like an artist, and my own head painted with great care and study from a mirror." Ibid., 282.

95. Ammi Robbins to Thomas Robbins, Mar. 13, 1812, cited in "Reuben Moulthrop," *Connecticut Historical Society Bulletin*, Apr. 1955, 51.

CHAPTER THREE

1. The life of Elizabeth Freeman is discussed in Catharine Maria Sedgwick, "Mumbet," unpublished ms., Catharine Maria Sedgwick Papers, Massachusetts Historical Society; Mary Kelley, ed., *The Power of Her Sympathy: The Autobiography and Journal of Catharine Maria Sedgwick* (Boston: Massachusetts Historical Society, 1993), 69–71, 124–126; and Theodore Sedgwick, *The Practicability of the Abolition of Slavery: A Lecture* (New York: J. Seymour, 1831). Freeman's legal case is discussed in Arthur Zilversmit, "Quok Walker, Mumbet, and the Abolition of Slavery in Massachusetts," *William and Mary Quarterly*, 3rd ser., 25:4 (Oct. 1968), 614–624. The quote is from Sedgwick, "Mumbet."

2. My discussion of Betsey Way Champlain's life is drawn from Ramsay MacMullen's invaluable collection of the Way Champlain family's correspondence, *Sisters of the Brush: Their Family, Art, Lives, and Letters, 1797–1833* (New Haven, CT: Past Times, 1997).

3. This argument is developed at length in my "Reading and the Problem of Accomplishment," in *Reading Women: Literacy, Authorship, and Culture in the Atlantic World, 1500–1800*, ed. Heidi Brayman Hackel and Catherine E. Kelly (Philadelphia: University of Pennsylvania Press, 2007), 124–143. See also "RUDIMENTS OF TASTE and a POLITE FEMALE EDUCATION," *Juvenile Port-Folio and Literary Miscellany* 1:38 (Jul. 3, 1813), 150 ; and the letters of the fictional Miss Penelope Airy, who supports herself with her needle after the premature deaths of her parents, in [Judith Sargent Murray], *The Gleaner. A miscellaneous production. In three volumes. By Constantia* (Boston: I. Thomas and E. T. Andrews, 1798), 176–178.

4. Susan Ridley Sedgwick's titles included *The Morals of Pleasure: Illustrated by Stories Designed for Young Persons* (1829), *Allen Prescott: or, The Fortunes of a New England Boy* (1834), *Alida; or, Town and Country* (1844), and *Walter Thornley, or, A Peep at the Past* (1859). On Susan Ridley Sedgwick's life and place within the Sedgwick clan, see Kelley, *Power of Her Sympathy*, 90–94; Timothy Kenslea, *The Sedgwicks in Love: Courtship, Engagement, and Marriage in the Early Republic* (Boston: Northeastern University Press, 2006), 48–50, 225n48. On the fraught relation between creative women and publicity in the nineteenth century, see Mary Kelley, *Private Woman, Public Stage: Literary Domesticity in Nineteenth-Century America* (New York: Oxford University Press, 1984). The problem of publicity for female artists is discussed in Anne Sue Hirshorn, "Anna Claypoole, Margaretta, and Sarah Miriam Peale: Modes of Accomplishment and Fortune," in *The Peale Family: Creation of a Legacy, 1770–1870*, ed. Lillian B. Miller (Washington, DC: Abbeville Press in association with the Trust for Museum Exhibitions and the National Portrait Gallery, Smithsonian Institution, 1996), 220–247. On manners and gaze control, see C. Dallett Hemphill, *Bowing to Necessities: A History of Manners in America, 1620–1860* (New York: Oxford University Press, 1999), 79, 111.

5. Elizabeth Way Champlain to Mary Way, May 1822 and 1819, in MacMullen, *Sisters of the Brush*, 242, 129; Lizzie W. Champney, "Sea-Drift from a New England Port," *Harper's Monthly Magazine* 60:355 (Dec. 1879), 62. Betsey Champlain's career is summarized in MacMullen, *Sisters of the Brush*, 33–44. For a detailed description of taking the likeness of a corpse, see Betsey Way Champlain to Eliza Way, ca. 1822, in ibid., 242–243. On the vogue for mourning miniatures more generally, see Robin Jaffee Frank, *Love and Loss: American Portrait and Mourning Miniatures* (New Haven, CT: Yale University Press, 2000), 119–154.

6. Frank, *Love and Loss*, 7. For a different perspective on the psychological resonances of miniatures, see Susan Stewart, *On Longing: Narratives of the Miniature, the Gigantic, the Souvenir, the Collection* (Durham, NC: Duke University Press, 1993), 125–127. Katherine C. Reider astutely analyzes the gifting of miniatures in the construction and perpetuation of status in "Gifting and Fetishization: The Portrait Miniature of Sally Foster Otis as a Maker of Female Memory," unpublished paper in the author's possession. On oil portraits and lineage, see Margaretta M. Lovell, *Art in a Season of Revolution: Painters, Artisans, and Patrons in Early America* (Philadelphia: University of Pennsylvania Press, 2005), 10–11, 26–93, 94–140. On exchange and status more generally, see Marcia Pointon, "'Surrounded by Brilliants': Miniature Portraits in Eighteenth-Century England," *Art Bulletin* 83:1 (Mar. 2001), 48–71; Anne A. Verplanck, "The Social Meanings of Portrait Miniatures in Philadelphia, 1760–1820," in *American Material Culture: The Shape of the Field*, ed. Ann Smart Martin and J. Ritchie Garrison (Winterthur, DE: Henry Francis du Pont Winterthur Museum, 1997), 195–223.

7. On miniature prices, see Reider, "Gifting and Fetishization"; Verplanck, "Social Meanings of Portrait Miniatures," 195–223, 201–203; Mona Leithiser Dearborn, *Anson Dickinson: The Celebrated Miniature Painter* (Hartford: Connecticut Historical Society, 1983), 155–168; MacMullen, *Sisters of the Brush*, 24, 92.

8. The Way Champlain papers contain multiple references to female patrons. On the dynastic dimensions of oil portraits, see Lovell, *Art in a Season of Revolution*, 141–183.

9. See Eliza Champlain to Betsey Way Champlain, Jan. 1818, in MacMullen, *Sisters of the Brush*, 98. The request appears in a letter written by Eliza Champlain, Betsey Champlain's daughter. Way's business and her faltering eyesight encouraged her to dictate letters through Eliza when the young woman was visiting.

10. The history of the correspondence and its preservation is described in MacMullen, *Sisters of the Brush*, 477–478n2.

11. Kelley, *Power of Her Sympathy*, 68, 125–126; Sedgwick, "Mumbet."

12. The tombstone inscription is quoted in Kelley, *Power of Her Sympathy*, 71n33. See also T. Sedgwick, *Practicability*, 18. Authorities disagree about who delivered the lecture; some attribute it to Henry Dwight Sedgwick, others to Theodore Sedgwick II. I have followed the lead of Sedgwick specialists.

13. See, e.g., Sidney Kaplan, *The Black Presence in the Era of the American Revolution, 1770–1800* (Washington, DC: New York Graphic Society in association with the Smithsonian Institution Press, 1973), which describes the image as "lovingly painted in watercolors," 217. For similar references, see Jon Swan, "The Slave Who Sued for Freedom," *American Heritage* (Mar. 1990), 51–55.

14. On racialized aesthetics and the representation of race in the long eighteenth century, see Gwendolyn DuBois Shaw, *Portraits of a People: Picturing African Americans in the Nineteenth Century* (Andover, MA: Addison Gallery of American Art, 2006); David Bindman, *Ape to Apollo: Aesthetics and the Idea of Race in the Eighteenth Century* (London: Reaktion, 2002); Marcus Wood, *Blind Memory: Visual Representations of Slavery in England and America, 1780–1865* (London: Routledge, 2000); and Albert Boime, *The Art of Exclusion: Representing Blacks in the Nineteenth Century* (Washington, DC: Smithsonian Institution Press, 1990).

15. Frederick Douglass, "A Tribute for the Negro," *North Star* (Apr. 7, 1849) and "Negro Portraits," *Liberator* 19:6 (Apr. 20, 1849). On Douglass's interest in his depictions within portraits, see John Stauffer, *The Black Hearts of Men: Radical Abolitionists and the Transformation of Race* (Cambridge, MA: Harvard University Press, 2001), 45–56; and Marcy J. Dinius, *The Camera and the Press: American Visual and Print Culture in the Age of the Daguerreotype* (Philadelphia: University of Pennsylvania Press, 2012), 192–232.

16. Hannah Farnham Sawyer Lee, *Memoir of Pierre Toussaint, Born a Slave in St. Domingo* (Boston: Crosby, Nichols, and Company, 1854), 34, 59. Empahsis in original. See also Arthur Jones, *Pierre Toussaint* (New York: Doubleday, 2003). On Antonio Meucci, his career in the Americas, and his black students and sitters, see Patricia Brady, "Black Artists in Antebellum New Orleans," *Louisiana History: The Journal of the Louisiana Historical Association* 32:1 (Winter 1991), 5–28.

17. Lee, *Memoir*, 27. On African Americans' strategies and aims as sitters and for examples of their portraits, see Shaw, *Portraits of a People*.

18. Euphemia Toussaint's image can be viewed in the digital collections of the New-York Historical Society.

19. Elizabeth Maddock Dillon, "The Secret History of the Early American Novel: Leonora Sansay and Revolution in Saint Domingue," *Novel* 40:1/2 (Fall 2006/Spring 2007), 77–103, 89; Leonora Sansay, *Secret History; or, The Horrors of St. Domingo*, ed. Michael J. Drexler (Buffalo, NY: Broadview, 2007), 65, 95; Susan Branson and Leslie Patrick, "Étrangers dans un Pays Étrange: Saint-Domingan Refugees of Color in Philadelphia," in *The Impact of the Haitian Revolution in the Atlantic World*, ed. David P. Geggus (Columbia: University of South Carolina Press, 2001), 196–197.

20. Charles W. Peale, "Account of a Negro, or a Very Dark Mulatto, Turning White," *Massachusetts Magazine; or, Monthly Museum* 3:12 (Dec. 1791), 744.

21. On Peale's portrait of Mamout, see Shaw, *Portraits of a People*, 78. David Steinberg ("Charles Willson Peale Portrays the Body Politic," in Miller, *Peale Family*) suggests that Mamout's rumpled collar signals his marginal capacity for full participation in the social order. But especially in light of Peale's participation in the fin-de-siècle fascination with blacks who seemed to turn white, it seems more logical to locate his marginalization of Mamout in his rendering of the sitter's flesh. See also Kariann Akemi Yokota, *Unbecoming British: How Revolutionary America Became a Postcolonial Nation* (New York: Oxford University Press, 2011), 192–225; John Wood Sweet, *Bodies Politic: Negotiating Race in the American North, 1730–1830* (Baltimore, MD: Johns Hopkins University Press, 2003), 271–312; and Joanne Pope Melish, *Disowning Slavery, Gradual Emancipation and "Race" in New England, 1780–1860* (Ithaca, NY: Cornell University Press, 1998), 119–162.

22. Andrew J. Cosentino, "Charles Bird King, American Painter, 1785–1862" (Ph.D. diss., University of Delaware, 1976), 156; Cosentino, "Charles Bird King; an Appreciation," *American Art Journal* 6 (May 1974), 54–71, 57. See also Cosentino, *The Paintings of Charles Bird King (1785–1862)* (Washington, DC: National Collection of Fine Arts by the Smithsonian Institution Press, 1977).

23. On Native Americans as a "red" race, see esp. Nancy Shoemaker, "How Indians Got to Be Red," *American Historical Review* 102:3 (Jun. 1997), 625–644; and Alden T. Vaughn, "From White Man to Redskin: Changing Anglo-American Perceptions of the American Indian," *American Historical Review* 87:4 (Oct. 1982), 917–953. Vaughn presciently noted the extent to which the perception of skin color is culturally constructed or rooted in "social perceptions which can change to meet the psychological needs of the observer." 918.

24. See John Murdoch, Jim Murrell, Patrick J. Noon, and Roy Strong, *The English Miniature* (New Haven, CT: Yale University Press, 1981), 85–157.

25. My account of the process draws on T. S. Cummings, "Practical Directions for Miniature Painting," printed in William Dunlap, *History of the Rise and Progress of the Arts of Design in the United States*, ed. Rita Weiss, 2 vols. (1834; repr., New York: Dover, 1969), vol. 2, pt. 1, 10–13. As we have seen, Dunlap himself struggled with the technical aspects of miniature painting; see Dunlap, "Autobiography of the Author," in Dunlap, *History*, 1:269–270. For further discussions about the technical difficulties presented by ivory miniatures, see Murdoch et al., *English Miniatures*, 16–19, 163–195; Frank, *Love and Loss*, 1–13, 155–230; Carol Aiken, "Materials and Techniques of the American Portrait Miniaturist," in Dale T. Johnson, *American Portrait Miniatures in the Manney Collection* (New York: Metropolitan Museum of Art, 1991), 13–26; and Harry B. Wehle and Thomas C. Bolton, *American Miniatures, 1730–1850* (New York: Doubleday, 1927).

26. See Murdoch et al., *English Miniatures*, 16–19, 163–195; Frank, *Love and Loss*, 1–13, 155–230; Johnson, *American Portrait Miniatures*, 13–26; and Wehle and Bolton, *American Miniatures*.

27. For a complementary discussion about racialized portraiture in eighteenth-century Britain, see Angela Rosenthal, "Visceral Culture: Blushing and the Legibility of Whiteness in Eighteenth-Century British Portraiture," *Art History* 27:4 (Sept. 2004), 563–592. The literature on sensibility is too large and complex to be cited here in any detail. But on sensibility among eighteenth-century and early nineteenth-century Anglo-American elites, see esp. Sarah Knott, *Sensibility and the American Revolution* (Chapel Hill: University of North Carolina Press for the Omohundro Institute of Early American History and Culture), 2009; David S. Shields, *Civil Tongues and Polite Letters in British America* (Chapel Hill: University of North Carolina Press for the Omohundro Institute of Early American History and Culture, 1997); and Jay Fliegelman, *Declaring Independence: Jefferson, Natural Language, and the Culture of Performance* (Stanford, CA: Stanford University Press, 1993).

28. Thomas Jefferson, *Notes on the State of Virginia* (Boston: Lilly and Wait, 1832), 144–145. On the political and cultural significance of transparent skin as an index of individual sentiment and character, see Fliegelman, *Declaring Independence*, 192–195. On sensibility and the Anglo-American response to slavery, see, e.g., Christopher Leslie Brown, *Moral Capital: Foundations of British Abolitionism* (Chapel Hill: University of North Carolina Press for the Omohundro Institute of Early American History and Culture, 2006); and Philip Gould, *Barbaric Traffic: Commerce and Antislavery in the Atlantic World* (Cambridge, MA: Harvard University Press, 2003).

29. Roxann Wheeler, *The Complexion of Race: Categories of Difference in Eighteenth-Century British Culture* (Philadelphia: University of Pennsylvania Press, 2000), esp. chap. 1, 2–48.

30. Samuel Stanhope Smith, *An Essay on the Causes of the Variety of Complexion and Figure in the Human Species*, 2nd ed. (New Brunswick, NJ: J. Simpson & Co., 1810), 49, 66, 67–68, 162, 168. Scholarly discussions of Smith include Wheeler, *Complexion of Race*, 251–253; Scott Juengel, "Countenancing History: Mary Wollstonecraft, Samuel Stanhope Smith, and Enlightenment Racial Science," *ELH* 68 (2001), 897–927; and Winthrop Jordan, *White over Black: American Attitudes Toward the Negro, 1550–1815* (Chapel Hill: University of North Carolina Press for the Omohundro Institute of Early American History and Culture, 1968), 486–488.

31. "Complexion in the Human Species," *Port-Folio*, Jul. 1814, 30.

32. "Familiar Letters on Physiognomy," *Visitor* 1 (1809), 148.

33. Oliver Goldsmith, *An History of the Earth, and Animated Nature*, 4 vols. (Philadelphia: Mathew Carey, 1795), 1:375.

34. "On Flattery," in Betsey Way Champlain to Eliza Way Champlain, late Aug. 1819, in Way Champlain Papers, box 2, folder 3, American Antiquarian Society.

35. Although Champlain insisted that the dialogue between Jane and Frederick was "nothing more than the picture of fancy," she added that it was "so near . . . to what I have seen, that my

conscience never even frowned at me for writing it," a claim borne out in descriptions of her encounters with actual sitters. For a fuller discussion of the cultural resonances of ivory portrait miniatures, see Chapter 2.

36. See, for example, Charles Hayter, *An Introduction to Perspective, Practical Geometry, Drawing and Painting; a New and Perfect Explanation of the Mixture of Colours; with Practical Directions for Miniature, Crayon, and Oil Painting*, 6th ed. (London: Samuel Bagster and Sons, 1845); and John Payne, *The Art of Painting in Miniature on Ivory in the Manner at Present Practised by the Most Eminent Artists in the Profession . . .*, 8th ed. (London: Richard Holmes Laurie, 1820).

37. Arthur Parsey, *The Art of Miniature Painting on Ivory* (London: Longman, Rees, Orme, Brown, and Green, 1831).

38. L. Mansion, *Letters upon the Art of Miniature Painting* (London: Ackermann, 1822), 3–4, 10–11, 179.

39. Ibid., 10–11.

40. Emma E. Kendrick, *Conversations on the Art of Miniature Painting; dedicated, with the sanction of her grace the Duchess of Rutland, to the Honorable Misses Forester* (London: published for the author, 1830), 7, 23.

41. Kendrick, Ibid., 89, 65–66.

42. P[eter] F. Cooper, *The Art of Making and Colouring Ivorytypes, Photographs, Talbotypes, and Miniature Painting on Ivory, &c. by PF Cooper, Miniature, Portrait, Pastil, and Equestrian Painter, and Photographer* (Philadelphia: published by the author, 1863), 28.

43. J. Dougall, *The Cabinet of the Arts; Being a New and Universal Drawing Book*, 2nd ed. (London: Ackermann, 1821), 226.

44. Ibid., 268.

45. Cooper, *Art*, 26.

46. John Russell, *Elements of Painting with Crayons* (Dublin, 1773), 70–75.

47. Mr. Hayter, *Introduction to Perspective, Drawing, and Painting* (London: Black, Parry, & Co., 1815), 180–181.

48. W. M. Craig, *A Course of Lectures on Drawing, Painting, and Engraving, Considered as Branches of Elegant Education* (London: Longman, Hurst, Rees, Orme, and Brown, 1821), 350–355.

49. Dougall, *Cabinet*, 268–270.

50. See Mary Way to Betsey Way Champlain, ca. 1814, in MacMullen, *Sisters of the Brush*, 27–30; Mary Way to Eliza Champlain, Dec. 1816, in ibid., 59.

51. Betsey Way Champlain to Eliza Champlain, Nov. 16, 1824, in ibid., 322–323.

52. Betsey Way Champlain to Eliza Champlain, 1822, in ibid., 264.

53. Betsey Way Champlain to Eliza Champlain, Jan. 1825, in ibid., 327; William Champlain to Eliza Champlain, Feb. 13, 1825, in ibid., 328.

54. Sweet, *Bodies Politic*; Melish, *Disowning Slavery*. Barbara Ryan situates Elizabeth Freeman and Catharine Maria Sedgwick's fiction in the context of racialized service and dependence in *Love, Wages, and Slavery: The Literature of Servitude in the United States* (Urbana: University of Illinois Press, 2006), chap. 1.

55. Last will and testament of Elizabeth Freeman, Oct. 18, 1829, Sheffield Historical Society (www.mumbet.com; accessed Feb. 1, 2007).

56. T. Sedgwick, *Practicability*, 16, 18; Kelley, *Power of Her Sympathy*, 69; Sedgwick, "Mumbet."

57. "African Americans and the End of Slavery in Massachusetts," online exhibition, Massachusetts Historical Society (http://www.masshist.org/endofslavery/?queryID=54; accessed Oct. 15, 2007).

58. This perspective significantly revises the standard historical accounts of race in North America, which associate nineteenth-century whiteness with masculinity, commerce, and politics. Women, and the family more generally, enter the equation only when abolitionist and feminist agitators together raise the specter of race and slavery in the private sphere. The classic accounts are David Roediger, *Wages of Whiteness: Race and the Making of the American Working Class* (New York: Verso, 1991); Noel Ignatiev, *How the Irish Became White* (London: Routledge, 1995); Karen Sanchez-Eppler, *Touching Liberty: Abolition, Feminism, and the Politics of the Body* (Berkeley: University of California Press, 1993); Jean Fagan Yellin, *Women and Sisters: The Anti-Slavery Feminists in American*

Culture (New Haven, CT: Yale University Press, 1989); and Louise Michele Newman, *White Women's Rights: The Racial Origins of Feminism in the United States* (New York: Oxford University Press, 1999). Scholars considering the visual representation of race and racial identity look to the Civil War to structure their inquiries. In their telling, the nineteenth-century imaginary juxtaposed black/slave/South against white/free/North. See, e.g., Mary Niall Mitchell's "'Rosebloom and Pure White,' or So It Seemed," *American Quarterly* (Sept. 2002), 369–410.

CHAPTER FOUR

1. The ongoing efforts to secure the funding necessary to restore The Woodlands and maximize its potential as a historic site and neighborhood hub are chronicled on the organization's website (www.woodlandsphila.org). For an account of the organization's status and aims as of January 2015, see Kristen A. Graham, "Woodlands Rebirth: Backers Aim to Restore Historic W. Phila. Estate," *Philadelphia Inquirer*, Jan. 6, 2015.

2. On the history of the Hamilton family, see James A. Jacobs, "The Woodlands," HABS No. PA-1125, Historic American Buildings Survey (HABS), National Park Service, U.S. Department of the Interior (hereafter cited as HABS No. PA-1125); James A. Jacobs, "William Hamilton and The Woodlands: A Construction of Refinement in Philadelphia," *Pennsylvania Magazine of History and Biography* 130:2 (Apr. 2006), 181–209, 184–185; and John W. Jordan, ed., *Colonial and Revolutionary Families of Pennsylvania: Genealogical and Personal Memoirs*, 4 vols., (1911; repr., Baltimore, MD: Genealogical Publishing, 2004), 1:519–527.

3. On the Hamiltons' position within the proprietary gentry, see Stephen Brobeck, "Revolutionary Change in Colonial Philadelphia: The Brief Life of the Proprietary Gentry," *William and Mary Quarterly*, 3rd ser., 33:3 (Jul. 1976), 410–434, esp. 416.

4. Jacobs speculates that only one other contemporary Philadelphia mansion, John Penn's Lansdowne, possessed a two-story portico and that it was divided into two levels; Jacobs, "William Hamilton and The Woodlands," 192. Jacobs (HABS No. PA-1125, 25–30) provides an extended and invaluable discussion of the history of Hamilton's mansion and scholars' attempts to recover that history.

5. Thompson Westcott, *The Historic Mansions and Buildings of Philadelphia with Some Notice of Their Owners and Occupants* (Philadelphia: Walter H. Barr, 1895), 419–421. On Philadelphia's loyalists, see Wilbur Henry Siebert, *The Loyalists of Pennsylvania* (Columbus: Ohio State University, 1920; repr., Boston: Gregg, 1972).

6. Casca, "A Hint to Traitors and Those Tories," *Pennsylvania Evening Post*, Jul. 16, 1778, 241.

7. J. Thomas Scharf and Thompson Westcott, *History of Philadelphia 1609–1884*, 3 vols. (Philadelphia: L. H. Everts & Co., 1884), 1:387.

8. Westcott, *Historic Mansions*, 421.

9. William Hamilton to Tilghman, Apr. 1779, Historical Society of Pennsylvania (hereafter cited as HSP).

10. *Minutes of the Supreme Executive Council of Pennsylvania, from Its Organization to the Termination of the Revolution*, 6 vols. (Harrisburg, PA: Theo. Fenn & Co., for the State of Pennsylvania, 1853), 6:495, 499, 549; Westcott, *Historic Mansions*, 422; John Cadwalader to William Hamilton, Oct. 16, 1780, HSP. On the role of the Supreme Executive Council in Pennsylvania's evolving treatment of loyalists, see Henry J. Young, "Treason and Its Punishment in Revolutionary Pennsylvania," *Pennsylvania Magazine of History and Biography* 90:3 (1966), 287–313.

11. Abigail Adams to John Quincy Adams, Feb. 16, 1786, in *The Adams Family Correspondence*, ed. Margaret A. Hogan et al., 11 vols. (Cambridge, MA: Belknap Press of Harvard University Press, 2005–), 7:66; William Hamilton to Dr. Thomas Parke, Jul. 28, 1785, HSP; William Hamilton to Dr. Thomas Parke, Sept. 24, 1785, HSP.

12. William Hamilton to Dr. Thomas Parke, Sept. 24, 1785, HSP; Abigail Adams to Isaac Smith, Jun. 30, 1785, in *The Adams Family Correspondence*, ed. Richard Alan Ryerson et al., 11 vols. (Cambridge, MA: Belknap Press of Harvard University Press, 1993–), 6:201; Abigail Adams to Elizabeth Storer Smith, Aug. 29, 1785, in ibid., 316.

13. Abigail Adams to John Quincy Adams, Jan. 22, 1786, in *Adams Family Correspondence*, 6:12, 24; William Hamilton to Dr. Thomas Parke, Sept. 24, 1785, HSP.

14. Abigail Adams to Mary Smith Cranch, Sept. 30, 1785, in *Adams Family Correspondence*, 6:393; Abigail Adams II to John Quincy Adams, Jan. 22, 1786, in ibid., 7:13, Abigail Adams to John Quincy Adams, Feb. 16, 1786, in ibid., 67.

15. Abigail Adams to John Quincy Adams, Jul. 7, 1785, in *Adams Family Correspondence*, 6:208.

16. Abigail Adams to Charles Storer, May 22, 1786, in ibid., 7:187; Abigail Adams II to John Quincy Adams, Oct. 1, 1785, in ibid., 6:432; Abigail Adams to Charles Storer, May 22, 1786, in ibid., 7:187; Abigail Adams II to John Quincy Adams, Feb. 8, 1786, in ibid., 25.

17. Quoted in Jacobs, "The Woodlands," 51.

18. William Hamilton to Dr. Thomas Parke, Jul. 28, 1785, HSP; William Hamilton to Dr. Thomas Parke, Sept. 24, 1785, HSP.

19. William Hamilton to Dr. Thomas Parke, Sept. 24, 1785, HSP; William Hamilton to Dr. Thomas Parke, Mar. 8, 1786, HSP.

20. William Hamilton to Dr. Thomas Parke, Sept. 24, 1785, HSP; Abigail Adams to Elizabeth Cranch, Sept. 2, 1785, in *Adams Family Correspondence*, 6:328.

21. William Hamilton to Thomas Parke, Aug. 22, 1785, HSP; William Hamilton to Thomas Parke, Mar. 8, 1786, HSP.

22. William Hamilton to Thomas Parke, Sept. 24, 1785, and Jul. 28, 1785, HSP.

23. The best account of The Woodlands' grounds and garden is Aaron V. Wunsch, "Woodlands Cemetery," Historic American Landscapes Survey (HALS) No. PA-5, National Park Service, U.S. Department of the Interior, 2003–2004. The discussion that follows leans heavily on his research. See also Karen Madsen, "To Make His Country Smile: William Hamilton's Woodlands," *Arnoldia Arboretum* 42:2 (Spring 1989), 14–24. On Philadelphia's garden history and Hamilton's place within it, see Elizabeth McLean, "Town and Country Gardens in Eighteenth-Century Philadelphia," in *British and American Gardens in the Eighteenth Century: Eighteen Illustrated Essays on Garden History*, ed. Robert P. Maccubbin and Peter Martin (Williamsburg, VA: Colonial Williamsburg Foundation, 1984), 136–147. On gardens and colonial gentility, see Richard L. Bushman, *The Refinement of America: Persons, Houses, Cities* (New York: Random House, 1993), 127–132.

24. William Hamilton to William Tilghman, Apr. 1779, quoted in Wunsch, "Woodlands Cemetery," 23.

25. John Dixon Hunt, *The Picturesque Garden in Europe* (London: Thames and Hudson, 2002), 35. Hunt offers a useful survey of the rise of the picturesque garden in England and Europe. See also Nikolaus Pevsner, ed., *The Picturesque Garden and Its Influence Outside the British Isles* (Washington, DC: Trustees for Harvard University, Dumbarton Oaks, 1974).

26. Wunsch, "Woodlands Cemetery," 8–9, 25–26.

27. Julian Ursyn Niemcewicz, *Under Their Vine and Fig Tree: Travels Through America in 1797–1799, 1805, with Some Further Account of Life in New Jersey*, trans. Metchie J. E. Budka, Collections of the New Jersey Historical Society at Newark (Elizabeth, NJ: Grassman, 1965), 52.

28. On labor at The Woodlands' grounds, see Wunsch, "Woodlands Cemetery," 11; Joseph Ewan and Nesta Ewan, "John Lyon, Nurseryman and Plant Hunter, and His Journal, 1799–1814," *Transactions of the American Philosophical Society* 53:2 (1963), 1–69; U. P. Hedrick, *A History of Horticulture in America to 1860* (New York: Oxford University Press, 1950), 404–405.

29. Hamilton initially tried to buy the mill in order to tear it down; the greenhouse placement appears to have been his second choice. L.G. to Eliza, [n.d., ca. 1788], Society Collection, HSP.

30. The quotes are drawn from L. G. to Eliza, [n.d., ca. 1788], Society Collection, HSP. For other contemporary accounts, see J. Francis Fisher, "Philadelphia Social Scene and Remarks," ms., J. Francis Fisher Papers, box 10, folder 7, Cadwalader Collection, Series 9, HSP; [Joseph Dennie], "American Scenery," *Port Folio*, 3rd ser., Dec. 1809. For scholarly attempts to reconstruct the grounds, see McLean, "Town and Country Gardens"; Madsen, "To Make His Country Smile"; and esp. Wunsch, "Woodlands Cemetery."

31. Quoted in John Summerson, *Architecture in Britain, 1530–1830* (New Haven, CT: Yale University Press, 1991), 394.

32. William Hamilton to Dr. Thomas Parke, Sept. 24, 1785, HSP; William Hamilton to Dr. Thomas Parke, Mar. 8, 1786, HSP.

33. Fisher, "Philadelphia Social Scene and Remarks"; Catherine Ann Carosino, "The Woodlands: Documentation of an American Interior" (M.A. thesis, University of Pennsylvania, 1997), 122, 187.

34. Carosino, "Woodlands," 169, 171.

35. On mirrors at Woodlands, see ibid., 19, 34, 97, 122, 143, 147, 187, 188, 216, 219; Timothy Preston Long, "The Woodlands: A Matchless Place" (M.A. thesis, University of Pennsylvania, 1991), 62; Jacobs, "William Hamilton and The Woodlands," 200. On the comparable use of mirrors in the Bingham house, see Amy Hudson Henderson, "Furnishing the Republican Court: Building and Decorating Philadelphia Homes, 1790–1800" (Ph.D. diss., University of Delaware, 2008), 250, 275.

36. Dr. Charles Drayton's 1806 memoirs, reproduced in Carosino, "The Woodlands," 19; L. G. to Eliza, [n.d., ca. 1788], Society Collection, HSP. On illusions, pleasure, and visuality, see Wendy Bellion, *Citizen Spectator: Art, Illusion, and Visual Perception in Early National America* (Chapel Hill: University of North Carolina Press for the Omohundro Institute of Early American History and Culture, 2011).

37. In addition to purchasing paintings from noted artists like Wertmüller and Wollaston, James Hamilton contributed funds to send young Benjamin West to study in Italy. See Jacobs, "William Hamilton and The Woodlands," 204.

38. Fisher, "Philadelphia Social Scene and Remarks"; Laura, "The Woodlands, for the Portfolio," *Port Folio* (Feb. 1809). Jacobs, "William Hamilton and The Woodlands," offers a detailed discussion of Hamilton's collection.

39. Doris Devine Fanelli, "History of the Portrait Collection," in *Independence National Historical Park and Catalogue of the Collection*, ed. Karie Diethorn (Philadelphia: American Philosophical Society, 2001), 155; Fisher, "Philadelphia Social Scene and Remarks"; Laura, "The Woodlands, for the Portfolio"; Harriet Manigault, *The Diary of Harriet Manigault, 1813–1816* (Rockland, ME: Colonial Dames of America, 1976), 61.

40. Long, "Woodlands: A Matchless Place," 63, 66; L. G. to Eliza, [n.d., ca. 1788], Society Collection, HSP; HABS No. PA-1125, 63–65; Jacobs, "William Hamilton and The Woodlands," 200–201; Carosino, "The Woodlands," 19. Jacobs, "The Woodlands," provides the fullest discussion of The Woodlands' hidden service areas. Thomas Jefferson took similar steps to conceal the dependencies at Monticello by sinking them into the ground; he famously devised a set of revolving service doors to stand in for the conventional jib doors.

41. John C. Fitzpatrick, A.M., ed., *The Diaries of George Washington, 1748–1799*, 4 vols. (Boston: Houghton Mifflin, 1925), 3:220–221; Thomas Twining, *Travels in America 100 Years Ago* (New York: Harper and Brothers, 1893), 162–163. William Hamilton resided at Bush Hill from the summer of 1787, when new construction on The Woodlands house began in earnest, until the fall of 1789. HABS No. PA-1125, 34, 39.

42. Twining, *Travels in America*, 162–163; Eliza Cope Harrison, ed., *Philadelphia Merchant: The Diary of Thomas P. Cope, 1800–1851* (South Bend, IN: Gateway, 1978), 160; Rufus Wilmot Griswold, *The Republican Court; or, American Society in the Days of Washington* (New York: Appleton, 1867), 267. James Jacobs ("William Hamilton and The Woodlands") argues that Hamilton's hospitality is best understood as genteel performance.

43. In the 1990s, David S. Shields and Fredrika Teute wrote a series of conference and symposium papers that alerted a generation of scholars to the importance of the republican court and manners more generally in the early republic. The papers were later published, along with scholars' responses, in a special issue of the *Journal of the Early Republic* 35:2 (Summer 2015), 160–301. See also Catherine Allgor, *Parlor Politics: In Which the Ladies of Washington Help Build a City and a Government* (Charlottesville: University of Virginia Press, 2000).

44. William Hamilton to George Washington, Mar. 17, 1792, undated "List of Plants, from Mr Hamilton's," in *The Papers of George Washington, Presidential Series*, ed. Philander Chase, 17 vols. (Charlottesville: University of Virginia Press, 1987), 10:120–121; William Hamilton to George Washington, Mar. 6, 1797, in *The Papers of George Washington, Retirement Series*, ed. Dorothy Twohig, 4 vols. (Charlottesville: University of Virginia Press, 1998), 1:11–12. Washington and Hamilton initially met in 1774, when the former was in Philadelphia attending the Continental Congress.

45. William Hamilton to Thomas Jefferson, Jan. 16, 1803, in *Thomas Jefferson's Garden Book, 1766–1824, with Relevant Extracts from His Other Writings*, ed. Edwin Morris Betts (Philadelphia: American Philosophical Society, 1944), 284.

46. For examples of Hamilton's gifts to Jefferson, see ibid., 305, 363, 366. On Jefferson's gifts to Hamilton, see ibid., 307, 320. On Hamilton as a recipient of seeds from the Lewis and Clark expedition, see ibid., 337. See also Madsen, "To Make His Country Smile."

47. Thomas Jefferson to William Hamilton, Jul. 1806, in Betts, *Jefferson's Garden Book*, 322–323; Thomas Jefferson to William Hamilton, May 7, 1809, in *The Papers of Thomas Jefferson, Retirement Series*, ed. J. Jefferson Looney, 10 vols. (Princeton, NJ: Princeton University Press, 2004), 1:191–192.

48. George Washington to William Hamilton, Mar. 6, 1797, in Twohig, *Papers of George Washington, Retirement Series*, 1:12; Thomas Jefferson to William Hamilton, May 7, 1809, in Looney, *Papers of Thomas Jefferson, Retirement Series*, 1:192; William Hamilton to George Washington, Feb. 20, 1784, *The Papers of George Washington, Confederation Series*, ed. W. W. Abbot and Dorothy Twohig, 6 vols. (Charlottesville: University of Virginia Press, 1992), 1:136; William Hamilton to Thomas Jefferson, Oct. 5, 1805, *The Thomas Jefferson Papers, Series I, The General Correspondence, 1606–1827*, Library of Congress American Memory Project (http://memory.loc.gov; accessed Jun. 27, 2011).

49. George Washington to William Hamilton, Jan. 15, 1784, in Abbot and Twohig, *Papers of George Washington, Confederation Series*, 1:48.

50. Thomas Jefferson to William Hamilton, Jul. 26, 1806, in Betts, *Thomas Jefferson's Garden Book*, 322–323; Thomas Jefferson to William Hamilton, Mar. 1, 1808, in Betts, *Thomas Jefferson's Garden*, 366; Thomas Jefferson to William Hamilton, May 7, 1809, in Looney, *Papers of Thomas Jefferson, Retirement Series*, 1:192.

51. James Hamilton's portrait is discussed in Helmut von Erffa and Allen Staley, *The Paintings of Benjamin West* (New Haven, CT: Yale University Press for the Barra Foundation, 1986), 514–516; Fanelli, "History of the Portrait Collection," 155.

52. On West's portrait of William and Ann Hamilton, see von Erffa and Staley, *Paintings of Benjamin West*, 516. On the depiction of affection in late eighteenth-century family portraits, see Margaretta M. Lovell, "Reading Eighteenth-Century American Family Portraits: Social Images and Self-Images," *Winterthur Portfolio* 22:4 (Winter 1987), 243–264.

53. Harrison, *Philadelphia Merchant*, 184; Jacobs, "William Hamilton and The Woodlands," 197; André Michaux, *Travels West of the Alleghenies*, ed. Rueben Gold Thwaites (Cleveland, OH: Arthur H. Clark, 1904), 134; Scharf and Westcott, *History of Philadelphia*, 873. Eberlein's hoax is described in HABS No. PA-1125, 21.

54. On Malcolm's and Groombridge's paintings, see Martin P. Snyder, *City of Independence: Views of Philadelphia Before 1800* (New York: Praeger, 1975), 167–170, 178–179. On Groomsbridge's role in the quarrel over the Columbianum, see Bellion, *Citizen Spectator*, 69–71, 75–77.

55. William Russell Birch, *The Country Seats of the United States*, ed. Emily T. Cooperman (Philadelphia: University of Pennsylvania Press, 2009), 43, 68. The only other estate whose house contents Birch mentioned was his own, Springland. See also Michael J. Lewis, "William Birch and the Culture of Architecture in Philadelphia," *Studies in the History of Gardens and Designed Landscapes* 32:1 (Feb. 2012), 35–49; Emily T. Cooperman and Lea Carson Sherk, *William Birch: Picturing the American Scene* (Philadelphia: University of Pennsylvania Press, 2011), 129–159; Martin P. Snyder, "William Birch: His 'Country Seats of the United States,'" *Pennsylvania Magazine of History and Biography* 81:3 (Jul. 1957), 225–247. The ceramics depicting The Woodlands are in the collections of the Philadelphia Museum of Art.

56. Laura, "The Woodlands, for the Portfolio," 180.

57. [Dennie], "American Scenery," 505. Dennie regularly capitalized on opportunities to hold William Hamilton up as both an exemplar of taste and a promoter of the fine arts.

58. George Beck, Esq., "On the River Schuylkill," *Ladies' Literary Cabinet*, Mar. 31, 1821, 167. The poem was initially published in the *Western Review*. On Beck's career and his relationship with Hamilton, see J. Hall Pleasants, *Four Late Eighteenth Century Anglo-American Landscape Painters* (Worcester, MA: Antiquarian Society, 1942), 22–30.

59. Scholarly discussions of the Anglo-American interest in perception include Wendy Bellion, "Illusion and Allusion: Charles Willson Peale's 'Staircase Group' at the Columbianum Exhibition,"

American Art 17:2 (Summer 2003), 18–39; Wendy Bellion, "Pleasing Deceptions," *Common-place* 3:1 (Oct. 2002); Edward Cahill, "An Adventurous and Lawless Fancy: Charles Brockden Brown's Aesthetic State," *Early American Literature* 36:1 (2001), 31–70; Jonathan Crary, *Techniques of the Observer: Vision and Modernity in the Nineteenth Century* (Cambridge, MA: MIT Press, 1990); and Peter de Bolla, *The Education of the Eye: Painting, Landscape, and Architecture in Eighteenth-Century Britain* (Stanford, CA: Stanford University Press, 2003).

60. The literature on the transatlantic rise of the picturesque is far too large to be cited here in any detail. My thinking about the connections between picturesque gardens, perception, and literary culture has been influenced by John Marshall, "The Problem of the Picturesque," *Eighteenth-Century Studies* 35:3 (2002), 413–437; and John Dixon Hunt, "*Ut Pictura Poesis, Ut Pictura Hortus,* and the Picturesque," in *Gardens and the Picturesque: Studies in the History of Landscape Architecture* (Cambridge, MA: MIT Press, 1992), 105–136. For useful discussions of the picturesque in early American letters, see Edward Cahill, *Liberty of the Imagination: Aesthetic Theory, Literary Form, and Politics in the Early United States* (Philadelphia: University of Pennsylvania Press, 2012), 49–51, 99–137; Larry Kutchen, "'The Vulgar Thread of the Canvas': Revolution and the Picturesque in Ann Eliza Bleecker, Crèvecoeur, and Charles Brockden Brown," *Early American Literature* 36:3 (2001), 395–425; and Dennis Berthold, "Charles Brockden Brown, Edgar Huntly, and the Origins of the American Picturesque," *William and Mary Quarterly*, 3rd ser., 41:1 (Jan. 1984), 62–84.

61. Looker-on, "On a Taste for the Picturesque," *Monthly Magazine and American Review*, Jul. 1800; "Distinctions Between the Beautiful and the Picturesque," *Literary Magazine*, Jun. 1806; "Sketch of a Summer Passage up the Ohio," *Philadelphia Minerva*, Sept. 2, 1797; "Temple of the Muses," *Philadelphia Repository and Weekly Register*, Aug. 20, 1803. A search of the American Antiquarian Society Periodical collection database for essays printed before 1809 with "picturesque" included in the title registered more than 150 results; those with picturesque in the text numbered 191. However imprecise, this suggests something about the pervasiveness of the "picturesque" in the early national period.

62. [Hugh] Blair, "On Criticism and Genius," *Boston Magazine*, Dec. 1793; "General Reflections on Taste," *Columbian Magazine*, Feb. 1790; A Lover of the Polite Arts, "Influence of Taste upon Manners," *American Weekly Museum or Universal Magazine*, Jun. 1792.

63. "The German School of painting," *Literary Magazine and American Register*, Apr. 3, 1805; "The Fine Arts," *Massachusetts Magazine*, Aug. 1796; "Strictures upon the Work of Mr. West," *Philadelphia Repository and Weekly Magazine*, Jan. 12, 1805; "Wertmuller," *Analectic Magazine*, Jun. 1815.

64. L.G. to Eliza [n.d., ca. 1788], Society Collection, HSP.

65. Birch, *Country Seats*, 43.

66. *Poulson's American Daily Advertiser*, Jun. 8, 1813; *Columbian*, Jun. 11, 1813; *Boston Gazette*, Jun. 14, 1813.

67. Thomas Jefferson to William Hamilton, Apr. 22, 1800, in *Papers of Thomas Jefferson*, ed. Barbara B. Oberg, 40 vols. (Princeton, NJ: Princeton University Press, 2004), 31: 533–535.

68. Niemcewicz, *Under Their Vine and Fig Tree*, 53; François Alexandre Frédéric, duc de La Rochefoucauld-Liancourt, *Travels Through the United States of North America, the Country of the Iroquois, and Upper Canada, in the Years 1795, 1796, and 1797*, 2nd ed., 4 vols. (London: R. Phillips, 1800), 1:76, 482–483.

69. On the importance of omissions in structuring narratives of nation formation, see Michel-Rolph Trouillot, *Silencing the Past: Power and the Production of History* (Boston: Beacon, 1995). Sarah J. Purcell offers a suggestive discussion of problems posed by loyalists in postwar commemorations in *Sealed with Blood: War Sacrifice and Memory in Revolutionary America* (Philadelphia: University of Pennsylvania Press, 2002), 67–71.

70. As Maya Jasanoff points out, even the Treaty of Paris did not put an end to confiscations; some states viewed the Treaty's protection of loyalist property as a violation of states' rights and enacted anti-loyalist legislation in defiance of the Treaty. Jasanoff, *Liberty's Exiles: American Loyalists in the Revolutionary World* (New York: Alfred A. Knopf, 2011), 319.

71. Robert M. Calhoon, "The Reintegration of the Loyalists and the Disaffected," in *Tory Insurgents: The Loyalist Perception and Other Essays*, rev. and exp. ed., ed. Robert M. Calhoon et al.

(Columbia: University of South Carolina Press, 2010), 350–369; Jasanoff, *Liberty's Exiles*, 317–320. Ruma Chopra, *Unnatural Rebellion: Loyalists in New York City* (Charlottesville: University of Virginia Press, 2011), emphasizes the failure of state legislatures to enforce Congress's recommendations (205–208).

72. As Robert M. Calhoon rightly notes, if scholars have produced a "richly varied portrayal of loyalist reintegration as a social and political process," they have been "far less successful in recreating the interior experiences that underlay that process." See "Reintegration of the Loyalists," 362.

73. See, e.g., Jacobs, "William Hamilton and The Woodlands."

74. William Hamilton to Dr. Thomas Parke, Sept. 24, 1785, HSP.

75. For Birch's reference to national character and nationalism, see Birch, *Country Seats*, 43; entries for July 1806 and May 1809, in Betts, *Thomas Jefferson's Garden Book*, 323, 411.

76. On oratory, see Thomas Jefferson, "Autobiography, Aug. 25, 1789," in *The Papers of Thomas Jefferson, Digital Edition*, ed. James P. McClure and J. Jefferson Looney (Charlottesville: University of Virginia Press, 2009–2015) (http://rotunda.upress.virginia.edu/founders/TSJN.html). On architecture, see "From Thomas Jefferson to James Buchanan and William Hay, 13 August 1785," Founders Online, National Archives (http://founders.archives.gov/documents/Jefferson/01-08-02-0293) (original source: *The Papers of Thomas Jefferson*, vol. 8, *25 February–31 October 1785*, ed. Julian P. Boyd [Princeton, NJ: Princeton University Press, 1953], 366–368). On military size, see Thomas Jefferson to Nathaniel Macon, May 14, 1801; on parliamentary protocol, see Thomas Jefferson to George Wythe, Apr. 7, 1800; on carriage decoration, see Thomas Jefferson to Enoch Edwards, Mar. 30, 1801, all in *Papers of Thomas Jefferson, Digital Edition*.

77. Bushman, *Refinement of America*, 181–207. On the contradictions engendered by Americans' continued desire for and reliance on English goods, see Kariann Akemi Yokota, *Unbecoming British: How Revolutionary America Became a Post-colonial Nation* (New York: Oxford University Press, 2011).

CHAPTER FIVE

1. The preceding description is drawn from "Columbian Museum, Near the Mall, Boston . . . ," 1799 broadside, Massachusetts Historical Society.

2. Charles Willson Peale wanted a place in history and he got one. Among the many studies that attend to his museum as well as his painting, see David C. Ward, *Charles Willson Peale: Art and Selfhood in the Early Republic* (Berkeley: University of California Press, 2004); Laura Rigal, *The American Manufactory: Art, Labor, and the World of Things in the Early Republic* (Princeton, NJ: Princeton University Press, 1998); David C. Ward, "Democratic Culture: The Peale Museum, 1784–1850," in *The Peale Family: Creation of a Legacy, 1770–1870*, ed. Lillian C. Miller (Washington, DC: Abbeville Press in association with the Smithsonian Institution, 1996), 260–276; David R. Brigham, *Public Culture in the Early Republic: Peale's Museum and Its Audience* (Washington, DC: Smithsonian Institution Press, 1995); Susan Stewart, "Death and Life, in That Order, in the Works of Charles Willson Peale," in *The Cultures of Collecting*, ed. John Elsner and Roger Cardinal (London: Reaktion, 1994): Sidney Hart and David C. Ward, "The Waning of an Enlightenment Ideal: Charles Willson Peale's Philadelphia Museum, 1790–1820," *Journal of the Early Republic* 8:4 (Winter 1988), 389–418; and Charles Coleman Sellers, *Mr. Peale's Museum: Charles Willson Peale and the First Popular Museum of Natural Science and Art* (New York: W. W. Norton, 1980).

The secondary material on other early national museums is sparse. See James M. Lindgren, "'That Every Mariner May Possess the History of the World': A Cabinet for the East India Marine Society of Salem," *New England Quarterly* 68:2 (Jun. 1995), 179–205; Ellen Fernandez Sacco, "Spectacular Masculinities: The Museums of Peale, Baker, and Bowen in the Early Republic" (Ph.D. diss., University of California, Los Angeles, 1998); *Extracts from the Journals of Ethan A. Greenwood: Portrait Painter and Museum Proprietor*, ed. Georgia Brady Barnhill (Worcester, MA: American Antiquarian Society, 1993), hereafter cited as *Extracts*; Thompson R. Harlow, "The Life and Trials of Joseph Steward," *Connecticut Historical Society Bulletin* 46:4 (Oct. 1981); Loyd Haberly, "The Long Life of Daniel Bowen," *New England Quarterly* 32:3 (Sept. 1959), 320–332; and Ralph W. Thomas, "Reuben Moulthrop, 1763–1814," *Connecticut Historical Society Bulletin* 21:4 (Oct. 1956).

3. Georges Didi-Huberman uses the transience of the material to meditate on the genre's equally transient place in art history. See Didi-Huberman, "Viscosities and Survivals: Art History Put to the

Test by the Material," in *Ephemeral Bodies: Wax Sculpture and the Human Figure*, ed. Roberta Panzanelli (Los Angeles: Getty Research Institute, 2008), 154–170.

4. Madame Tussaud, and European waxwork more generally, has begun to attract scholarly attention. See Kate Berridge, *Madame Tussaud: A Life in Wax* (New York: Morrow, 2006); Teresa Ransom, *Madame Tussaud: A Life and a Time* (Stroud, UK: Sutton, 2003); and Michelle E. Bloom, *Wax-Work: A Cultural Obsession* (Minneapolis: University of Minnesota Press, 2003).

5. For useful overviews of the relationship between natural sciences and social sciences, see Johan Heilbron, "Social Thought and Natural Science," in *The Cambridge History of Science*, vol. 7, *The Modern Social Sciences*, ed. Theodore M. Porter and Dorothy Ross (Cambridge: Cambridge University Press, 2003), 40–57; and I. Bernard Cohen, "Preface and Introduction" and "An Analysis of the Interactions Between the Natural Sciences and the Social Sciences," in *The Natural Sciences and the Social Sciences: Some Critical and Historical Perspectives*, ed. I. Bernard Cohen (Dordrecht, Netherlands: Springer, 1994), vii–x, 1–100.

6. Hannah Webster Foster, *The Coquette*, ed. Cathy N. Davidson (New York: Oxford University Press, 1986), 113.

7. *Columbian Centinel*, Feb. 20, 1799 (p. 23), Feb. 1799, and Jul. 4, 1804; *New York Daily Advertiser*, Jul. 4, 1818. See also *New England Palladium and Commercial Advertiser*, Dec. 8, 1818; *Boston Commercial Gazette*, Aug. 9, 1821. See also Ward, *Charles Willson Peale*, 82, 101–105; *Extracts*, 138, 143; and Haberly, "Long Life of Daniel Bowen," 324.

8. *Extracts*, 154, 143.

9. Fernandez Sacco, "Spectacular Masculinities," 12–13, 20–21, 40; Harlow, "Life and Trials of Joseph Steward," 105–107.

10. Hart and Ward, "Waning of an Enlightenment Ideal," 405–412. The quote is on 405.

11. Brigham (*Public Culture in the Early Republic*) does a remarkable job of reconstructing the demographics of Peale's audience; he is less successful at teasing out viewer responses.

12. Kristin Olsen, *Daily Life in 18th-Century England* (Westport, CT: Greenwood, 1999), 154, 157, 203; Joseph Roach, "Celebrity Erotics: Pepys, Performance, and Painted Ladies," *Yale Journal of Criticism* 16:1 (2003), 211–230; Pamela Pilbeam, *Madame Tussaud and the History of Waxworks* (London: Humbledown and London, 2003), 1–4, 8–16; Troy Bickham, "'A Conviction of the Reality of Things': Material Culture, North American Indians and Empire in Eighteenth-Century Britain," *Eighteenth-Century Studies* 39:1 (Winter 2005), 30.

13. (Boston) *Evening Post*, Sept. 1, 1740.

14. Martha C. Codman, ed., "Diary of Katherine Greene Amory, Oct. 1775," in *The Journal of Mrs. John Amory* (Boston: Merrymount, 1923), 12; Abigail Adams to Mary Smith Cranch, Jul. 25, 1784, in *The Adams Family Correspondence*, ed. Richard Alan Ryerson, 11 vols. (Cambridge, MA: Belknap Press of Harvard University Press, 1993–), 5:376–377.

15. *Pennsylvania Gazette*, Aug. 15, 1756; John Thomas Scharf and Thompson Westcott, *History of Philadelphia, 1609–1884* (Philadelphia: L. H. Evert, 1884), 887; *New York Gazette and Weekly Miscellany*, Jun. 4, 1770. See also Jason Shaffer, *Performing Patriotism: National Identity in the Colonial and Revolutionary American Theater* (Philadelphia: University of Pennsylvania Press, 2007); Margaretta Lovell, "Bodies of Illusion: Portraits, People, and the Construction of Memory," in *Possible Pasts: Becoming Colonial in Early America*, ed. Robert Blair St. George (Ithaca, NY: Cornell University Press, 2000), 270–301; and Heather S. Nathans, *Early American Theater from the Revolution to Thomas Jefferson: Into the Hands of the People* (Cambridge: Cambridge University Press, 2003).

16. Charles Coleman Sellers, *Patience Wright: American Artist and Spy in George III's London* (Middletown, CT: Wesleyan University Press, 1976), 34–38, 40.

17. Joan B. Landes, "Wax Fibers, Wax Bodies, and Moving Figures: Artifice and Nature in Eighteenth-Century Anatomy," *Ephemeral Bodies*, 41–65.

18. William Shippen Jr. to Benjamin Franklin, May 14, 1767, in *Papers of Benjamin Franklin*, vol. 14, *January 1 Through December 31, 1767*, ed. Leonard W. Labaree (New Haven, CT: Yale University Press, 1970), 148; Sellers, *Patience Wright*, 34.

19. Evelyn M. Accomb, "The Journal of Baron Von Closen," *William and Mary Quarterly*, 3rd ser., 10:2 (Apr. 1953), 196–236; 206; John Adams to Abigail Adams, May 10, 1777, in *The Adams Family*

Correspondence, ed. L. H. Butterfield, 11 vols. (Cambridge, MA: Belknap Press of Harvard University Press, 1963–), 2:235–236; George Washington, diary, July 4, 1787, *The Diaries of George Washington*, ed. Donald Jackson and Dorothy Twohig, 6 vols. (Charlottesville: University of Virginia Press, 1979), 5:174. For the complete contents of Chovet's collection, see "List of Articles Contained in the Anatomical Museum of the Pennsylvania Hospital," in *Catalogue of the Medical Library Belonging to the Pennsylvania Hospital* (Philadelphia: printed for the hospital by Archibald Bartram, 1806), 121–127. On Chovet's career, see William Snow Miller, "Abraham Chovet: An Early Teacher of Anatomy in Philadelphia," *Anatomical Record* 5:4 (Apr. 1911), 147–172; and John H. Appleby, "Human Curiosities and the Royal Society," *Notes and Records of the Royal Society of London* 50:1 (Jan. 1996), 14. For discussions that locate anatomical display in a wider cultural context, see Alexander Nemerov, *The Body of Raphael Peale: Still Life and Selfhood, 1812–1824* (Berkeley: University of California Press, 2001); and Michael Sappol, *A Traffic of Dead Bodies: Anatomy and Embodied Social Identity in Nineteenth-Century America* (Princeton, NJ: Princeton University Press, 2002).

20. On English waxwork, see Henrietta Irving Bolton, "Curious Relics of English Funerals," *Journal of American Folklore* 7:26 (Jul.–Sept. 1894), 233–236; Paul S. Fritz, "The Trade in Death: The Royal Funerals in England, 1685–1830," *Eighteenth-Century Studies* 15:3 (Spring 1982), 291–316; and Paul S. Fritz, "From 'Public' to 'Private': The Royal Funerals in England, 1500–1800," in *Mirrors of Mortality: Studies in the Social History of Death*, ed. Joachim Whaley (New York: St. Martin's, 1991), 61–79.

21. "Effigies of the Royal Family of England," *New York Weekly Journal*, Jul. 3, 1749, reprinted in *The Arts and Crafts in New York, 1726–1776: Advertisements and News Items from New York City Newspapers*, ed. Rita Susswein Gottesman, 3 vols. (New York: New-York Historical Society, 1938), 1:389–390. See also *New York Gazette*, Oct. 9, 1749; *Boston Gazette*, Aug. 27, 1745; *Boston Gazette*, May 7, 1751; Brendan McConville, *The King's Three Faces: The Rise and Fall of Royal America, 1688–1776* (Chapel Hill: University of North Carolina Press for the Omohundro Institute of Early American History and Culture, 2006), 132–137, 308.

22. On effigies during the Imperial Crisis, see Kenneth Silverman, *A Cultural History of the American Revolution* (New York: Thomas Y. Crowell, 1976), 75–81. John Mein's story is regularly recounted in histories of the Revolution; for a full discussion, see ibid., 144–145. See also Charles Willson Peale, autobiography manuscript, quoted in ibid., 75; Robert Blair St. George, *Conversing by Signs: Poetics of Implication in Colonial New England Culture* (Chapel Hill: University of North Carolina Press, 1998), 250–251, 252–254, 258–259. St. George emphasizes the continuities between New Englanders' use of effigies and early modern popular politics.

23. Brandon Brame Fortune, "Portraits of Virtue and Genius: Pantheons of Worthies and Public Portraiture in the Early American Republic, 1780–1820" (Ph.D. diss., University of North Carolina, Chapel Hill, 1987), 34–86. My understanding of republican pantheons is indebted to her fine analysis.

24. "On Emulation," *Boston Magazine*, Feb. 1786, quoted in Fortune, "Portraits of Virtue and Genius," 91; Charles Willson Peale is quoted in ibid., 92. Fortune is especially sensitive to the relationship between "naturalism" and "convention" in the portrayal of republican worthies. On the importance of emulation in the early republic, see William Huntting Howell, "'A More Perfect Copy Than Heretofore': Imitation, Emulation, and American Literary Culture" (Ph.D. diss., Northwestern University, 2005); J. M. Opal, "Exciting Emulation: Academies and the Transformation of the Rural North, 1780s–1820s," *Journal of American History* 91:2 (2004), 445–470; and J. M. Opal, *Beyond the Farm: Ambition and the Transformation of Rural New England, 1770s–1820s* (Philadelphia: University of Pennsylvania Press, 2008).

25. Fortune, "Portraits of Virtue and Genius." The range of goods incorporating these motifs is suggested in Wendy C. Wick, *George Washington: An American Icon* (Washington, DC: Smithsonian Institution, 1982); and Noble E. Cunningham Jr., *Popular Images of the Presidency from Washington to Lincoln* (Columbia: University of Missouri Press, 1991). On the incorporation of political symbols into everyday life, see Leora Auslander, *Cultural Revolutions: Everyday Life and Politics in Britain, North America, and France* (Berkeley: University of California Press, 2009).

26. On the connections between aesthetic and political theory in early national America, see esp. Jay Fliegelman, *Declaring Independence: Jefferson, Natural Language, and the Culture of Performance*

(Stanford, CA: Stanford University Press, 1993); Eric Slauter, *The State as a Work of Art: The Cultural Origins of the Constitution* (Chicago: University of Chicago Press, 2007); and Edward Cahill, *Liberty of the Imagination: Aesthetic Theory, Literary Form, and Politics in the Early United States* (Philadelphia: University of Pennsylvania Press, 2012).

27. John Adams to Abigail Adams, May 10, 1777, in *Adams Family Correspondence*, 2:235–236.

28. Benjamin Silliman to G. S. Silliman, Jun. 5, 1801, in George P. Fisher, *Life of Benjamin Silliman, M.D., LL.D.* (New York: Charles Scribner and Son, 1866), 72; Benjamin Silliman, *A Journal of Travels in England, Holland, and Scotland and of Two Passages over the Atlantic, in the Years 1805 and 1806*, 2 vols. (New York: D. G. Bruce, 1810), 2:172.

29. "Wax Figures," in Francis Leiber, Edward Wigglesworth, and Thomas Gamaliel Bradford, eds., *Encyclopedia Americana* (Philadelphia: Carey, Lea, and Carey, 1833), v. XIII, p. 97. Cf. Susan Stewart, who writes that collections carry with them the "dream of animation," the fantasy that the "collection might come to life." Stewart, "Death and Life," 204.

30. Aphra Behn, "The Lady's Looking-Glass to Dress Herself By," in *The Plays, Histories, and Novels of the Ingenious Mrs. Behn, with Life and Memoirs*, 6 vols. (London: Johan Pearson, 1871), 6:204; Samuel Richardson, *The History of Clarissa Harlowe in a Series of Letters in Eight Volumes*, 8 vols. (London: James Carpenter, 1811), 3:28; Ann March-Caldwell, *Evelyn Marston*, 3 vols. (London: Hurst and Blackett, 1856), 2:41; Frances Trollope, *The Three Cousins*, 3 vols. (London: Henry Colburn, 1847), 2:243.

31. Sir Joshua Reynolds, *Discourses on Art*, ed. Robert R. Wark (New Haven, CT: Yale University Press, 1997).

32. Sir Joshua Reynolds, "Discourse XI. Genius," in *The Works of Sir Joshua Reynolds . . . in 3 Volumes*, ed. Edmond Malone, Esq. (London: T. Cadell and W. Davies, 1809), 2:46–47.

33. Advertisement in *Village Record, or Chester* (PA) *and Delaware Federalist*, Jan. 12, 1820; *Stockbridge* (MA) *Western Sun*, Jan. 30, 1797.

34. "Washington Museum and Gallery of Paintings," *Poulson's American Daily Advertiser*, Aug. 9, 1819; "Wax-Work," *New Hampshire Gazette*, Feb. 9, 1802; "The Columbian Museum, at the Head of the Mall, Boston," 1799 broadside; "Wonderful Woman!!" *Columbian Centinel*, Feb. 6, 1811; "Wax-Work, Moulthrop and Street," *Connecticut Journal*, Feb. 20, 1800; "Museum, Joseph Steward," *Connecticut Courant*, Jan. 5, 1801; "The American Museum," (Boston) *Evening Post*, May 2, 1810; "Museum and Wax-Work," *Columbian Gazetteer*, Oct. 16, 1794, in Gottesman, ed., *Arts and Crafts in New York, 1777–1799*, 2:391. "Columbian Museum," *Columbian Centinel*, Dec. 16, 1797.

35. "The Naked Truth," *Poulson's Daily Advertiser*, Nov. 8, 1806; "New Museum of Wax-Work," *Connecticut Courant*, May 13, 1807; "Museum, Joseph Steward," *Connecticut Courant*, May 1, 1801; "Columbian Museum, at the Head of the Mall"; "Tammany Museum Belonging to G. Baker," *American Minerva and New York Daily Advertiser*, Feb. 15, 1796.

36. "Wax Work, as Large as Life," *Pennsylvania Gazette*, Jul. 7, 1790; "Museum of Wax Figures, Natural and Mechanical Curiosities," *Poulson's American Daily Advertiser*, Jun. 21, 1813; "Bowen's Columbian Museum," *Columbian Centinel*, Dec. 16, 1797.

37. *Extracts*, 147, 149, 152, 155, 156, 162, 163, 169, 174; Lemuel Catchpenny, "Wax Work," *Aeronaut: A Periodical Paper*, Jul. 22, 1817.

38. "Wax Exhibition, R. Letton," 1808, Connecticut Historical Society Broadsides Collection, L651wa.

39. On the problems of clothing disguise, and authenticity, see, e.g., Richard Bushman, *The Refinement of America: Persons, Houses, Cities* (New York: Random House, 1993); David Waldstreicher, "Reading the Runaways: Self-Fashioning, Print Culture, and Confidence in Slavery in the Eighteenth-Century Mid Atlantic," *William and Mary Quarterly*, 3rd ser., 56:2 (Apr. 1999), 243–272; David Waldstreicher, "Why Thomas Jefferson and African Americans Wore Their Politics on Their Sleeves: Dress and Mobilization Between the American Revolutions," in *Beyond the Founders: New Approaches to the Political History of the Early American Republic*, ed. Jeffrey L. Pasley et al. (Chapel Hill: University of North Carolina Press, 2004), 79–106; and Karen H. Halttunen, *Confidence Men and Painted Women: A Study of Middle-Class Culture in America, 1830–1870* (New Haven, CT: Yale University Press, 1982).

40. "From the *Argus*: Demolition of the Exhibition of Wax-Work," *Salem Gazette*, Oct. 18, 1791. The essay originally appeared in the Boston *Argus*, Oct. 11, 1791.

41. Charles Edward Lester, *The Artist, the Merchant, and the Statesman of the Age of the Medici to Our Own Times* (New York: Paine and Burgess, 1845), 57–58.

42. See, e.g., the readings of the museum that appear in Hart and Ward, "Waning of an Enlightenment Ideal"; Ward, "Democratic Culture"; Ward, *Charles Willson Peale*, 95–110; and Brooke Hindle, "Charles Willson Peale's Science and Technology," in *Charles Willson Peale and His World*, ed. Edgar P. Richardson et al. (New York: Harry N. Abrams, 1982), 106–169.

43. William Parker Cutler and Julia Perkins Cutler, *Life, Journals and Correspondence of Rev. Manasseh Cutler, LL.D. By His Grandchildren*, 2 vols. (Cincinnati, OH: Robert Clarke, 1888), 1:260–261. See also Lillian B. Miller et al., eds., *Selected Papers of Charles Willson Peale and His Family*, vol. 5, *The Autobiography of Charles Willson Peale* (New Haven, CT: Yale University Press, 2000), 221–225; Sellers, *Mr. Peale's Museum*, 69–80.

44. Sellers, *Mr. Peale's Museum*, 60.

45. Charles Willson Peale, broadside [1792], in *Selected Papers of Charles Willson Peale and His Family*, vol. 2, *The Artist as Museum Keeper*, ed. Lillian B. Miller (New Haven, CT: Yale University Press, 1988), 12; Charles Willson Peale, "To the Citizens of the United States of America [1790]," in *Selected Papers of Charles Willson Peale and His Family*, vol. 1, *Artist in Revolutionary America*, ed. Lillian B. Miller (New Haven: Yale University Press, 1983), 581; Charles Willson Peale to Isaac Weaver, and Resolutions, Feb. 11, 1802, in Miller, *Selected Papers of Charles Willson Peale*, 1:396. Emphasis in the original.

46. Charles Willson Peale, "The Autobiography of Charles Willson Peale," in Miller et al., *Selected Papers of Charles Willson Peale*, 5:225.

47. [Joseph Dennie], "Peale's Museum," *Port Folio*, 3rd ser., Nov. 7, 1807, 293.

48. Ward, "Democratic Culture," 265.

49. Guides to the Philadelphia Museum that described its contents and layout were available to patrons onsite and were also widely reprinted, with minor variations over time. This description is based on "Account of the Philadelphia Museum," *Literary Magazine*, Nov. 1804, 576–579. On the move to the State House, see Sellers, *Mr. Peale's Museum*, 152–154, 210–211.

50. "Account of the Philadelphia Museum."

51. Sellers, *Mr. Peale's Museum*, 153; Ward, *Charles Willson Peale*, 102; Fernandez Sacco, "Spectacular Masculinities," 95.

52. On observation, see Lorraine Daston, "The Empire of Observation, 1600–1800," in *Histories of Scientific Observation*, ed. Lorraine Daston and Elizabeth Lunbeck (Chicago: University of Chicago Press, 2011), 81–114. Quotes are from Charles Willson Peale, "Address to Citizens of Philadelphia," Jul. 18, 1816, in *Selected Papers of Charles Willson Peale and His Family*, vol. 3, *The Belfield Farm Years*, ed. Lillian B. Miller et al. (New Haven, CT: Yale University Press, 1992), 415–416.

53. Miller et al., *Selected Papers of Charles Willson Peale*, 2:130.

54. "Columbian Museum, at the Head of the Mall"; Haberly, "Long Life of Daniel Bowen," 323–324.

55. "Columbian Museum, Milk Street," 1804 broadside; "Columbian Museum," 1805 broadside, both at Massachusetts Historical Society; Haberly, "Long Life of Daniel Bowen," 327–328.

56. The 1795 *Historical and Descriptive Catalogue of Peale's Museum* indicates that holdings dropped from eighty-seven items to sixty-nine. Sacco, "Spectacular Masculinities," 55–56.

57. On the interior of and arrangement of Greenwood's museum, see *Extracts*, 137–145 passim.

58. Tellingly, Peale fretted that the handbills he printed to publicize his museum smacked of "Bowen's plans to make money. No matter, provided I do not disgrace the Character of a Naturalist by too much puffing." See Sellers, *Mr. Peale's Museum*, 154.

59. Maximilian Prince of Wied, "Travels in the Interior of North America," trans. Hannibal Evans Lloyd, in *Early Western Travels, 1748–1846*, ed. Reuben Golde Thwaites, 3 vols. (Cleveland, OH: Arthur H. Clarke, 1906), 1:49.

60. Frederick Marryat, *A Diary in America, with Remarks on Its Institutions in 3 Vols.* (London: Longman, Orne, Brown, Green, and Longmans, 1839), 1:291–293.

61. *Diary of William Bentley, D.D.*, vol. 2, *January 1793—December 1807* (Salem, MA: Essex Institute, 1907). See entries for Feb. 12, 1800, 330; and Mar. 12, 1798, 261.

62. For pertinent case studies, see Bickham, "'Conviction'"; Lindgren, "'That Every Mariner.'" The classic discussion of museums as representations and enforcers of hierarchy remains Tony Bennett, *The Birth of the Museum: History, Theory, Politics* (London: Routledge, 1995).

63. Several years after installing the models of Blue Jacket and Red Pole, Peale painted *Captain Joseph Brant (Thayendanegea)* for his museum's gallery. Charles Coleman Sellers, "'Good Chiefs and Wise Men': Indians as Symbols of Peace in the Art of Charles Willson Peale," *American Art Journal* 7:2 (Nov. 1975), 10–18; Sellers, *Mr. Peale's Museum*, 91–94; Brigham, *Public Culture in the Early Republic*, 125–129. On the Shawnee delegation's experiences in Philadelphia, see John Sugden, *Blue Jacket: Warrior of the Shawnees* (Lincoln: University of Nebraska Press, 2000), 213–215.

64. See, e.g., John Wood Sweet's analysis of abolitionist images in *Bodies Politic: Negotiating Race in the American North, 1730–1830* (Baltimore, MD: Johns Hopkins University Press, 2003).

65. In the past two decades, scholars working in various disciplines and employing a variety of theoretical and methodological frameworks have begun to trace the ways that race in general and whiteness in particular are imbricated in U.S. national identity. Although that literature is far too large to be cited here, a representative sample addressing the early republic might include Elizabeth Maddock Dillon, "Slaves in Algiers: Race, Republican Genealogies, and the Global Stage," *American Literary History* 16:3 (Fall 2004), 407–436; Sweet, *Bodies Politic*; Pauline Schloesser, *The Fair Sex: White Women and Racial Patriarchy in the Early American Republic* (New York: New York University Press, 2002); Dana D. Nelson, "Consolidating National Masculinity: The Scientific Discourse of Race in the Post-Revolutionary United States," in *Possible Pasts: Becoming Colonial in Early America*, ed. Robert Blair St. George (Ithaca, NY: Cornell University Press, 2000); Dana D. Nelson, *National Manhood: Capitalist Citizenship and the Imagined Fraternity of White Men* (Durham, NC: Duke University Press, 1998); Matthew Frye Jacobsen, *Whiteness of a Different Color: European Immigration and the Alchemy of Race* (Cambridge, MA: Harvard University Press, 1998); Peter S. Onuf, "'To Declare Them a Free and Independent People': Race, Slavery, and National Identity in Jefferson's Thought," *Journal of the Early Republic* 18:1 (Spring 1998), 1–46; and Noel Ignatiev, *How the Irish Became White* (New York: Routledge, 1995).

66. This analysis is indebted to Barbara M. Benedict, *Curiosity: A Cultural History of Early Modern Inquiry* (Chicago: University of Chicago Press, 2001). As Benedict writes, "Rather than becoming a subject of classification in a moral or sociological system, the collector or the spectator of an exhibition systematizes his or her own experience and objectifies time [or history] and nature according to individual desire and memory" (202–203).

67. *Diary of William Bentley*, vol. 2, Mar. 12, 1798, 261. See also James Elkins, *The Object Stares Back: On the Nature of Seeing* (New York: Simon and Schuster, 1996); and Peter de Bolla, *The Education of the Eye: Painting, Landscape, and Architecture in Eighteenth-Century Britain* (Stanford, CA: Stanford University Press, 2003).

68. See, e.g., Manasseh Cutler's account of his visit to Peale's museum, where he mistook Peale's wax self-portrait for the original. Cutler recalled that the wax man "had no motion; but he appeared to me to be as *absolutely* alive as the other." Cutler and Cutler, *Life, Journals, and Correspondence*, 1:260. As Jay Fliegelman has observed, unlike portraits, which are always obviously representations, wax figures were representations masquerading as embodiment. Fliegelman, *Declaring Independence*, 87.

69. Rigal, *American Manufactory*, 117, 119, 129–130. See also Catherine O'Donnell Kaplan, *Men of Letters in the Early Republic: Cultivating Forms of Citizenship* (Chapel Hill: University of North Carolina Press, 2008).

70. *Extracts*, Dec. 9, 1823, 163. To be sure, Greenwood was also worried about competition from the circus, as Chapter 2 demonstrates. Yet the point about spectators holds.

CHAPTER SIX

1. The most comprehensive account of Washington's portraits, both painted and engraved, remains W[illiam] S[pohn] Baker, *The Engraved Portraits of Washington, with notices of the originals*

and brief biographical sketches of the painters (Philadelphia: Lindsay and Baker, 1880). On Peale's Washingtons, see Baker, *Engraved Portraits*, 14–31; on Wright, see Baker, *Engraved Portraits*, 48.

2. [New York] *Daily Advertiser*, Sept. 2, 1789, quoted in William Kelby, comp., *Notes on American Artists, 1754–1820* (New York: New-York Historical Society, 1922), 33–34. Noble E. Cunningham Jr. surveys Washington memorabilia in *Popular Images of the Presidency from Washington to Lincoln* (Columbia: University of Missouri Press, 1991).

3. The literature on Washington-as-national-symbol is far too large to be cited in any detail. But the range is suggested by the following works: Catherine Albanese, *Sons of the Fathers: The Civil Religion of the American Revolution* (Philadelphia: Temple University Press, 1976); Garry Wills, *Cincinnatus: George Washington and the Enlightenment* (Garden City, NY: Doubleday, 1984); Paul K. Longmore, *The Invention of George Washington* (Berkeley: University of California Press, 1988); Max Cavitch, "The Man That Was Used Up: Poetry, Particularity, and the Politics of Remembering George Washington," *American Literature* 75:2 (Jun. 2003), 247–274.

4. Brendan McConville revisits Anglicization with an eye toward the prominence of the monarch in *The King's Three Faces: The Rise and Fall of Royal America, 1688–1776* (Chapel Hill: University of North Carolina Press for the Omohundro Institute of Early American History and Culture, 2006); see esp. 146–152. See also Jack P. Greene, *Pursuits of Happiness: The Social Development of Early Modern British Colonies and the Formation of American Culture* (Chapel Hill: University of North Carolina Press, 1988). On material culture and Anglicization, see T. H. Breen, *The Marketplace of Revolution: How Consumer Politics Shaped American Independence* (New York: Oxford University Press, 2004); and "An Empire of Goods: The Anglicization of British America," *Journal of British Studies* 25:4 (Oct. 1986), 467–469. On the 1740s as a turning point in Anglicized consumption, see Cary M. Carson, "The Consumer Revolution in Colonial British America: Why Demand?" in *Of Consuming Interests: The Style of Life in the Eighteenth Century*, ed. Cary Carson, Ronald Hoffman, and Peter J. Albert (Charlottesville: University of Virginia Press, 1994), 483–697. Eliga Gould usefully summarizes the literature on Anglicization throughout the British Empire in "A Virtual Nation: Greater Britain and the Imperial Legacy of the American Revolution," *American Historical Review* 104:2 (Apr. 1999), 476–489.

5. Richard H. Saunders, *John Smibert: Colonial America's First Portrait Painter* (New Haven, CT: Yale University Press, 1995), 96; Graham Hood, *The Governor's Palace in Williamsburg: A Cultural Study* (Williamsburg, VA: Colonial Williamsburg Foundation, 1991), 146, 184. For general discussions of royal portraiture in the colonies, see Hood, *Governor's Palace*, 111, 129, 170; Saunders, *John Smibert*, 96–98; McConville, *King's Three Faces*, 128–137; and John Gorham Palfrey, *History of New England during the Stuart Dynasty*, 3 vols. (Boston: Little, Brown, 1882), 3:402–403.

6. Saunders, *John Smibert*, 94–95. Adams is quoted in Gordon S. Wood, *The Radicalism of the American Revolution* (New York: Vintage, 1993), 16–17.

7. Lady Victoria Manners and G. C. Williamson, *John Zoffany, R.A., His Life and Works, 1735–1810* (London: J. Lane, 1920), 24–26.

8. E. McSherry Fowble, *To Please Every Taste: Eighteenth Century Prints from the Winterthur Museum* (Alexandria, VA: Art Services International, 1991), 25; George Francis Dow, comp., *The Arts and Crafts in New England, 1704–1775* (Topsfield, MA: Wayside, 1927), 37.

9. Marcia Pointon, *Hanging the Head: Portraiture and Social Formation in Eighteenth-Century England* (New Haven, CT: Yale University Press, 1993), 53–78; Dow, *Arts and Crafts in New England*, 36–37, 20. See also Brandon Brame Fortune, "Portraits of Virtue and Genius: Pantheons of Worthies and Public Portraiture in the Early American Republic, 1780–1820" (Ph.D. diss., University of North Carolina, Chapel Hill, 1987), 1–33.

10. Joan Dolmetsch, "Prints in Colonial America: Supply and Demand," in *Prints in and of America to 1850*, ed. John D. Morse (Charlottesville: University of Virginia Press, 1970), 53–74; E. McSherry Fowble, *Two Centuries of Prints in America, 1680–1880: A Selective Catalogue of the Winterthur Museum Collection* (Charlottesville: University of Virginia Press, 1987); Fowble, *To Please Every Taste*.

11. Dolmetsch, "Prints in Colonial America," 53; Dow, *Arts and Crafts in New England*, 34, 20.

12. Cadwalader Colden, quoted in Arthur S. Marks, "The Statue of King George III in New York and the Iconology of Regicide," *American Art Journal* 13:3 (Summer 1981), 61–82; the quote is on 61.

Other accounts of the statue and its destruction include McConville, *King's Three Faces*, 309–310; and Kenneth Silverman, *A Cultural History of the American Revolution: Painting, Music, Literature, and the Theatre in the Colonies and the United States from the Treaty of Paris to the Inauguration of George Washington, 1763–1798* (New York: Thomas Y. Crowell, 1976), 90, 324.

13. On Richardson's influence in Anglo-America, see Margaretta M. Lovell, *Art in a Season of Revolution: Painters, Artisans, and Patrons in Early America* (Philadelphia: University of Pennsylvania Press, 2005), 11; and Richard H. Saunders and Ellen G. Miles, *American Colonial Portraits, 1700–1776* (Washington, DC: Smithsonian Institution Press, 1987), 45.

14. The defaced portrait is on display in Thyatira Presbyterian Church in Salisbury, North Carolina.

15. Silverman, *Cultural History*, 431; Longmore, *Invention of George Washington*, 98, 210; Barry Schwartz, *George Washington: The Making of an American Symbol* (New York: Free Press, 1987), 37; Margaret Brown Klapthor and Howard Alexander Morrison, *George Washington: A Figure upon the Stage* (Washington, DC: National Museum of American History, Smithsonian Institution, 1982), 18–21.

16. Washington Irving, "Rip Van Winkle, A Posthumous Writing of Diedrich Knickerbocker" (1819) (http://www.bartleby.com/195/4.html). Marcus Cunliffe makes a complementary argument in "The Two Georges: The President and the King," *American Studies International* 24:2 (Oct. 1986), 53–73.

17. See, e.g., Carrie Rebora Barratt and Ellen G. Miles, *Gilbert Stuart* (New Haven, CT: Yale University Press; New York: Metropolitan Museum of Art, 2004), 133–191; William M. S. Rasmussen and Robert S. Tilton, *George Washington: The Man Behind the Myths* (Charlottesville: University of Virginia Press, 1999), 216–217; Ellen G. Miles, *George and Martha Washington: Portraits from the Presidential Years* (Washington, DC: Smithsonian Institution; Charlottesville: University of Virginia Press, 1999).

18. On the Lansdowne portrait and its copies, see Barratt and Miles, *Gilbert Stuart*, 166–183. Marianna Jenkins, in *The State Portrait: Its Origin and Evolution* (New York: College Art Association, 1947), discusses the conventions of state portraiture. It is possible that the copy of Ramsay's George III and Queen Charlotte displayed in the mansion of Virginia's royal governor was Washington's first exposure to state portraiture; see Hood, *Governor's Palace*, 184–185, for speculations on the effect of Ramsay's paintings. See also *Journals of the Continental Congress, 1774–1789*, ed. Worthington C. Ford et al., 34 vols. (Washington, DC, 1904–1937), 24:494–495; 29:869. For recent examination of the political and intellectual anxieties prompted by the relationship between the presidency and kingship following Washington's election, see Kathleen Bartaloni-Tuazon, *For Fear of an Elective King: George Washington and the Presidential Title Controversy* (Ithaca, NY: Cornell University Press, 2014).

19. Phoebe Lloyd Jacobs, "John James Barralet and the Apotheosis of George Washington," *Winterthur Portfolio* 12 (1977), 115–137; the quote is on 123. For similar arguments about the problems posed by republican representation that cast it as a technical dilemma for artists, see Wendy C. Reaves, *George Washington, An American Icon: The Eighteenth-Century Graphic Portraits* (Washington, DC: Smithsonian Traveling Exhibition Service and the National Portrait Gallery, 1982). On the European flavor of American classicism, see Caroline Winterer, *Mirror of Antiquity: American Women and the Classical Tradition, 1750–1900* (Ithaca, NY: Cornell University Press, 2007), esp. 102–141.

20. Reaves, *George Washington*, is the authoritative source on Washington's print portraits before 1800. On the European likenesses, see Reaves, *George Washington*, 18–26. Art historians who focus on portraiture as a genre have generally been preoccupied with the accuracy of different Washington portraits and have overlooked the extent to which an inauthentic or merely inaccurate Washington functioned just as well abroad as an authentic one.

21. In this sense, the likenesses of Washington that circulated in Europe at the end of the eighteenth century operated much like the paintings and prints of the "four Indian kings" who had taken England by storm almost a hundred years earlier and who symbolically incorporated America into European power structures. The best discussion of the Indian kings is Eric Hinderaker, "The 'Four Indian Kings' and the Imaginative Construction of the British Empire," *William and Mary Quarterly*, 3rd ser., 53:3 (Jul. 1996), 487–526; pictorial representations of the "kings" are discussed on 505–517.

22. Charles-Guillaume-Frederic Dumas to George Washington, May 28, 1785, in *Papers of George Washington Confederation Series*, ed. W. W. Abbott, 6 vols. (Charlottesville: University of Virginia Press, 1992), 3:23 (hereafter cited as PGWCS).

23. Lillian B. Miller, ed., *The Selected Papers of Charles Willson Peale and His Family*, vol. 1, *Charles Willson Peale: Artist in Revolutionary America, 1735–1791* (New Haven, CT: Yale University Press, 1983), 330–331. Peale's portrait fully realized its diplomatic subtext. Gérard is posed beside two female figures, representing France and the United States; the Pennsylvania State House appears in the background.

24. Martha Elena Rojas, "Diplomatic Letters: The Conduct and Culture of United States Foreign Affairs in the Early Republic" (Ph.D. diss., Stanford University, 2003), 13–49; the quote is from 32–33. Although Rojas is concerned with the exchange of texts rather than objects, my discussion is indebted to her analysis of diplomatic cultures. On diplomatic portrait exchanges in a different context, see Natasha Eaton, "Between Mimesis and Alterity: Art, Gift, and Diplomacy in Colonial India, 1770–1800," *Comparative Studies in Society and History* 46:4 (Oct. 2004), 816–844.

25. Comte de Solm to George Washington, Aug. 4, 1785, in *PGWCS*, 3:172; Rochambeau to George Washington, Sept. 9, 1784, in ibid., 1:71.

26. Order of Congress, Jul. 15, 1779, in *Journals of the Continental Congress*, 14:736–739. On diplomatic protocol as an index of power, see Benjamin H. Irvin, *Clothed in Robes of Sovereignty: The Continental Congress and the People Out of Doors* (New York: Oxford University Press, 2011), 165–202.

27. On Miralles's career, see Light Townsend Cummins, *Spanish Observers and the American Revolution, 1775–1783* (Baton Rouge: Louisiana State University Press, 1991), 115–167; and Helen Matzke McCadden, "Juan de Miralles and the American Revolution," *Americas* 29:3 (Jan. 1973), 359–375.

28. Miller, *Selected Papers of Charles Willson Peale and His Family*, vol. 1, *Artist in Revolutionary America*, 303–304; McCadden, "Juan de Miralles," 362.

29. Lillian B. Miller, "The Legacy," in *The Peale Family: Creation of a Legacy, 1770–1870*, ed. Lillian B. Miller (Washington, DC: Abbeville, 1996), 41–97; the quote is on 65.

30. Reaves, *George Washington*, 88.

31. See, e.g., Marcus Cunliffe, *George Washington, Man and Monument* (Boston: Little, Brown, 1958); Wills, *Cincinnatus*; Schwartz, *George Washington*; Longmore, *Invention of George Washington*; Joseph J. Ellis, *His Excellency: George Washington* (New York: Knopf, 2004); and François Furstenberg, *In the Name of the Father: Washington's Legacy, Slavery, and the Making of a Nation* (New York: Penguin, 2006).

32. Quoted in Longmore, *Invention of George Washington*, 176. On the wider purposes of emulation in the early American republic, see William Huntting Howell, *Against Self-Reliance: The Arts of Dependence in the Early United States* (Philadelphia: University of Pennsylvania Press, 2015).

33. Mason L. Weems, *The Life of Washington*, ed. Marcus Cunliffe (Cambridge, MA: Belknap Press of Harvard University Press, 1962), 2, 169; George Washington Parke Custis, *Recollections and Private Memoirs of Washington, by his adopted son, a memoir of the author, by his daughter, and illustrative and explanatory notes by Benson J. Lossing* (Philadelphia: J. W. Bradley, 1861), 262–263.

34. Custis, *Recollections*, 463–464.

35. Quoted in Fortune, "Portraits of Virtue and Genius," 92.

36. The forensic reconstruction is described in detail in Jeffrey H. Schwartz, "Putting a Face on the First President," *Scientific American* (Feb. 2006), 84–91.

37. Ellis, *His Excellency*, 11–12, 44–45, 68–69; Ron Chernow, *Washington, a Life* (New York: Penguin, 2010), 29–30, 121–122, 468; Richard Brookhiser, *Founding Father: Rediscovering George Washington* (New York: Free Press, 1996), 111; italics in the original. This preoccupation has not gone unnoticed. See Jill Lepore, "His Highness: George Washington Scales New Heights," *New Yorker*, Sept. 27, 2010; and Michiko Kakutani, "Washington's Standing in Locker Room Line-Up," *New York Times*, Feb. 6, 1996.

38. William Spohn Baker, comp., *Early Sketches of George Washington: Reprinted with Biographical and Bibliographical Notes* (Philadelphia: Lippincott, 1893), 26–27, 31, 53.

39. Abigail Adams to John Adams, Jul. 26, 1775, in *The Adams Family Correspondence*, ed. L. H. Butterfield, 11 vols. (Cambridge, MA: Belknap Press of Harvard University Press, 1963), 1:246.

40. Baker, *Early Sketches*, 78, 77.

41. *Memory of Washington: Comprising a Sketch of His Life and Character; and National Testimonials of Respect* (Newport, RI: Oliver Farnsworth, 1800), 8, 9.

42. Custis, *Recollections*, 431, 488, 492. Comparable accounts appear throughout the memorial compendia that were published following Washington's death. See, e.g., *Memory of Washington*; *Washington's Political Legacies* (Boston: printed for John Russell and John West, 1800); *The Washingtoniana* (Lancaster, PA: printed and sold by William Hamilton, 1802). William Spohn Baker's *Early Sketches* offers a preliminary bibliographic history of each "sketch," making it possible to trace circulation and in some cases determine when a manuscript description appeared in print.

43. On ritual and civic culture, see, e.g., Irvin, *Clothed in Robes of Sovereignty*; Sandra Moats, *Celebrating the Republic: Presidential Ceremony and Popular Sovereignty* (DeKalb: Northern Illinois University Press, 2010); Leora Auslander, *Cultural Revolutions: Everyday Life and Politics in Britain, North America, and France* (Berkeley: University of California Press, 2009); David Waldstreicher, *In the Midst of Perpetual Fetes: The Making of American Nationalism, 1776–1820* (Chapel Hill: University of North Carolina Press for the Omohundro Institute of Early American History and Culture, 1997); Simon P. Newman, *Parades and the Politics of the Street: Festive Culture in the Early American Republic* (Philadelphia: University of Pennsylvania Press, 1997); and Ann Fairfax Withington, *Toward a More Perfect Union: Virtue and the Formation of American Republics* (New York: Oxford University Press, 1991).

44. This summary draws on the accounts in Terry W. Lipscomb, *South Carolina in 1791: George Washington's Southern Tour* (Columbia: South Carolina Department of Archives and History, 1993); *George Washington and Delaware* (Dover: Public Archives Commission of Delaware, 1932); Howard W. Preston, *Washington's Visits to Rhode Island, Gathered from Contemporary Accounts* (Providence, RI: Oxford, 1932); Archibald Henderson, *Washington's Southern Tour, 1791* (Boston: Houghton Mifflin, 1923); and "Journal of William Loughton Smith, 1790–1791," *Proceedings of the Massachusetts Historical Society*, 3rd ser., 51 (Oct. 1917), 35–39. See also Moats, *Celebrating the Republic*.

45. "Account of the Preparations at Gray's Ferry," *Columbian Magazine*, May 1789; Silverman, *Cultural History*, 605.

46. On Washington's Boston visit, see *Massachusetts Centinel*, Oct. 28, 1789. Charleston's celebration differed from others more in degree than kind. For a detailed description of the extravaganza, see Henderson, *Washington's Southern Tour*, 144–198; the description of the Exchange Building is on 188. See also Lipscomb, *South Carolina in 1791*; Preston, *Washington's Visits*, 17.

47. Quoted in Thomas E. V. Smith, *The City of New York in the Year of Washington's Inauguration* (New York: Anson D. F. Randolph, 1889).

48. Lipscomb, *South Carolina in 1791*, 16; Elizabeth Montgomery, *Reminiscences of Wilmington, in Familiar Village Tales Ancient and New* (Philadelphia: T. K. Collins, 1851), 110–111.

49. "Extract of a Letter from a Lady in Charleston to Her Friend in This City," *Connecticut Courant*, Jun. 6, 1791.

50. "Account of the PRESIDENT'S Reception at Trenton," *Massachusetts Magazine*, May 15, 1789. Apparently, the story made a vivid impression on readers, for contributors were still referring to it six months later; see "The Dreamer. No. X," *Massachusetts Magazine*, Nov. 11, 1789. News of the encounter may well have spread south to inspire the welcome prepared by Washington's former aide-de-camp, Benjamin Smith of North Carolina, in 1791. When the presidential party reached the river landing at Smith's Belvidere plantation, it was met by thirteen white-gowned young women who represented the original colonies; the women preceded the president on the path toward the mansion, strewing flowers along his path. Henderson, *Washington's Southern Tour*, 119. For more examples of tears, see Smith, *City of New York*, 222.

51. Silverman, *Cultural History*, 607; Theodore Sedgwick to Pamela Dwight Sedgwick, Feb. 23 1791, box 5, folder 11, Sedgwick II Papers, Massachusetts Historical Society; Elizabeth Mankin Kornhauser, *Ralph Early: The Face of the Young Republic* (New Haven, CT: Yale University Press, 1991), 140.

52. Cf. Eric Thomas Slauter, *The State as a Work of Art: The Cultural Origins of the Constitution* (Chicago: University of Chicago Press, 2009). I am indebted to Slauter's analysis of Federalists'

aestheticization of the Constitution. On the Cult of Washington that emerged during his first administration, see Jeffrey L. Pasley, *The First Presidential Contest: 1796 and the Founding of American Democracy* (Lawrence: University Press of Kansas, 2013), 137. The standard account of the relationship between early partisanship and nationalism remains David Waldstreicher's *In the Midst of Perpetual Fetes.*

53. Quoted in Silverman, *Cultural History*, 428. On authentic portrait prints, see Baker, *Engraved Portraits*; and Reaves, *George Washington.*

54. Reaves, *George Washington*, 35; Dorinda Evans, "Survival and Transformation: The Colonial Portrait in the Federal Era," in *The Portrait in Eighteenth-Century America*, ed. Ellen G. Miles (Newark: University of Delaware Press, 1993), 123–137.

55. Johann Caspar Lavater, *Essays on Physiognomy Designed to Promote Knowledge and the Love of Mankind . . .* 3 vols. (London: printed for John Murray 1789), 3:435–437. Lavater's thoughts on Washington and Franklin were reprinted in the *Columbian Magazine* in March 1788. On Lavater's influence within the United States and the application of physiognomy to early national portraiture, see Christopher J. Lukasik, *Discerning Characters: The Culture of Appearance in Early America* (Philadelphia: University of Pennsylvania Press, 2011), 32–54, 121–152. If this preoccupation with physiognomic accuracy was especially in regard to representations, it was not limited to him. On efforts to capture precise images of the founding generation, see Fortune, "Portraits of Virtue and Genius," 183–186. Trish Loughran frames this issue as an attempt to realize the Federalist fantasy of an extended republic in *The Republic in Print: Print Culture in the Age of U.S. Nation-Building, 1770–1870* (New York: Columbia University Press, 2007), 161–169, 197–221.

56. (New York) *Daily Advertiser*, Sept. 24, 1787, quoted in Kelby, *Notes on American Artists*, 31–32; *Pennsylvania Packet*, Mar. 3, 1790, quoted in Reaves, *George Washington*, 36; (Pennsylvania) *Commercial Advertiser*, Jun. 27, 1800, quoted in Reaves, *George Washington*, 60; *Philadelphia Gazette*, Jan. 1, 1800, quoted in Reaves, *George Washington*, 66.

57. Rembrandt Peale, *Portrait of Washington* (Philadelphia: s.n., 1824). On Peale and *Patriae Pater*, see Wendy Bellion, *Citizen Spectator: Art, Illusion, and Visual Perception in Early National America* (Chapel Hill: University of North Carolina Press for the Omohundro Institute for Early American History and Culture, 2011), 287–327; and William Oedel, "The Rewards of Virtue: Rembrandt Peale and Social Reform," in Miller, *Peale Family*, 163–167.

58. Richard Peters to Rembrandt Peale, Jun. 24, 1824, and General Daniel Udree to Rembrandt Peale, May 4, 1824, in Peale, *Portrait of Washington*, 16, 12–13.

59. Stuart's attitudes are related in William Dunlap, *History of the Rise and Progress of the Arts of Design in the United States*, ed. Rita Weiss, 3 vols. (1834; repr., New York: Dover, 1969), 1:198–199. Dunlap's own sighting of Washington is described in ibid., 252. On Washington copies as cash, see William Dunlap to his wife, Jan. 1, 1806, quoted in Cunningham, *Popular Images*, 16.

60. Leora Auslander distinguishes between commemorative objects that were commercially and domestically produced, emphasizing the significance of the latter and paying scant attention to the former in *Cultural Revolutions*, 103–108.

61. See, e.g., Cunningham, *Popular Images*; Reaves, *George Washington*. On the acceleration of tributes to Washington, including those that took the form of visual and material culture, see Gerald E. Kahler, *The Long Farewell: Americans Mourn the Death of George Washington* (Charlottesville: University of Virginia Press, 2008); and Phoebe Lloyd Jacobs, "John James Barralet and the Apotheosis of George Washington," *Winterthur Portfolio* 12 (1977), 115–137.

62. This summary is based on searches of newspaper advertisements between 1780 and 1830 in America's Historic Newspapers and on searches of the collections database at the Winterthur Museum, Gardens, and Library.

63. See, e.g., Cunningham, *Popular Images*; Reaves, *George Washington*; Jacobs, "John James Barralet," 12; Christina H. Nelson, "Transfer-Printed Creamware and Pearlware for the American Market," *Winterthur Portfolio* 15:2 (Summer 1980), 93–115.

64. See, e.g., Cunningham, *Popular Images.*

65. For information on print sizes and costs, see Reaves, *George Washington*; Kelby, *Notes on American Artists*; Alfred Coxe Prime, ed., *The Arts and Crafts in Philadelphia, Maryland, and South*

Carolina, 2 vols. (New York: Da Capo, 1969); and Rita Susswein Gottesman, *The Arts and Crafts in New York: Advertisements and News Items from New York City Newspapers*, 3 vols. (New York: printed for the New-York Historical Society, 1938). On medals, see Cunningham, *Popular Images*, 165–166.

66. "Columbian Museum," *Columbian Centinel*, Dec. 12, 1797; "The Portrait of His Excellency the President of the United States," *Porcupine's Gazette*, Jul. 16, 1798. Smith's advertisements ran for a year; he also offered a sample portrait to Washington himself.

67. Cunningham, *Popular Images*, 180–186. Cunningham (180) notes one detailed description of *The Entry*, a caricature satirizing the pomp that attended Washington's inauguration and the only reference to a caricature of Washington created during his presidency; there are no known extant copies of *The Entry*.

68. The following discussion is based on "Day v. Jarvis," *American Law Journal* 1 (1808), 175–176. Emphases in the original. For a fuller discussion of the case, see H. E. Dickson, "Day vs. Jarvis," *Pennsylvania Magazine of History and Biography* 63:2 (Apr. 1939), 169–188.

69. Unfortunately, because Jarvis's deposition was ex parte, it could not be read aloud in court and never entered the court records; therefore it is impossible to determine what the "test of criticism" consisted of.

70. Andrew W. Robertson, "Voting Rites and Voting Acts: Electioneering 1790–1820," in *Beyond the Founders: New Approaches to the Political History of the Early Republic*, ed. Jeffrey L. Pasley, Andrew W. Robertson, and David Waldstreicher (Chapel Hill: University of North Carolina Press, 2004), 67. Jeffrey L. Pasley's marvelously refreshing *First Presidential Contest*, which pays close attention to the construction of candidates' images and messages with an eye toward the public, is the exception to Robertson's rule. For suggestive studies that examine the democratization of political culture in the early republic with an eye toward electoral mechanics, see Alan Taylor, " 'The Art of Hook & Snivey': Political Culture in Upstate New York During the 1790s," *Journal of American History* 79:4 (Mar. 1993), 1371–1396; "From Fathers to Friends of the People: Political Personas in the Early Republic," *Journal of the Early Republic* 11:4 (Winter 1991), 465–491; and Ronald P. Formisano, *The Transformation of Political Culture: Massachusetts Parties, 1790s–1840s* (New York: Oxford University Press, 1983). Although its ambitions extend well beyond the concerns sketched here, John L. Brooke's *Columbia Rising: Civil Life on the Upper Hudson from the Revolution to the Age of Jackson* (Chapel Hill: University of North Carolina Press for the Omohundro Institute of Early American History and Culture, 2013) offers a sweeping account of the origins and transformation of political culture in the early republic.

71. M. J. Heale, *The Presidential Quest: Candidates and Images in American Political Culture, 1787–1852* (London: Longman, 1982), 2–3.

72. On the role of the press in partisan politics, see Pasley, *First Presidential Contest*; and Jeffrey L. Pasley, *The Tyranny of Printers: Newspaper Politics in the Early American Republic* (Charlottesville: University of Virginia Press, 2001).

73. George Washington to Francis Hopkinson, May 16, 1785, in PGWCS 2:561–562; George Washington to Henry Lee, Jul. 3, 1792, in *Papers of George Washington, Presidential Series*, ed. Philander D. Chase (Charlottesville: University of Virginia Press, 2001), 10:515–516.

74. Cunningham, *Popular Images*, 16.

75. Cf. Cathy Matson and Peter Onuf, "Toward a Republican Empire: Interest and Ideology in Revolutionary America," *American Quarterly* 37:4 (Autumn 1985), 496–531, on the privileging of production over consumption in early national political economy.

76. Delaplaine is quoted in Wendy Wick Reaves, *American Portrait Prints: Proceedings of the Tenth Annual American Print Conference* (Charlottesville: University Press of Virginia, 1984), 40.

77. George Washington, "Farewell Address, 1796," Avalon Project, Yale University Law School (http://avalon.law.yale.edu/18th_century/washing.asp; accessed Apr. 24, 2015).

EPILOGUE

1. For scholarly discussions of Lafayette's tour, see esp. Sarah J. Purcell, *Sealed with Blood: War, Sacrifice, and Memory in Revolutionary America* (Philadelphia: University of Pennsylvania Press, 2002), 171–209; Lloyd Kramer, *Lafayette in Two Worlds: Public Cultures and Personal Identities in an*

Age of Revolutions (Chapel Hill: University of North Carolina Press, 1996), 185–226; Stanley J. Idzerda, Anne C. Loveland, and Marc H. Miller, eds., *Lafayette, Hero of Two Worlds: The Art and Pageantry of His Farewell Tour of America, 1824–1825* (Flushing, NY: Queens Museum, 1989). For discussions of Lafayette's return that attend to visual and material culture, see Zara Anishanslin, "'This Is the Skin of a Whit Man': Visual Memory and Materiality of Violence in the American Revolution," in *The Revolution Reborn*, ed. Michael Zuckerman (Philadelphia: University of Pennsylvania Press, forthcoming); and Anishanslin, "Lafayette's Farewell Tour and the Material Memory of the Revolution," unpublished paper. Contemporary newspaper accounts of the tour are collected and annotated in Edgar Ewing Brandon, *Lafayette, Guest of the Nation; A Contemporary Account of the Triumphal Tour of the General Lafayette Through the United States in 1824–1825, as Reported by the Local Newspapers*, 3 vols. (Oxford, OH: Oxford Historical Press, 1950–1957).

2. Brandon, *Lafayette, Guest of the Nation*, 1:66, 117, 46.

3. Ibid., 2:48. See also William Ogden Wheeler, comp., *The Ogden Family in America, Elizabethtown Branch, and Their English Ancestry* (Philadelphia: printed by J. B. Lippincott for private distribution, 1907), 107. I am indebted to Stephen Davidson, a public historian active in the Loyalist Research Network and Upper Empire Loyalists' Association of Canada, for additional background on Ogden.

4. Brandon, *Lafayette, Guest of the Nation*, 3:52, 1:247, 86–87; Eliza Susan Quincy, "Journal of Lafayette's visit to Boston, (1824–1835)," 18, in Quincy, Wendell, Holmes and Upham Family Papers, Massachusetts Historical Society.

5. Marc H. Miller, "Lafayette's Farewell Tour and American Art," in Idzerda et al., *Lafayette, Hero of Two Worlds*, 145–194; the quote is on 145.

6. See, e.g., *The order of exercises in the chapel of Transylvania University: a collection of original pieces in honour of the arrival of General La Fayette. . . .* (Lexington, KY: [s.n.], May, 1825); *Honour to the Brave; Merited Praise to the Disinterested: A Description of the Grand Fete given Given at Washington Hall by the Citizens of France to Gen. La Fayette* (New York: G. F. Hopkins, 1824).

7. Brandon, *Lafayette, Guest of the Nation*, 1:207, 2:67, 3:57, 147.

8. Ibid., 2:38–40.

9. See, e.g., Purcell, *Sealed with Blood*, 179–180, 190–192; Kramer, *Lafayette in Two Worlds*, 218–219, 220–226.

10. The best overview of the visual and material culture associated with Lafayette's return is Miller, "Lafayette's Farewell Tour and American Art." My discussion of the range of artifacts produced to honor Lafayette is based on the remarkable Lafayette Memorabilia Collection, David Bishop Skillman Library, Lafayette College, Easton, PA. See also Purcell, *Sealed with Blood*, 181–186.

11. See entries for Sept. 3, 1824, and Sept. 10, 1824, in Marquis de Lafayette Reception Committee Papers 1824, Historical Society of Pennsylvania (hereafter cited as HSP).

12. Ongoing negotiations between Rembrandt Peale and the Committee are recorded in Marquis de Lafayette Reception Committee Papers 1824, HSP, Aug.–Sept. 1824, passim. Benjamin Franklin Peale's request was noted in ibid., Sept. 23, 1824. It is not clear from the records whether or not the reception committee paid the museum to compensate it for lost business.

13. Noel Robertson to Helen Robertson, Jul. 25, 1825, Robertson Family Papers, HSP; [?] Stansom to William Tilghman, Oct. 30, 1824, William Tilghman Papers #659, HSP. On religion and taste in the early republic, see Richard L. Bushman, *The Refinement of America: Persons, Houses, Cities* (New York: Vintage, 1993), 313–352.

Index

Page numbers in italics refer to figures.

Bartram, John, 131
Beach, Clementina, 39
Beach, Mary, 43
beauty, 4, 38, 54, 128, 151; linked to visual perception, 6–7, 23–25
Beck, George, 149–150
Bell, John, 213, 214
belles lettres, 4, 65, 108
Bentley, Rev. William, 50, 188, 190–192
Bethlehem Female Seminary, 20, 26, 39, 42, 45, 52
Bingham, Anne Willing, 126, 128
Birch, William, 147, 149, 152, 156, 157
Blacks, 102–103, 111. See also race
Blair, Hugh, 1, 4, 6, 23–25
blindness, 69–70, 73, 79, 98
Blue Jacket, 189
Bonaparte, Joseph, 146
Boston, 95, 152; during American Revolution, 167–168; art displayed in, 67, 68, 167, 197; art galleries in, 67, 85; artists in, 62, 68, 74–75, 76, 83, 85, 90; art market in, 83, 85, 198–199, 201; art training in, 63; museums in, 56, 59, 87, 174, 182, 184, 186, 227; George Washington in, 216; waxworks in, 163, 175–176
Boucher, Jonathan, 213
Bowditch, Nathaniel, 238
Bowen, Daniel: as museum keeper, 160, 161, 169, 171, 174, 175, 178, 184–185, 227; museum mentioned in *The Coquette*, 1, 161, 193. See also Columbian Museum
Brace, John P., 22, 36, 52
Bristol Academy, 19
British monarchs, representations of, 167, 197–200, 201, 202, 204. See also George III
Burke, Edmund, 4, 23
Bush Hill, 121, 122, 124, 133, 139, 141
Bushman, Richard, 157

Cadwalader, John, 125
Cahill, Edward, 5
capitalism, 7, 194
Causes of the Variety of Complexion (Smith), 107
Champlain, Eliza, 77, 80, 81, 90, 113, 118; difficulties earning a living, 83, 84, 88–89
Champlain, Elizabeth (Betsey) Way, 12, 65, 94; as connoisseur, 77–78, 81; difficulties earning a living, 92, 95–96; "Flattery," 108–109; refines painting technique, 114–115, plate 10; self-portrait, 9, 97–98, 117–118, plate 3
Champlain, George, 93
Charleston (South Carolina), 208; art displayed in, 167, 168; art market in, 83–85, George Washington in, 216–217
Cheever, Henry, 1, 2, 24, 25, 26
Chernow, Ron, 213
Chester, Caroline, 14, 15, 16, 24, 36–38
Chew, Benjamin, 127
Chovet, Abraham, 166, 171
Christ Healing the Sick in the Temple (West), 68

civic celebrations, 5, 193, 196, 214; and July 4th, 33, 56, 161–162, 166; and Lafayette, 237–240, 241, 242
Clark, Ann W., 52–53
class, 12, 15, 77, 94, 106; artists and, 58, 77; education and, 16–21, 48–50; laboring class, 20, 107, 158, 241; middle class, 4, 6, 12, 82, 94, 97, 105, 147
Clermont Seminary, 41, 51
color, 61–62, 65; ability to perceive, 70, 72–73, 78, 81; complexion and, 99–100, 107–108, 111–115; miniature portraits and, 105–106
The Columbiad (Barlow), 168
Columbian Museum, 1, 2, 159, 161, 171, 182, 184, 185, *187*. See also Bowen, David
Columbianum, 61, 147
commodities, 7, 9, 12, 53; art as, 57, 77, 109; British, 8–9, 157–158, 193, 244; ideas as, 49; Lafayette depicted on, 238–239; George Washington depicted on, 196, 226–237
connoisseurs and connoisseurship, 7–8
connoisseurship, 6, 50, 51, 225; compared to taste, 7–8; Ethan Allan Greenwood and, 56, 66–68; William Hamilton and, 143, 146; Way Champlain family and, 77–82
consumer market, 7, 9, 57, 82, 201, 233
consumers, 9, 10, 147; of art, 88, 98, 223, 228; women as, 97. See also patrons
consumption, 53–54, 156, 196, 225; and political culture, 231–234, 244
Continental Army, 124, 125, 201, 202, 207, 238; and battle at Trenton (New Jersey), 217, 240; George Washington and, 211
Continental Congress, 166, 204, 206
Conversations upon the art of miniature painting (Kendrick), 110, 111–112
Cope, Thomas, 139, 146
Copley, John Singleton, 29, 30, 61, 62, 69, 82, 85
The Coquette (Foster), 1–2, 161
Cornwallis, Gen. Charles, 125, 202, 240
Cosway, Richard, 106
country houses, 120–121. See also Birch, William; Leasowes; Stourhead; Stowe; The Woodlands
The Country Seats of the United States (Birch), 147, 149, *149*
A Course of Lectures on Drawing, Painting and Engraving (Craig), 113
The Court of Death (Peale), 80, 85
Cowper, William, 24, 42, 52
Cox, James, 41
Cult of Washington, 225
Custis, George Washington Parke, 212, 214
Cutler, George Younglove, 36, *37*
Cutler, Manasseh, 178–179

Danaë Receiving Jupiter in a Shower of Gold (Wertmuller), 137
Dartmouth College, 55, 91
Day, Augustus, 228–231, 233

Acknowledgments

Republic of Taste has been a joy to work on, which is a good thing given that I have worked on it for a very long time. Its parts took shape as a series of talks and shorter essays. I am grateful for the generous feedback I received at Rider University, Lehigh University, Texas A&M University, the University of Delaware, and the University of Rochester and at seminars and symposia sponsored by the American Antiquarian Society, the McNeil Center for Early American Studies (MCEAS), the Omohundro Institute of Early American History and Culture (OIEAHC), the Huntington Library, Yale University Art Gallery, and Oregon State University. I am especially grateful to the larger community of Early Americanists who listened, queried, and pushed me at meetings of the American Studies Association, the OIEAHC , the Society of Early Americanists, and especially the Society for Historians of the Early American Republic. Portions of this book appeared in *New Views of New England: Studies in Material and Visual Culture, 1680–1830*; *Reading Women: Literacy, Authorship, and Culture in the Atlantic World, 1500–1800*; and *Common-place*.

Republic of Taste garnered a good deal of financial support, all the more remarkable given the budget constraints that confront libraries, museums, and universities. I am therefore especially grateful for the research funding extended by the American Antiquarian Society, the Library Company of Philadelphia, the McNeil Center for the Humanities, the National Endowment for the Humanities, the Winterthur Museum and Library, and the Oklahoma Humanities Council. This external support has been supplemented by generous contributions from the University of Oklahoma's History Department, College of Arts and Sciences, and vice president for research. As the book moved to press, the University of Oklahoma's provost, Kyle Harper; vice president for research, Kelvin Droegemeier; dean of the College of Arts and Sciences, Kelly Damphousse; and chair of the History Department, James Hart, partnered to offset the book's production costs. Special thanks are due to Ramsay MacMullen, who graciously allowed reproduction and publication of Elizabeth Way Champlain's paintings.

Research requires time, money, and travel—but any historian will tell you that getting to the sources is only half the battle. Once you are there, librarians, archivists, and curators make all the difference. I thus owe a good deal to the staffs of the Connecticut Historical Society, the Massachusetts Historical Society, the Boston Athenaeum, the Historical Society of Pennsylvania, the New-York Historical Society, and the University of Oklahoma's Bizzell Library. I offer special thanks to Jim Green, Connie King, Phil Lapsansky, and Nicole Joniec at the Library Company; to Gretchen Buggeln, Jeanne Solensky, Emily Guthrie, Rosemarie Krill, and Kasey Grier, who enriched two idyllic fellowships at Winterthur; and to John Hench, Paul Erickson, Tom Knoles, Marie Lamoreaux, Laura Wasowicz, and especially Gigi Barnhill at the American Antiquarian Society. I am particularly indebted to Caroline Sloat, formerly the director of book publications at the American Antiquarian Society, who dragged me out of the reading room one dreary February day and took me to Old Sturbridge Village to meet curator and historian Lynne Zacek Basset. The two of them took me "backstage" and let me see (and touch!) the kinds of things I wanted to write about; nothing has been the same since.

I generally characterize myself as a lucky person and nowhere is my luck more pronounced than when I begin to count my colleagues both at home and abroad. At the University of Oklahoma, Robert A. Griswold and James S. Hart have been exemplary department chairs, stalwart allies, and true friends; my fellow faculty are as nice as they are smart. History Department staff Barbara Million, Rhonda George, Christa Seedorf, Kelly Kunc Guinn, Janie Adkins, Tanya Miller, and Bobby Collings pushed the paper and juggled the balls demanded by teaching, research, and travel. Superb advice was proffered at one point or another by Angela Woollacott, Pat Cohen, Bob Shalhope, and Paul Gilje. I offer special and heartfelt thanks to Trudy Powers, Catherine Preus, Paul Erickson, Matt Bahar, and Bryan Rindfleisch (for their work on *Common-place*) and to Kate Tyler Wall and Jayson Porter (for their work on the *Journal of the Early Republic*). More times than I can count, they took care of business so that I didn't have to; quite simply, their efforts made this book possible. The final stages of writing and the endless stages of revision benefited from the scrappy crew of writers who congregate at #TheGraftonLine. Like so many others, I signed on to L. D. Burnett's Facebook group for the word counts and stayed for the community, the counsel, and the hashtags.

I was fortunate to begin work on this book around the same time that a number of scholars far more gifted than I were also turning their attention to visual and material culture. For their conversation, insights, and example, I thank Linzy Brekke-Aloise, Zara Anishanslin, Wendy Bellion, Martin Bruckner, Amy Hudson Henderson, Kate Haulman, Hunt Howell, David Jaffee, Chris

Lukasik, Marla Miller, Eric Slauter, and Susan Stabile. I am every bit as grateful for the community cultivated by Dan Richter and administered by Amy Baxter-Bellamy at Penn's MCEAS. This book became real, and I became far smarter, as a consequence of an MCEAS postdoc in 2006–2007. It was a glorious year, made all the better by the comradeship of Brian Connolly, Yvie Fabella, Charlie Foy, Candice Harrison, Hunt Howell, Jess Lepler, Heather Miyano Kopelson, Michelle McDonald, Roderick McDonald, Katie Paugh, Yvette Piggush, Jared Richman, George Boudreau, the late Dallett Hemphill, and the other gifted and engaged scholars who have helped make 3355 Woodland Walk the very best place to think about all things early American.

Given that both reading and imagination play key roles in *Republic of Taste*, it is not surprising that it was written with three imagined readers very much in mind. David Jaffee, Mary Kelley, and David Shields may not be pleased with the result but they must surely be relieved to see it finally finished. A few hardy souls served as more than inspiration; they served as real readers. This book is much better for the sharp eyes and sharper minds of David Chappell, Brian Connolly, Paul Gilje, Heidi Brayman Hackel, Rich Hamerla, Kate Haulman, Hunt Howell, David Jaffee, David Levy, Tod Kelly, Marla Miller, Josh Piker, David Shields, and Caroline Winterer, who read and critiqued portions of the manuscript. This book is also much the better for its connection to the University of Pennsylvania Press. My editor, Peter Agree, saw potential in the project before almost anyone else did. I am deeply grateful for the efforts of Ann Fabian, Dan Richter, and the anonymous reader for the press who read the entire manuscript, tempering justice with mercy. I am grateful, too, for Dan's lesson in the fine art of the table of contents. I am delighted to offer thanks here to the people at Penn Press who turned my virtual text into an artifact: Amanda Ruffner, the press's production staff, and most especially Erica Ginsburg, who has been a pillar of patience and good sense.

That the years spent working on this book were so much fun is due in no small part to the folks who distracted me from it. Stephanie Patterson, Jaime Parker, and Kim Jackson taught me a thing or two about holding body and soul together. The "AOD" welcomed me with open arms despite the fact that I cannot ride a mountain bike; it might have helped that I can cook. Warm thanks to Dewayne Norvill and Arian Davis, Tobin and Jenny Vigil, Steve Hach, Ricky Dyer, Joanna Dyer, Luke and Christa Short, Michele and Tim Stephens, Mathias Rudolf, and Ryan Lenhart. A number of colleagues did double duty and became much-loved friends: Josh Piker, Francesca Sawaya, Judy Lewis, Heidi Brayman Hackel, Todd Shepherd, Said Gahia, Liz Miller, Matthew Stratton, Jess Lepler, Candice Harrison, and Hunt Howell have given me more than they can imagine.

As ever, my deepest debts are to my family, real and fictive. The Loves and Dentons have always held me close, despite the miles that separate us. I have relished the opportunity to worm my way into the Hamerla-Battle-Carpenter-Thomas clan. The Steckler-Kellys remain a source of joy, laughter, and recipe ideas. Robyn Lily Davis, Billy Jackson, Randy Soto, and Timmy Way have been the bestest. Frankie, Sammie, and Perrie—our funny, funny girls—make every single day better. Lastly, mostly, there is Rich Hamerla. When I take stock of the last eighteen years, it is easy to see that the finest things that have come to me have all come from him. This book is for him, with love.